Blockchain Technology Solutions for the Security of IoT-Based Healthcare Systems

Cognitive Data Science in
Sustainable Computing

Blockchain Technology Solutions for the Security of IoT-Based Healthcare Systems

Edited by

Bharat Bhushan
School of Engineering and Technology (SET), Sharda University, Greater Noida,
Uttar Pradesh, India

Sudhir Kumar Sharma
Department of Information and Technology, Institute of Information Technology &
Management, Guru Gobind Singh Indraprastha University, Delhi, India

Muzafer Saračević
Department of Computer Science, University of Novi Pazar, Novi Pazar, Serbia

Azedine Boulmakoul
Department of Computer Science, FST Mohammedia - Hassan II University of
Casablanca, Casablanca, Morocco

Series Editor
Arun Kumar Sangaiah
School of Computing Science and Engineering, Vellore Institute of Technology
(VIT), Vellore, Tamil Nadu, India

ACADEMIC PRESS
An imprint of Elsevier

ISBN : 978-0-323-99199-5

For information on all Academic Press publications
visit our website at https://www.elsevier.com/books-and-journals

Publisher: Mara Conner
Editorial Project Manager: Zsereena Rose Mampusti
Production Project Manager: Punithavathy Govindaradjane
Cover Designer: Christian Bilbow

Typeset by STRAIVE, India

Working together
to grow libraries in
developing countries

www.elsevier.com • www.bookaid.org

Contents

5. Performance investigation of several convolutional neural network models in healthcare systems

Hala Shaari, Jasmin Kevric, Muzafer Saračević, and Nuredin Ahmed

6. The classification of the investigations and punishment for crime syndicates that relate to intrusions against IoT-based healthcare systems

Joshua Ojo Nehinbe, Jimmy Adebesin Benson, and Linda Chibuzor

10. The use of blockchain technology in IoT-based healthcare: A concise guide
Deepak Sharma and Sudhir Kumar Sharma

11. Applications of blockchain technology for improving security in the internet of things (IoT)
Qasem Abu Al-Haija, Mohammad Alnabhan, Eyad Saleh, and Mohammad Al-Omari

Contributors

Numbers in parentheses indicate the pages on which the authors' contributions begin.

Qasem Abu Al-Haija (199), Department of Computer Science/Cybersecurity, King Hussein School of Computing Sciences, Princess Sumaya University for Technology (PSUT), Amman, Jordan

K. Adalarasu (133), Department of Electronics and Instrumentation Engineering, School of Electrical and Electronics Engineering, SASTRA Deemed to be University, Thanjavur, Tamil Nadu, India

Saša Adamović (77,151), Faculty of Informatics and Computing, Singidunum University, Belgrade, Serbia

Nuredin Ahmed (97), National Board for Technical and Vocational Education, Tripoli, Libya

Mohammad Alnabhan (199), Department of Computer Science/Cybersecurity, King Hussein School of Computing Sciences, Princess Sumaya University for Technology (PSUT), Amman, Jordan

Mohammad Al-Omari (199), Department of Business Information Technology, King Talal School of Business Technology, Princess Sumaya University for Technology (PSUT), Amman, Jordan

Satish Anamalamudi (1), Department of Computer Science and Engineering, SRM University-AP, Mangalagiri, Andhra Pradesh, India

T. Arunkumar (133), School of Computer Science & Engineering, Vellore Institute of Technology (VIT), Vellore, Tamil Nadu, India

A.K.M. Bahalul Haque (223), Software Engineering, LUT University, Lappeenranta, Finland

Jimmy Adebesin Benson (113), NHS England, London, United Kingdom

Bharat Bhushan (45,223,241,263), School of Engineering and Technology (SET), Sharda University, Greater Noida, Uttar Pradesh, India

Raj Chaganti (241,263), Department of Computer Science, University of Texas at San Antonio, San Antonio, TX, United States

Linda Chibuzor (113), Northamptonshire Healthcare NHS Foundation Trust, Nottingham, United Kingdom

Murali Krishna Enduri (1), Department of Computer Science and Engineering, SRM University-AP, Mangalagiri, Andhra Pradesh, India

Milan Gnjatović (77), University of Criminal Investigation and Police Studies, Beograd, Serbia

Sai Sri Vineeth Gudapati (167), University of Southern Mississippi, Hattiesburg, MS, United States

Koduru Hajarathaiah (1), Department of Computer Science and Engineering, SRM University-AP, Mangalagiri, Andhra Pradesh, India

M. Jagannath (133), School of Electronics Engineering, Vellore Institute of Technology (VIT), Chennai, Tamil Nadu, India

Saumya Kakandwar (45), School of Engineering and Technology (SET), Sharda University, Greater Noida, Uttar Pradesh, India

Saptadeepa Kalita (241), School of Engineering and Technology (SET), Sharda University, Greater Noida, Uttar Pradesh, India

Jasmin Kevric (97), Faculty of Engineering and Natural Sciences, International BURCH University, Sarajevo, Bosnia and Herzegovina

Avinash Kumar (45,241,263), School of Engineering and Technology (SET), Sharda University, Greater Noida, Uttar Pradesh, India

H.M. Lavanya (1), Department of Computer Science and Engineering, NITK (National Institute of Technology Karnataka) Surathkal, Mangaluru, Karnataka, India

Nemanja Maček (77), Academy of Technical and Art Applied Studies, School of Electrical and Computer Engineering; Faculty of Computer Sciences, Megatrend University, Belgrade, Serbia

Joshua Ojo Nehinbe (113), ICT Security Solutions, Lagos, Nigeria

Ahmed J. Obaid (241), Kufa University, Faculty of Computer Science and Mathematics, Kufa, Iraq

Nikola Pavlović (151), Faculty of Informatics and Computing, Singidunum University, Belgrade, Serbia

Dalibor Radovanović (151), Faculty of Informatics and Computing, Singidunum University, Belgrade, Serbia

Nick Rahimi (167), University of Southern Mississippi, Hattiesburg, MS, United States

Rehab A. Rayan (23), Department of Epidemiology, High Institute of Public Health, Alexandria University, Alexandria, Egypt

Eyad Saleh (199), Department of Computer Science/Cybersecurity, King Hussein School of Computing Sciences, Princess Sumaya University for Technology (PSUT), Amman, Jordan

Abdur Rashid Sangi (1), School of Artificial Intelligence and Big Data, Yibin University, Sichuan, China

Marko Šarac (151), Faculty of Informatics and Computing, Singidunum University, Belgrade, Serbia

Muzafer Saračević (77,97,151), Department of Computer Science, University of Novi Pazar, Novi Pazar, Serbia

Hala Shaari (97), Faculty of Engineering and Natural Sciences, Department of Information Technologies, International BURCH University, Sarajevo, Bosnia and Herzegovina

Deepak Sharma (183), Department of Information and Technology, Institute of Innovation Technology & Management, Guru Gobind Singh Indraprastha University, Delhi, India

Sudhir Kumar Sharma (183), Department of Information and Technology, Institute of Information Technology & Management, Guru Gobind Singh Indraprastha University, Delhi, India

Sonal Shristi (241,263), School of Engineering and Technology (SET), Sharda University, Greater Noida, Uttar Pradesh, India

Ben Othman Soufiene (263), PRINCE Laboratory Research, ISITcom, Hammam Sousse, University of Sousse, Sousse, Tunisia

Christos Tsagkaris (23), Faculty of Medicine, University of Crete, Heraklion, Greece

S. Varsha (133), Department of Electronics and Instrumentation Engineering, School of Electrical and Electronics Engineering, SASTRA Deemed to be University, Thanjavur, Tamil Nadu, India

Nikola Vukobrat (77), Faculty of Informatics and Computing, Singidunum University, Belgrade, Serbia

Imran Zafar (23), Department of Bioinformatics and Computational Biology, Virtual University of Pakistan, Lahore, Punjab, Pakistan

About the editors

Bharat Bhushan is an Assistant Professor of the Department of Computer Science and Engineering (CSE) at the School of Engineering and Technology, Sharda University, Greater Noida, India. He received his undergraduate degree (B-Tech in Computer Science and Engineering) with distinction in 2012, received his postgraduate degree (M-Tech in Information Security) with distinction in 2015, and his doctorate degree (PhD Computer Science and Engineering) in 2021 from Birla Institute of Technology, Mesra, India. Dr. Bhushan has earned numerous international certifications such as CCNA, MCTS, MCITP, RHCE, and CCNP. He has published more than 100 research papers in various renowned international conferences and SCI indexed journals, including Journal of Network and Computer Applications (Elsevier), Wireless Networks (Springer), Wireless Personal Communications (Springer), Sustainable Cities and Society (Elsevier), and Emerging Transactions on Telecommunications (Wiley). He has contributed more than 30 chapters in various books and has edited 15 books from the most respected publishers, including Elsevier, Springer, Wiley, IOP Press, IGI Global, and CRC Press. He has served as keynote speaker (resource person) in numerous reputed faculty development programs and international conferences held in different countries including India, Iraq, Morocco, China, Belgium, and Bangladesh. He has served as a reviewer/editorial board member for several reputed international journals. In the past, he worked as an assistant professor at HMR Institute of Technology and Management, New Delhi and Network Engineer in HCL Infosystems Ltd., Noida. In the year 2021, Stanford University (United States) listed Dr. Bharat Bhushan in the Top 2% Scientists list. In addition to being the senior member of IEEE, he is also a member of numerous renowned bodies including IAENG, CSTA, SCIEI, IAE, and UACEE.

Sudhir Kumar Sharma is currently a Professor and Head of the Department of Computer Science, Institute of Information Technology & Management affiliated to GGSIPU, New Delhi, India. He has had extensive experience for over 21 years in the field of computer science and engineering. He obtained his PhD degree in Information Technology in 2013 from USICT, Guru Gobind Singh Indraprastha University, New Delhi, India. Dr. Sharma obtained his M-Tech degree in Computer Science and Engineering in 1999 from the Guru Jambheshwar University, Hisar, India, and MSc. degree in Physics from the University of Roorkee (now IIT Roorkee), Roorkee, in 1997. His research interests include machine learning, data mining, and security. He has published more than 60 research papers in various prestigious international journals and international conferences. He is a life member of CSI and IETE. Dr. Sharma is lead guest editor of the special issue on Multimedia Tools & Applications, Springer. He was a convener and volume editor of two international conferences, namely ICETIT-2019 and ICRIHE-2020. Dr. Sharma has authored and edited seven computer science books in the fields of internet of things, WSN, blockchain, and cyber-physical systems for Elsevier, Springer, and CRC Press, United States. He was selected as a reviewer/editorial board member for several reputed international journals. He has also served as a speaker, session chair, or co-chair at various national and international conferences.

Muzafer Saračević is a Full Professor at the University of Novi Pazar, Serbia. His research work covers the areas of software engineering and programming, applied mathematics, cryptography, and data protection. He graduated in computer sciences (cryptography) at the Faculty of Informatics and Computing in Belgrade, obtained his master's degree from the University of Kragujevac, Faculty of Technical Sciences, and completed his PhD (field of computational geometry) at the University of Nis, Faculty of Science and Mathematics in 2013 (Serbia). He has authored/coauthored several university textbooks and over 170 scientific papers printed in international and national journals, and proceedings of international and national scientific conferences. He has published scientific papers and chapters in journals and monographs of international publishers including Elsevier, Springer, Taylor and Francis, IEEE, Wiley, IET, TechScience Press, MDPI, De Gruyter, IGI Global, and IOP Science. Dr. Saracevic has authored/coauthored articles in highly ranked and prestigious journals such as Future Generation Computer Systems (Elsevier), IEEE Transactions on Reliability (IEEE), IET Intelligent Transport Systems, International Journal of Computer Mathematics (Taylor and Francis), Mathematics (MDPI), etc. He is a member of the editorial board for 15 journals and has reviews for more than 40 international journals and many conferences.

Azedine Boulmakoul is a Professor in the Department of Computer Science at FST Mohammedia—Hassan II University of Casablanca, where he has been since 1994. He received his PhD and "Habilitation à Diriger des Recherches" from the Claude Bernard University of Lyon in 1990 and 1994, respectively. In 1987, he was lecturer assistant at the ENTPE School (Ecole Nationale des Travaux Public de l'Etat Lyon France). For the period 1987–88, he was appointed Assistant Professor at INSA de Lyon. Between 1987 and 1994, he joined the National Institute for Research on Transportation and Safety (INRETS-Paris, www.ifsttar.fr) for real time intelligent systems research and development. He is President of the Innovative Open Spatial Information Systems Association: www.iosis.ma. He has received many awards for his contributions to research and business development, including French Academy of Sciences, R&D Maroc Awards and Distinction Medal from Moroccan Ministry of Higher

Education and Research, and Distinction Medal from Istanbul International Inventions. He also contributes to intellectual property of industrial patents. Dr. Boulmakoul has had several years in R&D and in studies and business consulting. He has chaired several conferences and program committees. He is the author of over 300 papers (in books, journals and conferences, patents, etc.) on computer science. He holds 10 patents deriving from his research. His research interests include intelligent real time systems, logic for artificial intelligence, fuzzy systems theory, distributed frameworks, data analytics, complex systems, information systems engineering, transportation, and computer engineering.

Preface

In the recent past, a huge range of connected wireless devices have emerged, thereby dramatically increasing the overall data generated by internet of things (IoT) systems. The IoT, or Industry 4.0, has led a digital revolution that has not bypassed the healthcare sector, making it necessary to switch to sophisticated medical sensors from the already prevalent wearable IoT e-health devices. Due to advances in precision medicine and the rise of genetic research, healthcare systems have witnessed a novel approach to disease treatment and prevention that incorporates an individual patient's lifestyle, surroundings, and genetic makeup. Furthermore, recent advances in information technology (IT) have enabled the development of health data tracking tools, large health information databases, and the engagement of individuals in their own healthcare. Therefore, integration of IT and healthcare has fostered transformative and revolutionary change in the health IT field. Intelligent medical systems, or e-health, are among the most widely accepted applications of IoT, where the medical data is sensitive and highly vulnerable to any unauthorized access.

However, lightweight IoT devices, having shallow energy footprints and decentralized topology, are incapable of withstanding the challenges related to healthcare data privacy and security. As conventional security schemes are inapplicable for such systems, there is an urgent need for secured, distributed, lightweight, and scalable safeguards. Furthermore, the current IoT-based healthcare systems are incapable of sharing data between platforms in an efficient manner and holding them securely at the digital and physical levels. To this end, blockchain technology guarantees a fully autonomous secure ecosystem by exploiting the combined advantages of smart contracts and global consensus. Healthcare systems can be transformed by enhancing the accuracy of electronic health records (EHRs) and enhancing connections among heterogeneous systems. Blockchain technology supports EHR management, enables remote patient monitoring, and plays a vital role in sharing, storing, and retrieving remotely gathered health data. It promises to answer the data integrity dilemma and facilitates better data-level collaboration between providers and payers, adopting the principle of securely storing the electronic health records (EHRs). Furthermore, blockchain is useful in the pharmaceutical industry to solve issues related to counterfeit medications that might have serious consequences for patients. It can also benefit the field of health insurance claims in preserving data auditability, transparency, and immutability.

Based on the scope and diversity of the topics covered, this book will serve as a valuable and useful resource to scholars, researchers, a wide range of professionals, material developers, technology specialists, and methodologists dealing with the multifarious aspects of data privacy and security enhancement in blockchain-based IoT healthcare systems. This book is designed to be the first reference choice at research and development centers, academic institutions, university libraries, and for industries and institutions dealing with current research topics and challenging issues related to IoT healthcare systems.

Chapter 1

Integration of E-health and Internet of Things

Koduru Hajarathaiah[a], Satish Anamalamudi[a], Murali Krishna Enduri[a], Abdur Rashid Sangi[b], and H.M. Lavanya[c]

[a]Department of Computer Science and Engineering, SRM University-AP, Mangalagiri, Andhra Pradesh, India, [b]School of Artificial Intelligence and Big Data, Yibin University, Sichuan, China, [c]Department of Computer Science and Engineering, NITK (National Institute of Technology Karnataka) Surathkal, Mangaluru, Karnataka, India

1. Introduction

State-of-the-art distributed networks have become ubiquitous and are able to touch almost every corner of the globe. This in turn affects human life in previously unimaginable ways through complete automation [1]. With these developments, the existing Internet architecture is going to enter into a new era with more pervasive connectivity where a very wide variety of applications can be connected to the World Wide Web (WWW). This concept has come to be known as the "Internet of Things" (IoT), which can be defined as an interaction between the physical and digital worlds through constrained capabilities. The digital world in general will interact with the physical world with the help of sensors and actuators. The Internet of Things (IoT) can be depicted as a combination of sensors and actuators that provide and receive the information that is being digitalized and placed into bidirectional networks to transmit user data for use in different services. In general, multiple different sensors can be attached to a single device in order to measure a broad range of physical variables or phenomena and then transmit the sensed data to either the cloud or a server for data analysis [2,3]. The sensing can be analyzed and is understandable as a service model that is shown in Fig. 1. With this service model, we can redefine the Internet of Things as computing and networking capabilities that are being embedded in any kind of object (healthcare, vehicles, industrial applications, etc.). These kinds of capabilities can be used to query the state of the object through sensing capabilities and to change its state of behavior.

With the IoT, a new kind of world can be created with interconnection of all the devices and appliances through distributed internetworking [4]. For the

Blockchain Technology Solutions for the Security of IoT-Based Healthcare Systems.
https://doi.org/10.1016/B978-0-323-99199-5.00016-1

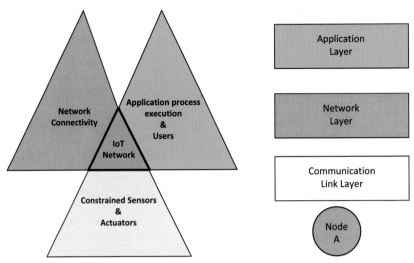

FIG. 1 Architecture of IoT systems.

interconnection with different networks, IoT devices are designed to be equipped with embedded sensors, actuators, microprocessors, and transceivers. IoT is a combination of various technologies that work together to provide thing-to-thing communication. Sensors, along with the actuators, are constrained devices that help to interact with the physical domain. The application data that is collected by the sensors has to be routed, stored, and processed intelligently in order to trigger useful operations from the sensed information. It is noteworthy that the term sensor can be any mobile device or even a washing machine that count as a sensor node to provide the input from its current state. Actuator can be defined as a device which can be used to effect the change in the environment, such as the temperature monitor of a patient in a hospital. The processing and the storage of the application data that was sent by the generating sensors can occur at the edge of the network itself (gateways) or at the remote server.

The limitation of an IoT object is with its storage and processing capabilities due to constrained resources, which are often related to size, node energy, transmission power, and computational ability. Along with the constrained challenges, data collection and data handling need to be taken care of during network communication. The communication in between IoT devices is mainly with wireless (unguided medium) technology because, in general, they will be installed at geographically different locations, and narrow band radio channels are often highly unreliable with high rates of channel distortion. In such a scenario, assuring the reliable communication to the application data without too many packets drops and retransmissions is a significant issue in the communication technologies [5]. Currently, state-of-the-art IoT devices, such as automated blood pressure monitoring or other healthcare devices, consist of the combination of communication and sensing capabilities. Sensing capabilities are constantly increasing to incorporate better communication and sensing tools in automated healthcare systems.

The basic architecture of IoT systems is categorized into four layers, namely:

1. Object sensing layer
2. Data exchange layer
3. Information integration layer
4. Application data generation layer

Consumers of the sensor data can communicate with the sensor network via the information integration layer, which is responsible for all the communication and transactions. In addition, new requirements and challenges to exchange the data along with information filtering and data integration is significant in the network architecture [6,7]. The use of distributed cloud technologies continues to grow exponentially due to the increase in deployment of constrained IoT devices. New infrastructure platforms, along with the software applications, have begun to be deployed in the IoT networks. With the Internet of Things (IoT), an integrated communication within the interconnected devices and platforms can be engaged in both the virtual and physical world. Remote digital healthcare-based IoT systems makes the transmission of medical data as a routine daily task [8,9]. Hence, it is significant to develop efficient scheduling and routing protocols to efficiently transmit and receive the patient's diagnostic data within the IoT environment. Smart IoT devices can be interconnected with the traditional Internet through wired or wireless networks [10].

In this work, the existing constrained protocol stack of the sensor network is being amended with the IETF 6LoWPAN adaptation layer to compress the IPv6 address along with other header fields of the transport and network layer. In addition, a point-to-point reactive AODV-RPL routing protocol is being proposed to support asymmetric bidirectional constrained links. It is crucial to implement the asymmetric links to share the network load, especially in the constrained IoT networks. This will help to reduce packet drops and enhance the performance of the overall network. For medical applications, the network throughput plays a prominent role in transmitting the patient data to the destination within predetermined timeslots.

2.   Overview of protocol stack in IoT networks

The IETF (Internet Engineering Task Force) propose 6LoWPAN (IPv6 over low-power wireless personal area network) as a standard communication protocol stack for low power radio devices. 6LoWPAN support in traditional sensor networks enables routing to public switched networks through an IPv6 address. However, without modifications in the IP protocol stack, it is difficult to enable routing in sensor networks to operate in the heterogeneous networks.

This is because the traditional IP protocol stack is mainly designed with the assumption of operating with high data supportable rates, whereas in IoT networks it is completely constrained in terms of radio and network resources. One approach to integrate the traditional wireless networks with the IPv6-enabled sensor network is with the support of tunneling. However, the implementation of tunneling in IPv6 transition is difficult to interoperate the heterogeneous networks because IPv6 is mainly used for 6LoWPAN protocol, which runs over the IPv6 network. This will not provide a way to utilize an existing IPv4 routing infrastructure to carry IPv6 traffic that was generated through IoT networks.

IETF 6LoWPAN is a constrained protocol specification proposed to enable the IPv6 standards to be used in low-power constrained wireless networks, specifically with the Institute of Electrical and Electronics Engineers IEEE 802.15.4 standard. It is being managed and maintained by the IETF 6LoWPAN working group. The reason for introducing 6LoWPAN protocol stack to IoT networks is that the existing IPv6 is too bulky (in terms of header formats and packet sizes) for IPv6-enabled wireless sensor networks. In 6LoWPAN networks, a new layer, called the adaptation layer, is introduced in between the network and MAC/PHY layer without disturbing the main functionality of the IPv6 protocol [11]. In traditional wireless (infrastructure or ad hoc) networks, the IPv6 maximum transmission unit (MTU) is 1280 bytes, which can be supported by 2.4 GHz or 5 GHz spectrum bands through IEEE 802.11 a/b/g/n standards. However, the transmission of the same 1280 bytes with IPv6 maximum transmission unit (MTU) is difficult to achieve in constrained narrow bands over IEEE 802.15.4 standard. To deal with this, IETF 6loWPAN group propose a new layer called adaptation layer, which performs fragmentation and reassembly to transmit/receive the minimal packets over IEEE 802.15.4 standard. The detailed overview and the operation of the adaptation layer in 6LoWPAN networks is explained in IETF standard RFC4944 [12].

The IETF proposed 6LoWPAN protocol stack consists of low-power wireless area networks (LoWPANs), which are collection of IPv6 subnetworks. In the sense, 6LoWPAN contains a collection of 6LoWPAN nodes that share a similar IPv6 address prefix (first 64-bits of a 128-bit IPv6 address). Like nodes in wireless ad hoc networks, 6LoWPAN nodes can play the dual role of host or router along with one or more gateway routers. In general, we have three types of 6LoWPANs networks, namely simple LoWPANs, extended LoWPANs, and ad hoc LoWPANs [13], as shown in Fig. 2. The first type, simple LoWPAN, will be connected through one LoWPAN edge router to another wired or wireless IP(IPv6 or IPv4) network. The second type of 6LoWPAN, extended LoWPAN, contains multiple edge/gateway routers along with a high speed backbone link to interconnect them [12]. The third type of 6LoWPAN, ad hoc LoWPAN, in general won't be connected to the Internet and only operates without an infrastructure.

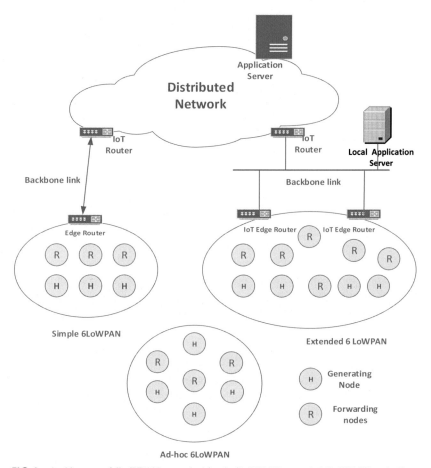

FIG. 2   Architecture of 6LoWPAN networks (simple 6LoWPAN, extended 6LoWPAN, and ad hoc 6LoWPAN).

Fig. 3 shows the 6LoWPAN protocol stack in comparison with the traditional IP protocol stack. It is noteworthy that 6LoWPAN is almost identical to a traditional IPv6 implementation, but with two major differences [13,14]:

- The proposed 6LoWPAN stack, in general, only supports IPv6 addresses, because of which, a new adaptation layer (LoWPAN) has been implemented in the protocol stack to optimize and compress the IPv6 over constrained narrow bank link layers.
- 6LoWPAN is specifically designed to work with IEEE 802.15.4 standard at the data link and physical layer.

The rest of this chapter is organized as follows. Section 3 briefly describes the existing scheduling protocols for IoT networks; following which, a new scheduling protocol is proposed for the end-to-end traffic flows with resource

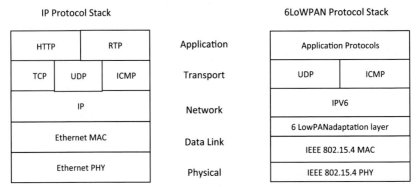

FIG. 3   6LoWPAN adaptation layer in the TCP/IP protocol stack.

reservation protocols. Section 4 explains about the reactive routing protocols along with a detailed explanation of implementing the asymmetric bidirectional data links. The support of asymmetric bidirectional data links is of the utmost importance in machine-critical applications. Section 5 explains about the simulation/experimental analysis for the proposed AODV-RPL with asymmetric bidirectional links. Finally, Section 6 presents the conclusion and future work.

3.   Scheduling protocols for best effort IoT networks

In constrained IoT networks, designing an optimal distributed scheduling algorithm is significant to maximize the utilization of CPUs and enhance the performance of the IoT networks in terms of throughput, and to minimize the end-to-end latency along with the power consumption. In general, the applications of IoT networks include repeated tasks that, in general, will be executed in various constrained sensor nodes, which may result in higher sensing cost with reduced node and network lifetime. This kind of issue can be resolved by simply assigning similar tasks within the specific region in a single network system. However, in reality, selecting the single network system for execution is always a challenging task. In addition, the selection of an efficient scheduling algorithm will avoid the repeated execution of the same distributed process, which may lead to unnecessary internode IoT communication.

The data flow of 6LoWPAN-IoT networks is usually depicted as a directed acyclic graph (DAG) whose vertex in the given network graph represents the constrained nodes and its communication edges depict the communication in between two IoT nodes for the application data transmission. In addition, the operation of the best effort scheduling protocols can be separated into two categories, namely, application task selection and node/network resource allocation. In first case, the application task selection scenario is proposed to determine the sequence of multiple traffic flows from different applications. These tasks, in general, can be divided in different ways as long as the successive dependencies cannot be violated [15]. Hence, the task execution phase may be implemented in different ways. Furthermore, the resource allocation phase is divided into two different traffic flows, namely, best-effort traffic flows and per-flow deterministic traffic flows. Scheduling protocols in the constrained distributed systems have been widely investigated by many researchers to efficiently utilize the shared medium with reduced collision rate due to channel contention. Brandt et al. [16] propose a low-rate cost-based scheduling algorithm for smart utility based IoT grids. The proposed algorithm aims to minimize the end-to-end delay with minimal packet drops along with consideration of the node channel utilization. Over the last few years, active research has been initiated in terms of the evaluation of the IEEE 802.15.4 wireless standard for constrained data transmission through scheduling protocols [17].

The proposed idea is to apply the GTS allocation mechanism to enhance and efficiently utilize the channel bandwidth through the scheduling concept with the assistance of IEEE 802.15.4 standard [18]. The 6TiSCH architecture within the 6LOWPAN networks is shown in the Fig. 4. It represents a reference protocol stack that is being implemented and tested within open-source simulators and supported by IETF and ETSI efforts. One of the major goals is to assist other network bodies to easily adopt the protocol stack as a whole in the IPv6-based IoT protocol stack. RPL is a standard routing protocol that is being proposed by IETF to route the data in constrained IoT networks. Until now, there is no need was identified to propose a specific Objective Function for 6TiSCH network [19]. The existing "Minimal 6TiSCH Configuration" describes the operation of proactive based RPL routing protocol (routing protocol for low-power and lossy networks) over a static schedule used in a slotted aloha fashion.

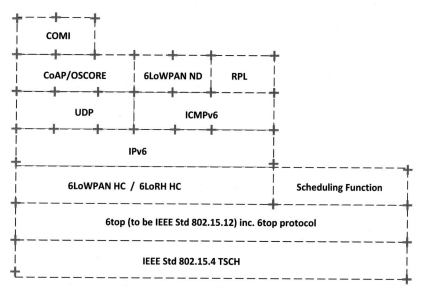

FIG. 4   Scheduling function in 6LoWPAN-IoT networks.

This works well for active slots that may be used for transmission or reception of both one-to-one (unicast) and one-to-many (multicast frames) [20].

The existing 6LoWPAN header compression in the 6LoWPAN adaptation layer is being proposed to compress the IPv6 and transport layer headers (specifically UDP headers), whereas 6LoWPAN routing header (6LoRH) is used to compress the IPv6 data packets, along with RPL packet information (RPI). The physical layer of the IEEE802.15.4 standard is designed to support the low-power scenarios targeting the use of unlicensed ISM spectrum bands, in both 2.4 GHz and 5 GHz industrial, scientific, and medical (ISM) bands. This introduces a new requirement in terms of designing a new frame size, constrained data rate, and efficient utilization of assigned narrow bands to achieve reduced collision probability along with reduced packet error rate. In addition, the node should transmit the data in an acceptable transmission range with limited node transmission power.

Based on the IETF 6LoWPAN and 6lo, it is recommended to support the PHY layer with a frame size of up to 127 bytes. Hence, it is clear that a new layer within the network and datalink layer of the 6LOWPAN stack is introduced to support the data compression along with the fragmentation to support the 127-byte frame at the data link of the IEEE 802.15.4 6TiSCH networks. The existing scheduling functions is most suitable for best effort traffic flows, which aggregate the data from different flows or different neighbor nodes, and can be best suited for nondeterministic best effort applications like pollution monitoring or soil pollution detection. However, the existing scheduling protocols in the current literature may not be suitable for real-time deterministic traffic flows such as critical healthcare monitoring. The best example is that one can't transmit the heartbeat monitoring or blood pressure monitoring information within a predicted time through existing best effort scheduling protocols through a proactive-based RPL routing protocol. Hence, it is significant to tightly couple the scheduling protocol with reactive routing protocol at the network layer to support the per-flow traffic flows for the deterministic traffic flows. In the next section, we will see how the existing RPL protocol works can't be used for the deterministic traffic flows in IoT networks.

4. Routing protocol for best effort IoT networks

The routing protocol design plays a pivotal role in determining the performance of the constrained networks with minimal node energy consumption. For this purpose, IETF has developed a proactive IPv6 routing protocol for low-power and lossy networks (RPL). Constrained nodes within the LLN network that are running the RPL protocol are connected by constructing a destination oriented directed acyclic graph (DODAG). Root node (LLN boarder router) initiates the DIO control messages with metric container options to form a DODAG for a specific instance. With this, each node within the LLN network is able to select its parent node (best candidate of intermediate node) within a set of next-hop

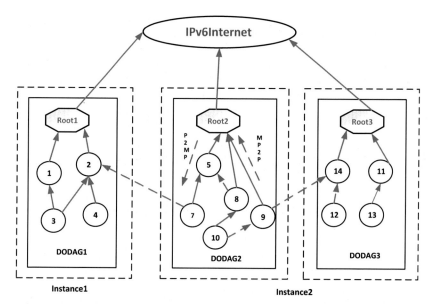

FIG. 5   DODAG in RPL routing protocol.

neighbors (called parent set, parent list) to forward data from leaf node to root node. Later, the root node can either send the data back to the LLN network (point-to-point links) or send it to outside networks. RPL, the IPv6 distance vector routing protocol for low-power and lossy networks (LLNs), is designed to support multiple traffic flows through a root-based destination-oriented directed acyclic graph (DODAG) (see Fig. 5) [7].

In the traditional RPL protocol, the data packets have to either traverse the root in nonstoring mode (source routing) or need to traverse a common ancestor in storing mode (hop-by-hop routing) for point-to-point (P2P) traffic flows. Such P2P traffic flows may result in suboptimal routes and may suffer severe traffic congestion near the DAG root [11,12]. To discover optimal paths for P2P traffic flows in the traditional RPL protocol, a reactive-based P2P-RPL [11] protocol specifies a temporary DODAG with origin node acting as temporary root. The temporary origin node initiates the "P2P route discovery mode (P2P-RDO)" with an address vector for both nonstoring mode (H = 0) and storing mode (H = 1) [7]. Subsequently, each intermediate router adds its IP address and multicasts the P2P-RDO message, until the message reaches to the target node. Later, the target node unicasts the "discovery reply" option back to the origin node. The design of P2P-RPL can be efficient for source routing (non-storing mode), but much less efficient for hop-by-hop routing (storing mode), due to the extra address vector overhead. In fact, when the P2P-RDO message is being multicast from the source hop-by-hop, receiving nodes are able to determine a next-hop toward the source in symmetric links. When the target node subsequently replies to the source along the established forward route, receiving nodes can determine the next hop toward target node. In other words, it is efficient to use routing tables for the P2P-RDO message instead of "address vector" for hop-by-hop routes (H = 1) in symmetric links.

Traditional RPL and reactive P2P-RPL both specify the use of a single DODAG in networks of symmetric links. However, application-specific routing requirements that are defined by the IETF ROLL Working Group for constrained networks [13–15] call for routing metrics and constraints related to asymmetric bidirectional links. For this, Winter et al. [7] describe the bidirectional asymmetric links for traditional RPL with paired DODAGs, for which the DAG root (DODAGID) is common for two instances. With this, application-specific routing requirements for bidirectional asymmetric links in base RPL can be satisfied, but P2P-RPL for paired DODAGs require two DAG roots, namely one for the origin node and another for the target node, due to temporary DODAG formation. For bidirectional asymmetric links in constrained networks, AODV-RPL specifies P2P route discovery, utilizing traditional RPL with a new mode of operation (MoP). For asymmetrical links, AODV-RPL has two multicast messages: one from the origin node to the target node and another from target node to origin node. With AODV-RPL, no address vector is needed for symmetrical links, significantly reducing the control packet size. That is important for constrained LLN networks. With proposed proactive based RPL, point-to-point links are suboptimal due to traversal of data packets to the root in nonstoring mode (source routing), or to traverse a common ancestor in storing mode (hop-by-hop routing). To avoid suboptimal routes in the storing mode of LLN, a reactive-based AODV-RPL protocol is proposed with the support of both symmetrical and asymmetrical links.

4.1   Reactive-based AODV-RPL protocol for deterministic IoT networks

With AODV-RPL, point-to-point routes from Origin_node to Target_node within an LLN network are "on-demand." In other words, route discovery in AODV-RPL is not invoked unless the Origin_node has application data for delivery to the Target_node but the existing routes do not satisfy the application's requirements. Routes discovered by AODV-RPL are point-to-point; meaning that the routes are not constrained to traverse a root node (global DAG). Unlike traditional RPL [7] and P2P-RPL [11], AODV-RPL can enable asymmetric communication paths in networks with bidirectional asymmetric links. For this, AODV-RPL enables discovery of two routes: namely one from Origin_node to Target_node, and another from Target_node to Origin_node. AODV-RPL also enables symmetric routing along paired DODAGs based on the "S" bit (see Figs. 6 and 7).

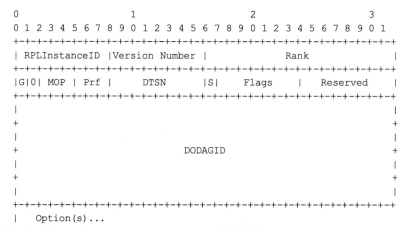

```
0                   1                   2                   3
0 1 2 3 4 5 6 7 8 9 0 1 2 3 4 5 6 7 8 9 0 1 2 3 4 5 6 7 8 9 0 1
+-+-+-+-+-+-+-+-+-+-+-+-+-+-+-+-+-+-+-+-+-+-+-+-+-+-+-+-+-+-+-+-+
| RPLInstanceID |Version Number |              Rank             |
+-+-+-+-+-+-+-+-+-+-+-+-+-+-+-+-+-+-+-+-+-+-+-+-+-+-+-+-+-+-+-+-+
|G|0| MOP | Prf |     DTSN      |S|    Flags    |    Reserved   |
+-+-+-+-+-+-+-+-+-+-+-+-+-+-+-+-+-+-+-+-+-+-+-+-+-+-+-+-+-+-+-+-+
|                                                               |
+                                                               +
|                                                               |
+                           DODAGID                             +
|                                                               |
+                                                               +
|                                                               |
+-+-+-+-+-+-+-+-+-+-+-+-+-+-+-+-+-+-+-+-+-+-+-+-+-+-+-+-+-+-+-+-+
|    Option(s)...
```

FIG. 6   DIO modification to support asymmetric AODV-RPL.

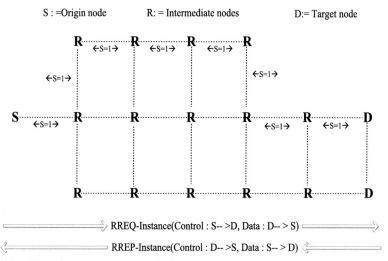

FIG. 7   AODV-RPL with symmetric paired instances.

4.2   Overview of AODV-RPL mode of operation (MoP)

In AODV-RPL, reactive route discovery is invoked by forming a temporary DAG rooted at the OrigNode. Paired DODAGs (RREQ-Instance and RREP-Instance) are constructed according to the AODV-RPL mode of operation (MoP) during route formation between the OrigNode and TargNode. The RREQ-Instance is formed by multicasting a route control message from OrigNode to TargNode, whereas the RREP-Instance is formed by multicasting (asymmetric), or unicasting (symmetric) a route control message from

TargNode to OrigNode. Intermediate routers in LLN network join the paired DODAGs based on the rank (objective function zero (OF0)) as calculated from the DIO message. In this chapter, the RREQ message represents the AODV-RPL DIO message with RREQ option from OrigNode to TargNode. Similarly, the RREP represents the AODV-RPL DIO message with RREP option from TargNode to OrigNode. Subsequently, the RREQ-Instance is used for application data transmission from TargNode to OrigNode and RREP-Instance is used for application data transmission from OrigNode to TargNode. The AODV-RPL mode of operation (MoP) defines a new bit called the symmetric bit, "S," which is added to the traditional RPL-DIO message as shown in Fig. 8. During the route discovery control multicast, OrigNode sets the "S" bit to 1 in the RREQ-Instance message. It is noteworthy that rows of 32-bits each in Fig. 6 are broken up into constituent fields so that the number of bits in each field may be quickly determined by visual inspection.

An LLN node originating the AODV-RPL message supplies the following information in the DIO header:

- "S" bit: Symmetric bit is added in the traditional DIO object.
- MOP: Mode of operation in the DIO object is "TBD(5)" for AODV-RPL DIO message.
- RPLInstanceID: RPLInstanceID in the DIO object is the InstanceID of AODVInstance (RREQ-Instance). The InstanceID for RREQ-Instance MUST be always an odd number.
- DODAGID: For RREQ-Instance: DODAGID in the DIO object MUST be the IPv6 address of the device that initiates the RREQ-Instance.

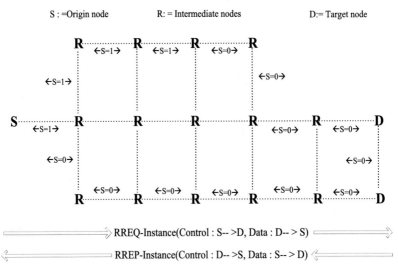

FIG. 8   AODV-RPL with asymmetric paired instances.

- For RREP-Instance: DODAGID in the DIO object MUST be the IPv6 address of the device that initiates the RREP-Instance.
- Rank: Rank in the DIO object is the rank of the AODV-RPL Instance.
- Metric container options: AODV-Instance messages may carry one or more DODAG Metric container options to indicate the relevant routing metrics and constraints.

The "S" bit in the DIO base object is set to mean that the route from OrigNode to TargNode is symmetric. When the RREQ-Instance arrives over an interface that is known to be symmetric, and the "S" bit is set to 1, then it remains set at 1, as illustrated in Fig. 8. When the RREQ-Instance arrives at any of the intermediate nodes over a link that is not known to be symmetric, or is known to be asymmetric, then the "S" bit in the DIO base object is set to be 0.

The expected transmission count (ETX) value is used as an indication of whether the link at the intermediate node is symmetric (S = 1) or asymmetric (S = 0). When the "S" bit arrives already set to be "0" then it is again set to be "0" on retransmission at the intermediate nodes (see Fig. 7). Based on the "S" bit received in DIO-RREQ-Instance, the TargNode decides whether or not the route is symmetric before transmitting the RREP-Instance message upstream toward the OrigNode.

4.3   RREQ option

The RREQ option that is defined for the RREQ-Instance in AODV-RPL is shown in Fig. 4. OrigNode supplies the following information in the RREQ option of the RREQ-Instance message:

- Type: The type of the RREQ option.
- Orig SeqNo: Sequence number of OrigNode.
- Dest SeqNo: When it is nonzero, the last known sequence number for Targ-Node for which a route is desired.
- TargNode IPv6 Address: IPv6 address of the TargNode that receives RREQ-Instance message. This is the same address as in the RREQ option (see Fig. 9) of AODV-RPL.

To establish the upstream route from TargNode, OrigNode start multicasts the RREQ-Instance message to its one-hop neighbors. Subsequently, each intermediate node (Ri) computes the rank for RREQ-Instance and creates a routing table entry for the upstream route toward the OrigNode when the routing metrics/constraints are satisfied. For this, (Ri) must use the asymmetric link metric measured in the upstream direction, from Ri to its upstream neighbor that multicast the RREQ-Instance message. When the path toward the TargNode is not known at the intermediate node, then it multicasts the RREQ-Instance message with updated rank information to its next-hop neighbors until the message reaches the TargNode (Fig. 2). Based on the "S" bit in the received RREQ

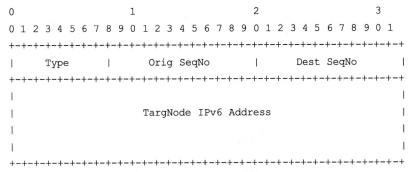

FIG. 9   RREQ option format for DIO object in AODV-RPL.

option of DIO object, the TargNode will decide whether the reply message (RREP option) should unicast or multicast back to the OrigNode. As described in gratuitous RREP, there are certain circumstances where intermediate node (Ri) MAY unicast a gratuitous RREP toward the OrigNode, thereby helping to minimize the control multicast overhead during the route discovery process from OrigNode to TargNode.

4.4   RREP option

The RREP option is defined to unicast or multicast the following information from TargNode to OrigNode (Fig. 10):

- Type: The type of the RREQ option.
- Dest SeqNo: The sequence number for the TargNode for which a route is established.
- Prefix Sz: The size of the prefix for which the route to the TargNode is available. This allows routing to other nodes on the same subnet as the TargNode.
- "G" bit: "G" bit is briefly described below.

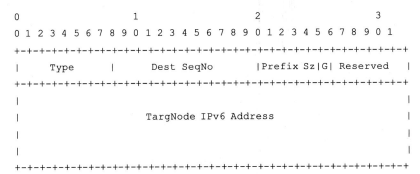

FIG. 10   DIO RREP option format for AODV-RPL MoP.

- TargNode IPv6 address: IPv6 address of the TargNode that receives the RREP-Instance message. This address must be in the RREP option of AODV-RPL.

The IP address of the OrigNode is available as the DODAGID in the DIO object (see Fig. 6). When the TargNode receives a RREQ option in DIO object with the "S" bit as "1" (as illustrated in Fig. 7) then it unicasts the RREP option with the "S" bit set to "1." In this case, route discovery control messages and application data in between OrigNode and TargNode for both RREQ-Instance and RREP-Instance are transmitted along the symmetric links. When the TargNode receives the RREQ message with the "S" bit as "0" (as shown in Fig. 3) then it starts to multicast the RREP message with the "S" bit set to "0." Intermediate nodes create a routing table entry for the path toward the TargNode while processing the RREP-Instance to the OrigNode. Once the OrigNode receives the RREP message, it starts transmitting application data to the TargNode along the path as discovered through RREP messages. Similarly, application data from TargNode to OrigNode is transmitted through the path that is discovered from the RREQ message.

4.5 Gratuitous RREP

Under some scenarios, an intermediate node that receives a DIO-RREQ message may transmit a "gratuitous" RREP message back to the OrigNode instead of continuing to multicast the RREQ message toward the TargNode. For these circumstances, the "G" bit of the RREP option is provided to distinguish the gratuitous RREP sent by the intermediate node from the RREP sent by the Targ-Node. When an intermediate node, let's say "R," receives a RREQ message and has recent information about the cost of an upstream route from TargNode to "R," then "R" may unicast the gratuitous RREP (GRREP) message to the OrigNode. "R" determines whether its information is sufficiently recent by comparing the value it has stored for the sequence number of TargNode against the DestSeqno in the incoming RREQ message. "R" also must have information about the metric information of the upstream route from TargNode. The GRREP message must have PrefixSz $==0$ and the "G" bit set to "1." "R" should also unicast the RREQ message to TargNode, to make sure that Targ-Node will have a route to OrigNode. This operation helps to minimize the route control multicast storm in between OrigNode and TargNode.

5. Experimental results

In this chapter, we report the simulation experiments conducted on Cooja simulator [16] for studying performance of the symmetric link AODV-RPL. The wireless medium is configured to use the DGRM (Directed Graph Radio Medium) radio propagation model with wireless links having a packet reception ratio (PRR) of 80% in both the directions. The MAC is configured to use CSMA/CA with radio duty cycling disabled. The maximum transmission retry limit is set to three. The RPL is configured to use storing mode of operation. It is important to note that Contiki, by default, uses the minimum DIO interval of 2^{12} ms to enable nodes to join the network in the duty cycled MAC environment. Considering the delay-sensitive P2P applications where AODV-RPL is expected to be used, we reduced it to 2^3 ms, which is the minimum value recommended by RPL [7]. The mote type is chosen to be Z1. IPv6 packets are fragmented to 127 bytes at the 6LoWPAN adaptation layer [6]. The application data size is chosen to be 40 bytes. In this study, data from source to destination is transmitted with different packet transmission delays (0.2–1.6 s). Performance is measured in terms of "packet delivery ratio (PDR)," average packet delay, and number of hops from source to destination. Furthermore, performance of AODV-RPL is compared with default RPL [7]. Fig. 6 briefly describes the network topology that was used to simulate AODV-RPL with asymmetric links. The number of nodes within the network topology is chosen to be 16. Node-1 is assumed to be an LLN border router where LLN traffic is rerouted through a traditional wired backbone network. In our simulation setup, source transmits the application data with a delay of 0.2, 0.4, 0.6, 0.8, 1, 1.2, 1.4, and 1.6 "seconds" to destination.

Later, packet delivery ratio and average delay is calculated for source (node 10) to destination (node 11) with the application packet-size as 40 bytes. In addition, hop-count is calculated for source (node-10) to the destination. The transmission path taken by the default RPL is: 10-11-6-2-3, 10-5-2-1-3, and AODV is: 10-5-2-3. As the number of hops taken by AODV-RPL is less, the packet delivery ratio for AODV-RPL is better in comparison with default-RPL for source (node 10) to destination (node 3), as shown in Fig. 11. In addition, the delay comparison between AODV-RPL and default-RPL is shown in Fig. 8. Default RPL has higher delays in comparison with AODV-RPL for source (node 10) to destination (node 3) as shown in Fig. 12. Fig. 13 shows the PDR and delay with respect to interpacket arrival time from node 10 (source) to node 15 (destination) for the topology shown in Fig. 11.

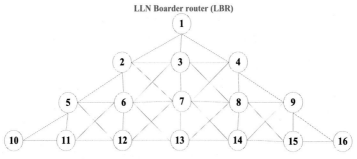

FIG. 11 Network topology with 16 nodes in Cooja simulator.

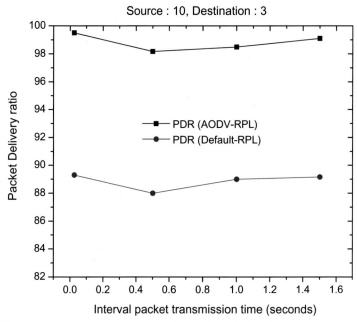

FIG. 12   Packet delivery ratio with respect to interpacket arrival time.

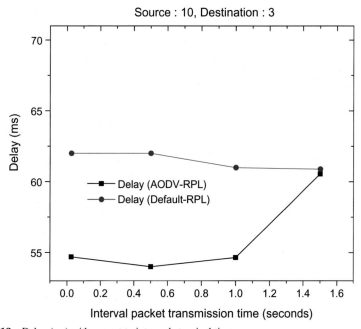

FIG. 13   Delay (ms) with respect to interpacket arrival time.

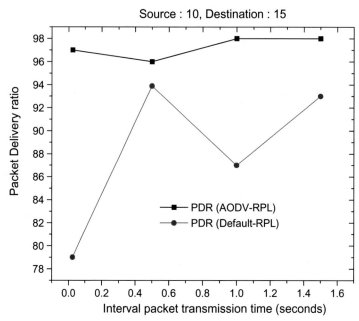

FIG. 14   Packet delivery ratio with respect to interpacket arrival time.

Paths taken by default RPL are: 10-5-2-1-3-8-15, 10-5-2-1-4-8-15, 10-5-6-3-8-f, and AODV-RPL are: 10-11-6-13-14-15, 10-5-12-7-14-15, 10-5-2-3-4-8-15. Figs. 16 and 17 present the PDR and delay with respect to interpacket arrival time from node 7 (source) to node 2 (destination) for the topology.

The path taken by the default RPL is: 7-4-1-2, whereas AODV-RPL is being traversed through 7-3-2. The PDR for default-RPL and AODV-RPL is very close in Figs. 12 and 14. This clearly shows that PDR for default-RPL and AODV-RPL is almost equal when there is little hop-count difference between default-RPL and AODV-RPL. We also see that there is much less difference in the delay statistics between default-RPL and AODV-RPL when there is little hop-count difference between default-RPL and AODV-RPL (Fig. 15).

When the LLN network is dense, RPL relies on established routes, whereas AODV-RPL creates a fresh routing entry (Fig. 16). In a dense network, storing-mode RPL will route the packets through a common ancestor of source and destination. This clearly shows that RPL packets will have a higher number of hop-count when compared with AODV-RPL. Even though RPL smartly chooses the source-destination path, the path establishment is achieved only after delivery of a few packets between source and destination (see Fig. 17).

In addition, RPL relies on preestablished routes, which will route the packets based on the old network state. Hence, default-RPL performs poorly for on-demand delay-sensitive P2P applications. Based on the simulation

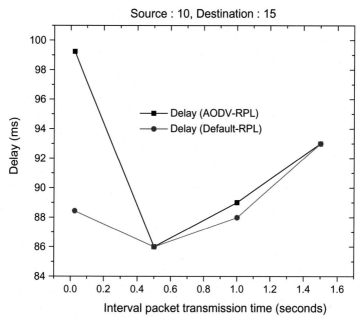

FIG. 15 Delay (ms) with respect to interpacket arrival time.

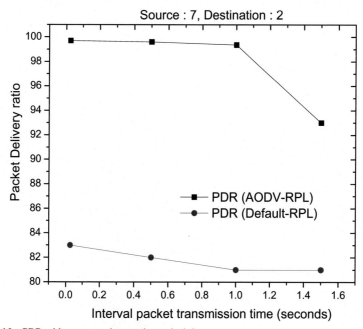

FIG. 16 PDR with respect to interpacket arrival time.

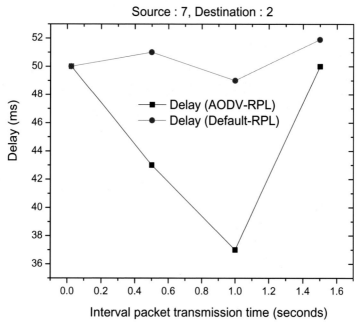

FIG. 17 Delay (ms) with respect to interpacket arrival time.

observations, AODV-RPL reduces the route-convergence time and transmits the data with minimal hop-count when compared with default-RPL.

6. Conclusion

In this chapter, reactive routing protocol with asymmetric and symmetric link-based data transmission is proposed to transmit point-to-point data at the network layer of LLN networks. In addition, per-hop scheduling protocol is proposed to integrate along with the reactive routing protocols. With this, critical medical healthcare applications can be transmitted through the reactive protocols at the network layer and scheduling protocol at the data link layer. Following this, the performance of the proposed reactive AODV-RPL routing protocol has been simulated and tested in Cooja simulator. From the simulation results, we observed that the packet delivery rate is higher for AODV-RPL when compared with the default proactive RPL routing protocol. Furthermore, transmission delay for AODV-RPL is less when compared with the default-RPL. In the future, we will use a network setup with 80-node to simulate, test, and analyze the performance of AODV-RPL with asymmetric links. In addition, performance of AODV-RPL with multiple source and multiple destination nodes is going to be tested, and performance metrics are going to be tested with default-RPL. Since, AODV-RPL is achieving better throughput with minimal delays, it can be used along with the per-flow scheduling protocols to enhance the performance of critical healthcare systems when transmitted through deterministic constrained traffic flows.

References

[1] F. Michahelles, Internet of things reality check, IEEE Pervasive Comput. 16 (2) (2017) 90–91.

[2] M. Wollschlaeger, T. Sauter, J. Jasperneite, The future of industrial communication: automation networks in the era of the internet of things and industry 4.0, IEEE Ind. Electron. Mag. 11 (1) (2017) 17–27.

[3] K.J. Singh, D.S. Kapoor, Create your own internet of things: a survey of IoT platforms, IEEE Consum. Electron. Mag. 6 (2) (2017) 57–68.

[4] T. Watteyne, A. Molinaro, M.G. Richichi, M. Dohler, From MANET To IETF ROLL standardization: a paradigm shift in WSN routing protocols, IEEE Commun. Surv. Tutorials 13 (4) (2011) 688–707.

[5] M.R. Palattella, et al., Standardized protocol stack for the internet of (Important) things, IEEE Commun. Surv. Tutorials 15 (3) (2013) 1389–1406.

[6] T.H. Lee, H.S. Chiang, L.H. Chang, M.C. Hsieh, C.H. Wen, K.M. Yap, Modeling and performance analysis of route-over and mesh-under routing schemes in 6LoWPAN, in: 2013 IEEE International Conference on Systems, Man, and Cybernetics, Manchester, 2013, pp. 3802–3806.

[7] T. Winter, P. Thubert, A. Brandt, J. Hui, R. Kelsey, P. Levis, K. Pister, R. Struik, J.P. Vasseur, R. Alexander, RPL: IPv6 Routing Protocol for Low-Power and Lossy Networks, RFC, Mar 2012, https://doi.org/10.17487/RFC6550.

[8] A.K.M.B. Haque, B. Bhushan, G. Dhiman, Conceptualizing smart city applications: requirements, architecture, security issues, and emerging trends, Expert Syst (2021), https://doi.org/10.1111/exsy.12753.

[9] B. Bhushan, C. Sahoo, P. Sinha, A. Khamparia, Unification of Blockchain and Internet of Things (BIoT): requirements, working model, challenges and future directions, Wirel. Netw. 27 (1) (2021).

[10] N. Shabbir, S.R. Hassan, Routing protocols for wireless sensor networks (WSNs), in: Wireless Sensor Networks - Insights and Innovations, 2017, pp. 197–228, https://doi.org/10.5772/intechopen.70208.

[11] M. Goyal, E. Baccelli, M. Philipp, A. Brandt, J. Martocci, Reactive Discovery of Point-to-Point Routes in Low-Power and Lossy Networks, RFC 6997, 2013.

[12] M. Goyal, E. Baccelli, A. Brandt, J. Martocci, A Mechanism to Measure the Routing Metrics along a Point-to-Point Route in a Low-Power and Lossy Network, RFC 6998, August 2013.

[13] M. Dohler, T. Watteyne, T. Winter, D. Barthel, Routing Requirements for Urban Low-Power and Lossy Networks, RFC 5548, May 2009.

[14] K. Pister, P. Thubert, S. Dwars, T. Phinney, Industrial Routing Requirements in Low-Power and Lossy Networks, RFC 5673, October 2009.

[15] A.R. Sangi, M. Alkatheiri, S. Anamalamudi, et al., Cognitive AODV routing protocol with novel channel-route failure detection, Multimed. Tools Appl. 79 (2020) 8951–8968.

[16] A. Brandt, J. Buron, G. Porcu, Home Automation Routing Requirements in Low-Power and Lossy Networks, RFC 5826, April 2010.

[17] M.S. Alkatheiri, A.R. Sangi, A. Anamalamudi, Physical unclonable function (PUF)-based security in internet of things (IoT): key challenges and solutions, Handbook of Computer Networks and Cyber Security, 2020.

[18] J. Martocci, P. De Mil, N. Riou, W. Vermeylen, Building Automation Routing Requirements in Low-Power and Lossy Networks, RFC 5867, June 2010.

[19] J. Eriksson, F. Österlind, N. Finne, N. Tsiftes, A. Dunkels, T. Voigt, R. Sauter, P.J. Marrón, COOJA/MSPSim: interoperability testing for wireless sensor networks, Proceedings of the 2nd International Conference on Simulation Tools and Techniques (Simutools '09), ICST (Institute for Computer Sciences, Social-Informatics and Telecommunications Engineering), 2009.

[20] S. Anamalamudi, A.R. Sangi, M. Alkatheiri, A.M. Ahmed, AODV routing protocol for Cognitive radio access based Internet of Things (IoT), Futur. Gener. Comput. Syst. 83 (2018) 228–238.

Chapter 2

Industry 4.0 technologies for healthcare: Applications, opportunities, and challenges

Rehab A. Rayan[a], Imran Zafar[b], and Christos Tsagkaris[c]
[a]Department of Epidemiology, High Institute of Public Health, Alexandria University, Alexandria, Egypt, [b]Department of Bioinformatics and Computational Biology, Virtual University of Pakistan, Lahore, Punjab, Pakistan, [c]Faculty of Medicine, University of Crete, Heraklion, Greece

1. Introduction

The growing population and the hopes worldwide regarding better therapies and quality of life are overwhelming the healthcare system. Hence, healthcare globally is still among the most crucial economic and societal challenges, demanding further modern and innovative solutions in science and technology [1]. In this regard, information and communication technologies (ICTs) have favorably influenced accessibility, productivity, and quality of a good deal of healthcare procedures [2]. E-health, which refers to applying ICTs to healthcare, has grabbed much attention, and significantly boosted investment in funding and research [3]. E-health grows with technologies growing; hence the term has gradually changed [4], the latest changes in respect of a trend known as Industry 4.0 (I4.0). The principle of I4.0 is considered to be a formal, apparent dedication for boosting technologies and the needed social and legal structures for grasping their real potential, as shown in Fig. 1 [5].

Technically, the fourth industrial revolution is founded primarily upon the cyber-physical systems (CPS) principle that integrates communication, computing, and control; and depends on specific technology domains: the Internet of Things (IoT), which is characterized by the widespread collection of sophisticated and coordinated objects like smartphones and sensors; cloud computing, which provides virtual limitless utilities like computing, storage, and communication resources; and big data analytics, which extract values from massive data volumes.

Smart health, usually used for adopting ICT-enabled healthcare solutions, is described as the clinical and population health field applying intelligent

Blockchain Technology Solutions for the Security of IoT-Based Healthcare Systems.
https://doi.org/10.1016/B978-0-323-99199-5.00011-2

23

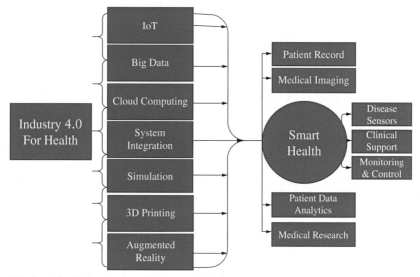

FIG. 1 A detailed mechanism of Industry 4.0 in the healthcare system.

portable techniques like smartphones, sensors, robots, smart cards, and tele-health solutions over the Internet [6], or using IT for intelligent management of health and medical services [7]. However, it is Health 4.0, adopting the three major trends of IoT, big data, and cloud computing, which is revolutionizing the e-health ecosystem, the same way Industry 4.0 is doing for the production field [8]. There are multidisciplinary applications for Health 4.0, such as monitoring health, disease prevention, smart medications, precision medicine, telemedicine, assisted living, and rehabilitation. However, although developing and adopting power-efficient, incredibly reliable, and Internet-based communications has become common practice, the definition of IoT remains confusing to a certain extent [9].

Health is an attractive field for applying IoT [10], which could transform modern healthcare with innovative technological, economic, and societal patterns, hence contributing significantly to the general reduction in healthcare costs with better health results; however, transformation of the views of the system's stakeholders is required [11]. Growth in wireless technologies linked to enhanced functionality improves the timely monitoring of physiological parameters, simplifying the continuity of care for chronic disorders, enabling early detection, and controlling health conditions. Thus, medical, diagnostic, and imaging sensors are vital for meaningfully integrating IoT in healthcare [10].

With the IoT, smart devices could connect to collect new data regarding consumers and settings to support decisions [12]. The Wearable Internet of Things (WIoT) [13] applies telehealth solutions to digitalize the ecosystem. Involving both biosensors and WIoT could monitor data for better personal daily living by targeting attitudes, habits, and wellbeing, among others, and link patients to healthcare facilities. The Internet of Health Things (IoHT) leverages smartphone applications, wearables, and other linked sensors and devices [14]. The Internet of Medical Things (IoMT) [15] comprises implantables and wearables connected to a mobile phone, smartwatch, and the Internet. The Internet of Nano Things (IoNT) [1] uses IoT in nanomedicine for further precise tracking, diagnosis, and therapeutics for agile prevention, chronic management, and monitoring. The Internet of Mobile-Health Things (m-IoT) [16] links power-efficient personal-area networks and the growing 4G network, exhibiting the global portability of connected utilities.

This chapter is meant to guide researchers and experts in ICTs in solving the issues of the healthcare system and those in healthcare information systems and digital transformation, to see the novel principles and techniques of IT and envision the evolution of Health 4.0 effectively and profitably. Through exploring literature, this chapter reviews adopting and integrating Industry 4.0 technologies in healthcare, reshaping the conventional techniques of delivering products and services.

The chapter introduces the key technologies and patterns relevant to Health 4.0, including ICTs, the IoT, cloud computing, and big data. It examines their major applications in monitoring health, disease prevention, smart medication, personalized health, and telemedicine. It shows an application case in the pharmaceutical industry, opportunities, and limitations, along with some future insights.

2. Literature review

2.1 ICT for Health 4.0

The IoT includes gadget sets, computers, and household appliances that allow the sharing of interfaces and data, including hardware, programming, sensors, and networking capabilities [17]. These devices can then distribute and join forces all over the Internet, potentially by monitoring and control. The Internet of Services (IoS) paradigm will intelligently connect gadgets to meet their goals properly with a long-term revenue stream; consequently, manufacturers need to analyze their business models carefully [18]. Multiple suppliers will experience this and develop their business. Increased profit requires large-scale development and for IoS to be promoted. Competent organization should be versatile and smart objects should be transmitted. A surprising misunderstanding is that this is not simply a cost-saving process; in fact, for revenue and profit growth, it is a distinct business practice. IoT, IoS, and so on will adopt the Industry 4.0 standard since it enables the virtualization of physical processes and their transformation into health facilities with the presence of products such as biomedical implants, biosensors, smart devices, and smart drugs [19]. To modularize various forms of medicine, the programs will then turn these things around, enabling patients and healthcare practitioners to be autonomous, connecting devices and technology, and moving toward personalized medicine [20].

Smart Industry 4.0-compatible equipment are context-aware and allow people to perform tasks [21]. The term situation-aware implies that the computer may consider depth data, for instance, the QR code, place, and position of an object. These systems rely on data to complete their real-life and virtual assignments. Real-world information, e.g., temperature, position, running time, and an instrument's condition, is compared to virtual data, such as e-documents, interactive content, and simulation performance. Clinics and distributed healthcare offer factory-close structures, such as general practice (GP) networks, public nurses, clinics, and so on, to facilitate context-conscious help for people and the proper use of machinery during the tasks that can occur in the hospital information systems (HIS) or procedures IT systems. In medical facilities and configurations, they often link current vulnerabilities to real-time data, as this is limited and makes it difficult to represent workflows accurately, and the position of the patient or specialist or her/his status is also not known. The regular fall-out of this can be a disruption to the operating schedules of the medical professionals waiting for a patient in an intensive care unit, or clinicians waiting for extended periods in accident and emergency (A&E) and outpatient fields. All operations in the manufacturing fields need to be considered by smart medical plants [22].

Recent advances in the capacity of computers to store and process information have made it possible to build and extend different innovations that profoundly impact the everyday lives of the people of the world. While some of the most influential innovative technologies were achieved in the last century, their creation has only recently generated major fundamental shifts. Important examples are artificial intelligence, computer mining, and deep learning, among others. These developments in integrating the digital, physical, and biological worlds were then responsible for the so-called Fourth Industrial Revolution [21].

Healthcare is one business aiming to positively affect the revolution of 4.0 [5]. The concept of Health 4.0 addresses the broad possibility of applying the technology of Industry 4.0 to changes in healthcare. The wellness of man must begin from a common understanding of illness and disease. Technology, from the point of view of a clinical awareness of the disease, its successful diagnosis, or the practice of medicine itself, has been prevalent in the field. In the practice of healthcare, the intersection of ICTs and health is traditionally called health-IT. Using ICTs in medicine for knowledge processing and the provision of care is a combination that can strengthen the provision of medical care and, as a result, improve health outcomes. The World Health Organization (WHO) agreed in 2007 that there were four key elements of e-health: (1) systemic reform in the provision of health care, (2) cooperation with investors and the private sector in improving access and suitability to technology, (3) awareness where technical technologies can be used, (4) development of standard and practice uniforms.

We adopted a qualitative approach in evaluating publications, integrating the method for measuring. Because of their importance, the criteria defined for the purposes and reach of our research were: "health," "healthcare," "cloud technology," and "artificial intelligence," demonstrating the use of these medical technologies: IoT, cloud computing, and big data. According to analysis and evidence, their growth in terms of academic interest and success is inclusive. We agree that, concerning Health 4.0, other variables, both scientific and not, may be considered, but they are secondary or technologically supported at a lower sophistication than the above foundations. The 5G ecosystem, the principles and technological standards of which are still being developed and under intensive debate, undoubtedly plays a crucial role in these. Of necessity, the potential for these emerging technologies (e.g., near-zero latency, increased standard of service characteristics, and Gbps upload rates) is anticipated to provide many ways to boost the omnipresent development of healthcare initiatives.

2.2 IoT in Health 4.0

Within Industry 4.0, the International Telecommunication Union offers a fundamental description of the IoT as the move from anywhere in a network, denoting more to connectivity for all [23]; it initially concentrated on digital identification and machine-to-machine communication (M2M). The IoT-compliant artifacts, such as RFID and wireless sensor networks (WSNs), have a wide variety of concepts and connotations and all share specific strict requirements in terms of size, power consumption, and processing capacities, for example. Wireless body area networks (WBANs) comprise wireless tools attached to or embedded in the human body and are of specific healthcare interest (sensors and actuators).

Because of these dynamically varying conditions, IoT-related issues are often handled by invoking several complementary layers, i.e., from largest to smallest: (i) sensing unit (composed of sensors and actuators); (ii) propagation layer (transmitting sensing data to higher levels); (iii) processing layer (responsible for processing and decision-making); and (iv) application layer (use of data). Although constructing and integrating a low-power, highly stable, and Internet-enabled communication stack is an accepted prerequisite, some aspects of the IoT concept still seem unclear. In the following, we respond to demands and related problems and opportunities in-depth and address them.

As implemented in the industry (e.g., manufacturing processes), the current IoT view aligns with I4.0. We can see this as a move beyond IoT, either integrating comprehensive coordination and processing systems or adding IoT technology to already automated processes, resulting in a range of alternative choices (and challenges). Healthcare has proven to be among the most desirable industries for IoT use. Contemporary healthcare's fascinating technical, economic, and social prospects reshape the advancement of this paradigm: IoT is undeniably the primary enabler for dispersed healthcare applications, contributing significantly to the ultimate decrease in healthcare costs and increasing patient happiness, while players in the system expect behavioral improvements. The development of smart devices with associated improvements in efficiency strongly supports the tracking of hematological responses in actual environments, promoting integrated chronic illnesses services, early diagnosis, and emergency medical management. In this context, sensor devices for medical diagnostics and imaging are key to meaningfully integrating IoT in the healthcare domain [24]. However, general-purpose connected devices (PDAs, tablets, and smartphones) often enjoy the benefits of a wide range of applications.

IoT, for example, allows situations in which electronic sensors communicate with other connected devices to attract additional information and understanding of both individuals and the decision-making setting. A variety of variants have already been established in the healthcare industry, each with its peculiarities, inspired by the prime IoT paradigm. To enter an environment for electronic services, the WIoT aims to integrate telemedicine technologies. Using body-worn detectors, WIoT makes data recording useful for optimizing the total daily quality of life (e.g., reflecting on variables such as attitudes, health, habits, etc.) and links patients to medical infrastructures. The IoHT is focused on a mix of smartphone platforms, wearable technology, and other wireless networks, and optimizes professional-grade measurement in medical instruments that are often context-aware. The IoMT refers to applications composed of ingestible and communication capabilities linked to a direct smartphone or fitness tracker linked to the network, which act as a personal portal. IoNT relates to the use of IoT in nanomedicine, the application of proactive surveillance, preventive healthcare, management of chronic conditions, and follow-up care to integrate more personalized monitoring, diagnosis, and treatment [25]. The m-IoT envisages a networking model between low-power private-area networks and growing 4G networks, representing the basic characteristics of the geographic mobility of participating organizations [26].

2.3 Cloud and fog computing in Health 4.0

Cloud computing "or merely fog computing" is a term that mainly describes capable maneuverability technologies "with minimal user interference, i.e., high-definition contracting of cloud computing (computational complexity, processing, and related development platforms)." Fog computing thus optimizes operations because it does not require careful configuration and resource planning, enabling short-term wage-per-use pricing even without the immediate contribution of the customer [27]. Cloud users take advantage of limitless on-demand resources and can either exploit or give all as-a-service: with further variants such as function-as-a-service (also known as "serverless computing"), in which the most common services are classified as infrastructure, network, or software as-a-service (IaaS, NaaS, and SaaS, respectively). Importantly, to the degree that, according to several hypotheses, it is considered as one of the outermost layers of the IoT, fog computing is important to meet a lot of IoT requirements. The ongoing migration to operating systems is motivated by a pattern that emerged in the last millennium: i.e., the expansion of investigation aimed at identifying wireless sensors that have given them more knowledge and versatility, allowing certain functions to be migrated to the cloud, with the associated virtualization and accessibility (and economic) benefits [28].

Admittedly, over the decades, many shortcomings in cloud computing systems have become clear, particularly related to synchronization between target computers and cloud-supported computer infrastructure solutions: usability, coordination, cost, and continuity of communications all contribute to the limitations on many uses of cloud technology. This trend has further sped up ubiquitous mobile devices, strongly undermining the cloud model. Indeed, in various cases, particularly for healthcare, the cloud does not meet all the requirements of many applications, resulting in the need for unique architecture. Various meanings, terms, and phrases have been developed with the concepts suggested as outlined in the following. Edge computing attempts to move some cloud computing technology to the edge of the network, close to virtual computers and still partially reliant on users' device resources, distributing the load between end nodes and conventional cloud storage arrays and offering neighborhood-term stability and higher capacity, while also improving latency rates.

The distinctive benefits of this strategy in suppressing transformation costs and maximizing facilities are incredibly significant in the healthcare situation. Cloud computing satisfies the medical industry's IT criteria to simplify clinical practices, support the implementation of medical standards, and allow and motivate further innovations [29]. In medicine, the application of cloud technologies is now called healthcare as a service (HaaS). HaaS solutions have the same benefits of free, on-demand, and almost unlimited computer storage, and networking capabilities relative to the conventional explanations for cloud adoption technologies in more complex applications and in the IoT model. We have found other factors to be important, such as ease of data exchange, the versatility of data processing, and flexibility.

Cloud and fog computing benefit from technology related to mobile and personal computers to handle the rise of digital data and demands for medical care anytime and anywhere. The general enhancement of the quality of service is judged by relevant contributions to the healthcare sector: since many mobile devices and artifacts are now more aware of everyday encounters with patients and healthcare practitioners, usability and touch latency may be severe issues, affecting predictability, interrupting decision-making processes, and disrupting delivery. The mobile cloud tends to alleviate or fix these concerns and provides applications with relevant knowledge, ensuring more user-friendly and higher quality goods and versatile integration performance [30]. To sum up, blockchain, fog, and remote cloud technologies make up an integral aspect of Health 4.0, with major advantages for the development of both health science and services (improving efficiency, making them accessible for a wider number of people than currently possible, and improving patient outcomes).

2.4 Big data in Health 4.0

The concept of big data has a highly contentious definition and scope. Over time, the focus has moved from the dataset properties in reaction to existing structures (a dataset that could not be gathered, handled, and processed by general computers within an acceptable reach according to the Apache Hadoop concept) to be outlined in the project to strategically extract value from enormous amounts of a large variety of data sources by requiring. The biggest and best-known set of big data-related properties was captured by a widely agreed and concise characterization focused on five Vs [31]: (i) volume (increases in data scale); (ii) velocity (time limits are obtained and analyzed); (iii) complexity (data comprises different sorts, i.e., structured or unstructured format data); (iv) authenticity (data of different extents); (v) utility (that this whole framework is targeted at creating revenue economically).

This 5-V characterization shows the powerful context-dependent existence of big data, which is defined regarding applications (value) and technological constraints (volume, speed, variety, veracity). These unusual requirements, which challenge the capabilities accessible through the recognition of big data, have sparked tremendous progress in data processing strategies and tools over the last two decades, including leveraging cloud computing as an enabler for the new virtual frameworks. We focus on an overall technical analysis of the evolution of big data. In fact, and overwhelmingly in industry 4.0 systems, big data and main dimensions are clearly implied in Industry 4.0. It is of paramount importance to be mindful of the broad variety of available datasets to consider the actual usefulness of big data for health care 4.0 [32].

Internet-based networking site data is the most traditional type of big data, which has previously overshadowed big data applications and advocated for the right skills [33]. In the sense of I4.0, this data is used more reliably in an automatic manner to tune the value chain, directed initially at targeted ads and market analysis. From a certain point of view, everything in supply chain management should be seen as an attempt to promote some immediate input directly into the architectural-production-delivery loop from in-the-wild data analysis. Social media is reshaping the essence of health-related experiences, changing the way health care practitioners interpret patient information, and sharing medical expertise with what is solely concerned with the health industry. Social media and related technology are radically changing the practice of medicine, especially social networking sites and feeds, social media networks, and online discussion groups, as access to web content offers increasingly valuable information.

Academic evidence is still a significant source of biomedical data (although there is a growing availability of organized resources). Indexing and cataloging require dedicated online text mining tools, allowing users to scan and download relevant literature quickly and efficiently. Finally, substantial amounts are now being generated and collected at an exponential pace and size from diverse biological data sources (e.g., bioengineering, microbiomics, bioinformatics, metatranscriptomics, epigenomes, metagenomics, etc.), as the expense of data processing and interpretation declines with technical advances. This term can be broken into four distinct levels: data at the molecular level, data at the tissue level, data at the patient level, and population data. Table 1 presents contemporary literature regarding: (i) ICTs in Health 4.0, (ii) IoT in Health 4.0, (iii) cloud and fog computing in Health 4.0, and (iv) big data in Health 4.0.

3. Findings

3.1 Applications for Health 4.0

Both corporate policy and empirical consensus note the role of healthcare in being a catalyst for the main pillars shaping the I4.0 vision. IoT is used for wireless networking in all its facets, concerns, and bases, promoting a biomedical application in diverse ways, ranging from long-term treatment of the elderly and home security to rapid recovery services for healthcare. Since these configurations increasingly produce greater volumes of a broad range of data by enabling them to draw value from its high-speed collection, detection, and analysis, big-data technologies and new-generation frameworks are required. The need to evaluate these enormous quantities of data further pushes for a transition to cloud architecture, necessary for the safe and efficient analysis of both transport and communication prerequisites. Researchers and doctors are developing innovative innovations thanks to IoT, cloud and fog, and big data that can quickly and effectively renew integrated healthcare delivery or even provide exciting new insights to address and resolve long-lasting health challenges.

3.1.1 Health monitoring

The study demonstrates how the IoT model, facilitated by developments in mobile communication networks as well as smart devices and sensor systems, often organized in WSN and WBAN, together with mobility including on-demand cloud and fog services including big data technologies, can provide a powerful forum to support robust security activities [34]. The final configuration requires medical data to be accessed, which potentially allows for the processing of health-related statistical information and the implementation of new forms of cloud technologies that can supplement or replace current hospital information systems. This type of automated technique means that the likelihood of committing errors is drastically reduced, particularly compared to approaches that require manual input. Clinicians' remote-control methods

TABLE 1 Tabular presentation of contemporary literature regarding ICTs in Health 4.0

Author, Year	Focus	Topic	Key findings
Khan, 2017 [17]	ICT for Health 4.0	Healthcare monitoring system on the Internet of Things (IoT) with a focus on the use of RFID.	Proposal of a comprehensive healthcare monitoring system based on the combination of the IoT and RFID tags. Presentation of experimental results supporting the robust output of this model in a wide range of health emergencies.
Abdel-Basset et al., 2020 [18]	ICT for Health 4.0	Literature review and a new model for the fusion of the Internet of Intelligent Things (IoIT) in remote diagnosis of obstructive sleep apnea (OSA).	A combination of AI and IoT modalities leads to the formation of the IoIT framework. This framework has major potential in OSA diagnosis.
de Paula Ferreira et al., 2020 [19]	ICT for Health 4.0	State-of-the-art review about the role of simulation in Industry 4.0.	A conceptual framework of principles for modeling and simulation in Industry 4.0 illustrated with the presentation of 10 simulation-based approaches in this context.
Ho et al., 2020 [20]	ICT for Health 4.0	Technologies enabling personalized and precision medicine.	AI- and IoT-based approaches to precision medicine can use population-wide data to improve individualized treatment strategies.
Aheleroff et al., 2020 [21]	ICT for Health 4.0	A case study of IoT-based smart applications in the context of Industry 4.0.	IoT-based smart systems can integrate conventional home appliances into a smart home system facilitating big data analytics, customer satisfaction, and energy efficiency.
Friis, 2020 [22]	ICT for Health 4.0	Original study about inactive hermeneutics and smart medical technologies.	Continuous human interpretative enactments can improve any application of the information output because they enhance statistical repetition by means of meaning-generating interpretative processes.

Author	Category	Title	Description
Giuseppe Aceto et al., 2020 [5]	ICT for Health 4.0	Taxonomies, perspectives, and challenges in the frame of information and communication technologies (ICTs) in healthcare.	A survey providing an up-to-date picture of healthcare novelties supported by the ICTs advancements with a focus on critical healthcare departments and domains.
Thakar and Pandya, 2017 [26]	IoT in Health 4.0	A survey of IoT-enabled devices in healthcare	Smart devices can enhance preventive and urgent interventions, decreasing the total cost and burden of healthcare provision.
Gupta and Paiva, 2020 [24]	IoT in Health 4.0	Challenges related to the integration of IoT in healthcare.	Data protection, a collaboration between healthcare services and the IoT industry, and synchronized delivery of information to several healthcare stakeholders represent the main challenges of IoT in healthcare,
Suresh et al., 2020 [23]	IoT in Health 4.0	Intelligent production systems in the intersection of IoT and additive manufacturing.	Digital 3D data can accelerate additive manufacturing processes, increasing both their efficacy and quality.
Nižetić et al., 2020 [25]	IoT in Health 4.0	Opportunities and challenges for a smart and sustainable future in the frame of the IoT.	IoT technologies in environmental sustainability, IoT-based smart cities, e-health, ambient assisted living systems, and reduction in transportation carbon emissions based on the IoT are the most potent and challenging fields.
Rouzbeh et al., 2020 [27]	Cloud and fog computing in Health 4.0	Open-source technologies enabling collaborative cloud computing for healthcare data.	Proposal of a novel architecture for a software-hardware-data ecosystem based on open-source technologies (Apache Hadoop, Kubernetes, and JupyterHub). Evaluation of the system by analyzing a clinical database of 69M patients.
Paliwal, 2020 [28]	Cloud and fog computing in Health 4.0	E-governance in the cloud environment.	Critical analysis of challenges and requirements for the implementation of cloud-based e-governance services in India.

Continued

TABLE 1 Tabular presentation of contemporary literature regarding ICTs in Health 40—cont'd

Author, Year	Focus	Topic	Key findings
Narkhede et al., 2020 [29]	Cloud and fog computing in Health 4.0	Bibliometric analysis of cloud computing research	Bibliometric analysis of 750 identified research papers published between 2011 and 2017.
Vyas et al., 2020 [30]	Cloud and fog computing in Health 4.0	Fog data in remote monitoring systems.	Decentralized data use can improve remote monitoring systems' function, equipment monitoring, and smart equipment maintenance.
Reinhardt et al., 2020 [31]	Big Data in Health 4.0	Healthcare Industry 4.0 in the pharmaceutical sector.	A survey assessing the perceptions of Industry 4.0 in the pharmaceutical industry globally. Despite the growth of the sector, a comprehensive understanding of Industry 4.0 has not been achieved. This is leading to delays in the integration of its full potential into the pharmaceutical industry.
Sarangi et al., 2021 [32]	Big Data in Health 4.0	Fog computing with IoT, cloud computing, big data, and machine learning in the context of Healthcare Industry 4.0.	Role and application of machine learning infrastructure, fog computing architectures, and relevant case studies.
Galetsi et al., 2020 [33]	Big Data in Health 4.0	Theoretical framework, techniques, and prospects of big data analytics.	A critical review of several pragmatic examples highlighting the implementation of big data advances in healthcare.

consist of three components: (i) processing and data storage machines for capturing perceptual and speech data; (ii) remote center communication technology and data transmission systems; and (iii) data analysis techniques for extracting physiological and activity data from clinically relevant data. Applications, depending on the type of sensors used, may be either physical or electrical. The use of advanced medical and environmental equipment, such as accelerometers and gyroscopes (often incorporated into portable devices), monitors for temperature and humidity, ECG, glucose, blood pressure, and gas sensors, allows continuous tracking of the patient's physiological and physical condition.

To maximize the advantage of infinite storage, flexible computing resources, and high service efficiency of future computational modeling, IoT systems will transfer this knowledge to remote locations where big data processing can be carried out. This solution requires an external secure network connection for remote storage, cloud medical record processing, and retrieval, and presents several problems related to network access and traffic. Health tracking is mentioned among the practical applications that promote growth under the 5G wireless network infrastructure's extremely stable telecommunications standards. Fog computing at smart gateways, providing tools such as automatic data mining, distributed storage, and notification systems on the fringes of the network to mitigate the concerns posed by the implementation of remote cloud services, are other moves to overcome these obstacles in improving health management networks [35]. Flickering approximation often plays a key role (e.g., comprehensive brain management systems using EEG-based brain-computer interfaces or semantic-related facilities). Fog-based architectures can also be designed to provide the tools for the implantation of medical instruments in living tissue to improve and restore human beings, such as artificial organs, the brain imaging network, and to activate the cardiovascular system.

3.1.2 Prevention and self-management

Health 4.0 combines broad-scale self-management strategies [36]. Indeed, big-data technology facilitates the implementation of a transition from cure to prevention. Besides practical tasks, researchers have researched how cognitive techniques can be created, such as displaying measuring data temporarily and storing information while still being able to provide individuals with effective input. These solutions may include algorithms for disease prevention including, for example, identifying modifiable risk factors and designing techniques for optimizing health behavior. Management of chronic illnesses is one of the most relevant examples of this self-management for wellbeing. For example, these mechanisms can include guidelines for awareness and provision of healthy eating and preparing exercise programs to monitor and avoid diabetes and obesity.

3.1.3 Smart medication and monitoring

Drug management problems are pervasive in elderly and sick patients and amplify suicidal tendencies. Related problems are addressed by control of opioid usage. These systems are a valuable tool for disease control professionals because they provide a systematic means of evaluating the success of treatment. Early implementations for the elderly took advantage of the combined use of sensor networks and smartcards. There are currently several smartphone applications with features such as setting alerts, prescribing reminders, and monitoring opioid intake, based on the critical importance of the duration of drug administration of drug therapies to reach maximum effectiveness and decrease side effects. There are also advanced methods (such as compact or interchangeable detectors, and integrated software communication and intellectual ability). Here, smart drugs are known as advanced electronics, delivery systems, or medicines with digital value-added (e.g., through a wireless link to an Internet-enabled computer or direct Internet contact that allows communication to a remote machine capable of compiling, storing, and analyzing data). We expect future smart drugs to accumulate a range of micro- and macro-level metadata that will offer new insights into diseases, assist with service design, and facilitate personal care.

3.1.4 Precision medicine

Personalized healthcare is designed to be user-centered, i.e., taking patient-specific decisions (rather than stratifying patients into traditional categories of treatment). It is vital to collect data from multiple sources (e.g., from both patients and the environment), as similar data collection facilitates decision-making and implementation of health and social care [37]. Conventional outlets can be compact with monitors or therapy monitoring systems, such as dropping alarms, implantable insulin pumps, defibrillator vests, etc. (or even implantable micro- and nanotechnologies). These characteristics represent the vision of I4.0 (namely, user centrality and data convergence from various heterogeneous sources, including wearable devices, to deliver highly customized services). They specifically define sector 4.0 and are further stressed, depending heavily on everyone's genetic constitution. A detailed comprehension of everyone's biology (personalized omics) affects predisposition, sampling, diagnosis, prognosis, pharmacogenomics, and tracking. Therefore, big-data analytics is essential, both at the individual and community level, for the adoption of personalized healthcare.

3.1.5 Cloud-based health information systems

In several ways, cloud-based applications have been universally adopted to improve and automate the design, implementation, and distribution of information networks to store, retrieve, and exchange patient documents, administrative healthcare data, or diagnostic images. These architectures increase data collection (e.g., the affected computers are often equipped with mobile interfaces for cloud providers to manage and exchange health records). This is useful to exchange information between various medical structures or between patients and healthcare professionals, as they are frameworks to combine data in many formats, sometimes of healthcare [38].

3.1.6 Telemedicine for disease monitoring

The first visible attempts made at operational telepathology, i.e., external capture, delivery, and analysis of pathology specimens, date back to the 1980s, when the incorporation of robotic microscopy, video imaging, databases, and subsequent groundbreaking wireless telecommunications networking was developed as technology promoting telepathology services [39]. As there are many grants available today that show how ICT facilitates a variety of telemedicine, telepathology, and disease detection applications, this promise has proved true. Two classifications of research are available: (i) generic constructs applicable to most cases of use, and (ii) study focused on individual diseases such as cancer diagnosis, cardiovascular disease, diabetes, Parkinson's disease, and Alzheimer's disease. These monitoring systems can be applied both to feed large-scale experiments and to specific treatments tailored to the outcomes. Surgery is therefore predicted in the future to become even more transparent.

Camcorders are frequently incorporated into operating room lighting for open operations. The laparoscopic procedure is also theoretically denoted by several observers. These instruments are channels, which allow the physical presence of the professional to be avoided. If an active camera bearer is used throughout the process and the remote consultant can switch the camera, hence the telepresence occur. The implementation of this proposed system, where the surgeon and his/her simulator are physically separated from the operating theater, is described as telesurgery [24]. The existence of restricted virtual paths to the edge fog networks will support in this regard since the best-effort Internet links are not enough to support several application groups (for example, if the aim is to replicate the effect of a locally controlled microscope). For example, it would allow remote sites to cooperate using complex diagnostics as supporting tools for decision making.

4. Transformation case of the pharmaceutical industry

Pharmaceutical agents are struggling to improve their performance in terms of manufacturing processes and supply chain. Once such a transformation is planned, there are considerations regarding its feasibility, its functionality, and sufficient return on investment. The latter is so important that the company puts on hold 1 year's work and investment when the estimated return would not outweigh the expenses. The pharmaceutical company turned to digital experts, who suggested strengthening the plan and its estimated outcome by adopting a design compatible with Industry and Health 4.0. In the frame of an Industry 4.0 roadmap, the plan was revised to prioritize performance and value. Technological modalities were adjusted to the company's plans for growth and not the opposite. Performance was prioritized over the adoption of the latest novelties, while homogeneous mapping of procedures and decision-making processes was established at the company level [40].

Digital world solutions including blockchain and AI were adopted and adjusted according to the data storage, flow, and processing capacity of the company. The personnel were thoroughly trained to combine their experience and expertise with the innovative technologies. The company's leadership came to understand that performance should be placed ahead of technology. Conventional technology could be better than sophisticated novelties, if it were consistent with the existing business planning and expertise [41]. Real-time monitoring of processes and data collection became possible by replacing paperwork with designated electronic devices, particularly tablets [42]. In the end, revising the transformation plan in line with Industry 4.0 improved the returns. The return on investment was increased four times in a timeframe shorter than expected. Industry 4.0 modification is still on the way, following the pace of the business plan rather than manipulating it [31].

5. Opportunities and challenges

Health 4.0 has been conceptualized through the wisdom pyramid, as shown in Fig. 2. This structure enables us to break down the digital underpinning of Health 4.0 to an order of:

- Foundations of digital data (data/information)
- Representations of digital knowledge (knowledge)
- Learning, prediction, and decision-making based on digital knowledge (wisdom)

The wisdom pyramid system provides a comprehensive basis for the evaluation of the opportunities and challenges arising from data/information and digital knowledge representation and learning. Wisdom, defined as deep expertise

FIG. 2 The wisdom pyramid.

in various healthcare domains, pertains to the ability to collect, store, and process existing data. Upon analysis, such data can be transformed to evidence-based decision-making supported by machine learning (ML) and artificial intelligence (AI) [43].

A prominent level of expertise oriented to decision-making represents an opportunity and a challenge at the same time. For the origin of the required data, we understand they derive from a network of innovative digital technologies spanning from smartphones, wearable devices, and social media networks, to medical imaging and conventional monitoring devices interconnected within the IoMT [5]. Such a level of monitoring can upgrade healthcare services, making precision and evidence-based medicine services more accessible. The cost of implementing such networks is considerable, while there is a lack of sufficient data related to its cost-effectiveness [44]. Confidentiality is a challenging point as well, given that biometric data can be used by insurance companies or employers as selection criteria.

Knowledge repositories such as PubMed, and Cochrane library are aligned with semantic sensor networks (SSNs) providing AI modalities including but not limited to machine learning, recognition of patterns, processing of speech and language, semantic reasoning, visual data processing, and computational/computer vision [45]. The capacity to incorporate such an immense amount of knowledge is a revolution to learning curves. Such tools supporting decision-making could substitute years of formal training and experience. This very feature is risky, though. Neglecting systematic education and training may harm the integrity of future physicians and researchers. Doctor-patient communication may be significantly decreased [46]. Machine-driven decision-making may lack personalization and rational-critical thinking. An automated staging system suggesting invasive surgical treatment to an old and frail patient can only be avoided with humane consideration [47]. Finally, yet importantly, cooperative decision-making may be replaced by machine-backed paternalism, with the physician dictating the suggestion of an algorithm.

Merging digital data foundations, digital knowledge representation, and digital knowledge learning and prediction is expected to support remote healthcare facilities and practitioners. The provision of an equivalent level of care in urban centers and remote centers has been a serious challenge. Despite the allocated resources, distance and time have always hindered healthcare services in remote settings [48]. Health 4.0 applications in remote healthcare include, but are not limited to, telehealth in terms of prevention and management of conditions, assisted ambient living, monitoring of infectious diseases outbreaks, clinical decision-making support systems, close monitoring and care of vulnerable individuals/population groups, mental health, health promotion, and literacy. We expect these applications to transform the current perception of individual and community care, ameliorating the patients' experience and empowering healthcare workers in remote contexts [31,43].

6. Future insights

ICTs are highly influential on humanity, especially in the health domain. The promising technologies of Health 4.0 are transforming future healthcare provision into widespread and ongoing access to precise healthcare programs. Wearables, IoT, and its health-driven subfields such as the Internet of Health or Medical Things, are major pillars supporting Health 4.0, especially wireless body area networks, including nanoscale biosensors. The effects on wellness and life quality for healthy and sick individuals are easily seen in better habits and real-time therapies that are enhanced during hospitalization, and in decreased health costs. In addition, big data analysis tools and models involving artificial intelligence technologies could quickly extract the hidden value in huge volumes of data using pervasive wearable sensors that would enable studying, disclosing, and benefiting the massive future populations with prior unrecognized trends and relations for better-promoting prevention and treatment potentials.

Technologies like fog and cloud computing and the growing 5G telecommunication networks, leveraged with the IoT, are as yet working in the background. They would be required for the innovative applications to build the perverseness of the healthcare services and the needed functionality at a reasonable cost. Such technologies are challenging for future medical applications in terms of, for example: devices' security, connections, and procedures; confidentiality and ethical considerations regarding thorough monitoring prioritization and massive digitalization of health procedures; great platform complexity, confining or hindering complete understanding and hence management; the fast track technological revolution, making it difficult to cope with laws and public awareness; and the interdisciplinary Health 4.0 itself, involving several technological domains and, notably, also including nontechnical ones.

Some well-known limitations such as security and privacy are highly investigated. Leveraging various technologies and applying them to novel scenarios requires more research of alternative solutions, which is complicated by the interaction among some solutions and other problems, such as improving security, which usually leads to more complexity regarding transparency and understanding of the system, hindering awareness and laws, and halting rapid innovation.

7. Conclusions

This chapter aims to guide researchers and experts in ICTs and those in healthcare information systems and digital transformation, to see the novel principles and techniques of IT, and to envision the evolution of Health 4.0 effectively and profitably. This chapter discussed the powerful technologies of the Fourth Industrial Revolution, referred to as the IoT, big data analytics, and fog and cloud computing, and emphasized their applications in health. Healthcare is shifting toward ICT-based e-health and would see a more crucial transformation under Health 4.0, where ICTs could enhance conventional procedures and systems such as cloud-derived health information systems, health tracking of vital and physiological indicators, and smart medications; and promote novel unpreceded techniques and applications, like better living ecosystems, home care rehabilitation, and precision medicine. The chapter also highlighted several technological advantages and disadvantages and ended with future recommendations.

References

[1] E. Omanović-Mikličanin, M. Maksimović, V. Vujović, The future of healthcare: nanomedicine and Internet of Nano Things, Folia Med. Fac. Med. Univ. Saraeviensis 50 (2015).

[2] G. Aceto, V. Persico, A. Pescapé, The role of information and communication technologies in healthcare: taxonomies, perspectives, and challenges, J. Netw. Comput. Appl. 107 (2018) 125–154, https://doi.org/10.1016/j.jnca.2018.02.008.

[3] P. Germanakos, C. Mourlas, G. Samaras, A mobile agent approach for ubiquitous and personalized eHealth information systems; 2005. In Proceedings of the Workshop on 'Personalization for e-Health' of the 10th International.

[4] C. Pino, R.D. Salvo, A Survey of Cloud Computing Architecture and Applications in Health, Atlantis Press, 2013, pp. 1649–1653, https://doi.org/10.2991/iccsee.2013.413.

[5] G. Aceto, V. Persico, A. Pescapé, Industry 4.0 and health: internet of things, big data, and cloud computing for healthcare 4.0, J. Ind. Inf. Integr. 18 (2020) 100129, https://doi.org/10.1016/j.jii.2020.100129.

[6] M. Bamiah, S. Brohi, S. Chuprat, J.A. Manan, A study on significance of adopting cloud computing paradigm in healthcare sector, in: 2012 Int. Conf. Cloud Comput. Technol. Appl. Manag. ICCCTAM, 2012, pp. 65–68, https://doi.org/10.1109/ICCCTAM.2012.6488073.

[7] J.H. Park, M.K. Kim, A study on the potential needs and market promotion of smart health in Korea, in: 2013 Int. Conf. ICT Converg. ICTC, JEJU ISLAND, Korea (South): IEEE, 2013, pp. 824–825, https://doi.org/10.1109/ICTC.2013.6675489.

[8] G. Aceto, V. Persico, A. Pescapé, A survey on information and communication technologies for Industry 4.0: state-of-the-art, taxonomies, perspectives, and challenges, IEEE Commun. Surv. Tutorials 21 (2019) 3467–3501, https://doi.org/10.1109/COMST.2019.2938259.

[9] Z. Sheng, S. Yang, Y. Yu, A.V. Vasilakos, J.A. Mccann, K.K. Leung, A survey on the ietf protocol suite for the internet of things: standards, challenges, and opportunities, IEEE Wirel. Commun. 20 (2013) 91–98, https://doi.org/10.1109/MWC.2013.6704479.

[10] S.M.R. Islam, D. Kwak, M.D.H. Kabir, M. Hossain, K.-S. Kwak, The internet of things for health care: a comprehensive survey, IEEE Access 3 (2015) 678–708, https://doi.org/10.1109/ACCESS.2015.2437951.

[11] J. Couturier, D. Sola, G.S. Borioli, C. Raiciu, How Can the Internet of Things Help to Overcome Current Healthcare Challenges, 2012.

[12] J. Santos, J.J.P.C. Rodrigues, B.M.C. Silva, J. Casal, K. Saleem, V. Denisov, An IoT-based mobile gateway for intelligent personal assistants on mobile health environments, J. Netw. Comput. Appl. 71 (2016) 194–204, https://doi.org/10.1016/j.jnca.2016.03.014.

[13] S. Hiremath, G. Yang, K. Mankodiya, Wearable internet of things: concept, architectural components and promises for person-centered healthcare, in: 2014 4th Int. Conf. Wirel. Mob.

Commun. Healthc. - Transform. Healthc. Innov. Mob. Wirel. Technol. MOBIHEALTH, 2014, pp. 304–307, https://doi.org/10.1109/MOBIHEALTH.2014.7015971.

[14] N. Terry, Will the Internet of Things Disrupt Healthcare?, Social Science Research Network, Rochester, NY, 2016, https://doi.org/10.2139/ssrn.2760447.

[15] N.K. Jha, Internet-of-medical-things, in: Proc. Gt. Lakes Symp. VLSI 2017, New York, NY, USA: Association for Computing Machinery, 2017, p. 7, https://doi.org/10.1145/3060403.3066861.

[16] R.S.H. Istepanian, S. Hu, N.Y. Philip, A. Sungoor, The potential of Internet of m-health Things "m-IoT" for non-invasive glucose level sensing, in: 2011 Annu. Int. Conf. IEEE Eng. Med. Biol. Soc, 2011, pp. 5264–5266, https://doi.org/10.1109/IEMBS.2011.6091302.

[17] S.F. Khan, Health care monitoring system in Internet of Things (IoT) by using RFID, in: 2017 6th Int. Conf. Ind. Technol. Manag. ICITM, 2017, pp. 198–204, https://doi.org/10.1109/ICITM.2017.7917920.

[18] M. Abdel-Basset, W. Ding, L. Abdel-Fatah, The fusion of internet of intelligent things (IoIT) in remote diagnosis of obstructive sleep apnea: a survey and a new model, Inf. Fusion 61 (2020) 84–100, https://doi.org/10.1016/j.inffus.2020.03.010.

[19] F.W. de Paula, F. Armellini, L.A. De Santa-Eulalia, Simulation in industry 4.0: a state-of-the-art review, Comput. Ind. Eng. 149 (2020) 106868, https://doi.org/10.1016/j.cie.2020.106868.

[20] D. Ho, S.R. Quake, E.R.B. McCabe, W.J. Chng, E.K. Chow, X. Ding, et al., Enabling Technologies for Personalized and Precision Medicine, Trends Biotechnol. 38 (2020) 497–518, https://doi.org/10.1016/j.tibtech.2019.12.021.

[21] S. Aheleroff, X. Xu, Y. Lu, M. Aristizabal, J. Pablo Velásquez, B. Joa, et al., IoT-enabled smart appliances under industry 4.0: a case study, Adv. Eng. Inform. 43 (2020) 101043, https://doi.org/10.1016/j.aei.2020.101043.

[22] J.K.B.O. Friis, Enactive hermeneutics and smart medical technologies, AI Soc. (2020), https://doi.org/10.1007/s00146-020-00944-w.

[23] A. Suresh, R. Udendhran, G. Yamini, Internet of things and additive manufacturing: toward intelligent production systems in industry 4.0, in: G.R. Kanagachidambaresan, R. Anand, E. Balasubramanian, V. Mahima (Eds.), Internet Things Industry 4.0: Design, Challenges and Solutions, Springer International Publishing, Cham, 2020, pp. 73–89, https://doi.org/10.1007/978-3-030-32530-5_5.

[24] N. Gupta, S. Paiva (Eds.), IoT and ICT for Healthcare Applications, Springer International Publishing, 2020, https://doi.org/10.1007/978-3-030-42934-8.

[25] S. Nižetić, P. Šolić, D. López-de-Ipiña González-de-Artaza, L. Patrono, Internet of things (IoT): opportunities, issues and challenges towards a smart and sustainable future, J. Clean. Prod. 274 (2020) 122877, https://doi.org/10.1016/j.jclepro.2020.122877.

[26] A.T. Thakar, S. Pandya, Survey of IoT enables healthcare devices, in: 2017 Int. Conf. Comput. Methodol. Commun. ICCMC, 2017, pp. 1087–1090, https://doi.org/10.1109/ICCMC.2017.8282640.

[27] F. Rouzbeh, A. Grama, P. Griffin, M. Adibuzzaman, Collaborative cloud computing framework for health data with open source technologies, ArXiv200710498 Cs (2020), https://doi.org/10.1145/3388440.3412460.

[28] N. Paliwal, E-governance paradigm with cloud environment, Res. J (2020). https://www.gyanvihar.org/journals/index.php/2020/03/14/e-governance-paradigm-with-cloud-environment/. (Accessed 9 December 2020).

[29] B.E. Narkhede, R.D. Raut, V.S. Narwane, B.B. Gardas, Cloud computing in healthcare - a vision, challenges and future directions, Int. J. Bus. Inf. Syst. 34 (2020) 1, https://doi.org/10.1504/IJBIS.2020.106799.

[30] T. Vyas, S. Desai, A. Ruparelia, Fog data processing and analytics for health care-based iot applications, in: S. Tanwar (Ed.), Fog Data Processing and Analytics for Health Care-Based IoT Applications, Springer, Singapore, 2020, pp. 445–469, https://doi.org/10.1007/978-981-15-6044-6_18.

[31] I.C. Reinhardt, D.J.C. Oliveira, Ring DDT. Current perspectives on the development of industry 4.0 in the pharmaceutical sector, J. Ind. Inf. Integr. 18 (2020) 100131, https://doi.org/10.1016/j.jii.2020.100131.

[32] A.K. Sarangi, A.G. Mohapatra, T.C. Mishra, B. Keswani, Healthcare 4.0: a voyage of fog computing with iot, cloud computing, big data, and machine learning, in: S. Tanwar (Ed.), Fog Computing for Healthcare 4.0 Environments Technical, Societal, and Future Implications, Springer International Publishing, Cham, 2021, pp. 177–210, https://doi.org/10.1007/978-3-030-46197-3_8.

[33] P. Galetsi, K. Katsaliaki, S. Kumar, Big data analytics in health sector: theoretical framework, techniques and prospects, Int. J. Inf. Manag. 50 (2020) 206–216, https://doi.org/10.1016/j.ijinfomgt.2019.05.003.

[34] C.-Z. Dong, F.N. Catbas, A review of computer vision–based structural health monitoring at local and global levels, Struct. Health Monit. 1475921720935585 (2020), https://doi.org/10.1177/1475921720935585.

[35] S. Tanwar (Ed.), Fog Computing for Healthcare 4.0 Environments: Technical, Societal, and Future Implications, Springer International Publishing, 2021, https://doi.org/10.1007/978-3-030-46197-3.

[36] V. Simpson, D. Xu, Difficulties with health self-management by older adults: the role of wellbeing, Geriatr. Nurs. (Lond.) (2020), https://doi.org/10.1016/j.gerinurse.2020.07.010.

[37] O. Chén, B. Roberts, Personalized Healthcare and Public Health in the Digital Age, 2020, https://doi.org/10.31219/osf.io/hmves.

[38] T. Benil, J. Jasper, Cloud based security on outsourcing using blockchain in E-health systems, Comput. Netw. 178 (2020) 107344, https://doi.org/10.1016/j.comnet.2020.107344.

[39] L.A. George, R.K. Cross, Remote monitoring and telemedicine in IBD: are we there yet? Curr. Gastroenterol. Rep. 22 (2020) 12, https://doi.org/10.1007/s11894-020-0751-0.

[40] S. Souchet, Industry 4.0 Case Studies - KPMG Global, 2020.

[41] L.M. Vizer, J. Eschler, B.M. Koo, J. Ralston, W. Pratt, S. Munson, "It's not just technology, It's people": constructing a conceptual model of shared health informatics for tracking in chronic illness management, J. Med. Internet Res. 21 (2019), https://doi.org/10.2196/10830, e10830.

[42] M. Sanchez, E. Exposito, J. Aguilar, Autonomic computing in manufacturing process coordination in industry 4.0 context, J. Ind. Inf. Integr. 19 (2020) 100159, https://doi.org/10.1016/j.jii.2020.100159.

[43] P.P. Jayaraman, A.R.M. Forkan, A. Morshed, P.D. Haghighi, Y.-B. Kang, Healthcare 4.0: a review of frontiers in digital health, WIREs Data Min. Knowl. Discovery 10 (2020), https://doi.org/10.1002/widm.1350, e1350.

[44] A.P. Dicker, H.S.L. Jim, Intersection of digital health and oncology, JCO Clin. Cancer Inform. 2 (2018) 1–4, https://doi.org/10.1200/CCI.18.00070.

[45] R. Haux, Health information systems – past, present, future, Int. J. Med. Inform. 75 (2006) 268–281, https://doi.org/10.1016/j.ijmedinf.2005.08.002.

[46] E. Bielli, F. Carminati, S. La Capra, M. Lina, C. Brunelli, M. Tamburini, A wireless health outcomes monitoring system (WHOMS): development and field testing with cancer patients using mobile phones, BMC Med. Inform. Decis. Mak. 4 (2004) 7, https://doi.org/10.1186/1472-6947-4-7.

[47] S. Latif, J. Qadir, S. Farooq, M.A. Imran, How 5G wireless (and concomitant technologies) will revolutionize healthcare? Futur. Internet 9 (2017) 93, https://doi.org/10.3390/fi9040093.

[48] S. Vishnu, S.R.J. Ramson, R. Jegan, Internet of medical things (IoMT) - an overview, in: 2020 5th Int. Conf. Devices Circuits Syst. ICDCS, 2020, pp. 101–104, https://doi.org/10.1109/ICDCS48716.2020.243558.

Chapter 3

Integrated machine learning techniques for preserving privacy in Internet of Things (IoT) systems

Saumya Kakandwar, Bharat Bhushan, and Avinash Kumar
School of Engineering and Technology (SET), Sharda University, Greater Noida, Uttar Pradesh, India

1. Introduction

This era is largely dominated by technology, which can be used to enhance human lives and living standards. There are many fields within this technology responsible for making our lives convenient, fast, and more responsive to day-to-day needs; the Internet of Things (IoT) is one of them [1]. IoT is technology where a network of interconnected devices or machines is capable of exchanging data among themselves without any human interference or assistance. IoT is responsible for the term "smart," used in our day-to-day life, such as smart cities that utilize smart machines, smart devices, and smart sensors, whose implementation could be found in healthcare to monitor blood pressure, heartbeat, and other related symptoms [2,3]. Li et al. [4] discussed smart community as an application of IoT, which refers to a paradigmatic class of cyber-physical systems with cooperating objects. To understand, the working of IoT, it is necessary to learn about its elements and whole architecture in order to integrate it with other technologies [5]. Ray et al. [6] summarized the current state-of-the-art of IoT architectures in various domains systematically. Burhan et al. [7] discussed the elements comprising an IoT network, its different layers, and the protocols used in all layers. Sandeep et al. [8] examined the security concerns and presented an architecture capable of all-round security that could enhance the capability of the system.

Machine learning (ML) is another vast field, which, over the time, has been defined in different ways. To state a few: Arthur Samuel, in 1959, defined it as a field of study that gives computers the ability to learn without being explicitly programmed, while Tom Mitchell in 1998 defined it as a well-posed learning

Blockchain Technology Solutions for the Security of IoT-Based Healthcare Systems.
https://doi.org/10.1016/B978-0-323-99199-5.00012-4
45

problem. There is also another fact associated with vast usage of ML, which is that it is very convenient, i.e., it can handle various kinds of data; and thus, models relating to different types of data could be handled using ML, and later it can train them with a targeted result and can be tested to get the desired outputs. ML is more suitable as it also provides ways to reduce errors after training and testing. Thus, it can be said that it is an optimal field to be integrated with other fields.

For instance, Cui et al. [9] discussed ML implementations in IoT and different techniques such as network management, device identity, etc., that are very useful. Banerjee et al. [10] presented an integrated system of IoT-based wireless sensor network (WSN), based on ML and hybrid optimization techniques (HOT), which can be deployed in the field of agriculture. Liang et al. [11] discussed the need for and benefits of using ML in IoT to overcome its challenges. Khattab et al. [12] and Bera et al. [13] provided ways in which the ML models can be deployed in respect to different issues in IoT. Tomovic et al. [14] discussed techniques to check denial-of-service (DoS) and distributed denial-of-service (DDoS) attacks in IoT networks using ML techniques. While there is no denying the fact that both ML and IoT are vast fields and serve various purposes at different levels to facilitate many roles required for the smooth functioning of human life today and in the future, in this chapter, our major concern is how these two fields can be combined together to yield better results in the security areas of IoT. This is due to the fact that IoT is directly involved in providing services to humans and security is a major concern to all of us today, so the chapter discusses these two fields and their limitations. ML can be used to enhance IoT and its security, thus making it more suitable for the public's usage [15].

The major contributions of this chapter are as follows:

- This chapter provides an overview of IoT, its elements, and its architecture layers, along with different protocols used in it required to deal with IoT implementation.
- This work presents in-depth analysis of major security issues In IoT, its causes, and the motivation to use ML to overcome the issues.
- This chapter categorizes and discusses different learning paradigms of ML with algorithms used under them and tabularizes its applications in IoT, which enhances its security.
- Finally, this work presents different solutions that can be adopted to use ML in IoT to enhance its security and other functionalities.

The rest of the chapter is organized as follows: Section 2 defines and discusses IoT elements, its architecture, comprising of different layers, and tabularizes protocols governing the layers; Section 3 presents the need to use ML in IoT due to various security issues and challenges present in IoT networks; Section 4 presents discussion related to ML, its learning procedures and algorithms, and the applicability of those algorithms in IoT and other related fields;

Section 5 presents the deployment of ML in IoT to improve its functionality and to overcome the previously mentioned challenges in IoT; and finally, Section 6 concludes the work, providing relevant future research directions.

2. IoT and its architecture

In this section, the different elements comprising an IoT network are discussed. The role of each element is elaborated and, further in this section, the architecture of an IoT network has been critically analyzed.

2.1 IoT elements

Understanding the architecture of the IoT involves first discussing its elements. In the following subsections, the four different elements comprising IoT architecture are discussed.

2.1.1 Identification

Identification of objects in IoT involves a process of recognition and address-separation, which ensures the correct identity of an item within the device. EPC (electronic item code) and uCode (ubiquitous codes) are among the recognition systems used by IoT. Moreover, one of the major steps during the recognition is to address the IoT artifacts, which will distinguish the entity's ID from its position, as executed by IPv4 and IPv6 [16–18]. However, IPv6 addressing is found to be more appropriate for remotely available low-power systems due to compressing of IPv6 headers by using 6LoWPAN [19].

2.1.2 Communication

The IoT uses various connectivity technologies for communication, which includes Bluetooth, 802.15.4 IEEE 802.11b/g/n, IEEE 802.15.4, and LTE-A, etc., operating at low power nodes to reduce the chances of failure in communication links [20–24]. One such technology is radio frequency identification (RFID), which is a wireless system having two components: tags and readers [25]. The reader is a device that has one or more antennas that emit radio waves and receive signals back from the RFID tag. Tags communicate their identity and other information to nearby readers through radio waves. These tags can be active tags, which have batteries, or passive, which are powered by the readers only. The RFID can be of low frequency (LF) with a short read range of 10 cm, high frequency (HF) with a reading range that lies between $10\,\mathrm{cm}^{-1}\,\mathrm{m}$, and ultrahigh frequency (UHF) with the highest data transfer speed, ranging up to 12 m. Wireless fidelity (Wi-Fi) is another networking system accessed by the IoT to transfer information. Wi-Fi has different versions—802.11a, 802.11b, 802.11g, 802.11n, and 802.11ac—each of which have different data speed, signal interference from outside sources, and cost. While the current versions of

Wi-Fi haven't proved very helpful for IoT applications, there are versions being developed specifically for IoT, such as Wi-Fi Hallow (802.11ah) and HEW (802.11ax). Several researches have also discussed other technologies including near field communication (NFC) and ultra-wideband (UWB) [26,27].

Bluetooth is another technology used within the IoT enabling interaction among different devices over a very short-range. Bluetooth 5.0 is cost-effective and is being used by many large infrastructures. Another useful version that has been developed is Bluetooth low energy (BLE), which is especially beneficial for low-powered devices, helping them to conserve energy. This version is capable of improving operational efficiency and availability of devices as it is faster than previous Bluetooth versions, thus making it ideal for IoT devices and applications. LTE (long-term evolution) and LTE-A (LTE advanced) are other technologies used for communication between different IoT devices. Fig. 1 shows different protocols and framework for communication in the IoT.

2.1.3   Sensing

Sensing is the process of collecting information from nearby associated devices and then transferring it to the cloud, delivery center, etc. The information collected then goes through a series of processes to achieve the required services. This is achieved through different sensing devices such as intelligent sensors, wearable detecting gadgets, etc. Different applications are provided by many organizations to screen and control the intelligent gadgets utilizing cell phones inside a building [28,29]. Another useful tool is single board computers (SBCs) with sensors and tacit TCP/IP [30,31]. Authentication protocols are also useful in identifying different IoT devices.

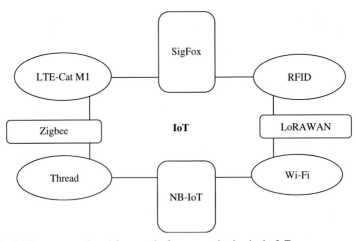

FIG. 1   Different protocols and frameworks for communication in the IoT.

2.1.4   Computation

Different reckoning units such as microchips, microcontrollers, etc., can be used to estimate the capability of an IoT system for computation. Various platforms have been created for computational function in IoT, such as Raspberry Pi, Intel Galileo, T-Mote sky, etc. Although all operating system (OS) cannot be suitable for computing platforms, real time operating systems (RTOS) serve the purpose efficiently—one such RTOS used for IoT is the Contiki RTOS—and different OS are suitable for different configurations of IoT infrastructure from a computational point of view [32–36].

2.2   IoT architecture layer

Fundamentally, IoT architecture can be defined as a three-layered design, which comprises of application, network, and perception layer [37–39]. Fig. 2 represents this three-layer architecture. Other models have also been proposed recently; for example, a four-layer architecture model is visualized in Fig. 3. Several researchers have also studied other different models providing more considerations to IoT architecture [40–42].

2.2.1   Perception layer

This layer comprises various sensors, which are responsible for collecting and analyzing the information from various resources. The sensors integrate to perform various functions. This layer uses several communication protocols to connect large numbers of homogenous and heterogeneous devices to the Internet. Some of the technologies/protocols used are presented in Table 1.

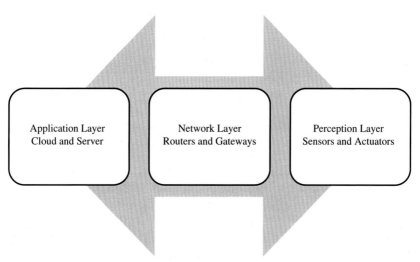

FIG. 2   Three-layer architecture model visualization.

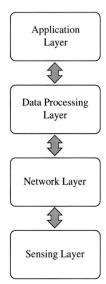

FIG. 3   Four-layer architecture model visualization.

2.2.2   Network layer

This layer determines the path for the data packets to be routed along from one host to another in the network. End-to-end security is provided through the IPsec protocol suite. This layer uses several protocols, which are discussed in Table 2.

2.2.3   Application layer

The application layer acts as an interface between the users and the network layer. It is meant to provide support to the users though high-performing applications. However, it is also vulnerable to threats of various security attacks. Some of the protocols used in this layer are given in Table 3.

2.3   IoT application and services

IoT is used at different levels to provide many services to mankind, be it services for day to day needs or professional needs. In this section, we will discuss some applications and services provided by the IoT.

2.3.1   Smart cities

Smart city is an outcome of various services efficiently combined together, such as smart utilities, disaster management, traffic management, intelligent homes with smart devices, and many more, which are capable of transmitting data using technologies like wireless and the cloud system. Basically, it represents

TABLE 1 Protocols in the perception layer.

Protocol name	Use	Range	Security model/mechanism	Security issues
Near field communication (NFC)	Used in card payments, biometric authentication, etc.	Exchanges the data over short-range distances.	Key-based systems	Security threats like data corruption, leakage, etc.
ZigBee	Provides authentic, low energy consuming, and cost-effective communication. It is present in the network layer and at the top of physical and MAC layer and comes under IEE 802.15.4 standard protocol.	Under personal area networks (PANs), it can provide range coverage 10–100 m.	Comprised of preinstalled keys which has had its security threatened by a new or unknown device. Trusted Center concept.	Sensitive nodes and data can be attacked.
Wi-Fi	Smart devices like phone, tablet, PCs, etc.	Range of 100 m with 900 MHz frequency.	Disabling service set ID(SSID) to detect unauthorized user. No physical connection required for any user to connect to the Internet.	Due to unencrypted communications. Insufficient network usage. Vulnerable to passive attacks like jamming, eavesdropping, etc.
Sigfox	Connects low-power devices like smartwatches.	Ranges up to 1000 km with 10 MHz frequency.	Uses cryptographic token mechanism for authenticating devices securely.	Vulnerable to hackers and not easy to maintain [43].

Continued

TABLE 1 Protocols in the perception layer—cont'd

Protocol name	Use	Range	Security model/mechanism	Security issues
Weightless	Used in low-power wide-area networks (LPWAN) for applications such as raffling sensing, industrial machine monitoring systems, etc.	Range covers up to 10 km.	Uses shift key methods to avoid interference, and 128-bit AES algorithm for encryption and authentication using shared secret key.	More prone to attacks such as DoS, replay attacks, etc.
Long-range WAN (LoRaWAN).	For WAN applications providing low power, cost effectiveness, scalability, etc. Provides multitenancy, multiple applications, and support network domains for long-range communication [43] and security.	Range is 5–15 km.	Use of session key, nonce value, and frame counters.	Vulnerable to attacks like replay, denial of service, eaves dropping, etc.

TABLE 2 Protocols in the network layer.

Protocol name	Use	Security mechanism	Security issue
Low-power wireless personal area network (6LowPAN)	Optimization of IPv6 packets routing.	Reducing the IP overhead through fragmenting and compressing the network header efficiently.	Vulnerable to sink-hole attacks, wormhole attacks, selecting forwarding, etc.
Routing protocol (RPL)	Designed by the Internet Engineering Task Force (IETF) for routing the information.	Tree data structure used via link-layer approach and cryptographic mechanism.	Attacks on integrity, availability of service, and confidentiality, etc.
Cognitive and opportunistic RPL (CORPL)	To frequently update node changes.	Lightweight attribute-based encryption (ABE) with opportunistic approach to forward the data to the neighboring node dynamically.	Extension of RPL and used in cognitive radio networks.
Channel-aware routing protocol (CARP)	To forward the data and initialize the network.	Nodes communicate with each other using relay nodes.	Certain situations make it difficult to control the packets.
6TiSCH	Synchronized backbone routers are used to link the network to the backbone.	Based on IPv6 multilink subnet spanning over high speed IEEE802.15.	Security, link management for the Ipv6 network layer, neighbor discovery, and routing.

an ecosystem of smart devices. The government itself today is planning to convert more and more ordinary cities into smart cities [44]. The smart city concept is executed in various steps and it creates major concerns for the security of its people. Thus, smart cities need to be a secured and sustainable service for the community built through the IoT system [45].

2.3.2   Smart home

Smart home adds more functionality to individual day to day life and increases responsiveness to the needs of the individual [46]. It provides an upgradation of

TABLE 3 Protocols in the application layer.

Protocol	Uses	Security model
Advanced message queuing protocol (AMQP)	A message-centric protocol providing point to point communication.	Uses protocols of transport layer security (TLS) and simple authentication and secure layer (SASL) authentication for security.
Message queue telemetry transport (MQTT)	Supports one to one, one to many, and many to many massaging.	Secure MQTT (sMQTT) has been proposed using lightweight attribute-based encryption (ABE).
Constrained application protocol (CoAP)	Unicast and multicast support is provided for the IOT network. To provide secure communication through datagram transport layer security (DTLS).	Based on the representational state transfer (REST) model with each resource having its own universal resource identifier (URI).
Extensible messaging and presence protocol (XMPP)	For instant messaging, improving mobility to remotely controlled robots.	SASL technique for authentication and TLS for secure communications.
Data distribution services (DDS)	To provide real-time applications via peer-to-peer communication.	Service plugin interface (SPI) is used.

simple human life to a more advanced and efficient life experience. Smart home comprises of many smart devices and machines linked together to share data. For instance, a smart home is capable of turning lights on automatically by monitoring the time stamps of the day relative to a person's usage of the lights. Therefore, smart home and devices need efficient communication with the surrounding conditions and environment [47].

2.3.3   Smart transport

An intelligent transportation system (ITS) is an important part of smart city, which majorly relies on communication and computational cooperation to manage traffic [48]. It aims to reduce the congestion due to traffic, leading to less wastage of time, cleaner air, and thus, lower energy consumption. In a nutshell, the goal is to provide more sustainability to the system and improve its ability to respond to a crisis. IoT devices such as sensors play an important role to operate the traffic and take action before any emergency situation occurs. Improving the traffic system on the existing roads also means reducing the need for new roads, which is very much more cost efficient.

2.3.4   Smart healthcare

Another notable applicability of IoT is the intelligent healthcare system (IHS), also known as e-healthcare, which uses IoT-enabled devices such as smart sensors to observe and track the health-related information of patients, resulting in improved ways to regulate it [49]. The different smart devices used in smart diagnosis of patients through the IoT help in more efficient management and enhanced responsiveness of the medical ecosystem. This, in turn, helps it to become more reliable and secure for its patients. Smart healthcare has also proved to be crucial for remote management of a healthcare system, thus providing more accessibility. One such example of smart healthcare was given by IBM, which used RFID to monitor handwashing of staff after checking every patient [25,50].

2.3.5   Smart agriculture

IoT has also been successful in helping the farming industry by providing sensors to retrieve, observe, and track data related to farming such as temperature of soil, environmental conditions, irrigation, power of hydrogen (pH) value, soil-moisture, and other factors responsible for a better yield of the crop. IoT-enabled applications can be installed to track the behavior of livestock or animals along with observing the harvest [51]. This will enhance productivity and will help farmers to avoid financial crises. Good agricultural productivity will also enhance the national economy. Therefore, intelligent agriculture systems (IAS) would be advantageous to be adopted and are serviced well with the help of IoT.

3.   IoT and its security

The IoT is a network of resource-constrained devices, making it more vulnerable to attack. Some vulnerabilities, security needs, and how these problems can be solved in order to provide a secure IoT network are discussed in the subsections below.

3.1   IoT security requirements

First and foremost, it is necessary to discuss the need to have a secure mechanism to transfer data with proper authentication, confidentiality, and availability [52]. Some major factors required for an IoT-enabled application to protect the fragile information are as follows:

- *Reliability*: The data transfer should be done between the legitimate nodes only.

- *Confidentiality*: The data transmission should be private, i.e.; no data should pass on to unauthorized nodes.
- *Incorruptibility*: Within an IoT network, before transferring the data it must be checked for its integrity; it should be ensured that the data is not corrupted (replaced, copied, or rewritten) by any means.
- *Secrecy*: A protected and reliable IoT network must secure the particularity of its users in order to conserve their privacy.
- *Accessibility*: The IoT-enabled services should be accessible to its legitimate users.

3.2   Security attacks in IoT and their sources

All the layers in an IoT architecture have different technologies enabling them to transfer data; this makes them vulnerable to various kinds of security threats and attacks. Some popular security attacks occurring at different layers in the IoT architecture along with their sources are discussed in the subsections below.

3.2.1   Perception layer attacks

The perception layer basically consists of various sensors used to collect information and later analyze it, such as temperature sensors, fire or smoke sensors, camera sensors, and many more. Some of the popular attacks include:

- *Node capturing*: This attack is most common in low polar sensors, hubs, or actuators. This could be replacing the node with a harmful new node (fake node injection), which will become part of the framework and thus, the security of entire IoT system is exposed to attacks.
- *Hardware interfering*: In these kinds of attacks, the nodes are physically damaged providing access over all the information.
- *Sleep deprivation*: This attack aims to deplete the power of the batteries, especially of low-powered IoT machines, which results in shutting down of the node.
- *Side channel attacks (SCA)*: Confidential information can be leaked easily through the side channels without attacking the node. Such information can be revealed by processors' micro-architecture, their electricity utilization, and radio communication.
- *Malicious code injection*: The Node's memory is injected with a malicious code. This makes certain unwanted changes in the software, providing them access to the node, conducting unwanted activities and exposing the entire security of IoT network.
- *Radio Frequency interference*: This attack can happen when the IoT application is running over RFID by infusing certain noisy signals on the carrier frequency signals.

3.2.2 Network layer attacks

- *Advance Persistent Threat (APT)*: It is an access attack wherein an unknown/unauthorized person breaches the IoT System and aims to collect valuable information by remaining undetected in the system.
- *Routing attack*: In this attack, routing pathways are blocked due to sharing of some malignant nodes. One form of attack, in which the attacker promotes some fake routing address to drive the network traffic, is known as a sink-hole attack. Other attacks under this category include wormhole attack, in which a wormhole is made between a device on the web and a weaker node. This can result in hacking of important security protocols in an IoT network [53].
- *Traffic analysis attack*: In this, an attack is made on the network by analyzing and predicting information gathered about the network.

Other attacks include Sybil, man in the middle, and spoofing attacks in which forging of fake IDs, secretly analyzing information between two parties, and masking the original data is done to gain control over the information at the network layer.

3.2.3 Application layer attacks

The application layer is meant to provide services to the users. This makes the application layer more prone to attacks involving identity stealing and privacy concerns. Some attacks are mentioned below.

- *Access control attacks*: This refers to attacking the access management system, which is essential to authenticate valid customers to access the information. Thus, the whole system's security is compromised to various cyber-attacks [54].
- *Sniffing attacks*: This is used to get confidential consumer details by using sniffers to track the traffic of the IoT network [55].
- *DoS attack*: This attack happens due to multiple unnecessary access being made disturbing and overwhelming the database system.
- *Reprogram attacks*: Attackers can try to reprogram the device if the architecture is not secured properly.
- *Service interruption attacks*: Several attacks, like DoS, illegally intruding into the system can cause the server to deny the service to legitimate clients or users by making the servers too busy [56].

3.3 IoT issues and challenges

IoT is based on the integration of various standards and enabling technologies with different sensing, connectivity, storage, computational, and other capabilities. However, the fragmentation of standards and diversities in deployed technologies produce significant challenges in providing full connectivity of everything [57,58]. This causes complex integration problems, and is one of the major challenges of IoT development. Numerous standardizing organizations, alliances, academic groups, and industries are working on IoT development, innovation, and standardization, but there is still a lack of a comprehensive framework with integrated standards under one IoT vision [59,60]. This causes many challenges that have been identified and discussed in this chapter.

Some of the most important challenges that IoT faces are related to traffic loads and various traffic models. Every day, more and more devices (things) are being connected to the Internet, and devices are becoming the major producers and consumers of traffic. This is the reason why traffic requirements arise and we need new traffic models, protocols, network capabilities, security mechanisms, etc. There is a need for simplification and adoption of the current IP (Internet protocol) architecture in order to enable seamless connectivity and effective management in a HetNet (heterogeneous networks) environment [61,62]. Some other challenges related to development of IoT include devices identification, addressing, interoperability, mobility, massive scaling, management, energy efficiency, security, and privacy, etc. Furthermore, future deployments of IoT need to achieve a sustainable smart world with the focus on green IoT-enabling technologies, which is another major issue.

3.4 Motivation for ML in IoT

ML refers to learning from past experience and datasets without being explicitly programmed and is largely based on mathematical techniques along with AI, optimization theory, information theory, and cognitive science [63]. Some of the popular fields using ML are natural language processing (NLP), speech recognition, facial recognition, etc. These are the fields where human intelligence and competence is not enough. Big tech companies like Google and Amazon are using ML extensively in many services, such as to detect and remove malware, analyzing threats in android applications, etc. Since ML works by predicting the output on datasets and improves its decision making based on previous experience, there are always possibilities for it to predict false positives and true negatives in some cases. This issue has been solved by adopting deep learning (DL), a subfield of ML and is inspired by the structure and functioning of human brain. DL has evolved such that it is able to work out the accuracy of its prediction by itself. Thus, with no doubt, DL is preferable—being more convenient and applicable—for IoT-based applications.

Large-scale deployment of IoT requires more innovative, vigorous, and well-grounded techniques rather than conventional ML/DL methods like clustering, analytics, allocation, etc. There can be several reasons to support the use of ML/Dl for IoT, one being the enormous data produced by IoT devices or applications, which can be used by ML/DL models to help IoT system in taking intelligent decisions. However, we cannot deny the fact that ML/DL models can be used for security reasons such as preventing attacks, privacy protection, malware, and malicious act prevention, etc. DL models can also be applied for sensing and recognition functions, which, as discussed earlier, happens at the perception layer of IoT architecture. They can be used to scrutinize and relate real-time human interaction with IoT-enabled smart devices and the physical environment. Some security related applications of ML in the real world are as follows:

- Identifying code in software that can be malevolent.
- Image recognition or facial recognition done in forensics.
- Identification of characters in various handwriting styles for privacy protection.
- Detecting of DDoS attack on IoT infrastructure.

Despite the use of ML/DL models in IoT systems and networks providing substantial benefits, there are some challenges that must be solved in order to deploy ML models to perform the above discussed tasks. Firstly, there is a need to build a well-fitted model to process diverse data from different IoT applications. This would require proper execution of processes like data preprocessing and feature engineering. Labeling the data is a bulky task in itself. Another challenge is to deploy these models in IoT devices designed with limited resource and storage capabilities for maximum output and cost-effectiveness [64]. Certain IoT applications with deprecatory infrastructure should also be considered while deploying the models. In conclusion, before deploying the ML/DL techniques, it is crucial to properly examine and evaluate the security problems associated with IoT.

4. Machine learning algorithms

In simple terms, machine learning is making the machine learn without explicitly programming it. It means, designing a model that perform accurate prediction on the basis of past data. To accomplish this, a model should be designed to learn and analyze the data fed as input, find patterns in them, and make accurate prediction as output. This can be done in various ways, for instance, sometimes the data can already be labeled whereas other times it can be unlabeled and the machine has to work to find existing patterns for itself among the input data, or it can be a mixture of both. Based on these criteria, there are four learning paradigms: supervised learning, unsupervised learning, semisupervised learning (SSL), and reinforcement learning [65–69]. Machine learning is used in various fields such as AI, statistics, optimization, and many others [70–72]. Various learning models and their applicability in IoT are discussed in the subsections below.

4.1 Supervised learning

As the name suggests, the learning here is supervised, i.e., labeled data are fed to the model. It requires human interference in order to make the model learn through already provided examples and cases. This learning paradigm is most suitable for classification and regression problems. The goal here is to build a decision model, which is trained on labeled data as input and desired output. The data set is divided into training and testing: after successfully training the model, it is tested for desired output. The model works to distinguish the values from the given input data and find new patterns and belongings to a new class. This is how a ML model works in the case of classification problems. Thus, a supervised model is one which builds a decision model from input data that are supervised (labeled) [73,74]. As mentioned earlier, supervised algorithms can broadly be classified as regression and classification problems. Some of the popular algorithms under each category are enumerated in the subsections below.

4.1.1   Regression techniques

Regression follows analytical modeling of data to produce a relation between the input variable and continuous output variables, which can be mathematically expressed. This mapping of data is useful in creating a prediction model to predict the desired output. This kind of model can be created using several underlying regression techniques such as linear regression, logistic regression, nonlinear regression, etc. [65,75,76].

Linear regression

This is a linear model, which creates linear relationships between input variables (x) and a single output variable (y). Thus, the output variable can be mathematically expressed as a linear combination of input variables. For instance, one dependent variable, which is the output, and one or more than one independent variable are input, and the bond between them is predicted by using this technique [77]. Every model needs to be trained to produce desired output; to train linear regression some techniques can be used such as ordinary least square technique [78]. This method helps to find the best possible values of x and y and thus the best fitting line [79].

Logistic regression

Unlike linear regression, the logistic regression technique is used when the dependent variable (y) is a categorical variable such as 0/1, true/false, or yes/ no, whereas in linear regression the output values are continuous [80]. This model works on the probability of output variable in the range 0 to 1 to classify the data [81]. Thus, when the model maps the input and output variable, a curved line is found on the graph instead of a straight line. This graphical behavior can also be explained by the use of sigmoid function, which is also known as logistic function. Sigmoid function is important to classify the output in classes lying between the values 0 to 1. It is also useful in binary classification of data.

Nonlinear regression

This is used to depict a nonlinear relationship between independent variables (x) and a dependent variable (y) [82]. Thus, it provides more flexibility than linear regression as the relation can be fitted in different types of curves. The resulting task is to find one that best fits the data using methods such as an iterative estimation algorithm [83].

4.1.2 Classification techniques

A model uses these methods to categorize objects in different classes based on the given training data. Therefore, it includes mapping of a discrete output function (y) to input variable (x). Some commonly used classification algorithms are elaborated in the subsections below.

Support vector machine (SVM)

This algorithm can be used for classification as well as regression problems, but is mostly used in classification. It involves the concept of "hyperplane." In this algorithm, the data items are plotted in an n-dimensional space (where "n" is number of features), then hyperplane is used to classify the data items [84]. Hyperplane is nothing but a decision boundary, whose dimensions are dependent on the number of features used. Support vectors are points that are close to the hyperplane and play a crucial role in classification, as using these support vectors, the margins of the classifier are maximized [85]. Thus, it can be concluded that SVM reduces the discrimination problem to a linear problem by finding the most suitable hyperplane [86]. Support vector machines can be both linear and nonlinear.

K nearest neighbor (KNN)

KNN is a versatile algorithm (which can be used for both classification and regression problems) that uses the nearest neighbors as data points having least distance from the new data point to be classified. "K" is the number of such data points taken into consideration [87]. Thus, it can be concluded that the classification of a data point depends on the distance metric and k. To find the distance, the most common method used is the Euclidian method. It is crucial to choose the optimum value of k to get the desired output.

Decision trees

A decision tree simply means representing all possible solutions graphically to reach a decision that is based on certain conditions. This forms a trees structure that has three nodes: a root node (parent), internal nodes (children), and leaf nodes (termination) [88]. Thus, it involves hierarchy of data in decision forms, which gives the desired output [89]. Table 4 depicts the possible roles of the abovementioned supervised learning algorithms in IoT.

TABLE 4 Some possible roles of supervised learning algorithms in IoT.

Algorithm	Role in IoT
Linear regression	• Can fix the energy issues in IoT and WSN. • To categorize unusual incoming sensor data using SVM and linear regression. • Using multiple linear regression model for evaluation method of IoT quality of experience (QoE). • To observe and supervise embedded applications linked with IoT using linear regression and least square method.
Logistic regression	• Used in different health-related areas in WSN and IoT. • To check dependability and strength of WSN network. • In heart disease detection in the initial stage through data collected from IoT devices.
Nonlinear regression	• Can be used in the technique to calculate the total power consumption in WSN networks. • To perform mobile target monitoring in WSNs.
Support vector machine	• Used in localizing nodes in WSN. • In online outlier detection in WSN. • Can be used in IoT applications to provide data safety and to check system intrusions.
K-nearest neighbors	• In intrusion detection system to identify abnormal nodes. • To increase the lifetime of a node in WSN. • To find the indoor position of Bluetooth low energy.
Decision tree	• To enhance data segregation in WSN. • Used to design a monitoring system to protect health hives. • Can be used in the deployment of IoT intelligent systems to keep track of health of cows to enhance production and milk quality.

4.2 Unsupervised learning

Contrary to supervised learning, the input data fed is unlabeled or unsupervised. Therefore, the model has to work to find patterns within the given unlabeled data to produce the result. These patterns are formed by observing common points in the input data [67]. Unsupervised learning has more practicality as there are more unlabeled data available than labeled data. Unsupervised learning includes some algorithms such as clustering, which is basically categorizing similar data points in clusters [90]. Some clustering methods are discussed below.

4.2.1 K-means clustering

As the name suggests, this is used to find clusters or groups (if they exist) in the given set of data [91]. K-means follows iterative clustering, which helps to produce the highest value for every iteration. Initially, the desired number of nonoverlapping clusters are considered, such that each data point is belonging to one cluster only. The simple rule to be taken care of while assigning the data points to the cluster is that the sum of squared distances between data points and the cluster's centroids is at minimum. For further information, there are works that explicitly explain the two basic steps followed to calculate K-means [92–95].

4.2.2   Fuzzy C-means clustering

This can be defined as an updated version of the K-means clustering method, introducing the concept of fuzziness in the system [96,97]. This algorithm works by a fuzzy classification method using the center of gravity of each class to represent them [98,99] (Table 5).

4.3   SSL

SSL is a ML paradigm that uses both labeled and unlabeled data to predict the output [103]. It was introduced to overcome the limitations of both supervised and unsupervised learning and thus, provides a middle ground between both learning methods. Initially, the model is trained on the labeled data, which are generally fewer than the unlabeled data. The training is continued until the result is not accurate. Then the unlabeled data are provided with pseudo labels linking them with labeled data. Again, the model is trained with all combined input and thus, improved accuracy is achieved. SSL uses the approach of supervised and unsupervised learnings but by extending or updating it. For example, semisupervised classification is an extended form of the supervised

TABLE 5 Some possible roles of unsupervised learning algorithms in IoT.

Algorithm	Role in IoT
K-means clustering	• Used in a routing protocol in WSN systems [69,100–146]. • Used to cluster the vast number of small datasets generated through various IoT devices or sensors [43]. • Employed in the initial stage of the approach used to manage the large requests of access from IoT devices [147].
Fuzzy C-means clustering	• Can be used in a routing protocol where fuzzy C-means clustering can be used as a centralized algorithm [100]. • Used in second layers of an IoT-based healthcare sensor system to evaluate the possibility of users being infected or not by chikungunya virus (CHV) [101]. • Used in intrusion detection systems in IoT networks [102].

classification technique [104,105], another one is semisupervised clustering, which is extended from the unsupervised clustering method [106,107].

4.4 Reinforcement learning

This learning method is different in context from the methods discussed so far. This learning paradigm is largely dependent on communication with the environment and observing actions [69]. The model, known as the agent in this learning method, learns to behave in an environment so as to increase its performance and receives rewards in return [108,109]. Thus, it is basically a feedback system, where the agent targets to maximize the reward, and therefore, efficacy is achieved [110]. It uses no labeled data and the learning is solemnly by its previous experience. This model is suitable for implementation in areas where there is sequential decision making along with long term goals, such as gaming, robotics, etc., Alpaydin et al. [111] have briefly discussed the steps taken in RL to make an agent learn and produce efficient result in an environment.

5. ML for IoT

The above sections briefly discussed the types of ML algorithms categorized broadly under different learning paradigms. Various learning algorithms can be included within an IoT network to fulfill several purposes like protecting privacy, securing it from attacks, and many more, as discussed in the subsections below.

5.1 ML for privacy—Protecting applications

IoT systems need access permissions, which can be administered and can be observed for doubtful authentication requests by deploying some ML models trained over data collected from past authentication and access behavior. While authenticating, original nodes are protected from being imitated from illegitimate nodes by determining a device's identity. Xiao et al. [112] discussed authorization in the physical layer using a wireless network process through radio channel information. Some authorization processes include ML linked with blockchain technologies [113]. However, this system has some drawbacks, such as the fact that using blockchain makes the process slow and thus incapable of exploiting larger datasets for model training.

IoT datasets are used by many public or private services to train various ML models, considering the fact that these could be a source of data leakage. This problem was solved by introducing privacy protecting structures based on ML approaches such as regression, clustering, linear regression, decision tree, SVM, logistic regression, and naïve Bayesian [114–125]. To learn the model without disclosing the data, a distributed deep learning model was also proposed

[126]. A two-server model where datasets were encrypted in the offline phase before being used in the model training was developed using neural network models with stochastic gradient descent, linear, and logistic regression techniques [126], while a structure was developed where both input data and learning parameters were made private [127].

5.2   ML-based authentication and access control in IoT

Signal strength as a physical channel property can be used for authentication in IoT, known as physical layer authentication [128]. ANN (artificial neural network) models are also used for authorization purposes in IoT [129]. Transmitters have some physical properties that are often rejected as communication impurities; these impurities, when evaluated, are termed authorization with physically unclonable function (PUF).

5.3   ML-based attack and mitigation in IoT

SSL (having features of both supervised and unsupervised learning) can be used for detecting attacks for IoT [130]. This structure was implemented through edge-based semifuzzy C-means clustering (ESFCM), which is extreme learning machine (ELM) algorithms combined with fuzzy C-means (FCM) [131]. ESFCM has increased rates for encountering distributed, attacks as it uses labeled data, but with decreased rate of accuracy as compared with other ML-based methods. Smart grids are one of the advance infrastructures of IoT, and therefore, these infrastructures are crucial for attack detection. Ozay et al. [132] elaborated various methods and techniques such as semisupervised learning, feature space fusion, supervised learning, and online learning algorithms for detecting attacks in smart grids [132], and concluded that SVM has better accuracy in attack detection in larger networks while K-NN works efficiently in smaller networks.

5.4   ML-based techniques to address DoS and distributed DoS (DDoS) attacks

The IoT provides a pool of chances for DDoS attackers and the frequency of DDoS attacks have increased in recent years [133]. One such attack was Mirai, a tribe of spywares that used simple day-to-day gadgets to set-off these attacks in many networks, which eventually led to disturbances in IoT-enabled services. The Mirai, like bots, had very intricate systems of growing and evolving. Several technologies and mechanisms have been researched to date that can help to prevent DDoS attacks happening in IoT network systems; nevertheless, the absence of a single unified technology makes it complex to implement on various IoT networks [134]. Intrusion detection and prevention methods are deployed at the gateways, routers, and entry points of IoT networks in conventional methods to discover DDoS attacks and attenuate them. In addition to these, several other technologies also help in mitigating DDoS attacks, such as fog and cloud computing [135].

Despite having developed some technologies, there is a need to develop more advanced and intelligent solutions that can also work upon the attacker's behaviors and properties. For this reason, using ML can benefit in providing some good optimized solutions with mechanisms to detect and attenuate DDoS attacks. A very similar mechanism using SVM in an SDN framework has been discussed for DDoS detection, providing accuracy of about 95.24%, which can also enhance some IoT-based applications [136]. Kokila et al. [137] proposed a very similar SVM-based system where the authors have also compared other methods, including random forest, bagging, and radial basis function (RBF), etc. SVM surpassed other methods with the same detection accuracy as mentioned in previous research. Not only SVM but other methods have also been leveraged in DDoS detection and mitigation, such as multivariate correlation analysis (MCA), which can be used on back-end servers for preventing these attacks by examining and distinguishing abnormal and normal activity patterns in the traffic [138].

5.5   ML-based anomaly or intrusion detection system (IDS) in IoT

Several ML technologies are available in the market for intrusion or anomaly detection [139]. Two such major techniques are traffic filtering and behavior-based models. However, these models do not work on 0-day vulnerabilities and, therefore, AI is adopted. These techniques work in SDN-governed IoT networks. Low-power 6LoWPAN operating IoT networks can use lightweight ML methods comprising of three techniques, one each from supervised (decision trees) and unsupervised learning (K-means), and one from hybrid learning for detecting anomalies [140]. The hybrid method, in spite of having a lower detection rate (71%–75%), than the other two methods, has better efficacy to be deployed in IDS systems. Nevertheless, artificial neural networks (ANN) and genetic algorithms can also be used in the gateway of IoT networks with anomaly detection [141]. A prediction rate of 99% can be found with respect to the training samples on two-input and three-input neurons. Other ML techniques can also be leveraged for IDS systems, such as the outlier detection method [142]. The conventional outlier detection was inappropriate for IoT systems as it used regression and statistical methods, which needed large storage. This problem was overcome by using nonparametric techniques [142]. Meanwhile, an IDS system which was optimized for energy and hardware using a three classifier system consisting of naïve Bayes, linear discriminant analysis (LDA), and decision trees was also designed. The accuracy archived was over 99%, which eventually reduced to about 30% with new attack cases. This shows the need for more advanced and optimized ML techniques in the future to detect new kinds of anomalies.

5.6   ML-based malware analysis in IoT

Malware stands for "malicious software," which is designed to damage the network or systems by exploiting various vulnerabilities of IoT devices, which can include security, authentication, and authorization. Android-based malware can be detected using random forest classifier. Malware detection in IoT-based wireless multimedia systems (WMS) is possible through a cloud-based technique using SVM [143]. Deploying principal component analysis (PCA), a one-class SVM and n-gram-based detector can help in protection of home-based routers against any DDoS attacks through malware detection [144]. This system proved to be efficient with 100% detection rate with no false negatives for PCA tested against popular malwares such as Mirai. Similarly, smart grid can be protected against false data injection and attacks using SVM and PCA techniques [145,146].

6.   Conclusion and future research direction

This chapter elaborated the security issues in IoT that need to be checked after discussing in brief about IoT and its architecture. The chapter also provided a detailed discussion on the security of IoT in all different layer and also, discussed ML and its algorithms that can be deployed within an IoT network to provide solutions to the security issues developing in IoT. Hence, ML can be integrated with IoT to enhance its security, reliability, and efficiency in all the ways discussed previously. The future research direction includes understanding some open issues and checking them. For instance, data abundance is a problem, as large amounts of data generated from smart cities are wasted and ML models cannot cope with them. Another issue is introduction of federated ML for IoT to surpass the conventional learning methods. Furthermore, there are still major concerns regarding data privacy in IoT networks, which remain unchecked. Thus, future work includes finding solutions to such issues.

References

[1] F. Wortmann, K. Flüchter, Internet of things, Bus. Inf. Syst. Eng. 57 (3) (2015) 221–224, https://doi.org/10.1007/s12599-015-0383-3.

[2] A. Zanella, N. Bui, A. Castellani, L. Vangelista, M. Zorzi, Internet of things for smart cities, IEEE Internet Things J. 1 (1) (2014) 22–32, https://doi.org/10.1109/jiot.2014.2306328.

[3] B.L. Risteska Stojkoska, K.V. Trivodaliev, A review of internet of things for smart home: challenges and solutions, J. Clean. Prod. 140 (2017) 1454–1464, https://doi.org/10.1016/j.jclepro.2016.10.006.

[4] X. Li, R. Lu, X. Liang, X. Shen, J. Chen, X. Lin, Smart community: an internet of things application, IEEE Commun. Mag. 49 (11) (2011) 68–75, https://doi.org/10.1109/mcom.2011.6069711.

[5] P. Aswale, A. Shukla, P. Bharati, S. Bharambe, S. Palve, An overview of internet of things: architecture, Protocols and challenges, in: Information and Communication Technology for Intelligent Systems, 2018, pp. 299–308, https://doi.org/10.1007/978-981-13-1742-2_29.

[6] P.P. Ray, A survey on internet of things architectures, J. King Saud Univ. – Comput. Inform. Sci. 30 (3) (2018) 291–319, https://doi.org/10.1016/j.jksuci.2016.10.003.

[7] M. Burhan, R. Rehman, B. Khan, B.-S. Kim, IOT elements, layered architectures and security issues: a comprehensive survey, Sensors 18 (9) (2018) 2796, https://doi.org/10.3390/s18092796.

[8] C.H. Sandeep, S.N. Kumar, P.P. Kumar, Security challenges and issues of the IOT system, Indian J. Public Health Res. Dev. 9 (11) (2018) 748, https://doi.org/10.5958/0976-5506.2018.01551.6.

[9] L. Cui, S. Yang, F. Chen, Z. Ming, N. Lu, J. Qin, A survey on application of machine learning for internet of things, Int. J. Mach. Learn. Cybern. 9 (8) (2018) 1399–1417, https://doi.org/10.1007/s13042-018-0834-5.

[10] A. Banerjee, A. Mitra, A. Biswas, An integrated application of iot-based WSN in the field of Indian agriculture system using hybrid optimization technique and machine learning, Agric. Inform. (2021) 171–187, https://doi.org/10.1002/9781119769231.ch9.

[11] F. Liang, W.G. Hatcher, W. Liao, W. Gao, W. Yu, Machine learning for security and the internet of things: the good, the bad, and the ugly, IEEE Access 7 (2019) 158126–158147, https://doi.org/10.1109/access.2019.2948912.

[12] A. Khattab, N. Youssry, Machine learning for IOT systems, in: Internet of Things (IoT), 2020, pp. 105–127, https://doi.org/10.1007/978-3-030-37468-6_6.

[13] S. Bera, S. Misra, A.V. Vasilakos, Software-defined networking for internet of things: a survey, IEEE Internet Things J. 4 (6) (2017) 1994–2008, https://doi.org/10.1109/jiot.2017.2746186.

[14] S. Tomovic, K. Yoshigoe, I. Maljevic, I. Radusinovic, Software-defined fog network architecture for IOT, Wirel. Pers. Commun. 92 (1) (2016) 181–196, https://doi.org/10.1007/s11277-016-3845-0.

[15] L. Xiao, X. Wan, X. Lu, Y. Zhang, D. Wu, IOT security techniques based on machine learning: how do IOT devices use AI to enhance security? IEEE Signal Process. Mag. 35 (5) (2018) 41–49, https://doi.org/10.1109/msp.2018.2825478.

[16] Z. Meng, Z. Wu, J. Gray, RFID-based object-centric data management framework for smart manufacturing applications, IEEE Internet Things J. 6 (2) (2019) 2706–2716, https://doi.org/10.1109/jiot.2018.2873426.

[17] N. Skoberne, O. Maennel, I. Phillips, R. Bush, J. Zorz, & Ciglaric, M., IPv4 address sharing mechanism classification and tradeoff analysis, IEEE/ACM Trans. Networking 22 (2) (2014) 391–404, https://doi.org/10.1109/tnet.2013.2256147.

[18] A.K. Al-Ani, M. Anbar, A. Al-Ani, D.R. Ibrahim, Match-prevention technique against denial-of-service attack on address resolution and duplicate address detection processes in ipv6 link-local network, IEEE Access 8 (2020) 27122–27138, https://doi.org/10.1109/access.2020.2970787.

[19] B.R. Al-Kaseem, Y. Al-Dunainawi, H.S. Al-Raweshidy, End-to-end delay enhancement in 6LoWPAN testbed using programmable network concepts, IEEE Internet Things J. 6 (2) (2019) 3070–3086, https://doi.org/10.1109/jiot.2018.2879111.

[20] W. Albazrqaoe, J. Huang, G. Xing, A practical bluetooth traffic sniffing system: design, implementation, and countermeasure, IEEE/ACM Trans. Networking 27 (1) (2019) 71–84, https://doi.org/10.1109/tnet.2018.2880970.

[21] R. Costa, J. Lau, P. Portugal, F. Vasques, R. Moraes, Handling real-time communication in infrastructured IEEE 802.11 wireless networks: the Rt-WIFI approach, J. Commun. Netw. 21 (3) (2019) 319–334, https://doi.org/10.1109/jcn.2019.000013.

[22] X. Cao, J. Chen, Y. Cheng, X.S. Shen, Y. Sun, An analytical MAC model for IEEE 802.15.4 enabled wireless networks with periodic traffic, IEEE Trans. Wirel. Commun. 14 (10) (2015) 5261–5273, https://doi.org/10.1109/twc.2015.2435006.

[23] L. Qu, R. Zhang, H. Shin, J. Kim, H. Kim, Performance enhancement of ground radiation antenna for Z -wave applications using tunable metal loads, Electron. Lett. 52 (22) (2016) 1827–1828, https://doi.org/10.1049/el.2016.1682.

[24] C. Zheng, Z. Hailin, A quasi-perfect resource allocation scheme for optimizing the performance of cell-edge users in FFR-aided LTE-a multicell networks, IEEE Commun. Lett. 23 (5) (2019) 918–921, https://doi.org/10.1109/lcomm.2019.2908372.

[25] X. Wang, J. Zhang, Z. Yu, S. Mao, S.C. Periaswamy, J. Patton, On remote temperature sensing using commercial UHF RFID tags, IEEE Internet Things J. 6 (6) (2019) 10715–10727, https://doi.org/10.1109/jiot.2019.2941023.

[26] A. Zhao, F. Ai, Dual-resonance NFC antenna system based on NFC chip antenna, IEEE Antennas Wirel. Propag. Lett. (2017) 1, https://doi.org/10.1109/lawp.2017.2749683.

[27] M.U. Rahman, A. Haider, M. Naghshvarianjahromi, A systematic methodology for the time-domain ringing reduction in UWB band-notched antennas, IEEE Antennas Wirel. Propag. Lett. 19 (3) (2020) 482–486, https://doi.org/10.1109/lawp.2020.2972025.

[28] M. Ayaz, M. Ammad-uddin, I. Baig, E.-H.M. Aggoune, Wireless sensor's civil applications, prototypes, and future integration possibilities: a review, IEEE Sensors J. 18 (1) (2018) 4–30, https://doi.org/10.1109/jsen.2017.2766364.

[29] X. Liu, B. Titurus, & Jiang, J. Z., Generalisable model development for fluid-inerter integrated damping devices, Mech. Mach. Theory 137 (2019) 1–22, https://doi.org/10.1016/j.mechmachtheory.2019.03.010.

[30] P.A. Da Rocha, W.D. De Oliveira, M.E. De Lima Tostes, An embedded system-based snap constrained trajectory planning method for 3D motion systems, IEEE Access 7 (2019) 125188–125204, https://doi.org/10.1109/access.2019.2939116.

[31] S. Ahmad, M.J. Arshad, Enhancing fast TCP's performance using single TCP connection for parallel traffic flows to prevent head-of-line blocking, IEEE Access 7 (2019) 148152–148162, https://doi.org/10.1109/access.2019.2946527.

[32] G. Yildirim, Y. Tatar, Simplified agent-based resource sharing approach for WSN-WSN interaction in IOT/CPS projects, IEEE Access 6 (2018) 78077–78091, https://doi.org/10.1109/access.2018.2884741.

[33] J. Ma, D. Yang, H. Wang, M. Gidlund, An efficient retransmission scheme for reliable end-to-end wireless communication over wsans, IEEE Access 6 (2018) 49838–49849, https://doi.org/10.1109/access.2018.2868099.

[34] M. Amjad, M. Sharif, M.K. Afzal, S.W. Kim, Tinyos-new trends, comparative views, and supported sensing applications: a review, IEEE Sensors J. 16 (9) (2016) 2865–2889, https://doi.org/10.1109/jsen.2016.2519924.

[35] E. Baccelli, C. Gundogan, O. Hahm, P. Kietzmann, M.S. Lenders, H. Petersen, K. Schleiser, T.C. Schmidt, M. Wahlisch, Riot: an open source operating system for low-end embedded devices in the IOT, IEEE Internet Things J. 5 (6) (2018) 4428–4440, https://doi.org/10.1109/jiot.2018.2815038.

[36] K.B. Lee, E.Y. Song, Sensor alert web service for IEEE 1451-based sensor networks, in: 2009 IEEE Intrumentation and Measurement Technology Conference, 2009, https://doi.org/10.1109/imtc.2009.5168608.

[37] F. Bing, The research of IOT of agriculture based on three layers architecture, in: 2016 2nd International Conference on Cloud Computing and Internet of Things (CCIOT), 2016, https://doi.org/10.1109/cciot.2016.7868325.

[38] M. Wu, T.-J. Lu, F.-Y. Ling, J. Sun, D. Hui-Ying, Research on the architecture of internet of things, in: 2010 3rd International Conference on Advanced Computer Theory and Engineering (ICACTE), 2010, https://doi.org/10.1109/icacte.2010.5579493.

[39] N. Kaur, S.K. Sood, An energy-efficient architecture for the internet of things (IOT), IEEE Syst. J. 11 (2) (2017) 796–805, https://doi.org/10.1109/jsyst.2015.2469676.

[40] D. Navani, S. Jain, M.S. Nehra, The internet of things (IOT): a study of architectural elements, in: 2017 13th International Conference on Signal-Image Technology & Internet-Based Systems (SITIS), 2017, https://doi.org/10.1109/sitis.2017.83.

[41] M.S. Virat, S.M. Bindu, B. Aishwarya, B.N. Dhanush, M.R. Kounte, Security and privacy challenges in internet of things, in: 2018 2nd International Conference on Trends in Electronics and Informatics (ICOEI), 2018, https://doi.org/10.1109/icoei.2018.8553919.

[42] L. Atzori, A. Iera, G. Morabito, The internet of things: a survey, Comput. Netw. 54 (15) (2010) 2787–2805, https://doi.org/10.1016/j.comnet.2010.05.010.

[43] X. Tao, C. Ji, Clustering massive small data for IOT, in: The 2014 2nd International Conference on Systems and Informatics (ICSAI 2014), 2014, https://doi.org/10.1109/icsai.2014.7009427.

[44] S. Kolozali, D. Kuemper, R. Tonjes, M. Bermudez-Edo, N. Farajidavar, P. Barnaghi, F. Gao, M. Intizar Ali, A. Mileo, M. Fischer, T. Iggena, Observing the pulse of a city: a smart city framework for real-time discovery, federation, and aggregation of data streams, IEEE Internet Things J. 6 (2) (2019) 2651–2668, https://doi.org/10.1109/jiot.2018.2872606.

[45] N. Mohammad, A multi-tiered defense model for the security analysis of critical facilities in smart cities, IEEE Access 7 (2019) 152585–152598, https://doi.org/10.1109/access.2019.2947638.

[46] D. Wang, B. Bai, K. Lei, W. Zhao, Y. Yang, Z. Han, Enhancing information security via physical layer approaches in heterogeneous IOT with multiple access Mobile edge computing in smart city, IEEE Access 7 (2019) 54508–54521, https://doi.org/10.1109/access.2019.2913438.

[47] P. Kumar, A. Braeken, A. Gurtov, J. Iinatti, P.H. Ha, Anonymous secure framework in connected smart home environments, IEEE Trans. Inf. Forensics Secur. 12 (4) (2017) 968–979, https://doi.org/10.1109/tifs.2016.2647225.

[48] K.C. Dey, A. Mishra, M. Chowdhury, Potential of intelligent transportation systems in mitigating adverse weather impacts on road mobility: a review, IEEE Trans. Intell. Transp. Syst. 16 (3) (2015) 1107–1119, https://doi.org/10.1109/tits.2014.2371455.

[49] S.U. Amin, M.S. Hossain, G. Muhammad, M. Alhussein, M.A. Rahman, Cognitive smart healthcare for pathology detection and monitoring, IEEE Access 7 (2019) 10745–10753, https://doi.org/10.1109/access.2019.2891390.

[50] A. Alabdulatif, I. Khalil, X. Yi, & Guizani, M., Secure edge of things for smart healthcare surveillance framework, IEEE Access 7 (2019) 31010–31021, https://doi.org/10.1109/access.2019.2899323.

[51] M. Ayaz, M. Ammad-Uddin, Z. Sharif, A. Mansour, E.-H.M. Aggoune, Internet-of-things (iot)-based smart agriculture: toward making the fields talk, IEEE Access 7 (2019) 129551–129583, https://doi.org/10.1109/access.2019.2932609.

[52] D. Airehrour, J.A. Gutierrez, S.K. Ray, Sectrust-RPL: a secure trust-aware RPL routing protocol for internet of things, Futur. Gener. Comput. Syst. 93 (2019) 860–876, https://doi.org/10.1016/j.future.2018.03.021.

[53] G. Ma, X. Li, Q. Pei, Z. Li, A security routing protocol for internet of things based on RPL, in: 2017 International Conference on Networking and Network Applications (NaNA), 2017, https://doi.org/10.1109/nana.2017.28.

[54] S.-Y. Tan, Comment on "Secure data access control with ciphertext update and computation outsourcing in fog computing for internet of things", IEEE Access 6 (2018) 22464–22465, https://doi.org/10.1109/access.2018.2827698.

[55] P. Anu, S. Vimala, A survey on sniffing attacks on computer networks, in: 2017 International Conference on Intelligent Computing and Control (I2C2), 2017, https://doi.org/10.1109/i2c2.2017.8321914.

[56] Z. Feng, & Hu, G., Secure cooperative event-triggered control of linear multiagent systems under DOS attacks, IEEE Trans. Control Syst. Technol. 28 (3) (2020) 741–752, https://doi.org/10.1109/tcst.2019.2892032.

[57] M. Condoluci, G. Araniti, T. Mahmoodi, M. Dohler, Enabling the IOT machine age with 5G: machine-type multicast services for innovative real-time applications, IEEE Access 4 (2016) 5555–5569, https://doi.org/10.1109/access.2016.2573678.

[58] A. Al-Fuqaha, M. Guizani, M. Mohammadi, M. Aledhari, M. Ayyash, Internet of things: a survey on enabling technologies, protocols, and applications, IEEE Commun. Surv. Tutorials 17 (4) (2015) 2347–2376, https://doi.org/10.1109/comst.2015.2444095.

[59] C. Sarkar, S.N. Akshay Uttama Nambi, R.V. Prasad, A. Rahim, R. Neisse, G. Baldini, Diat: a scalable distributed architecture for IOT, IEEE Internet Things J. 2 (3) (2015) 230–239, https://doi.org/10.1109/jiot.2014.2387155.

[60] M. Kim, H. Ahn, K.P. Kim, Process-aware internet of things: a conceptual extension of the internet of things framework and architecture, KSII Trans. Internet Inf. Syst. 10 (8) (2016), https://doi.org/10.3837/tiis.2016.08.032.

[61] M.R. Palattella, M. Dohler, A. Grieco, G. Rizzo, J. Torsner, T. Engel, L. Ladid, Internet of things in the 5G era: enablers, architecture, and business models, IEEE J. Sel. Areas Commun. 34 (3) (2016) 510–527, https://doi.org/10.1109/jsac.2016.2525418.

[62] B. Soret, K.I. Pedersen, N.T. Jørgensen, V. Fernández-López, Interference coordination for dense wireless networks, IEEE Commun. Mag. 53 (1) (2015) 102–109, https://doi.org/10.1109/mcom.2015.7010522.

[63] J. Qiu, Q. Wu, G. Ding, Y. Xu, S. Feng, A survey of machine learning for big data processing, EURASIP J. Adv. Signal Proc. 2016 (1) (2016), https://doi.org/10.1186/s13634-016-0355-x.

[64] S. Yao, Y. Zhao, A. Zhang, S. Hu, H. Shao, C. Zhang, L. Su, T. Abdelzaher, Deep learning for the internet of things, Computer 51 (5) (2018) 32–41, https://doi.org/10.1109/mc.2018.2381131.

[65] K. Das, R.N. Behera, A survey on machine learning: concept, algorithms and applications, Int. J. Innov. Res. Comput. Commun. Eng. 5 (2) (2017) 1301–1309.

[66] S.B. Kotsiantis, I.D. Zaharakis, P.E. Pintelas, Machine learning: a review of classification and combining techniques, Artif. Intell. Rev. 26 (3) (2006) 159–190, https://doi.org/10.1007/s10462-007-9052-3.

[67] T. Hastie, R. Tibshirani, J. Friedman, Unsupervised learning, in: The Elements of Statistical Learning, 2008, pp. 485–585, https://doi.org/10.1007/978-0-387-84858-7_14.

[68] O. Chapelle, B. Scholkopf, E. Zien, A., Semi-supervised learning (Chapelle, O. et al., eds.; 2006) [book reviews], IEEE Trans. Neural Netw. 20 (3) (2009) 542, https://doi.org/10.1109/tnn.2009.2015974.

[69] L.P. Kaelbling, M.L. Littman, A.W. Moore, Reinforcement learning: a survey, J. Artif. Intell. Res. 4 (1996) 237–285, https://doi.org/10.1613/jair.301.

[70] L. Breiman, Statistical modeling: the two cultures (with comments and a rejoinder by the author), Stat. Sci. 16 (3) (2001), https://doi.org/10.1214/ss/1009213726.

[71] G. Brewka, Artificial intelligence—a modern approach by Stuart Russell and Peter Norvig, prentice hall. Series in artificial intelligence, Englewood cliffs, NJ, Knowl. Eng. Rev. 11 (1) (1996) 78–79, https://doi.org/10.1017/s0269888900007724.

[72] J. Fulcher, Computational intelligence: an introduction, Stud. Comput. Intell. (2008) 3–78, https://doi.org/10.1007/978-3-540-78293-3_1.

[73] Y. Baştanlar, M. Özuysal, Introduction to Machine Learning, in: MiRNomics: MicroRNA Biology and Computational Analysis, 2013, pp. 105–128, https://doi.org/10.1007/978-1-62703-748-8_7.

[74] S. Suthaharan, Big data analytics, in: Machine Learning Models and Algorithms for Big Data Classification, 2016, pp. 31–75, https://doi.org/10.1007/978-1-4899-7641-3_3.

[75] P. Kashyap, Machine Learning for Decision Makers, 2017, https://doi.org/10.1007/978-1-4842-2988-0.

[76] M.K. Aery, C. Ram, A Review on Machine Learning: Trends and Future Prospects, 2017.

[77] P.S. Kott, A model-based look at linear regression with survey data, Am. Stat. 45 (2) (1991) 107–112, https://doi.org/10.1080/00031305.1991.10475779.

[78] S. Weisberg, Applied Linear Regression, Wiley Series in Probability and Statistics, 2005, https://doi.org/10.1002/0471704091.

[79] H.-S. Oh, Introduction to linear regression analysis, 5th edition by Montgomery, Douglas C., peck, Elizabeth A., and vining, G. Geoffrey, Biometrics 69 (4) (2013) 1087, https://doi.org/10.1111/biom.12129.

[80] C.-Y.J. Peng, T.-S.H. So, Logistic regression analysis and reporting: a primer, Underst. Stat. 1 (1) (2002) 31–70, https://doi.org/10.1207/s15328031us0101_04.

[81] C.Y.J. Peng, T.S.H. So, F.K. Stage, E.P. St. John, Research in, High. Educ. 43 (3) (2002) 259–293, https://doi.org/10.1023/a:1014858517172.

[82] R.S. Cármenes, Chapter 4 Nonlinear regression, in: Data Handling in Science and Technology, 1996, pp. 68–99, https://doi.org/10.1016/s0922-3487(96)80041-4.

[83] J.E. Dennis, D.M. Gay, R.E. Walsh, An adaptive nonlinear least-squares algorithm, ACM Trans. Math. Softw. 7 (3) (1981) 348–368, https://doi.org/10.1145/355958.355965.

[84] A. Chriki, H. Touati, H. Snoussi, SVM-based indoor localization in wireless sensor networks, in: 2017 13th international wireless communications and Mobile computing conference (IWCMC), 2017, https://doi.org/10.1109/iwcmc.2017.7986446.

[85] V.N. Vapnik, The Nature of Statistical Learning Theory, 1995, https://doi.org/10.1007/978-1-4757-2440-0.

[86] Y. Yuan, M. Zhang, P. Luo, Z. Ghassemlooy, L. Lang, D. Wang, B. Zhang, D. Han, SVM-based detection in visible light communications, Optik 151 (2017) 55–64, https://doi.org/10.1016/j.ijleo.2017.08.089.

[87] S. Thirumuruganathan, A Detailed Introduction to K-Nearest Neighbor (KNN) algorithm, Retrieved on July 21, 2010, p. 2015.

[88] A. Saettler, E. Laber, F.d.A. Mello Pereira, Decision tree classification with bounded number of errors, Inf. Process. Lett. 127 (2017) 27–31, https://doi.org/10.1016/j.ipl.2017.06.011.

[89] A. Bar-Or, D. Keren, A. Schuster, R. Wolff, Hierarchical decision tree induction in distributed genomic databases, IEEE Trans. Knowl. Data Eng. 17 (8) (2005) 1138–1151, https://doi.org/10.1109/tkde.2005.129.

[90] C.-F. Tsai, C.-W. Tsai, H.-C. Wu, T. Yang, ACODF: a novel data clustering approach for data mining in large databases, J. Syst. Softw. 73 (1) (2004) 133–145, https://doi.org/10.1016/s0164-1212(03)00216-4.

[91] M. Kaur, U. Kaur, A survey on clustering principles with K-means clustering algorithm using different methods in detail, Int. J. Comput. Sci. Mob. Comput. 2 (5) (2013) 327–331.

[92] A.C. Rencher, Classification analysis: allocation of observations to groups, in: Methods of Multivariate Analysis, 2002, pp. 299–321, https://doi.org/10.1002/0471271357.ch9.

[93] A.K. Jain, Data clustering: 50 years beyond K-means, Pattern Recogn. Lett. 31 (8) (2010) 651–666, https://doi.org/10.1016/j.patrec.2009.09.011.

[94] W.-L. Zhao, C.-H. Deng, C.-W. Ngo, K -means: a revisit, Neurocomputing 291 (2018) 195–206, https://doi.org/10.1016/j.neucom.2018.02.072.

[95] S.-S. Yu, S.-W. Chu, C.-M. Wang, Y.-K. Chan, T.-C. Chang, Two improved K-means algorithms, Appl. Soft Comput. 68 (2018) 747–755, https://doi.org/10.1016/j.asoc.2017.08.032.

[96] J. Nayak, B. Naik, H.S. Behera, Fuzzy C-means (FCM) clustering algorithm: a decade review from 2000 to 2014, in: Computational Intelligence in Data Mining, Vol. 2, 2014, pp. 133–149, https://doi.org/10.1007/978-81-322-2208-8_14.

[97] S. Chattopadhyay, D.K. Pratihar, S.C. De Sarkar, Developing fuzzy classifiers to predict the chance of occurrence of adult psychoses, Knowl.-Based Syst. 21 (6) (2008) 479–497, https://doi.org/10.1016/j.knosys.2008.03.006.

[98] Z. Cebeci, F. Yildiz, Comparison of k-means and fuzzy c-means algorithms on different cluster structures, J. Agric. Inform. 6 (3) (2015), https://doi.org/10.17700/jai.2015.6.3.196.

[99] N. Grover, A study of various fuzzy clustering algorithms, Int. J. Eng. Res. 3 (3) (2014) 177–181, https://doi.org/10.17950/ijer/v3s3/310.

[100] D.C. Hoang, R. Kumar, S.K. Panda, Fuzzy C-means clustering protocol for wireless sensor networks, in: 2010 IEEE International Symposium on Industrial Electronics, 2010, https://doi.org/10.1109/isie.2010.5637779.

[101] S.K. Sood, I. Mahajan, Wearable IOT sensor based healthcare system for identifying and controlling chikungunya virus, Comput. Ind. 91 (2017) 33–44, https://doi.org/10.1016/j.compind.2017.05.006.

[102] L. Liu, B. Xu, X. Zhang, X. Wu, An intrusion detection method for internet of things based on suppressed fuzzy clustering, EURASIP J. Wirel. Commun. Netw. 2018 (1) (2018), https://doi.org/10.1186/s13638-018-1128-z.

[103] X. Zhu, Semi-supervised learning, in: Encyclopedia of Machine Learning and Data Mining, 2017, pp. 1142–1147, https://doi.org/10.1007/978-1-4899-7687-1_749.

[104] U. Brefeld, T. Scheffer, Semi-supervised learning for structured output variables, in: Proceedings of the 23rd International Conference on Machine Learning - ICML '06, 2006, https://doi.org/10.1145/1143844.1143863.

[105] Z.-H. Zhou, M. Li, Semi-supervised learning by disagreement, Knowl. Inf. Syst. 24 (3) (2009) 415–439, https://doi.org/10.1007/s10115-009-0209-z.

[106] B. Kulis, S. Basu, I. Dhillon, R. Mooney, Semi-supervised graph clustering: a kernel approach, Mach. Learn. 74 (1) (2008) 1–22, https://doi.org/10.1007/s10994-008-5084-4.

[107] S. Basu, M. Bilenko, R.J. Mooney, A probabilistic framework for semi-supervised clustering, in: Proceedings of the 2004 ACM SIGKDD International Conference on Knowledge Discovery and Data Mining - KDD '04, 2004, https://doi.org/10.1145/1014052.1014062.

[108] J.A. Boyan, A.W. Moore, Generalization in reinforcement learning: safely approximating the value function, Adv. Neural Inf. Proces. Syst. (1995).

[109] W. Josemans, Generalization in Reinforcement Learning, University of Amsterdam, Leeuwarden, 2009.

[110] R.S. Sutton, Introduction: the challenge of reinforcement learning, in: Reinforcement Learning, 1992, pp. 1–3, https://doi.org/10.1007/978-1-4615-3618-5_1.

[111] E. Alpaydin, Introduction to Machine Learning, MIT press, 2014.

[112] L. Xiao, X. Wan, Z. Han, Phy-layer authentication with multiple landmarks with reduced overhead, IEEE Trans. Wirel. Commun. 17 (3) (2018) 1676–1687, https://doi.org/10.1109/twc.2017.2784431.

[113] A. Outchakoucht, H. Es-Samaali, J. Philippe, Dynamic access control policy based on blockchain and machine learning for the internet of things, Int. J. Adv. Comput. Sci. Appl. 8 (7) (2017), https://doi.org/10.14569/ijacsa.2017.080757.

[114] M. Upmanyu, A.M. Namboodiri, K. Srinathan, C.V. Jawahar, Efficient privacy preserving K-means clustering, in: Intelligence and Security Informatics, 2010, pp. 154–166, https://doi.org/10.1007/978-3-642-13601-6_17.

[115] Cui, Y. (n.d.). A Study on Privacy-Preserving Clustering. doi:https://doi.org/10.5353/th_b4357225.

[116] A. Gascón, P. Schoppmann, B. Balle, M. Raykova, J. Doerner, S. Zahur, D. Evans, Privacy-preserving distributed linear regression on high-dimensional data, Proc. Priv. Enh. Technol. 2017 (4) (2017) 345–364, https://doi.org/10.1515/popets-2017-0053.

[117] R.U. Haque, A.S. Hasan, Q. Jiang, Q. Qu, Privacy-preserving K-nearest neighbors training over blockchain-based encrypted health data, Electronics 9 (12) (2020) 2096, https://doi.org/10.3390/electronics9122096.

[118] A. Rooshenas, H.R. Rabiee, A. Movaghar, M.Y. Naderi, Reducing the data transmission in wireless sensor networks using the principal component analysis, in: 2010 Sixth International Conference on Intelligent Sensors, Sensor Networks and Information Processing, 2010, https://doi.org/10.1109/issnip.2010.5706781.

[119] P.K. Fong, J.H. Weber-Jahnke, Privacy preserving decision tree learning using unrealized data sets, IEEE Trans. Knowl. Data Eng. 24 (2) (2012) 353–364, https://doi.org/10.1109/tkde.2010.226.

[120] H. Yunhong, F. Liang, H. Guoping, Privacy-preserving SVM classification on vertically partitioned data without secure multi-party computation, in: 2009 Fifth International Conference on Natural Computation, 2009, https://doi.org/10.1109/icnc.2009.120.

[121] J. Vaidya, H. Yu, X. Jiang, Privacy-preserving SVM classification, Knowl. Inf. Syst. 14 (2) (2007) 161–178, https://doi.org/10.1007/s10115-007-0073-7.

[122] Y. Aono, T. Hayashi, L. Trieu Phong, L. Wang, Scalable and secure logistic regression via homomorphic encryption, in: Proceedings of the Sixth ACM Conference on Data and Application Security and Privacy, 2016, https://doi.org/10.1145/2857705.2857731.

[123] W. Xie, Y. Wang, S.M. Boker, D.E. Brown, PrivLogit: efficient privacy-preserving logistic regression by tailoring numerical optimizers, ArXiv (2016). abs/1611.01170.

[124] M. Huai, L. Huang, W. Yang, L. Li, M. Qi, Privacy-preserving naive bayes classification, in: Knowledge Science, Engineering and Management, 2015, pp. 627–638, https://doi.org/10.1007/978-3-319-25159-2_57.

[125] P. Li, J. Li, Z. Huang, C.-Z. Gao, W.-B. Chen, K. Chen, Privacy-preserving outsourced classification in cloud computing, Clust. Comput. 21 (1) (2017) 277–286, https://doi.org/10.1007/s10586-017-0849-9.

[126] P. Mohassel, Y. Zhang, SecureML: a system for scalable privacy-preserving machine learning, in: 2017 IEEE Symposium on Security and Privacy (SP), 2017, https://doi.org/10.1109/sp.2017.12.

[127] B.D. Rouhani, M.S. Riazi, F. Koushanfar, Deepsecure, in: Proceedings of the 55th Annual Design Automation Conference, 2018, https://doi.org/10.1145/3195970.3196023.

[128] L. Xiao, Y. Li, G. Han, G. Liu, W. Zhuang, Phy-layer spoofing detection with reinforcement learning in wireless networks, IEEE Trans. Veh. Technol. 65 (12) (2016) 10037–10047, https://doi.org/10.1109/tvt.2016.2524258.

[129] B. Chatterjee, D. Das, S. Maity, S. Sen, RF-PUF: enhancing IOT security through authentication of wireless nodes using in-situ machine learning, IEEE Internet Things J. 6 (1) (2019) 388–398, https://doi.org/10.1109/jiot.2018.2849324.

[130] S. Rathore, J.H. Park, Semi-supervised learning based distributed attack detection framework for IOT, Appl. Soft Comput. 72 (2018) 79–89, https://doi.org/10.1016/j.asoc.2018.05.049.

[131] I. Hafeez, A.Y. Ding, M. Antikainen, S. Tarkoma, Toward Secure Edge Networks: Taming Device-to-Device (D2D) Communication in IoT, 2017, [Online]. Available: www.arxiv.abs/1712.05958.

[132] M. Ozay, I. Esnaola, F.T. Yarman Vural, S.R. Kulkarni, H.V. Poor, Machine learning methods for attack detection in the smart grid, IEEE Trans. Neural Netw. Learn. Syst. 27 (8) (2016) 1773–1786, https://doi.org/10.1109/tnnls.2015.2404803.

[133] N. Vlajic, D. Zhou, IOT as a land of opportunity for ddos hackers, Computer 51 (7) (2018) 26–34, https://doi.org/10.1109/mc.2018.3011046.

[134] D. Yin, L. Zhang, K. Yang, A ddos attack detection and mitigation with software-defined internet of things framework, IEEE Access 6 (2018) 24694–24705, https://doi.org/10.1109/access.2018.2831284.

[135] Q. Yan, W. Huang, X. Luo, Q. Gong, F.R. Yu, A multi-level ddos mitigation framework for the industrial internet of things, IEEE Commun. Mag. 56 (2) (2018) 30–36, https://doi.org/10.1109/mcom.2018.1700621.

[136] J. Ye, X. Cheng, J. Zhu, L. Feng, L. Song, A ddos attack detection method based on SVM in software defined network, Sec. Commun. Netw. 2018 (2018) 1–8, https://doi.org/10.1155/2018/9804061.

[137] R.T. Kokila, S. Thamarai Selvi, K. Govindarajan, DDoS detection and analysis in SDN-based environment using support vector machine classifier, in: 2014 Sixth International Conference on Advanced Computing (ICoAC), 2014, https://doi.org/10.1109/icoac.2014.7229711.

[138] Z. Tan, A. Jamdagni, X. He, P. Nanda, R.P. Liu, A system for denial-of-service attack detection based on multivariate correlation analysis, IEEE Trans. Parallel Distrib. Syst. 25 (2) (2014) 447–456, https://doi.org/10.1109/tpds.2013.146.

[139] J.W. Branch, C. Giannella, B. Szymanski, R. Wolff, H. Kargupta, In-network outlier detection in wireless sensor networks, Knowl. Inf. Syst. 34 (1) (2012) 23–54, https://doi.org/10.1007/s10115-011-0474-5.

[140] P. Shukla, ML-IDs: |a machine learning approach to detect wormhole attacks in internet of things, in: 2017 intelligent systems conference (IntelliSys), 2017, https://doi.org/10.1109/intellisys.2017.8324298.

[141] J. Canedo, A. Skjellum, Using machine learning to secure IOT Systems, in: 2016 14th Annual Conference on Privacy, Security and Trust (PST), 2016, https://doi.org/10.1109/pst.2016.7906930.

[142] N. Nesa, T. Ghosh, I. Banerjee, Non-parametric sequence-based learning approach for outlier detection in IOT, Futur. Gener. Comput. Syst. 82 (2018) 412–421, https://doi.org/10.1016/j.future.2017.11.021.

[143] W. Zhou, B. Yu, A cloud-assisted malware detection and suppression framework for wireless multimedia system in IOT based on dynamic differential game, China Commun. 15 (2) (2018) 209–223, https://doi.org/10.1109/cc.2018.8300282.

[144] N. An, A. Duff, G. Naik, M. Faloutsos, S. Weber, S. Mancoridis, Behavioral anomaly detection of malware on home routers, in: 2017 12th international conference on malicious and unwanted software (MALWARE), 2017, https://doi.org/10.1109/malware.2017.8323956.

[145] M. Esmalifalak, N.T. Nguyen, R. Zheng, Z. Han, Detecting stealthy false data injection using machine learning in Smart Grid, in: 2013 IEEE Global Communications Conference (GLOBECOM), 2013, https://doi.org/10.1109/glocom.2013.6831172.

[146] M. Esmalifalak, L. Liu, N. Nguyen, R. Zheng, Z. Han, Detecting stealthy false data injection using machine learning in smart grid, IEEE Syst. J. 11 (3) (2017) 1644–1652, https://doi.org/10.1109/jsyst.2014.2341597.

[147] Y. Song, H. Zhang, X. Li, C. Zhu, H. Ji, Intelligent access scheme for internet of things supported by 5G wireless network, in: Communications and Networking, 2018, pp. 341–351, https://doi.org/10.1007/978-3-319-78139-6_35.

Chapter 4

Implementation of two factor authentication using face and iris biometrics

Nikola Vukobrat[a], Nemanja Maček[b,c], Saša Adamović[a], Muzafer Saračević[d], and Milan Gnjatović[e]

[a]Faculty of Informatics and Computing, Singidunum University, Belgrade, Serbia, [b]Academy of Technical and Art Applied Studies, School of Electrical and Computer Engineering, Belgrade, Serbia, [c]Faculty of Computer Sciences, Megatrend University, Belgrade, Serbia, [d]Department of Computer Science, University of Novi Pazar, Novi Pazar, Serbia, [e]University of Criminal Investigation and Police Studies, Beograd, Serbia

1. Introduction

Today, one of the main system security problems is the ability to generate strong enough cryptographic keys for user authentication, but still to keep the key simple enough for the user to remember it [1]. In order to preserve its complexity and to have a stronger key, it needs to contain upper and lower case letters, numbers, and special characters. The reason for this is to increase the number of characters that are available to generate the password; as a consequence of which, the number of possible password combinations grows exponentially and makes the process of breaking or guessing it more complicated [2].

The body of research on global password complexity shows that 62.6% of passwords contain only numbers, 24.3% of them contain just letters, while 12.4% have both numbers and letters. Just 0.7% of all passwords used in this research had a combination of numbers, letters, and special characters [3]. According to this, it is concluded that general password complexity, and by that, global system security, is very low. As a consequence, efforts to develop techniques that will improve the overall security level have intensified, not just in highly secure environments, but also in every security system globally.

Nowadays, one of the most successful areas in high security systems is biometrics [4], as this allows users to authenticate the system without remembering complex passwords. Instead, the user uses his/her unique characteristics, like a

Blockchain Technology Solutions for the Security of IoT-Based Healthcare Systems.
https://doi.org/10.1016/B978-0-323-99199-5.00004-5

fingerprint, voice, hand geometrics, handwriting, or retina [5], as well as the characteristics of the face and iris that will be described in this research.[a]

Biometrics can provide both single-factor and multifactor authentication, and therefore, one can differentiate two types of biometric systems: unimodal and multimodal [6]. Unimodal systems employ a single biometric sample, such as face or fingerprint. Multimodal systems employ two or more modalities belonging to the same person, such as face and fingerprint. Many consider unimodal biometrics to still not be secure enough because of the limitations in biometric technology or using low cost sensors [7]. Employing two or more modalities increases recognition accuracy, strengthens the proof, and reduces false rejection rates (FRR) and false acceptance rates (FAR).

Furthermore, from the application perspective, there are many possible implications of biometric authentication systems like this [8]. One of the focus domains of this research is healthcare. As concluded by many research papers [9–11], healthcare represents one of the most critical domains from the security perspective. Notably, highly sensitive data is stored in the vast healthcare systems around the world [12]. Therefore, the ways that system protection, authentication, and authorization are employed becomes crucial. So, our recommendations and research strive to improve many aspects of how security is (and will be) handled in the healthcare domain.

Further research will be used to explain how face and iris characteristics are extracted, prepared, and used to authenticate unique user. In addition, results from combining face and iris characteristics will be shown in a way where the face will represent the username, and iris represent the password for a certain user, in order to get the most reliable and secure system. This approach is the replacement for the typical username-password authentication scheme with two different biometric samples belonging to the same individual.

Major contributions of this chapter are:

- We introduce a multimodal biometric authentication system that uses the face and iris of the person as the parameters for the process itself.
- We present the implementation of a solution that uses the face and iris of the person for authentication, as well as the precision of the entire system during the authentication.
- We introduce an authentication system that uses the face and iris of the person as the parameters for the process itself.

The paper is organized into five sections. Face and iris recognition methods are provided in the second and third sections. In the fourth section, experimental evaluation and results are provided. Concluding remarks and future works are given in the last section.

---

a. The code that supports this research can be found on: https://github.com/NVukobrat/Two-factor-authentication-using-Face-and-Iris-Biometrics.

2. Face recognition

By and large, humans recognize each other by observing the main characteristics of the face. Relying on this fact, biometrics systems with capabilities of recognizing human faces have been developed. Face recognition is a convenient, nonintrusive authentication method. There are various feature extraction methods reported in the literature and, roughly, they can be classified either as geometric or photometric approaches. Past research based on face biometrics has shown that the face has unique characteristics that can be used to recognize a person with high precision [13]. In order to recognize a person using face biometrics, unique facial features need to be extracted. They will be used for comparison with facial features of a person that had been already stored in the database (see Fig. 1).

The method used for this process is based on information theory and dimensionality reduction of features. It is called Eigenface [14], and represents a technique for extracting important face features using the principal component analysis (PCA) algorithm.

2.1 Eigenface

Prior to this approach, most algorithms were based on facial geometry. This process involves comparing the characteristic facial features of one person with the same features of that person that were previously stored in the database.

Eigenface has been developed as an approach based on the theory of information. By studying key facial features and mutual correlations between them, a method has been developed in order to separate fundamental features from the nonessential. More precisely, it presents a person with the most important

FIG. 1 Face image, which can be used for authentication. *(Image from Unsplash.)*

characteristics [15], while neglecting others that are not of such importance for the process of authentication.

Considering the aspect of information theory, the most important features from the face have to be extracted as efficiently as possible, and then compared with other coded faces previously stored in the database.

From the mathematical point of view, we want to find the main components of the Eigenvectors and the covariance matrix has to be found. That matrix consists of the set of images, where each image is interpreted as a separate vector in a very large dimension.

Eigenvector can be identified as a set of features that together represent the variation between facial images. Each point on the face contributes to the final look of the Eigenvector, and thus the Eigenvector looks like a ghostly face that is called Eigenface. This method was inspired by the work of L. Sirovich and M. Kirby [16] showing the technique for representing a person using PCA. The paper discussed the possibility of presenting each person's face in a compressed form that reduces unimportant facial features. In addition, they managed to reconstruct the original face image from a compressed one. This was done by keeping a weight vector with a small number of elements that are projected onto a compressed face (see Fig. 2).

2.2   Computation of an Eigenface

First of all, we need to prepare training images of a range of faces [17] in order to get Eigenfaces. Faces should have the same dimensions so as to avoid problems during computation. If dimensions are different, they must be scaled to the same size. Before computing Eigenface, images needs to be transformed to gray scale, which is presented as a matrix with values ranging from 0 to 255.

The aim of further calculations is to find the vector that best fits the distribution of other facial images in the spatial area of all faces [18]. We define these

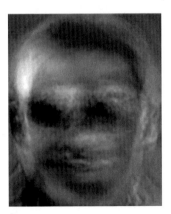

FIG. 2   Example of an Eigenface.

vectors as a subset of face images, which we call the "face area." These vectors are those that are derived from the correlation matrix corresponding to the original facial images. Since this matrix acts as a face when it appears in the image form, it is often called "Eigenfaces."

The next steps explain how to calculate Eigenface to its final form. Firstly, the average person's face is calculated. In order to do this, we need to load all faces for training into one matrix. This matrix is represented as the $M \times N$ matrix, where M represents the facial vector values that we converted from the matrix into the vector, while N represents the entire face vector. After loading all the persons in the matrix, the average person's face is calculated according to the following formula:

$$\overline{X} = \frac{1}{N} \sum_{i=1}^{N} x_i \tag{1}$$

An example is presented in Fig. 3.

The next step is normalizing the face. The faces are normalized by removing the average face obtained from Eq. (1) from each face. As a consequence of which, a difference matrix that represents the deviation of each face is established using the average face of $\overline{X}$. This can be presented in the following way:

$$D = X - \overline{X} \tag{2}$$

where X represents the $M \times N$ matrix with all the loaded training images.

An example of a normalized image can be seen in Fig. 4.

Further, it is necessary to calculate the correlation matrix, which represents the ratio between all facial vectors and the average face vector. The correlation matrix is calculated as:

$$C = D^T * D \tag{3}$$

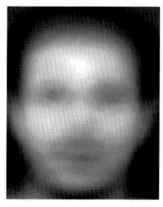

FIG. 3 Mean face of all training faces.

FIG. 4   Example of one normalized face.

The resulting matrix, C, represents the matrix of the $N \times N$ dimension. Using the correlation matrix Eigenvectors and Eigenvalues are calculated as:

$$CV = \lambda V \tag{4}$$

where V represents the set of the Eigenvector of the matrix C that is connected with the Eigenvalues λ.

In order to select the most representative collection of quality Eigenvectors, we need first to sort them by their values. After that, it will be enough to take only a few first vectors that are sorted from the best to the worse. The next step is getting Eigenfaces; these are obtained by mapping the difference matrix and the Eigenvector:

$$E = D*V \tag{5}$$

The last step is to normalize the Eigenvector [18]. The process of normalization is done by dividing the vector with the normalized vector:

$$\|v\|_p = \left[\sqrt{\sum_{i=1}^{n} |v_k|^p} \right]^{1/p} \tag{6}$$

where, in our case, $p = 2$.

This normalization is also called Euclidean normalization. The next step of normalization is removal of Eigenvectors with low Eigenvalues to eliminate noise. As a result of these two steps comes the matrix that representing a normalized Eigenface. An example of a few Eigenfaces is depicted in Fig. 5. This is the method for getting Eigenfaces from which vectors can be selected that will be used for the further classification process.

2.3   Classification using Eigenface

After obtaining the Eigenfaces, the next step is the classification of candidates by faces that have not passed through the system in the training process, as well

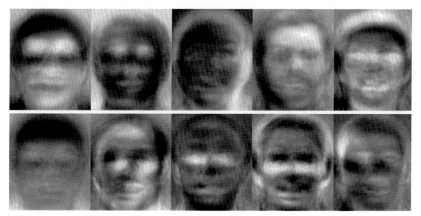

FIG. 5   Eigenfaces after normalization.

as all new candidates. Since Eigenfaces represent the ratio between faces with reduced dimensions, they contain the most important characteristics of the face, and they are ideal for authenticating the user. This means that the person's authentication process is the task of identifying patterns in the face image. Authentication of a person is done by counting the weight vectors for each person that will be used later to compare with the new face. Weight vectors are calculated using the face through which we have obtained our Eigenfaces. These weight vectors will be used for comparison with the new face vectors. They can be calculated while the system is idle, i.e., when there is no person trying to authenticate. These weight vectors are calculated using the formula:

$$W_{train} = D^T * E \tag{7}$$

where D represents the normalized training face, i.e., deviation matrix of each face from the average face, and E represents the now normalized Eigenface that contains the highest quality representations of the face.

In the next step, the person's face is recorded and it passes through the normalization phase (Eq. 2) to get the normalized D_{test} vector. Then we calculate the new face's weight vector (Eq. 7) in order to get W_{test}. Afterwards, it passes through all faces in order to obtain the difference between stored faces and the newly recorded face. That difference is calculated using the Euclidean vector normalization:

$$W_{diff(i)} = \sqrt{\sum_{i=1}^{n} |W_{train} - W_{test}|^2} \tag{8}$$

where $W_{diff(i)}$ is a comparison with a single training face.

By comparing all training faces, the W_{diff} weight vector is established and each element represents a deviation from the training face. This can be solved by applying the Euclidean distance representing the variation (Eq. 6) between the two vectors:

$$W_{diff(i)}d = \sqrt{\sum_{i=1}^{n}(q_i - p_i)^2} \qquad (9)$$

where a W_d vector is obtained, which contains weight differences between the new face and all other training faces.

Finally, a person is recognized by looking for the least distance from W_{diff} or the other W_d vectors. As a security factor, a certain threshold can also be adopted, so if a person's face does not cross over the threshold it can be classified as that of an intruder.

3.   Iris recognition

The iris is a circular membrane that lies between the cornea and the lens of the human eye. As depicted in Fig. 6, the iris surrounds the pupil of the eye and its center is close to the center of the pupil. The function of the iris is to control the amount of light that passes through the pupil, by adjusting the pupil size by contacting or relaxing the sphincter and dilator muscles around the pupil. The average diameter of the iris is 12 mm, while the pupil size may vary from 10% to 80% of the size of the iris diameter [19].

In order to recognize a person successfully by means of their iris, a few steps need to be performed. First of all, it is necessary to find the iris in the image and to do a complete segmentation of the iris, making it clear, and free from noise and from the rest of the image. After that, the normalization of the iris is followed by its transformation into a format that is suitable for further processing and extraction of a unique code. Finally, coding the extracted iris is done by filters. The main characteristics of the iris are selected and then used for further user authentications processes. Each of these steps will be described and explained in the following sections.

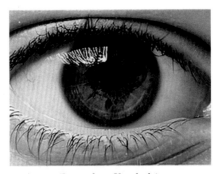

FIG. 6   Example of an eye image. *(Image from Unsplash.)*

3.1 Segmentation and normalization

Segmentation of the iris represents the process of isolating the iris from the image of a human eye. The iris can be represented as a space between two circles, one around the pupil and the other around the outer edge of the iris itself. Often, the flashes that occur in the iris area are eyelids and eyelashes. They appear from the upper and lower side of the iris and should be removed because they represent noise within the iris. The most important item is the iris pattern itself. These patterns are unique for every human being. Even the same person does not have the same iris pattern in both eyes, so in the authentication process, attention should be paid to these details.

The first step in the iris segmentation process is the extraction of edges and contours from the eye image. This step is necessary because the further process of iris extraction consists of identifying the patterns in the picture. Edges of objects are important for recognition of patterns. In order to extract edges in the image, "Canny edge" detector is used. The Canny edge detector [20] allows extraction of the most important contours from the image and drastic reduction of the number of data required for processing. This technique is mostly used in computer vision systems. An example of the output from Canny edge can be seen in Fig. 7, in which, the edges of the iris and pupil can be seen clearly.

To extract the edges using a Canny edge detector, it is necessary to remove the noise from the image; as a consequence of which, the algorithm will not report the false contours and edges. The noise from the image can be eliminated using a Gaussian filter, which will normalize and polish the image in order not to have too strong transitions:

$$g(x, y) = \frac{1}{2\pi\sigma^2} * e^{-\frac{x^2 + y^2}{2\sigma^2}} \tag{10}$$

where x and y represent a horizontal and vertical distance from the center, respectively.

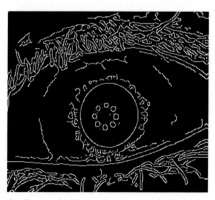

FIG. 7 Output image of a Canny edge detector.

After applying the Gaussian filter, the intensity and direction of the gradients need to be found. Since the edges of the picture can be in different directions, the Canny edge detector detects vertical, horizontal, and diagonal edges in order to successfully find all of them. The edges can be obtained by calculating:

$$G = \sqrt{G_x + G_y} \tag{11}$$

$$\Theta = a \tan 2\left(G_y, G_x\right) \tag{12}$$

where G_x and G_y represent the first derivative in the horizontal and vertical directions, respectively, and the angle is calculated using Eqs. (11) and (12).

In order not to have too many angles that have to be remembered, all of them are eventually rounded to 0, 45, 90, and 135 degrees. After determining the direction, we get a blurred image with recognizable edges, but a large proportion of them are incorrect and wide.

In order to extract thin and clean edges, we apply the nonmaximal compression edging technique to the image where most of the edges are blurred. The result of this process is an image with narrowed, clear, and thin edges. Still, in that image, a lot of details are present, and this can cause the noise that isn't isolated using the Gaussian filter. In order to eliminate these edges, upper and lower thresholds are applied. In this way, all the edges that are beyond these ranges are removed.

The final step in noise reduction is its elimination by following the correlation between edges. If some edges are poorly connected with others, they will be removed, while those that are well connected will be left as the most obvious edges. This is done by comparing each pixel with its neighbor pixels. If those pixels match their mutual pixel by intensity, they are considered as strong edge, otherwise, they are rejected. Hough transformation [21] is one of the standard computer vision algorithms through which we can search simple geometric patterns in the image, such as lines and circles. We define this transformation as:

$$\left[-(x - h_j) \sin \theta_j + (y - k_j) \cos \theta_j \right]^2 = a_j\left[(x - h_j) \cos \theta_j + (y - k_j) \sin \theta_j\right] \tag{13}$$

where a_j controls the curvature, k_j and h_j are the peaks of the parabola, and θ_j represents the angle relative to the x-axis.

When it comes to the iris, this transformation is an excellent solution for finding the edges of the pupil, iris, and eyelids. Circular transformation is used to find the outer edges of pupil and iris. This transformation is applied using the vertical Canny edge detector. The purpose of choosing it is based on empirical results as the best way to define the outer edges of the circles. Furthermore, in order to detect and remove eyelids, a linear transformation is applied. This transformation uses Canny edge detector with horizontal filters in order to detect lines in the image. An example of drawned pupil and iris circle can be seen in Fig. 8.

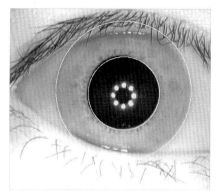

FIG. 8 Outer boundaries of iris and pupil.

The results of the Hough transformation are the coordinates of the center and the diameter of the circle, represented as:

$$x_c^2 + y_c^2 - r_c^2 = 0 \qquad (14)$$

The problem with this algorithm is that you have to define the thresholds manually, which can lead to errors and rejection of important edges, or the acceptance of too much noise. Furthermore, this transformation tends to be slow because it examines the pixels one by one on each edge to find the most suitable shapes.

The iris is segmented by detecting the largest circle in the image, which represents the outer edge of the iris. Then, the iris is cropped from the image, and inside that region, another circle, which represents the outer edge of the pupil, is found. The purpose of this process is to get the area of the iris that lies between these two circles without the disturbance of the pupil itself. In order to find the upper eyelid, the upper part of the iris is extracted and a line corresponding to the eyelid is found. The bottom edge of the eyelid is found in the same way. The last step is to remove the noise, which is done by extracting the area between the outer edges of iris and pupil. Then, the area above the upper eyelid and bellow the lower eyelid is removed. Additionally, the eyelashes are removed through the threshold, relaying on the fact that they vary considerably in color compared to the overall image.

Results of successful and unsuccessful segmentation are depicted on Figs. 9 and 10.

First, the outer edges of pupil and iris are found. Then, the locations of the eyelids are searched and their annulment is done so that the iris regions does not interfere with further comparison. Fig. 10 shows the iris regions that will not be considered during authentication, which leads to the classification of a person as an intruder, although it is valid.

In order to successfully compare more iris images of persons, it is necessary for the iris to have consistent dimensions. Therefore, it is important to normalize

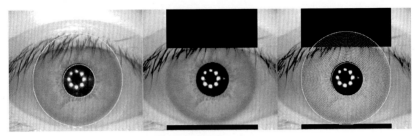

FIG. 9   An example of successful iris segmentation.

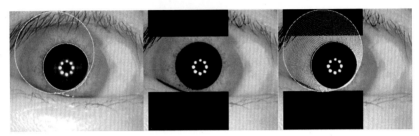

FIG. 10   An example of an unsuccessful iris segmentation process.

all of the irises at the same dimensions and in the correct format to make the comparison possible. Another problem that arises is that the pupil is not necessarily in the center of the iris. The consequences of this may be the occurrence of unwanted noise in poor normalization. All these problems can be solved by using Daugman's "Rubber Sheet Model."

Daugman's model [22] utilizes normalization of the iris from a circular shape into a rectangular shape. This method works by remapping each point of the iris (x, y) to the polar coordinates (r, θ), where r represents the diameter between the edges of the pupil and iris $[0, 1]$ and θ is the angle of the iris diameter $[0, 2\pi]$.

Mapping the iris from the Cartesian to the polar coordinate system is done by using the following equation:

$$I(x(r, \theta), y(r, \theta)) = I(r, \theta) \tag{15}$$

where $x(r, \theta)$ and $y(r, \theta)$ equal:

$$\begin{aligned} x(r, \theta) &= (1 - r)\, x_p(\theta) + r x_i(\theta) \\ y(r, \theta) &= (1 - r)\, y_p(\theta) + r y_i(\theta) \end{aligned} \tag{16}$$

Daugman's model also considers the problems with different pupil sizes, as well as the possible pupil movements in relation to the center of the iris. As a result of this method, the normalized iris is established.

The problem of displacement of the pupil is solved by the fact that the pupil center and the displacement vector between the center of the pupil and the

FIG. 11   An example of a normalized iris.

center of the iris have been taken as reference points for obtaining a normalized iris by Daugman's model [23]:

$$r' = \sqrt{\alpha\beta} \pm \sqrt{\alpha\beta^2 - \alpha - r_i{}^2} \qquad (17)$$

where α and β are obtained by:

$$\alpha = o_x^2 + o_y^2$$
$$\beta = \cos\left(\pi - \arctan\left(\frac{o_y}{o_x}\right) - \theta\right) \qquad (18)$$

Values o_x and o_y define the pupil shift vector in relation to the iris, r' is the distance between the outer edges of the pupil and the iris relative to the angle θ, and r_i is the diameter of the iris. In addition to creating a normalized iris, a noise mask is created. It is used for turning off iris noise during the comparison phase. This mask overlaps parts of the iris, eyelashes, and other elements that have been identified as noise. An example of a normalized iris can be seen in Fig. 11.

3.2   Iris coding using Gabor filters

In order to make the comparison of an iris successful, it is necessary that the paternal iris of the same persons be quite similar, even if they are partially deformed by a change in the light due to the expansion or contraction of the pupil. Solving this problem requires that only the key points that represent the uniqueness of each iris are extracted from the iris, while the others will be ignored. In this way, even if there are minor deformations in the iris itself, the total difference between the same iris will again be much lower than in the case of different ones, which enables the successful authentication of the person.

Extraction of main characteristic of the iris by coding is done using Gabor filters. For the iris encoding problem, we will use the 1D logarithmic Gabor filter. An example of a coded iris can be seen in Fig. 12. The iris noise mask is depicted in Fig. 13.

FIG. 12   An example of a coded iris. This form, along with the noise mask, is used for authentication of a person.

FIG. 13   Iris noise mask.

Gabor filters integrate the display of signals in a spatial domain and a spatial frequency domain. They work by modulating sine and cosine waves using the Gaussian method:

$$f(x) = a\, e^{-\frac{(x-b)^2}{2c^2}} \tag{19}$$

where a, b, and c represent arbitrarily real constants.

By further modulation, the Gaussian method successfully localizes the signal in the space, but in addition, it loses the localization in the space of frequencies. After localization, the signal is decomposed to the real and imaginary part, which is done using the pair of Gabor filters, where the real part is specified by cosine modulation, and the imaginary part by the sine. The combination of these two filters, both real and imaginary, is also called symmetric filters.

Although they are quite useful, Gabor filters have their drawbacks. The maximum filter permeability is limited to one octave of the signal, and in addition, Gabor filters are not optimal in the case of searching for wider spectral signal information with maximum spatial localization [24]. To address this part of the problem, we need to use Gabor filters that use a logarithmically scaled Gaussian method called the logarithmic Gabor filter:

$$G(f) = \exp\left(\frac{-\left(\log\left(f/f_0\right)\right)^2}{2\left(\log\left(\sigma/f_0\right)\right)^2}\right) \tag{20}$$

Using a logarithmic Gabor filter, we can encode the normalized iris. Since the normalized iris is constructed in two-dimensional form, we will apply the technique of one-dimensional logarithmic Gabor filters by breaking the normalized iris into several one-dimensional signals; then, each individual signal is encoded using Daugman's coding method [19] using a 2-D Gabor filter:

$$h_{\{Re,Im\}} = sgn_{\{Re,Im\}} \int_\rho \int_\phi I(\rho,\phi)\, e^{-i\omega(\theta_0-\phi)}\, e^{-\frac{(r_0-\rho)^2}{\alpha^2}} e^{-\frac{(\theta_0-\phi)^2}{\beta^2}} \rho\, d\rho\, d\phi \tag{21}$$

where $h_{\{Re,Im\}}$ is a complex bit whose real and imaginary values are 0 or 1, sgn is a sign that depends on the sign of the 2D integral, $I(\rho,\phi)$ is an image of the iris represented in polar coordinates, α and β represent the size of 2D waves, ω represents wave frequency, and (r_0, θ_0) represents the polar coordinates of each iris region for which the phase coordinates $h_{\{Re,Im\}}$ are calculated; this filter will produce two bits for each phasor.

The coding process will eventually produce a bit template that will contain the essential characteristics of the iris encoded in a series of bits. In addition, a noise mask corresponding to the fit iris regions will also be obtained. After that, we will use the encoded iris template, along with the noise mask, to compare it for the purpose of authenticating a person (see Fig. 12).

Fig. 13 shows the mask region of the iris that is not usable during the process of authentication.

3.3   Classification using Hamming distance

After full iris processing and finishing of the encoded template, we are ready to use this iris to authenticate other candidates. In order to authenticate candidates, we need to use a certain metric to determine the differences between the individual irises. In this case, Hamming distance is selected. The general Hamming distance [25] represents the distance of two elements that are compared. It can be a distance of two numbers, a string, a string of bits, and so on. In our case, this will be the distance of two encoded iris patterns. The general Hamming formula is defined as:

$$H(x, y) = \sum_{i=1}^{n} x_i \oplus y_i \tag{22}$$

The result of Hamming distance will be the sum of different elements in a series of elements over which distance is compared. A regular Hamming will not work best in our case, because there are noise masks that indicate which parts of the iris is not usable. For this reason, in this chapter, a modified version of Hamming distance [21] is used:

$$H = \frac{1}{N - \sum_{k=1}^{N} Xn_k \vee Yn_k} \sum_{j=1}^{N} X_j \oplus Y_j \wedge Xn_j \wedge Yn_j \tag{23}$$

where X_j and Y_j represent two encoded iris templates, X_n and Y_n represent the noise masks corresponding to X_j and Y_j, and N represents the sum of bits corresponding to each iris template.

Although, in theory, two irises of the same person should be the same, in practice, it is not the case. Due to the imperfection of all the images and the imperfection of the normalization process itself, a certain distance will arise between each iris.

Irises can often vary in images, especially because of the position itself: if the head is just slightly rotated aside the iris will also be rotated. These changes can cause significant difference even if iris is from same person. In order to solve this problem, Daugman's trick [19] is applied by moving the iris template into one or the other side for a number of bits. These iris shifts represent rotation of iris when it is not normalized, thus removing the problem if the iris is shifted during the iris capturing process. During the comparison, the new iris is rotated a couple of times and compared to the old ones. The distance between them is calculated, and in the end, the result is where the distance is smallest, i.e., more similar to the current iris. At the very end, it is seen whether the distance for a particular user does not exceed the threshold. If this is the case, the user is authenticated as valid and passes the system check.

4. Experimental evaluation and results

For maximum system precision, the face and iris are blended together in the person's authentication system. Authentication works by first creating a face image and a picture of an iris of a person trying to authenticate. Then, from face and iris, the main characteristics are extracted that uniquely identify the person. Finally, the derived characteristics are compared with the existing characteristics in the database that the person left in the process of applying for the system.

Since iris recognition is a more precise system, it is used as the ultimate confirmation that the person who represents the system is truly the one. More precisely, characteristics of the face are taken as the user name when the person is represented, while the characteristics of the iris are used as a password to confirm the person's identity. If both face and iris match and indicate that the same person is concerned, a person is authenticated as valid and can access the secured system or space. More detailed information on system accuracy can be found in Table 1.

The data in Table 1 represents the general precision of the system when the facial and iris features in the authentication process are aligned (precision was measured by a comparison of data from CASIA and ORL facial and iris databases). The threshold represents the percentage difference between the characteristics of a person. All persons who have a difference greater than the threshold are reported as intruders, while those with a percentage difference below the threshold are eligible and the authentication process is passed successfully. FAR (false acceptance rate) and FRR (false rejection rate) are metrics for checking the accuracy of biometric systems. FAR represents the percentage of intruders who enter the system, while FRR represents the number of valid persons reported as intruders in the authentication process. Depending on the security needs of the system, the threshold of acceptability is selected, which, according to characteristics, corresponds to the security needs system.

5. Conclusion

The algorithms presented in this chapter, as well as the entire solution, can be used in any system where security is an important factor. Applying these solutions removes the user's need to remember passwords because the user authenticates the system by simply approaching the camera, which creates a picture of his/her face and iris and uses that data for authentication.

Further plans for improving this system should focus on improving the process of segmentation of iris and face, as it has been established during the research that in the occurrence of errors in these phases there are significantly poorer results, which affect the further precision of the entire system.

TABLE 1 Results of system precision in relation to a certain threshold of acceptability.

Threshold	FAR	FRR
0.190000000000000	0.00000000000000000	84.9873737373737
0.195000000000000	0.00000000000000000	84.9873737373737
0.200000000000000	0.00938875938875939	84.9873737373737
0.205000000000000	0.00938875938875939	84.9873737373737
0.210000000000000	0.00938875938875939	84.9873737373737
0.215000000000000	0.00938875938875939	84.9873737373737
0.220000000000000	0.00938875938875939	84.9873737373737
0.225000000000000	0.00938875938875939	84.9873737373737
0.230000000000000	0.00938875938875939	84.6212121212121
0.235000000000000	0.01877751877751880	84.6212121212121
0.240000000000000	0.01877751877751880	84.2550505050505
0.245000000000000	0.01877751877751880	83.1565656565657
0.250000000000000	0.01877751877751880	82.0580808080808
0.255000000000000	0.02816627816627820	80.9595959595960
0.260000000000000	0.02816627816627820	79.8611111111111
0.265000000000000	0.03755503755503760	79.1287878787879
0.270000000000000	0.03755503755503760	78.0303030303030
0.275000000000000	0.03755503755503760	76.5656565656566
0.280000000000000	0.03755503755503760	75.8333333333333
0.285000000000000	0.03755503755503760	74.0025252525253
0.290000000000000	0.03755503755503760	73.2702020202020
0.295000000000000	0.03755503755503760	70.3409090909091
0.300000000000000	0.04694379694379690	68.8762626262626
0.305000000000000	0.04694379694379690	67.4116161616162
0.310000000000000	0.04694379694379690	65.2146464646465
0.315000000000000	0.05633255633255630	64.1161616161616
0.320000000000000	0.05633255633255630	62.6515151515152
0.325000000000000	0.05633255633255630	60.4545454545455
0.330000000000000	0.05633255633255630	55.6944444444444

Continued

TABLE 1 Results of system precision in relation to a certain threshold of acceptability—cont'd

Threshold	FAR	FRR
0.335000000000000	0.05633255633255630	54.5959595959596
0.340000000000000	0.05633255633255630	52.7651515151515
0.345000000000000	0.05633255633255630	49.1035353535354
0.350000000000000	0.05633255633255630	47.6388888888889
0.355000000000000	0.05633255633255630	46.1742424242424
0.360000000000000	0.05633255633255630	44.3434343434343
0.365000000000000	0.07511007511007510	43.2449494949495
0.370000000000000	0.07511007511007510	42.5126262626263
0.375000000000000	0.08449883449883450	40.3156565656566
0.380000000000000	0.09388759388759390	39.5833333333333
0.385000000000000	0.11266511266511300	38.4848484848485
0.390000000000000	0.13144263144263100	37.7525252525253
0.395000000000000	0.15960890960891000	35.9217171717172
0.400000000000000	0.16899766899766900	35.5555555555556
0.405000000000000	0.22533022533022500	34.0909090909091
0.410000000000000	0.30044030044030000	32.6262626262626
0.415000000000000	0.35677285677285700	29.3308080808081
0.420000000000000	0.42249417249417300	26.4015151515152
0.425000000000000	0.47882672882672900	25.3030303030303
0.430000000000000	0.58210308210308200	24.5707070707071
0.435000000000000	0.68537943537943500	23.4722222222222
0.440000000000000	0.87315462315462300	21.6414141414141
0.445000000000000	1.17359492359492000	19.8106060606061
0.450000000000000	1.82141932141932000	19.0782828282828
0.455000000000000	2.78846153846154000	17.2474747474747
0.460000000000000	5.14504014504015000	16.1489898989899
0.465000000000000	9.70797720797721000	14.3181818181818
0.470000000000000	18.3456358456358000	12.4873737373737
0.475000000000000	32.9639342139342000	10.2904040404040

TABLE 1 Results of system precision in relation to a certain threshold of acceptability—cont'd

Threshold	FAR	FRR
0.480000000000000	54.8303548303548000	6.99494949494950
0.485000000000000	78.0675343175343000	4.79797979797980
0.490000000000000	92.5825563325563000	3.33333333333333
0.495000000000000	96.4882802382802000	3.33333333333333
0.500000000000000	96.6666666666667000	3.33333333333333

The future development of this system should focus on the development of the face detection and iris feature in the picture. In addition to this component, development of the technique of cancelable biometrics should also be included in the plan. This technique should allow the facial and iris characteristic of the candidates to be stored in the database in such a way that if at some point they are taken from the database, they cannot be used to reattempt authentication. These two components, together with the already existing parts of the system, would round off the entire circle needed to make a completely secure biometric system.

References

[1] J.M. Haney, et al., ""We make it a big deal in the company": security mindsets in organizations that develop cryptographic products", in: Fourteenth Symposium on Usable Privacy and Security ({SOUPS} 2018), 2018.

[2] D. Florêncio, C. Herley, B. Coskun, Do strong web passwords accomplish anything? HotSec 7 (6) (2007) 159.

[3] C.F.A. Gomes, D.R. Pilar, A. Jaeger, L.M. Stein, Passwords usage and human memory limitations: a survey across age and educational background, PLoS One 7 (12) (2012).

[4] K. Delac, M. Grgic, A survey of biometric recognition methods, in: Proceedings. Elmar-2004. 46th International Symposium on Electronics in Marine, IEEE, 2004.

[5] A. Ross, A.K. Jain, S. Prabhakar, An introduction to biometric recognition, IEEE Trans. Circuits Syst. Video Technol. 14 (1) (2004) 4–20.

[6] M.O. Oloyede, G.P. Hancke, Unimodal and multimodal biometric sensing systems: a review, IEEE access 4 (2016) 7532–7555.

[7] M. Barni, et al., SEMBA: secure multi-biometric authentication, IET Biom. 8 (6) (2019) 411–421.

[8] D. Bhattacharyya, et al., Biometric authentication: a review, Int. J. u e Serv. Sci. Technol. 2 (3) (2009) 13–28.

[9] K.A. Shakil, et al., BAMHealthCloud: a biometric authentication and data management system for healthcare data in cloud, J. King Saud Univ. Comput. Inf. Sci. 32 (1) (2020) 57–64.

[10] J.J. Hathaliya, S. Tanwar, R. Evans, Securing electronic healthcare records: a mobile-based biometric authentication approach, J. of Inf. Secur. Appl. 53 (2020) 102528.

[11] J. Mason, et al., An investigation of biometric authentication in the healthcare environment, Array 8 (2020), 100042.

[12] K. Abouelmehdi, A. Beni-Hessane, H. Khaloufi, Big healthcare data: preserving security and privacy, J. Big Data 5 (1) (2018) 1–18.

[13] E. Vezzetti, F. Marcolin, Geometrical descriptors for human face morphological analysis and ecognition, Robot. Auton. Syst. 60 (6) (2012) 928–939.

[14] M. Turk, A. Pentland, Eigenfaces for Recognition, Massachusetts Institute of Technology, USA, 1991.

[15] M. Raza, J.H. Shah, M. Sharif, A. Azeem, Linear and Nonlinear PCA Based Face Recognition Techniques, Massachusetts Institute of Technology, USA, 1991.

[16] L. Sirovich, M. Kirby, Low-Dimensional Procedure for the Characterization of Human Faces, Brown University, Rhode Island, 1986.

[17] T.P. Singh, An Efficient Method for Feature Extraction of Face Recognition Using PCA, IFTM University, Moradabad, 2014.

[18] A.K. Bansal, P. Chawla, Performance Evaluation of Face Recognition Using PCA and N-PCA, Poornima Collage of Engineering, Jaipur, 2013.

[19] J. Daugman, How iris recognition works, in: International Conference on Image Processing, 2002.

[20] H. Liu, K.C. Jazek, Automated extraction of coastline from satellite imagery by integrating Canny edge detection and locally adaptive thresholding methods, Int. J. Remote Sens. 25 (5) (2010).

[21] J. Illingworth, J. Kittler, A Survey of the Hough Transform, University of Surrey, United Kingdom, 1988.

[22] J. Daugman, Iris Recognition, University of Cambridge, United Kingdom, 2006.

[23] L. Masek, Recognition of Human Iris Patterns for Biometric Identification, University of Westert Australia, Australia, 2003.

[24] D. Field, Relations between the statistics of natural images and the response properties of cortical cells, J. Opt. Soc. Am. 4 (12) (1987) 2379–2394.

[25] D.J. Fleet, M. Norouzi, R. Salakhutdinov, Hamming Distance Metric Learning, University of Toronto, Canada, 2012.

Chapter 5

Performance investigation of several convolutional neural network models in healthcare systems

Hala Shaari[a], Jasmin Kevric[b], Muzafer Saračević[c], and Nuredin Ahmed[d]

[a]*Faculty of Engineering and Natural Sciences, Department of Information Technologies, International BURCH University, Sarajevo, Bosnia and Herzegovina,* [b]*Faculty of Engineering and Natural Sciences, International BURCH University, Sarajevo, Bosnia and Herzegovina,* [c]*Department of Computer Science, University of Novi Pazar, Novi Pazar, Serbia,* [d]*National Board for Technical and Vocational Education, Tripoli, Libya*

1. Introduction

Artificial intelligence (AI) may provide faster services and assist in data analysis and diagnosis to find patterns that suggest a patient is more likely to have a certain condition in a challenging domain like healthcare services. AI adoption can be crucial in the medical domain since it can save lives by saving time.

Although the use of AI for diagnosing subjects is still in its early stages, there are interesting case scenarios of its use. Another way in which AI can improve healthcare is by automating administrative tasks. Image analysis takes a lot of time for doctors. Through AI image analysis, isolated areas that do not have easy access to health facilities could be supported by sending images of their rashes, injuries, and cuts to determine what care they need.

Brain diseases are among the most deadly [1] and neoplasm in children is the second most common of these disorders. Furthermore, brain tumors have surpassed leukemia as a primary cause of death for children [2]. Timely identification of brain diseases might assist to prepare better care plans and increase patients' survival rates or longevity. Magnetic resonance imaging (MRI) is a commonly employed imaging tool for diagnosing the human brain without a lot of radiation, which gives improved soft-tissue resolution.

With the rise of deep learning and its main emphasis on feature learning— automatic data representation learning, which is the main distinction between

Blockchain Technology Solutions for the Security of IoT-Based Healthcare Systems.
https://doi.org/10.1016/B978-0-323-99199-5.00008-2
97

deep learning methods and traditional machine learning—numerous automated research contributions to brain tumor analysis have been presented, for example, in computer-aided diagnosis, where the general process starts with data preprocessing and extraction, then feature reduction, and finally classification. Standard procedures for extraction, for instance, histogram extraction and local binary patterns, can detect a brain tumor through MRI images [3]. Recently, deep learning has gained prominence in the learning and training processes from medical imaging data [4]. In particular, convolutional neural networks (CNNs) show greater efficiency in the extraction of features than traditional hand-crafted features.

CNN finds applications in many areas, including image classification, language processing, forecasting, etc. The first significant success was achieved in 2012 when an error value of 0.23% was achieved on the MNIST (Modified National Institute of Standards and Technology) dataset. The goal is to classify the images, that is, to classify them in a certain category. In addition, CNN has found application in language processing, within which, the classification, prediction, and modeling of sentences is performed. Recurrent networks have priority in prediction and forecasts, but the convolutional ones have achieved results that are satisfactory and in line with the recurrent, so they can also be used in this regard.

Deep learning models are more powerful when employed in many training sets. These types of large data sets are generally not accessible in medical imaging compared with natural scene images. Consequently, techniques such as the data augmentation technique, which is a common technique in deep learning, are used to exploit research to overcome the obstacle of minimal labeling of data. With the correct data augmentation techniques, it is possible to incorporate variations in the training samples, which results in reduced overfitting during training but also increases the generalization of the trained network. Popular techniques for the task of data augmentation include rotation, translation, flipping, or the addition of noise [5].

Because of the self-learning ability, deep learning approaches could extract the hierarchy of image features easily compared to the manual extraction of machine learning tools. Hence, they obtain excellent outcomes and generalizability when trained on huge volumes of data. Furthermore, the rapid growth in the power of graphics processing unit (GPU) processing has allowed the improvement of deep learning algorithms and helped in the training of deep learning algorithms with a huge volume of images. Generally, the MRI image examination comprises huge quantities of image data and, therefore, increases the computational complexity [6].

The complexity problem in the discovery and identification of brain tumors is addressed by utilizing a graphics processing unit (GPU) [7,8].

Deep learning models are significantly faster when using GPUs rather than CPUs [9]. However, while GPUs bring performance improvements, they also increase hardware costs. An alternative approach to address the efficacy of deep learning models is to use the transfer of learning. Two transfer learning methods can be applied: the first method utilizing a pretrained network to derive attributes, and the second method by fine-tuning with the data of a pretrained configuration [10].

This study aims to investigate the behavior and execution of several convolutional neural networks (CNNs), with and without transfer learning, by adapting five different CNN models on MRI images of brain tumors.

This chapter is structured as follows. In Section 2, we discuss the related work for brain tumor analysis using CNN models and techniques. Section 3 shows the role of blockchain technology in medical imaging. Section 4 explains our proposed CNN models: SimpleConv, VGG, and ResNet. Section 5 presents the experiments followed by discussion of the results. Finally, Section 6 presents conclusions based on the experimental results.

2. Related works

Deep learning has been attracting growing attention recently, particularly the convolutional neural networks (CNNs), which are cutting-edge frameworks for image recognition and classification [11–13]. CNNs are built on the common concept of stacking multiple layers to understand a variety of different raw data abstractions. They automatically learn at different (low, high) levels using conventional filters, which are modified during the training procedure by learning the fundamental representational input attributes that are hierarchically complicated; avoiding the required pro-hand-crafted image attributes. Furthermore, convolutional neural networks do not need prior knowledge of the domain and can learn to do some tasks automatically simply by working through the dataset.

Convolutional neural systems have been utilized for decades, but were not common until 2012, when Krizhevsky et al. [14] used the AlexNet model and won the ImageNet Large Visual Recognition Challenge (ILSVRC). In 2014, Simonyan and Zisserman [15] proposed the VGG Net model—a similar but deeper CNN, which ranked second in the ILSVRC classification task. CNN models have become popular because of developments in computational technology such as powerful GPUs, improved learning algorithms [16–20], and the emergence of big data [21–23].

Many types of research have been conducted to automate brain tumor detection, segmentation, and classification using convolutional neural networks. CNN has been used to improve effectiveness in radiological activities by designing protocols based on the description of short texts [24]. Mohsen et al. [25] suggested a deep neural network (DNN) scheme to classify MRI into four classes of data. They trained a neural network with pulse-coupled feedback to segment the images. DWT (discrete wavelet transforms) then served as an extractor for the element. PCA (principal components analysis) was then utilized to decrease features and neural network backpropagation was selected as the classifier.

Kamnistas et al. [26] put forward an 11-layer deep 3D CNN for brain lesion segmentation. They developed this design to examine the shortcomings of existing configurations proposed for applications for segmentation of brain lesions. The authors then suggested a unique training approach that is not only computationally efficient but also offers an adaptive way of partially resolving segmentation difficulties' intrinsic class imbalance. Pereira et al. [27] suggested an automated segmentation process using (3 × 3) kernels CNN. They concluded that using small kernels offers a more profound architecture and gives confidence in overfitting problems if the weights are lower. Their preprocessing step involves normalization, although this is not typical in CNN-based segmentation methods.

Zhao et al. [28] created a system for automatic segmentation of brain tumors based on CNNs. The approach involves concentrating on local features alone in the convolutional CNNs. They created multiple scale CNNs that are three scale frames that could automatically identify the best three images of size scales and incorporate information around that pixel from different regions. Compared to traditional CNNs and the best two approaches in the Brain Tumor Segmentation (BraTS) challenge 2012 and 2013, this multiscale CNN system provides high precision in the segmentation of brain tumors.

Deep CNN training requires significant storage space and high computational power and, therefore, takes a long time. Repeated changes in architecture or features and eliminating overfitting make a tedious, time-consuming, and comprehensive process of deep learning from scratch. Transfer learning provides a better option by fine-tuning a pretrained CNN for a broad variety of labeled images that are accessible from any other category in the event of insufficient data, as Oquab et al. [29] reported. This helps to accelerate convergence while reducing computational complexity during training as Tajbakhsh et al. and Phan et al. [30,31] mentioned.

A deep transfer method for automated classification of brain images (normal and abnormal) with MRI has been suggested by Talo et al. [32]. The ResNet34 model has been used as a model of deep learning. Their model obtained 100% accuracy of classification on 613 MRI images. Swati et al. [33] used a pretrained CNN architecture and proposed a block-based transfer level approach.

Yang et al. [34] examined the role of transfer learning of MRI to accurately grade the type of brain tumor called gliomas. A private dataset of 113 pathologically reported glioma patients in a Chinese hospital was utilized. It consisted of 52 LGG (low-grade glioma) and 61 HGG (high-grade glioma) samples. AlexNet and GoogleLeNet models were developed and fine-tuned from scratch. Based on a 20% randomly selected test dataset, GoogleLeNet performed better than AlexNet in all cases, with test accuracy of 90%. Banerjee et al. [35] designed three-level ConvNet architectures (VolumeNet, PatchNet, and SliceNet) where images were handled in three different ways: patch mode, slice mode, and multiplanar mode. They trained proposed models that were implemented from scratch. Then fine tuning with transfer learning techniques was carried out on VGG and ResNet models. In addition, LOPO (leave one patient out)-based validation was completed on the selected datasets. The VolumeNet model provided the highest classification efficiency, achieving full training accuracy (100%) and 98% validation accuracy in just 20 epochs.

Both PatchNet and SliceNet model performance are fairly close on the validation set, with SliceNet achieving 94% accuracy on the train set. The implementation of the VGG and ResNet models shows comparable results, achieving an accuracy of 85% on the validation set. In [36], the authors proposed an ensemble implementation of deep learned features for analysis of medical images using mobile phones. Furthermore, the authors of [37] present a novel method for denoising multiple-coil magnetic resonance images.

3. The role of blockchain technology in medical imaging

In recent years, many researchers have been working on developing a viable solution for storing and sharing medical images in the healthcare field. Current methods rely on cloud-based centralized data centers, which increase maintenance costs, demand a huge amount of storage space, and create privacy issues when transferring data across a network. Medical record data breaches within major medical data centers have created significant challenges for any companies attempting to develop medical image processing technologies in recent years [38].

As a result of its decentralized character, blockchain technology has become one of the most significant study subjects, not only in the banking industry, but also throughout the healthcare field. Healthcare-based blockchain applications have been given special attention to allow the interoperable exchange of data between doctors, suppliers, and patients in real time [39,40]. Many companies utilize blockchain to manage patient identity, promote patient-centered healthcare, record and monitor tailored medical services, establish policies where patients may securely express their views on medical records and information with partners, and so forth.

Instead of depending on a single central control node, blockchain keeps data in a distributed network. The distributed ledger is the name given to this network. Data is kept in an immutable (nonmodifiable) format, making it exceedingly difficult to make unauthorized changes to the data. Data may only be added to the blockchain, and once a block has been recorded, it cannot be deleted or changed. As a result, the data is kept as a continually expanding list of records (blocks) that are added to one another (chain).

The distributed ledger base is distributed over multiple nodes as devices on a peer-to-peer network so that each node duplicates and saves the ledger identically and automatically updates it. The main advantage is that there is no central authority or server. During an update, every node creates a new transaction followed by a consensus process to determine the right copy. Other nodes are updated with the proper copy of the ledger after a consensus has been established. Security is done through encryption signatures and keys [41,42]. Database replication and computing confidence preserve data quality. This is different from other types of distributed ledge structures because of the structure of the blockchain, which consists of collected and structured data in blocks and secured by cryptography. Blockchain technology is, therefore, ideal for event recording, record management, transaction processing, asset tracking, and voting [42].

In general, the medical imaging sector has benefitted from blockchain technology more than other sections of the healthcare business. This is partially because it creates enormous, digital data sets that can be used analytically as well as training deep learning models. The medical imaging sector consists of a comprehensive technological stack, which offers considerable potential for innovation from hardware to intelligent software. It also provides improvements in processes and diagnostic accuracy and speed, which can yield demonstrable results in better patient care, cost reductions, and variability, as well as enhanced radiologist satisfaction [43].

A public blockchain or a private blockchain might be used to share medical images. Transactions may be added to a public blockchain, granting authorization to other hospital systems to access a patient's medical images. Individual users or organizations might be granted access to see images via transactions on a private blockchain. This would eliminate the requirement for medical imaging facilities to manufacture and import discs, as well as the necessity for patients to transfer them, potentially reducing the need for repeat imaging and wasting precious medical resources.

One especially efficient approach for blockchain-facilitated image sharing has been suggested by the authors of [44]. In this approach, three public/private key transactions on a blockchain enable secure image transmission by identifying the source of the image, its owners (the source and the patient), and enabling access to the image from its source after verification. According to this approach, an image is "published" as a public/private key set that the patient's private key may access. The blockchain containing these transactions is used to confirm that a requesting party—like a doctor or another hospital staff—is on a list allowed to obtain a certain imaging study and that the specific study matches these permissions.

In a recent study, a framework has been provided that creates an accurate collaborative model that uses numerous hospitals' data to detect CT images of COVID-19 patients. In cooperation with many hospitals with different types of CT scanners, a blockchain-based federated learning architecture is suggested. By adopting federated training, hospitals may retain data in private and just exchange weights and gradients, while data is being distributed across the hospitals via blockchain technology. The decentralized data-sharing architecture across several hospitals securely shares the data without hospital privacy being compromised. For training and evaluating the datasets, extensive experiments have been conducted on several deep learning tools. The Capsule

Network had the highest level of precision. The suggested model is intelligent since it may learn from shared data or sources among hospitals. Finally, because hospitals exchange their models' weights and gradients and/or private data for training a global and superior model, the suggested approach can aid in the detection of COVID-19 patients via lung screening [45].

4. Methodology

The methodology proposed is divided into three distinct phases: first, preparing images by applying some procedures to improve image quality; then, the data augmentation technique is executed to overcome the size and imbalanced dataset issue; finally, the proposed CNN models are implemented to identify a given image and whether or not it is tumorous.

4.1 Data acquisition and preprocessing

This study used the Brain Tumor Detection dataset provided by Kaggle [36]. The dataset contains 253 brain MRI Images divided into 2 folders: yes and no. Folder "yes" contains 155 tumorous brain images, whereas folder "no" contains 98 nontumorous brain images. Data preprocessing is the next step toward improving image quality. Three main procedures have been applied to all images in the dataset. First, since images came in various sizes in the dataset, we resized all images to have the shape (240, 240, 3). Second, normalization was employed so pixel values were scaled to 0–1. Finally, we cropped the image section containing only the brain based on Computer Vision (CV) techniques provided by Adrian Rosebrock [37].

4.2 Data augmentation

High quality and abundant data are crucial to the efficient deployment of different deep learning tools. Data augmentation is a technique for artificially expanding the amount of training data by creating custom images using the original collection of data. By this approach, variations are introduced into images that boost the model's ability to learn and better generalize possible unobserved data.

When the model is generalized by adding variance in the training dataset, then it becomes less susceptible to overfitting. To achieve the required accuracy, we expanded existing data by using eight different methods of augmentation (width shift range, height shift range, shear range, brightness range, rotation range, horizontal flip, vertical flip, and fill mode).

As mentioned above, 61% of the data (155 images) are tumorous, 39% of the data (98 images) are nontumorous. To balance the data, nine new images were generated for each image that falls under the "no" class and six images for each image that falls under the "yes" class. By applying these data augmentation techniques, our dataset is now composed of 1085 (52%) tumorous images and 980 (47%) nontumorous images, resulting in 2065 example images. Then, this augmented dataset was used with the proposed models.

4.3 The proposed CNN models

Five different CNN models have been implemented, and they are:

- SimpleConv model: One conventional layer.
- VGG-16 model: VGG-16 model.
- Resnet-50 model: Resnet-50 model.
- VGG-16TL model: VGG-16 model with transfer learning.
- Resnet-50TL model: Resnet-50 model with transfer learning.

All the models above have been trained using the augmented dataset to derive the best model for tumor analysis application. The dataset for all models was split into 70% for training, 15% for validation, and 15% for testing. The number of training iteration is set to 10 epochs for all models.

SimpleConv model is a one-layered CNN. It comprises a convolutional layer, a batch normalization layer, two pooling layers, and two fully connected layers. The first, flatten, layer is used to flatten the matrix of three dimensions into a one-dimensional vector. The second fully linked layer with a sigmoid activation function is then used for the two-class classification. Fig. 1 explains the SimpleConv model's architecture.

Layer (type)	Output Shape	Param #
input_1 (InputLayer)	[(None, 240, 240, 3)]	0
zero_padding2d (ZeroPadding2	(None, 244, 244, 3)	0
conv0 (Conv2D)	(None, 238, 238, 32)	4736
bn0 (BatchNormalization)	(None, 238, 238, 32)	128
activation (Activation)	(None, 238, 238, 32)	0
max_pool0 (MaxPooling2D)	(None, 59, 59, 32)	0
max_pool1 (MaxPooling2D)	(None, 14, 14, 32)	0
flatten (Flatten)	(None, 6272)	0
fc (Dense)	(None, 1)	6273

Total params: 11,137
Trainable params: 11,073
Non-trainable params: 64

FIG. 1 SimpleConv model architecture.

We also applied a VGG-16 model, which is a 16-layer CNN model developed by Simonyan and Zisserman [15]. The VGG-16 model uses serialized multiple 3×3 filters. Multiple smaller stacked kernels are more effective compared to a larger kernel because the multiple nonlinear layers increase the CNN's depth. The ability to learn hidden features thus improves with lower costs.

The Resnet-50 model that we implemented is a deep residual learning framework presented by He et al. [11]. The term "residual" refers to the subtraction of features that are related to the features learned from that layer's input. Compared to deep conventional CNN, these networks are relatively simple to train. In addition, they can solve the degrading accuracy problem. Resnet-50 architecture involves skipping connections together with substantial batch normalization. These skipping connections apply to a gated unit or repeated gated units. In comparison to VGG, it has a lower difficulty.

In the VGG-16TL model, transfer learning is used. A pretrained model is an already trained model on a large dataset (ImageNet) with several different categories of images. This allows us to use this model as an efficient feature extractor for new images. It is used as a simple feature extractor by freezing all the five convolution blocks in the VGG-16 model to ensure that their weights are not changed at each epoch. The first five blocks allow us to take advantage of the pretrained VGG-16 model as an efficient feature extractor. We then add our own fully connected, dense layers to determine whether the image is tumorous or not. Our own fully connected dense layers were: three different dense ReLU layers with different parameters followed by Softmax activation functions. Adam optimizer with $lr = 0.0003$ is used during training.

In the Resnet-50TL model, transfer learning is done on the pretrained Resnet-50 model. Resnet-50 was used as a simple feature extractor. The last predicting layer of the model was removed to incorporate transfer learning and replaced with our predicting layers. They are two dropout layers with a flatten layer and Sigmoid activation functions. In addition, Adam optimizer with $lr = 0.0003$ is used during training.

5. Results and discussion

This section addresses the experimental performance analysis of our CNN models. The experiments were carried out on Navoneel's dataset [36]. The dataset was created by professional radiologists using brain data from real MRI patients. Experiments were performed using the NVIDIA GTX-1050 with 4 GB memory and models have been developed using TensorFlow, with Keras in Python. As mentioned in the previous section, the dataset was divided into 70% for training, 15% for validation, and 15% for testing.

Accuracy is the most natural indicator of success and offers the ratio of correctly predicted observations. The plots demonstrate that the results of all proposed models yield relatively high results. Figs. 2–4 show the experiments' results for 10 epochs. Fig. 2 depicts the accuracy of the SimpleConv model,

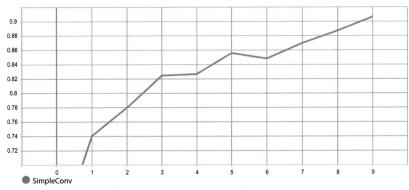

FIG. 2 SimpleConv model performance accuracy.

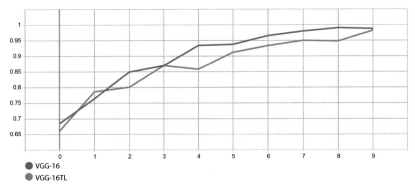

FIG. 3 VGG-16 and VGG-16TL models performance accuracy.

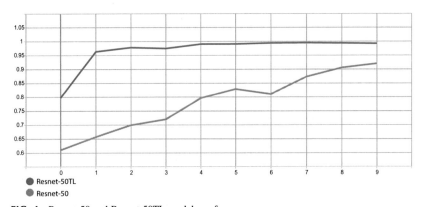

FIG. 4 Resnet-50 and Resnet-50TL models performance accuracy.

which yields surprisingly high results of 90% accuracy and 83% validation accuracy on training data, and 87% accuracy on the test data, with 0.88 f1 scores also on the test data.

Taking into account the simple architecture described in the previous section, these findings are very good. That might be due to the preprocessing techniques that were used on the dataset at the initial stage. In addition, using data augmentation methods has introduced variation and generalization to the training dataset.

Recently, many studies have proposed different CNN architectures, which also had accuracy results as high as our SimpleConv model. The authors of [35] proposed three separate models of CNNs: PatchNet, SliceNet, and VolumeNet, which have been created from scratch. In just 20 epochs, the plots in one of their experiments show that VolumeNet offers the highest rating efficiency during training, achieving the maximum testing accuracy set at 100%. Furthermore, the validation results of PatchNet and SliceNet are quite close: 90% for Patch-Net, and 92% for SliceNet. It is observed that SliceNet is 94% more accurate on the training set. The authors of [25] proposed a deep learning classifier that was combined with discrete wavelet transform (DWT) and principal components analysis (PCA). In all performance steps, the deep learning classifier provided strong results at 96.97%.

In Fig. 3, the accuracy that results from the two models are combined to examine experiment outcomes with and without the use of transfer learning. The VGG-16 model and VGG-16TL model showed similar accuracy results. The VGG-16 demonstrated its good classification capability, but the training took a long time. VGG-16 and VGG-16TL models both achieved 98% accuracy on the training dataset. However, it shows some differences in validation accuracy with 60% in the VGG-16 model and 92% in VGG-16TL.

Similarly, Fig. 4 shows the combined results of Resnet-50 and Resnet-50TL. Where Resnet-50 model is using transfer learning techniques, Resnet-50TL uses the 50 layers Residual Network provided by He et al. [11].

As in the VGG-16 model, the Resenet-50 model training was also time-consuming. However, the Resnet-50TL model (with transfer learning) yields slightly better accuracy at 99% over Resnet-50 (without transfer learning) with 92% on the training dataset.

The transfer learning technique is widely adopted because it leverages the performance of CNNs by lowering the common datasets using multiple CNN models. In addition, VGGNet and ResNet models have been employed to classify tumorous and nontumorous brain MRI images.

All methods achieved high accuracy irrespective of the time consumed at training. The pretrained Resnet-50 model achieved the highest accuracy with 99%. Our studies have shown the potential of CNNs for medical imaging, as using CNNs models provides remarkably good accuracy without the need for additional features extraction.

There are, however, various potential enhancements to this study. Above all, the proper size of the dataset is a crucial factor in the success of CNN models, while we addressed the mutational complexity of training time. The study [33] adapted transfer learning and fine-tuning into their new approach for brain tumor image classification. They used the VGG19 model and achieved 94.82% maximum classification accuracy. Furthermore, Ref. [32] introduced an approach that uses the ResNet34 model for automated classification of MRI brain tumors. On 613 MR images, their model achieved 100% classification accuracy. Moreover, Ref. [34] noted that GoogleLeNet and AlexNet can be useful in training new models as well as pretrained models. Pretrained Google-LeNet had a better performance than pretrained AlexNet with 94% and 92%, respectively, whereas AlexNet achieved 85% and GoogleLeNet achieved 90% when trained from scratch. As shown in Figs. 3 and 4, VGG-16 and Resnet-50 can be equally useful in the medical imaging domain for both the pretrained model and models that are trained from scratch, as also pointed out in [34].

Our findings indicate that the proposed CNN models are successful over the suggested models from other studies. Our proposed SimpleConv models, which were trained for 10 epochs, achieved 90% accuracy with a simple architecture compared to three different CNNs (PatchNet, SliceNet, and VolumeNet) proposed by [35]. These three models had deeper architecture than our SimpleConv models and they were trained for 20 epochs to achieve better results. Furthermore, the VGG-16TL model achieved 98% accuracy compared to 94.65% accuracy of VGG-16 pretrained models proposed by [33] with an epoch set maximum at 50. An equal number of iterations also presented two other pretrained models (AlexNet and VGG-19) with 89.95% and 94.82% accuracy, respectively.

6. Conclusion

This chapter presented a study to investigate the behavior and performance of several convolutional neural networks (CNNs), with and without transfer learning, by adapting five different CNNs models on MRI images of brain tumors. The main goal of this study was to explain and investigate (not compare) the various CNN models used in brain tumor analysis. To investigate the behavior and performance of CNN models, five different CNN models were adapted to analyze brain tumors on MRI images. Images were first prepared by applying some procedures to improve image quality. Then, a data augmentation technique was performed to overcome the size and imbalanced dataset issue.

Deep learning adaption for noninvasive brain tumor prediction can help doctors and radiologists taking better decisions and reducing human error. A variety of experiments have been performed by data augmentation techniques and transfer learning, and a large volume dataset will boost the results further. We explained our proposed CNN models: SimpleConv, VGG, and ResNet, and presented the experiments followed by discussion of the results. All CNN models were trained using the augmented dataset to derive the best model for tumor analysis application. The dataset for all models was split into 70% for training, 15% for validation, and 15% for testing, and the number of training iteration was set to 10 epochs for all models.

The findings suggest that all the proposed CNN models have achieved high overall accuracy, especially the Resnet-50 model, which achieved the highest accuracy with 99%. Our findings indicate that the proposed CNN models are successful over the suggested models from other studies. Our proposed Simple-Conv models, which were trained for 10 epochs, achieved 90% accuracy with a simple architecture compared to three different CNNs (PatchNet, SliceNet, and VolumeNet).

Other sophisticated pre-trained deep learning architectures may also be explored for brain research. Lastly, the proposed models can be applied to other tasks relevant to the different MRI data. In future work, there are, however, various potential enhancements to this study. Above all, the proper size of the dataset is a crucial factor in the success of CNN models.

The most important asset of any healthcare system is patient medical images. The majority of the time, medical images are dispersed across many systems, and sharing them is critical for building effective and unified healthcare. Furthermore, a centralized medical image data hosting site might be a single point of security attack. As the dispersed nature of health services has become more widely recognized, interest has increasingly shifted to decentralized designs and system interoperability, such as blockchain systems, to share these pretrained models' results securely and effectively.

References

[1] R.J. Dawe, L. Yu, J.A. Schneider, K. Arfanakis, D.A. Bennett, P.A. Boyle, Postmortem brain MRI is related to cognitive decline, independent of cerebral vessel disease in older adults, Neurobiol. Aging 69 (2018) 177–184, https://doi.org/10.1016/j.neurobiolaging.2018.05.020.

[2] S.C. Curtin, A.M. Minino, R.N. Anderson, Declines in cancer death rates among children and adolescents in the United States, 1999–2014, NCHS Data Brief (257) (2016) 1–8.

[3] N. Behzadfar, H. Soltanian-Zadeh, Automatic segmentation of brain tumors in magnetic resonance images, in: Proc.—IEEE-EMBS Int. Conf. Biomed. Heal. Informatics Glob. Gd. Chall. Heal. Informatics, BHI 2012, vol. 21, 2012, pp. 329–332, https://doi.org/10.1109/BHI.2012.6211580. no. 1–3.

[4] Y. LeCun, K. Kavukcuoglu, C. Farabet, Convolutional networks and applications in vision, in: ISCAS 2010–2010 IEEE International Symposium on Circuits and Systems: Nano-Bio Circuit Fabrics and Systems, 2010, pp. 253–256, https://doi.org/10.1109/ISCAS.2010.5537907.

[5] L. Perez, J. Wang, The Effectiveness of Data Augmentation in Image Classification using Deep Learning, *arXiv Prepr. arXiv1712.04621*, 2017, [Online]. Available: http://arxiv.org/abs/1712.04621.

[6] M.P. McBee, et al., Deep learning in radiology, Acad. Radiol. 25 (11) (2018) 1472–1480, https://doi.org/10.1016/j.acra.2018.02.018.

[7] R.R. Agravat, M.S. Raval, Deep learning for automated brain tumor segmentation in MRI images, in: Soft Computing Based Medical Image Analysis, Elsevier, 2018, pp. 183–201.

[8] M. Ben naceur, R. Saouli, M. Akil, R. Kachouri, Fully automatic brain tumor segmentation using end-to-end incremental deep neural networks in MRI images, Comput. Methods Prog. Biomed. 166 (2018) 39–49, https://doi.org/10.1016/j.cmpb.2018.09.007.

[9] B.J. Erickson, P. Korfiatis, T.L. Kline, Z. Akkus, K. Philbrick, A.D. Weston, Deep learning in radiology: does one size fit all? J. Am. Coll. Radiol. 15 (3) (2018) 521–526, https://doi.org/10.1016/j.jacr.2017.12.027.

[10] G. Litjens, et al., A survey on deep learning in medical image analysis, Med. Image Anal. 42 (2017) 60–88, https://doi.org/10.1016/j.media.2017.07.005.

[11] K. He, X. Zhang, S. Ren, J. Sun, Deep residual learning for image recognition, in: Proceedings of the IEEE Computer Society Conference on Computer Vision and Pattern Recognition, vol. 2016-Decem, 2016, pp. 770–778, https://doi.org/10.1109/CVPR.2016.90.

[12] Y. LeCun, Y. Bengio, G. Hinton, Deep learning, Nature 521 (7553) (2015) 436–444.

[13] C. Szegedy, et al., Going deeper with convolutions, in: Proceedings of the IEEE Computer Society Conference on Computer Vision and Pattern Recognition, vol. 07-12-June, 2015, pp. 1–9, https://doi.org/10.1109/CVPR.2015.7298594.

[14] A. Krizhevsky, I. Sutskever, G.E. Hinton, ImageNet classification with deep convolutional neural networks, Commun. ACM 60 (6) (2017) 84–90, https://doi.org/10.1145/3065386.

[15] K. Simonyan, A. Zisserman, Very deep convolutional networks for large-scale image recognition, in: 3rd Int. Conf. Learn. Represent. ICLR 2015—Conf. Track Proc, 2015.

[16] G.E. Hinton, S. Osindero, Y.W. Teh, A fast learning algorithm for deep belief nets, Neural Comput. 18 (7) (2006) 1527–1554, https://doi.org/10.1162/neco.2006.18.7.1527.

[17] G.E. Hinton, R.R. Salakhutdinov, Reducing the dimensionality of data with neural networks, Science 313 (5786) (2006) 504–507, https://doi.org/10.1126/science.1127647.

[18] S. Ioffe, C. Szegedy, Batch normalization: accelerating deep network training by reducing internal covariate shift, in: 32nd Int. Conf. Mach. Learn. ICML 2015, vol. 1, 2015, pp. 448–456.

[19] V. Nair, G.E. Hinton, Rectified linear units improve Restricted Boltzmann machines, in: ICML 2010—Proceedings, 27th International Conference on Machine Learning, 2010, pp. 807–814.

[20] N. Srivastava, G. Hinton, A. Krizhevsky, I. Sutskever, R. Salakhutdinov, Dropout: a simple way to prevent neural networks from overfitting, J. Mach. Learn. Res. 15 (1) (2014) 1929–1958.

[21] M. Everingham, The PASCAL visual object classes challenge 2008 (VOC2008) development kit, Challenge 2008 (2008) 1–24.

[22] L. Roux, D. Racoceanu, F. Capron, J. Calvo, E. Attieh, et al., MITOS-ATYPIA-14, 2014.

[23] O. Russakovsky, et al., ImageNet large scale visual recognition challenge, Int. J. Comput. Vis. 115 (3) (2015) 211–252, https://doi.org/10.1007/s11263-015-0816-y.

[24] Y.H. Lee, Efficiency improvement in a busy radiology practice: determination of musculoskeletal magnetic resonance imaging protocol using deep-learning convolutional neural networks, J. Digit. Imaging 31 (5) (2018) 604–610, https://doi.org/10.1007/s10278-018-0066-y.

[25] H. Mohsen, E.-S.A. El-Dahshan, E.-S.M. El-Horbaty, A.-B.M. Salem, Classification using deep learning neural networks for brain tumors, Futur. Comput. Inform. J. 3 (1) (2018) 68–71, https://doi.org/10.1016/j.fcij.2017.12.001.

[26] K. Kamnitsas, et al., Efficient multi-scale 3D CNN with fully connected CRF for accurate brain lesion segmentation, Med. Image Anal. 36 (2017) 61–78, https://doi.org/10.1016/j.media.2016.10.004.

[27] M.M. Thaha, K.P.M. Kumar, B.S. Murugan, S. Dhanasekeran, P. Vijayakarthick, A.S. Selvi, Brain tumor segmentation using convolutional neural networks in MRI images, J. Med. Syst. 43 (9) (2019) 1240–1251, https://doi.org/10.1007/s10916-019-1416-0.

[28] L. Zhao, K. Jia, Multiscale CNNs for brain tumor segmentation and diagnosis, Comput. Math. Methods Med. vol. 2016 (2016), https://doi.org/10.1155/2016/8356294.

[29] M. Oquab, L. Bottou, I. Laptev, J. Sivic, Learning and transferring mid-level image representations using convolutional neural networks, in: Proceedings of the IEEE Computer Society Conference on Computer Vision and Pattern Recognition, 2014, pp. 1717–1724, https://doi.org/10.1109/CVPR.2014.222.

[30] N. Tajbakhsh, et al., Convolutional neural networks for medical image analysis: full training or fine tuning? IEEE Trans. Med. Imaging 35 (5) (2016) 1299–1312, https://doi.org/10.1109/TMI.2016.2535302.

[31] H.T.H. Phan, A. Kumar, J. Kim, D. Feng, Transfer learning of a convolutional neural network for HEp-2 cell image classification, in: Proceedings—International Symposium on Biomedical Imaging, vol. 2016-June, 2016, pp. 1208–1211, https://doi.org/10.1109/ISBI.2016.7493483.

[32] M. Talo, U.B. Baloglu, Ö. Yıldırım, U. Rajendra Acharya, Application of deep transfer learning for automated brain abnormality classification using MR images, Cogn. Syst. Res. 54 (2019) 176–188, https://doi.org/10.1016/j.cogsys.2018.12.007.

[33] Z.N.K. Swati, et al., Brain tumor classification for MR images using transfer learning and fine-tuning, Comput. Med. Imaging Graph. 75 (2019) 34–46, https://doi.org/10.1016/j.compmedimag.2019.05.001.

[34] Y. Yang, et al., Glioma grading on conventional MR images: a deep learning study with transfer learning, Front. Neurosci. 12 (NOV) (2018) 804, https://doi.org/10.3389/fnins.2018.00804.

[35] S. Banerjee, S. Mitra, F. Masulli, S. Rovetta, Deep Radiomics for Brain Tumor Detection and Classification from Multi-Sequence MRI, arXiv Prepr. arXiv1903.09240, 2019, [Online]. Available: http://arxiv.org/abs/1903.09240.

[36] N. Chakrabarty, Brain MRI Images for Brain Tumor Detection, *Kaggle*, Apr. 2019. [Online]. Available: https://www.kaggle.com/navoneel/brain-mri-images-for-brain-tumor-detection.

[37] A. Rosebrock, Finding extreme points in contours with OpenCV, Resources (Apr. 2016). [Online]. Available http://www.pyimagesearch.com/2016/04/11/finding-extreme-points-in-contours-with-opencv/.

[38] Healthcare Data Breach Costs Remain Highest at $408...—Google Scholar. https://scholar.google.com/scholar?hl=en&as_sdt=0%2C5&q=Healthcare+Data+Breach+Costs+Remain+Highest+at+%24408+Per+Record&btnG=. (accessed Aug. 26, 2021).

[39] M. Zhang, Y.J.-P. Preprints, Blockchain for Healthcare Records: A Data Perspective, peerj.com, 2018, https://doi.org/10.7287/peerj.preprints.26942v1.

[40] M. Mettler, Blockchain technology in healthcare: the revolution starts here, in: 2016 IEEE 18th Int. Conf. e-Health Networking, Appl. Serv. Heal. 2016, Nov. 2016, https://doi.org/10.1109/HEALTHCOM.2016.7749510.

[41] S. Brakeville, B. Perepa, Blockchain Basics: Introduction to Distributed Ledgers, IBM Dev, 2018. https://developer.ibm.com/tutorials/cl-blockchain-basics-intro-bluemix-trs/. (accessed Aug. 26, 2021).

[42] S. Ray, The Difference Between Blockchains & Distributed, Towards Data Science, 2018. https://towardsdatascience.com/the-difference-between-blockchains-distributed-ledger-technology-42715a0fa92. (accessed Aug. 26, 2021).

[43] A. Alexander, M. McGill, A. Tarasova, C. Ferreira, D. Zurkiya, Scanning the future of medical imaging, J. Am. Coll. Radiol. 16 (4 Pt A) (2019) 501–507, https://doi.org/10.1016/j.jacr.2018.09.050.

[44] M.P. McBee, C. Wilcox, Blockchain technology: principles and applications in medical imaging, J. Digit. Imaging 33 (2020) 726–734.

[45] R. Kumar, A.A. Khan, J. Kumar, Zakria, N.A. Golilarz, S. Zhang, Y. Ting, C. Zheng, W. Wang, Blockchain-federated-learning and deep learning models for COVID-19 detection using CT imaging, IEEE Sens. J. 21 (14) (2021) 16301–16314, https://doi.org/10.1109/JSEN.2021.3076767.

Chapter 6

The classification of the investigations and punishment for crime syndicates that relate to intrusions against IoT-based healthcare systems

Joshua Ojo Nehinbe[a], Jimmy Adebesin Benson[b], and Linda Chibuzor[c]
[a]ICT Security Solutions, Lagos, Nigeria, [b]NHS England, London, United Kingdom, [c]Northamptonshire Healthcare NHS Foundation Trust, Nottingham, United Kingdom

1. Introduction

The classification of the investigation of and punishment for organized cyber-crimes is raising serious global ideological questions over social policy in contemporary healthcare delivery systems [1–4]. Recently, studies have indicated that healthcare systems that operate under the platform of the Internet of Things (IoT), otherwise known as IoT-based healthcare systems, have recorded laudable development during the Covid-19 pandemic, and resulted in positive outcomes for some patients [1,5]. However, the incidence of syndicates and faceless affiliations of gangsters in charge of organized criminal activities, and the variability in the power of jurisdiction and how this can influence the punishments for the gangsters or offenders, are current threats to a wider usage of IoT-healthcare systems. With this, forensic studies have shown that cyber laws are not functionally capturing all aspects of the IoT-based healthcare systems across the globe [3,6,7].

Further studies have also affirmed that these domains of the healthcare sector are immature and they are drastically evolving, in both developed and developing countries [8–10]. Nonetheless, serious threats due to organized criminal activities that some people perpetrate through the Internet, and the broadness of these aspects of healthcare services, have been observed as critical challenges

Blockchain Technology Solutions for the Security of IoT-Based Healthcare Systems.
https://doi.org/10.1016/B978-0-323-99199-5.00010-0
113

that might continue to confront forensic investigators and health mismanagement boards in establishing suitable measures to promote desirable healthcare services in the near future. For these reasons, experts agree that the above healthcare domains must be properly developed to deal with intrusions that are penal offenses and to boost demand and encourage patients to widely patronize the underlying healthcare services across the globe.

Another central issue here is how forensic investigators can accurately conduct thorough investigations of a loose affiliation of gangsters that intrude into IoT-based healthcare systems [11,12]. Firstly, it is difficult for these investigators to record detailed information about the suspects of organized crimes on the above healthcare systems and take inventory of all the items or exhibits recovered from each suspect without overemphasizing or confusing intrusions that are penal or criminal offenses with rehabilitative offenses, with minimal explanation. Secondly, affiliations of gangsters can carry out organized cyber attacks on IoT-based healthcare systems that may involve adult, minor offenders, serial offenders, and child suspects. Members of the syndicates that have been accused of cybercrimes against IoT-based healthcare systems may carryout different roles in their team.

Many complexities can crop up during investigations. For instance, the ringleader of the above syndicates might be actively involved (or less involved) in the recruitment and finances of the members of the organized cybercriminals than other members of the team. A suspect of proven crime may be guilty of many cyber offenses at a time [5,13]. Usually, the court should convict members of underworld organizations that have attacked the above healthcare systems on the basis of their roles and involvement. However, some child offenders might not be punished equally with an adult offender in the court of law. Some serial offenders that have escaped detection due to their previous involvement in different cybercrimes might be active members of the above syndicates but it might be impossible for the investigating police officers (IPOs) to re-arrest all of them. These fundamental issues can generate various discrepancies and controversial debates among the public, especially if the confessional statements of the above group of intruders are fallacious, misleading, and incoherent.

The motivation for this study is that studies on blockchain technology have suggested that inbuilt security measures can discourage the menace of organized cybercrimes on IoT-based healthcare systems. Therefore, the continuing usage of such healthcare systems requires some urgent measures in other to improve the security of all their components with proven technology. Thus, the objectives of this chapter are twofold. First, this chapter aims to model the investigative procedures that forensic investigators may encounter in the course of gathering evidence about organized cybercrimes on IoT-based healthcare systems from suspects. The second objective of this chapter is to adopt qualitative and quantitative methodologies to broadly discuss organized intrusions on the IoT-based healthcare systems on the basis of punitive and rehabilitative interventions. The punitive therapeutic intervention or penalization is meant to punish cyber offenses that might have caused or could cause significant or punitive damage to any of the human and nonhuman components of the IoT-based healthcare systems. Conversely, the rehabilitative therapeutic intervention is a kind of penalization that is meant for punishing organized groups of cyber offenders for committing insignificant offenses against any of the components of the IoT-based healthcare systems. The latter measure is meant to simultaneously restore both the IoT resources to their normal working conditions and the intruders to social norms.

There are numerous categories of punitive and rehabilitative strategies that are proposed in this chapter for the syndicates of intruders into IoT-based healthcare systems. However, the underlying fact is that the rehabilitation of the criminals that are punished for their involvement in organized cybercrimes on the above healthcare systems to become useful persons in society may be viewed differently in both legal and academic terms.

Thus, administration of justice on organized cybercrime is often influenced by the jurisdiction of the crime, existing cyber laws; element of the crime and the technicality of the allegations. The element of cybercrime is the underlying (or motivating) factor that induces a suspect to commit the crime. The elements of cybercrime can include considerations such as the intention of the suspect and the conditions the surround the allegation. For instance, a suspect of cyber crime may commit the act intentionally or unintentionally, accidentally or deliberately. Some physical disabilities of the organized cyber offenders may impede therapeutic measures and the recommendation of suitable rehabilitative strategies such as electrotherapy, community service, and exercise.

In essence, one of the major contributions of this chapter is its ability to pragmatically explore suitable models that forensic investigators and detectives can adopt to investigate and punish crime syndicates that relate to the intrusions on IoT-based healthcare systems. The chapter identifies potential challenges that could confront the above experts and the chapter further itemizes how these experts can practically overcome them while working on the intrusions involving IoT-based healthcare systems. The chapter also indicates a novel approach to pragmatically promote Internet security, protection of the electronic health data, and computational and networking aspects of IoT-based healthcare systems. The remainder of this chapter is organized as follows: Section 2 is the background to the topic; Section 3 discusses the newly proposed model for investigating and gathering evidence on organized intrusions on IoT-based healthcare systems; Section 4 enumerates the methodology for the study; Section 5 discusses and analyzes the results, together with the most important recommendations to safeguard the IoT-based healthcare systems; and Section 6 concludes the paper and suggests areas of future research on the above issues.

2. Background

Therapeutic measures meant to deal with cybercriminals on IoT-based healthcare systems can be divided into punitive and corrective interventions. These interventions are long-standing issues in cyber forensics. These have facilitated several calls for more punitive measures against cybercriminals across the globe. The aim of punitive therapeutic interventions is to punish cybercriminals. The examples of punitive measures include the imposition of exorbitant fines and terms of payment that are difficult for offenders to satisfy. It is a well-known fact that the power of detectives to detain suspects generally varies from one country to another [2,3,6,13,14]. In some countries, like the United Kingdom (UK), the police have special powers to detain suspects for up to 72h to continue their lines of enquiry and questioning, while in some countries, like Nigeria, the police should not keep a suspect in their custody for more than 24h without granting him/her bail or being charged to the court for trial.

Furthermore, the dynamic nature of risk analysis to ascertain various impacts of organized crimes on the above domain usually calls for more review [9]. Our survey has further shown that some policy makers and risk assessors often perceive intrusions and the punishment of serial intruders from different perspectives while formulating cyber laws [8,10,15]. We define an intrusion as an illegal penetration into private or corporate networks. Intrusions into IoT-based healthcare systems can cause partial or prolong interruption or entire disturbance of the IoT-based healthcare services, interference with IoT background services, invasion of privacy of the patients on the platforms, and infringement of corporate security policy, including serious data protection breaches. Intrusions on the IoT-based healthcare systems can have different objectives and different impacts on the victims. Some intruders may intend to steal and distort healthcare data that are stored in the IoT-based healthcare databases. Intrusions into the above healthcare services can also cause disruption of operating systems at the back-end of the above healthcare applications. It is also plausible that some repeat offenders among the above syndicates might have absconded from another country and rearrested and implicated concerning syndicate cybercrimes on the above healthcare systems in another country with or without the knowledge of the IPO. Yet, investigations may show that the intruders play lesser roles in their team. In other words, new members of an organized cybercrime against IoT-based healthcare systems might be responsible for deadly attacks on networks' services that obstruct legitimate service-users and paralyze activities of support staff working to recover the underlying services from the downtime caused by the attacks.

Basically, intrusions into the IoT-based healthcare networks are violation of corporate security policy of the health management board and the affected country should provide categories of punishments for all suspects of such crimes [7,10,11,14]. There is also the issue of stigmatization and reputational damage for corporate organizations or agencies that are the victims of the above categories of intruders. Unfortunately, considerable numbers of the existing measures designed to prosecute cyber criminals are not globally applicable to all aspects of the IoT-based healthcare systems. The IoT-based healthcare systems are assemblies of many networks of computers, electronic and home appliances (such as mobile and wearable devices) [9], the Internet, human and nonhuman elements, operating systems, and databases. Consequently, the criticality and resources required to complete the interrogation of crime cases on the organized sets of cybercriminals accused of intruding into the above healthcare systems is often underestimated at the initial stage of the case. The fact is that there are several ways to classify organized cybercrimes on the IoT-based healthcare systems [7,11,15]. However, the degree to which cybercrime acts and global cyber laws actually promote cybersecurity and protect intellectual property, data, computer and mobile systems, and their other auxiliary components, continues to generate substantial debates, with the rising cases of global gangsters and the impacts of the attacks on the victims [16]. Furthermore, a recent review of the standard measures for prosecuting syndicates of cyber offenders on the above healthcare systems put forward that forensic investigators might erroneously overlook the technicality of the issues regarding state laws and international laws. The bone of contention is that some of the punitive measures in cyber penal or criminal codes may not broadly cover all the existing categories of cybercrimes to date [3]. For instance, criminal laws in some developing countries like Nigeria do not permit detectives to take statements from the suspects of cybercrime without the presence of their relatives or lawyers [17]. Also, in the administration of criminal laws on cyber offenses, some federal laws may technically contradict some sections of the state laws in some countries, especially if the intruders reside in different countries. Consequently, some of the written punishments for cyber offenders may not significantly achieve social control in the long run if they are adapted to litigate and punish syndicates of intruders against the above healthcare domains. In other words, the premise is that some victims of above kinds of syndicate crimes on IoT-based healthcare systems may be indirectly subjected to penalization that can inflict undue pain, regret, and miscarriages of justice on them.

3.   Definitions of terms

- *Intrusion* is a kind of unauthorized access into a computer system [7,11]. It can involve an authorized act of a user with the intention to obtain or alter information in a computer or mobile system. Intrusion can signify an authorized activity that disrupts the functions of a computer or mobile system. It can denote the use of a computer system damaging the reputation of a person. Intrusion may occur when a person attempts to exceed his/her authorized privileges in a computer or mobile system.
- *IoT-based healthcare systems* are the combinations of the Internet of Things, computer systems, electronic and home appliances (such as wireless and wearable devices), healthcare networking, people, and clinical workflows and process involved in the delivering of healthcare services [11].
- *Rehabilitative punishment* is a kind of penalization that aims to achieve rehabilitation of the perpetrator of a cybercrime against IoT-based

healthcare systems [2,6,14]. This measure helps the convicted person to readapt and shift from his/her former state of mindset and achieve a good reputation. Rehabilitative punishment can come in the form of requiring the convict to participate in a course of mandatory moral education on the ethics of computer usage and IoT usage.

- *Cartel of cybercriminals* is a phrase to denote a consortium of independent organizations formed to limit competition and competitors by controlling the production and distribution of a product or service over the Internet.
- *Syndicate of cybercriminals* is a phrase to connote a loose affiliation of gangsters in charge of organized criminal activities on the Internet.
- *Accomplice of organized cybercrime* is a partner in committing an organized cybercrime against IoT-based healthcare systems.
- *Initiator of organized cybercrime* is the ringleader that masterminds the motive(s) of the syndicate.
- *Gini index* is a statistical concept to determine the proportion of repetitions in the confessional statements or criminal evidence in a dataset that is comprised of numbers and alphanumeric attributes [18].

3.1   A model for investigating organized intrusions on the IoT-based healthcare systems

Standard frameworks that investigators and litigators should follow in the course of issuing an arrest and charging organized cybercriminals that attack IoT-based healthcare systems are scarce [1,3,14]. Accordingly, the criticality of the above procedures is often unstressed in most of the existing cybercriminal laws. Thus, Fig. 1 illustrates a model that comprises of six phases to lessen the above challenges. The components of the model subsume arrest, investigation, bail, court trial, and conviction or acquittal. The arrest of the suspect of the organized cybercrime against the IoT-based healthcare systems involves the process

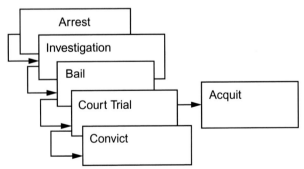

FIG. 1   A model for the arrest and trial of suspects of organized cybercrimes on IoT-based healthcare systems.

of identifying and capturing members of the team and the taking of each suspect into custody by a law enforcement agency such as the police.

Basically, misplacement of justice is not allowed in the investigations of the suspects of cybercrime in the above healthcare setting. In other words, the investigators of the crime must ensure that they track and arrest the right culprits [14]. Given the fact that a suspect cannot be detained in police custody more than 24 to 72 h before he/she is charged to court in most countries, it is imperative that the police should promptly arrest all the members of the syndicates and thoroughly investigate the allegations brought against each suspect within the limited resources available to them. In some developed countries, for instance, one of the problems is that the police try to establish the victim of the crime, and this is difficult because in such cases the organization and its patients are all victims. In addition, the level of harm the intrusions have caused to the victims is not always clearly established during preliminary arrest and interrogations of the suspects.

Furthermore, during investigation, it is pertinent that the police should conduct a thorough examination of each suspect after all the team members of the syndicates have been arrested [2,6,14,17]. This would not only enable the police to separate a suspect from a guiltless person, but to ascertain the depth of the offenses committed by each suspect of the cybercrimes on the IoT-based healthcare systems. The interrogators must also adopt a series of methods of investigations that suit organized cybercrimes. It is ethically important that the detectives should always accord each suspect compassionate treatment to achieve commendable results. Human rights laws generally require persons accused of a crime to be handled with respect and be accorded a fair hearing. A suspect of organized cybercrimes on the IoT-based systems might be allowed the opportunity to freely write what he/she knows about the allegations levied against the team while in police custody. All interrogations should be conducted in the interrogating room, which should be conducive to promoting decorum and good behavior for both the police and all suspects. There is need for the detectives to remove all stumbling blocks and impediments to fact finding in the interrogation room.

Moreover, the IoT-based healthcare systems are relatively new domains that are not exhaustively covered by the existing methods available to the police in interrogating suspects of cybercrimes in the above instances [5,9]. Therefore, the investigating police officer (IPO) in charge of the case must acquire the right skills to identify the motives, ringleader, and financiers of the team. The IPO should properly document the confessional statements he/she obtains from each suspect. The interrogators must restrict or control the interference of uninvited guests in and out of the interrogation rooms to avoid disturbance, digression, and sabotage. The victims of cyber attacks against IoT-based healthcare systems may be patients or corporate organizations. The patients may include mental health patients, pregnant women, and aging people who rely on wearable devices (like life-supporting appliances) as interventions to survive. The status of the health of the affected patients is very significant in determining suitable punishment for the cybercriminals that attack IoT-based healthcare systems. For instance, studies reveal that some service-users of IoT-based healthcare systems are patients that exhibit complex disorders [9]. This can include patients using wheelchairs, those with epilepsy or cognitive dysfunction, patients suffering chronic pain, and those feeding with the aid of tube that can require a length of time to set up [10]. The feeding tubes of some users of the above healthcare systems require proper online monitoring to accurately administer them. The corporate organizations working with the IoT-based healthcare systems may include multiagency organizations involved in social work and referral, hospital management boards, and vendors or third-party companies supporting the Internet and networking, devices, mobile appliances, and computer systems that underlie the healthcare delivery systems.

In addition, the outcomes of an investigation can incriminate some or all the suspects of a cybercrime on an IoT-based healthcare system. The IPO may, therefore, need to grant each suspect, or some suspects, the privilege to apply for bail and subsequently charge each suspect to court upon the completion of the investigations into the allegations the victims might have brought against the suspects. The IPO must ensure that the lawyers or families of each suspect in the above context must not face difficulties or being subjected to high-risk whenever they attempt to safely contact the suspects. It is better practice for the IPO to notify the victims or the petitioners of the above crime before he/she approves or grants bail to the suspects of the crime. The conditions to secure the bail must be accompanied with surety. The bailing conditions must be affordable and commensurate with legal provisions, otherwise, the suspects may inadvertently litigate the complainants for usurping their fundamental human rights. The most important thing is that the suspects' guarantors or lawyers must guarantee the availability of the suspects whenever the need arises.

The evidence the IPO may eventually gather from the complainants and suspects of the same cybercrime on the IoT-based healthcare systems may not be directly comparable. It is plausible that the IPO might have gathered evidence on different bases and determinants. For instance, the perspectives of the suspects might differ from the perspectives of the victims, defendants, and complainants of the allegations. For example, the time zones of the locations of all the syndicates at the time of the attacks may be at variance. Therefore, evidence gathered on reference periods and different timescales might be inadmissible in some courts of law due to the methods used for collating incriminating data from the IoT-based healthcare networks, software, and databases. For these reasons, potential cases of cybercrimes in the above context, which might have been used to serve as deterrents to others, may eventually drop out at any stage of the litigation process The investigations of suspects of cybercrimes against IoT-based healthcare systems may absolve all the suspects of the entire allegations that the complainants brought against them. Similarly, investigations may also have logical reasons to acquit some suspects and hold one or more suspects for further interrogations. The significance of these facts is that legal trial of suspects in the above context must be carried out in a competent law court and in accordance with legal provisions, constitutions, and cyber laws relevant to the IoT-based healthcare system of the country where the intrusions have occurred. The technicality of these cybercrimes and the available evidence may tremendously influence the outcomes of the court cases in the above domains. In the above model, the court may decide to convict the suspect on the basis of facts presented by the solicitors if the suspect is found guilty of the allegation(s) against him/her. On the other hand, the court may acquit the suspect if he/she is not found guilty of the allegation(s) levied against him/her. The court might also be lenient with the suspect if he/she has extenuating circumstances, for example, a terminal or life-altering condition/illness.

3.2 Models for gathering evidence of organized cybercrimes against IoT-based healthcare systems

The investigations of the syndicates that participate in cybercrime against IoT-based healthcare systems may demonstrate different patterns of operations. Suppose there are three members of a gang in such a scenario. All the members of the same gang may reside within the same geographic locations such as locations L1, L2, and L3. It is also possible that two or more members of the same gang reside in the same geographic locations. For instance, two suspects that reside in the locations L1 and L2, or L1 and L3, or L2 and L3 can be members of the same or different gangs. Hence, investigators of cyber crimes must be able to decipher the operating tactics of criminal gangs in other to get them arrested. It is conceivable that all the above three members may reside in different geographic locations. Gangsters that may reside in the same country may not necessarily live in the same geographic locations. Some syndicates in the above context that are international travelers may operate in more than one country. Studies on the organized cybercrimes suggest that incidence of cybercrime can initially be conceived by a ringleader or combination of one or more accomplices within the same or different geographic locations. Thus, organized cybercrimes on IoT-based healthcare systems can be categorized into simple crime scene and complex crime scene. The term "simple crime scene" is used to describe a cybercrime against the above healthcare systems that involves few initiators and small number of accomplices while "complex crime scene" is a kind of cybercrime that involves many initiators and accomplices and investigators must apply several tactics before they can trace and expose their connections.

The initiator provides intelligence and is the architect of the mode and time of cyber attacks on IoT-based healthcare systems for the organized cybercriminals, whereas an accomplice is a partner in carrying out the cybercrime on IoT-based healthcare systems. Technically, the accomplice is a co-conspirator in the organized cybercrime. Consequently, an accomplice in an organized cybercrime is a suspect before the law.

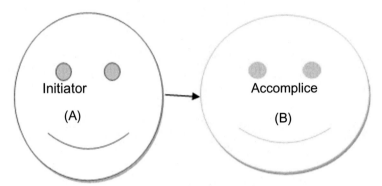

FIG. 2 The suspect (B) is known to the initiator (A) of the organized cybercrime.

Figs. 2 and 3 illustrate two possible categories of a simple form of organized cybercrime that investigators may encounter concerning the intrusions on IoT-based healthcare systems. Both models indicate that the initiator of the organized cybercrime is known to all accomplices in the crime. The implication is that the investigators can easily track all the accomplices once one of the team is arrested and properly interrogated.

Fig. 4 illustrates a complex form of organized cybercrimes that investigators may encounter on the IoT-based healthcare systems. The model indicates that the

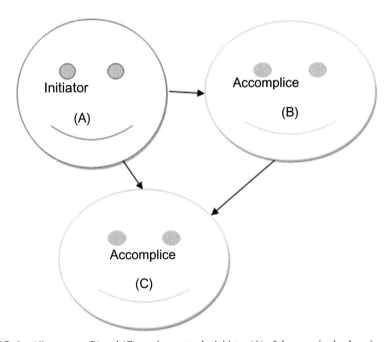

FIG. 3 All suspects, (B) and (C), are known to the initiator (A) of the organized cybercrime.

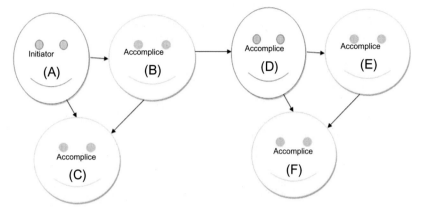

FIG. 4 A model for illustrating complex cybercrime on an IoT-based healthcare system.

initiator (A) of an organized cybercrime on an IoT-based healthcare system may be known to only a few of the accomplices, such as accomplices (B) and (C), at the crime scene. Meanwhile, accomplice (B) has recruited accomplice (D) without the knowledge of the initiator (A) of the organized cybercrime. Similarly, accomplice (D) has involved two other accomplices, (E) and (F), on his/her personal volition. The implication is that the investigators must be prudent and far-sighted in locating all the team members that are involved in the organized cybercrime and to arrest and gather sound evidence from them. One of the notable ways to track all the accomplices in this scenario is to track and establish their means of correspondence or conversation. Studies have shown that some organized cybercriminals may adopt social media, emails, and mobile phones to contact their team members. There may also be some unsuspecting or unknowing accomplices that could be include relatives, friends; former partners of the victims, or the spouse of the ringleader. The ringleader may tactically gather intelligence information from any of the above group of persons. However, during an investigation they would be classed as an accomplice because they would have divulged confidential information that has compromised an organizations' IoT-based healthcare system.

Studies have revealed that inmates that are approaching the end of their service term can form criminal gangs. Thus, the interrogators must thoroughly scrutinize the means of communication of some inmates that are approaching the end of their service term to get to the bottom of organized cybercrimes on IoT-based healthcare systems.

3.3 Challenges with the investigation of organized cybercrimes on IoT-based healthcare systems

Healthcare systems based on the platform of IoT services are a novel area of electronic healthcare services [8,9]. Intrusions on these domains would require intensive resources—more so than intrusions on aging computer networks [10,12]. Consequently, most agencies and detectives are likely to face some significant challenges during the course of investigating organized cybercrimes on IoT-based healthcare systems. For instance, most experts on cybercrimes still lack the technical skills essential for conducting thorough investigations of a loose affiliation of intruders and intrusions on IoT-based healthcare systems. The requirements of the investigations of some organized cybercrimes against the above healthcare systems may be resource-intensive. Investigators may need collaborations from detectives in another countries before some syndicates' members can be brought to book [8,11]. For this reason, some inexperienced detectives handling such cases for the first time may face tactical issues with how to accurately separate fabricated information or false evidence from honest information that is genuine but unconfirmed by confessional statements from other suspects accused or implicated as members of a gang carrying out organized cybercriminal activities in the above milieu.

Some developed and underdeveloped countries are political and economic rivals; this means there could be two or more nations that are unwilling to collaborate in fighting against crime syndicates. Unfortunately, detectives that are confronted with cybercrime issues that span such nations might lack the needed cooperation on how to conduct the arrest and trial of international suspects of crimes on IoT-based healthcare systems. Thus, such detectives might not be able to meet the deadlines to render their reports for litigation purposes. The courts might require additional evidence to prosecute the syndicates accused or implicated for carrying out cyber attacks on the above healthcare systems for a number of reasons. Such reports must be available to the lawyers of the complainants within a time limit for them to further file additional evidence require to litigate all the culprits. Furthermore, the complainants would need ample time to study and take decisions on the legality of the allegations and the outcomes of the investigations on their allegations. The complainants must equally be given the opportunity to ascertain the veracity of the case and whether to continue with the allegations or to just drop the case straightaway. Significant numbers of cybercrimes in the above categories are susceptible to ending up with inconclusive investigations and summary dismissal in the court of law, especially if they contain inadmissible and disjointed evidence that is prohibited by courts.

Fundamentally, confessional statements should be obtained from the suspects of organized cybercrimes on IoT-based healthcare systems that operate as syndicates, irrespective of their geographic locations. Presently, there are language barriers and acute shortages of automated tools that detectives can suitably adopt to translate, correlate, and harmonize diverse confessional statements involving numerous syndicates in different languages. These problems can deter attempts to ascertain the gravity of the complainants' allegations especially if there are no competent language translators to assist the detectives. The inconsistency of cyber laws to prosecute international suspects of intrusions on IoT-based healthcare systems is a potential issue that might also confront prosecutors and judges in pronouncing suitable punishments for cyber offenders in the above context.

There are insufficient lines of investigations and empirical evidence to assist detectives working on organized cybercrimes on IoT-based healthcare systems across the globe. The vulnerability of the physical components of the IoT-based healthcare systems to cyber attacks is not the same. Some hospitals may have stronger security to protect their computer resources than others. Forensically, gangs of cyber intruders might selectively compromise only the physical components (such as the networks' layers, wearable devices, mobile phones, and computers of patients) or the computational components (such as source codes and operating systems) of an IoT-based healthcare system. They might not necessarily compromise all the components of the above healthcare systems but their activities on the web might be on the basis of segregations of responsibilities. Furthermore, the IPO might be incompetent or unable to establish the depth of the involvement of the individual members of the crime syndicates in all cases. Some of the detective's work is made harder by organizations carrying out their own investigations and sometimes this is in parallel to the police investigations. These might result in the detectives having to obtain some of the key information from the organizations rather than obtaining them directly from the suspects. Suspects of cyber crimes in the above setting may unequally participate in the crime that they are held for. Hence, punitive interventions for each suspect should be proportionate to the role each suspect plays and their level of involvement in the allegations against them.

Lack of suitable datasets to train detectives and to simulate and statistically analyze various scenarios of organized cybercrimes on IoT-based healthcare systems are novel issues agencies might face in the next decade. The components of IoT-based healthcare systems vary from one organization to another. Some hospitals might decide to segment their healthcare services by deploying diversities of physical and computational components of the enabling IoT's platforms to capture clients with different economic status within the same country. Some wealthy private individuals might subscribe to receive both onshore and offshore IoT-based healthcare services. New technical and legal issues have emerged in the above domain in recent times. Privacy and human rights laws often forbid detectives to share crime data with researchers. It is also difficult for criminologists to synthesize criminal evidence that will be closely related to realistic evidence. For these reasons, pragmatic studies into the above categories of crime scenes have faced serious limitations over the years. In network forensics, for instance, datasets that indicate intrusions on a few segments of the above healthcare systems may have ethical, reliability, and validity issues. Furthermore, the above variability can compound investigations' tasks by making them cumbersome, demanding, and resource-intensive for detectives. In essence, the above limitations often affect the reliability and generalization of most empirical studies on the above social problems across the globe.

4.   Methodology for the study

This chapter adopted qualitative and quantitative empirical methods to propose suitable punishments for cybercriminals against IoT-based healthcare systems. We qualitatively interviewed 2 prosecutors and 44 anonymous experts selected across IT, social work, mental healthcare, adult nursing, strategy, and data analytics for the survey.

Suitable datasets for exploring organized cyber attacks on IoT-based healthcare systems are emerging trends and new challenges confronting researchers in this domain. Thus, we selected as samples Defcon-10 and Defcon-11 from the repositories of the Defcon datasets on the basis of the historic ways both datasets were simulated. Experimental analysis of the logs of Snort-IDS was carried out using both public trace files. In Fig. 5, by using clustering and C++ programming techniques, the logs of the above IDS were analyzed by log analyzer. The log analyzer has inbuilt rules that it adopted to receive the input log from terminal (A) and further used message description to cluster alerts from Snort-IDS into different groups. Alerts with the same message description were grouped together while alerts with different message descriptions were grouped differently. Thereafter, two reports were generated, and they were sent to terminal (C) for forensic analysis. The first report contained alerts in the sequence of $<date, IP\ address, message\ description>$ while the second report indicated sequence of $<IP\ address, date, message\ description>$. The above procedures were repeated for another dataset. The results obtained were presented to the above experts to adopt their expertise in their various fields to identify and classify potential cyber offenses among the above attacks that may correlate with the intrusions on IoT-based healthcare systems. The perceptions of the above respondents are discussed below.

5.   Results and analysis

The results indicate that the Defcon-10 dataset contains port scan attacks, fragmented attacks intended to cause buffer-overflow, directory traversal attacks, and IP spoofing attacks. Similarly, the Defcon-11 dataset indicates a collection of organized attacks that sought administrative privileges, hijacked sessions of file transfer protocol (FTP), probed the networks, and fragmented and spoofed packets. The dataset also contains directory traversal attacks, which signify intruders that tried to gain unauthorized access into protected files outside

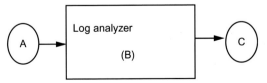

FIG. 5   Log analysis of the Internet trace files.

the root directory. Technically, the attack was a kind of buffer overflow attacks that exploited vulnerabilities in the file directories of web or FTP servers in order to compromise the passwords of vital files.

5.1 Classifications of cyber offenses from evaluative datasets

The combination of the quantitative analysis of the evaluative datasets and the thematic review of the perceptions of the respondents suggest the following intrusions are peculiar to services delivered via the platform of the Internet.

Some respondents believe that organized gangsters can alter the databases, operating systems, and systems files of IoT-based healthcare systems. They can illegally break into the back end and extract health-related reports from the IoT-based healthcare databases. It is also argued that some gangsters can deliberately infringe copyright laws by reusing the health records in the above healthcare systems in an unapproved manner. Furthermore, we evaluate the perceptions of the above participants on five specific cybercrimes that can have severe impacts on their victims. We specifically explore severe distributed denial of service (DDoS) attacks, buffer-overflow, password guessing, online stealing, and illegal leakage of IoT-related healthcare data. In Table 1, the respondents submit that proven suspects of the above cybercrime can be recommended for punitive therapeutic interventions like physiotherapy therapies, detention, and imprisonment in a proportionate manner.

Additionally, we assess the impacts of misinformation and defamation of character in relation to the IoT-based healthcare information and users. The results suggest that rehabilitative offenses that may require corrective therapeutic interventions such as temporary isolation, psychotherapy, and occupational and speech therapies, which could be recommended for the convicts of the above

TABLE 1 Categories of organized cyber offenses against IoT-based healthcare systems.

Type	Risk
Willful damage of hardware components of IoT-based healthcare systems	Low
Destruction of software resources like system files, databases, operating system	Low
Stealing of smart devices like wearable pendants, mobile phones, etc.	Medium
Illegal probing into the IoT networks	High
Defacement of the IoT websites	High
Spoofing and stealing of sensitive data from the IoT databases	High
Copyright infringements	High

group that are investigated, tried, and convicted of the erroneous publication and incorrect distribution of IoT-based healthcare information on social media, radio, or television, and unlawful sharing of official matters on IoT-based healthcare.

5.2 Recommendations for the management of IoT-based healthcare systems

The management aspect of IoT-based healthcare systems demands strict monitoring for stakeholders to thoroughly deal with the core issues mentioned and explicated above. Investigators should identify the novel aspects of the organized cybercrimes on IoT-based healthcare systems, and agencies should harmonize reports on the status of the organized cybercrimes on the above healthcare settings to ascertain the new trends, prevalence, and criticality of the problem across the globe.

Currently, it is possible that new researchers are experiencing the same challenges that have confronted past researchers in the above context. Forensic datasets and research models are urgently needed to assist investigators and pollsters to identify the significance of the confessional statements of syndicates, the improvement required, and the degree of the impacts of their activities from the perspectives of the families of the victims, complainants, and researchers in the domain of cybercrimes relating to IoT-based healthcare systems. Rigorous hardening of the back- and front-ends of IoT-based healthcare systems is recommended for the hospitals using such systems in order to deter organized cybercrimes.

Users of the IoT-services must be routinely trained to observe the basic security and precautionary measures necessary to improve the usage of wearable devices on the IoT-based healthcare systems. We recommend that organized cyber offenders that are willing to repent in the above context can be made to undergo occupational and speech therapies. These would enable them to acquire training on the ethical standards required in the usage of IoT-based healthcare systems and in engage in public discussions on the subject matter.

The above results indicate that economic strangulation statistically correlates with punishment of groups of cybercriminals on the IoT-based healthcare systems. Some experts agree that it is logical to identify and cut off all the commercial dealings of the organized cybercriminals accused of attacking the IoT-based healthcare systems. Forensic investigators working on the above healthcare domains may encounter uninteresting details among the confessional statements of the suspects in the above context. Thus, this chapter further suggests that investigators can adopt Gini index to statistically categorize organized intrusions into IoT-based healthcare systems to lessen the above challenges in the near future [1,18]. Fundamentally, *Gini Index* is an indicative of discrete and nonnegative distributions. For a given attribute and whenever the concept is equal to zero, it implies that the entire alert of the intrusion detection system

(IDS) or the evidence is grouped into one cluster. That is, they are the same or repeated events—mathematically:

$$GiniIndex(_{attribute}) = 1 - \sum_{i=1}^{n}(p(c_i))2 \qquad (1)$$

We then see that lack of appropriate datasets might be a major drawback in the above healthcare domains. Hence, we suggest the use of the above metric to understand large quantities of evidence or information at first sight. The attributes of alerts from their payloads for example, SI (source IP address), DI (destination IP address), TTL (time-to-live), and IPL (IP length) can be used to conduct forensic analysis of the activities of the syndicates of intrusions against the above healthcare systems in future [9]. The higher the Gini index, the more the items of evidence are different from each other.

6. Conclusion

Many academic discourses suggest that there is a need to foster IoT-based healthcare systems because they fundamentally lack pragmatic models that are inevitably critical for dealing with the syndicates of cyber intruders, and for marketing strategies, building trust, and expanding the numbers utilizing such healthcare services worldwide. Thus, this chapter has extensively discussed these issues and went further to broadly group the penalties for organized cyber intruders into punitive and rehabilitative therapies. Intrusions that call for punitive therapeutic interventions require the need to enforce disciplinary actions against the members of the syndicates. The argument is that their activities have caused (or would have caused) punitive damages to the victims of the crime. It is observed that most penal or criminal laws that are used for prescribing the punishment for organized cyber offenders under the local and international legal system are inadequate when adapted to treat syndicates that intrude into the IoT-based healthcare systems. Cybercrime is a division of global crime. Therefore, the campaigns for penal reform to capture organized cyber offenses that are punishable by law must increase across the globe to produce harmonized cyber laws that are adaptable to the above healthcare systems.

Intrusive measures may eventually require rehabilitative treatments to restore the IoT resources and the intruders to good social conditions. Therefore, some organized groups of intruders may deserve rehabilitative exercises to develop constructive attitudes and a constructive philosophy toward the usage and dissemination of information they have illegally extracted from or written on the IoT-based healthcare systems of the complainants or organizations. The goal of rehabilitative therapy is to help the organized cyber intruders to restore to a good standard of behavior in life. This chapter assumes that the organized cyber intruders might need social help to rehabilitate their gang members to a former state of good repute. Rehabilitative strategies must include correction intervention. This might occur in the form of mandating or sending members of the organized cyber intruders to attend correctional institutions. The chapter further states and clarifies several types of punishment and rehabilitative strategies for organized cyber intruders into the IoT-based healthcare systems.

Moreover, the chapter suggests that economic strangulation statistically correlates with punishment of a group of cyber criminals (by cutting off their commercial dealings) that are indicative of cartels, syndicates, and consortiums of independent organizations or organized online criminal gangsters. Conversely, we argue that corporal punishment, penance, and cruel and unusual punishment are poor therapeutic strategies for punishing organized intruders convicted of committing cybercrimes against IoT-based healthcare systems.

Finally, since the above domains cut across both social and scientific inventions, broad empirical studies are often required to evolve models that detectives can adopt to acquire investigative knowledge and deconstruct complex activities of syndicates of intruders into IoT-based healthcare systems. Research should formulate evidence-based forensic models to arrest all such intruders and discriminate between them on the basis of financier, first offender, minor offender, and serial offender. Further collaborative research is still needed to analyze and understand how econometric, statistical, and psychological techniques can be used to model various patters of operations of the above syndicates with the view to establish suitable benchmarks for quantifying dependable IoT-based healthcare systems. Future research should also assist forensic investigators to report and clearly describe the level of involvement of the members of the gangs discussed in this chapter in sufficient detail.

References

[1] I.K. Cevic, S. Gros, K. Slovenec, Systematic review and quantitative comparison of cyber attackScenario detection and projection, Electronics 9 (2020) 1722, https://doi.org/10.3390/electronics9101722.

[2] Federal Republic of Nigeria (FGN), Cybercrime ACT, 2015, 2015.

[3] Office of Legal Education Executive (OLE) Office for United States Attorneys, Prosecuting Computer Crimes; Computer Crime and Intellectual Property Section Criminal Division; OLE Litigation Series, 2010.

[4] R. Sethi, B. Bhushan, N. Sharma, R. Kumar, I. Kaushik, Applicability of industrial IoT in diversified sectors: evolution, applications and challenges, in: R. Kumar, R. Sharma, P.K. Pattnaik (Eds.), Multimedia Technologies in the Internet of Things Environment; Studies in Big Data, vol. 79, Springer, Singapore, 2021, https://doi.org/10.1007/978-981-15-7965-3_4.

[5] K. Goyal, K. Sharma, B. Bhushan, A. Shankar, IoT enabled technology in secured healthcare: applications, challenges and future directions, in: Cognitive Internet of Medical Things for Smart Healthcare, 2021, pp. 25–48, https://doi.org/10.1007/978-3-030-55833-8_2.

[6] Federal Republic of Nigeria (FGN), Cybercrimes (Prohibition, Prevention, etc) ACT, 2015, 2015.

[7] A.S. Tanenbaum, D.J. Wetherall, Computer Networks, fifth ed., Prentice Hall, India, 2021. ISBN: 978-9332518742.

[8] M. Arsh, B. Bhushan, M. Uppal, Internet of things (IoT) toward 5G network: Design require-ments, integration trends, and future research directions, in: A.E. Hassanien, S. Bhattacharyya, S. Chakrabati, A. Bhattacharya, S. Dutta (Eds.), Emerging Technologies in Data Mining and Information Security; Advances in Intelligent Systems and Computing, vol. 1286, Springer, Singapore, 2021, https://doi.org/10.1007/978-981-15-9927-9_85.

[9] W. Mwaura, Why IoT is the real; Department of Software development, Andela, USA, 2018, Available at: https://internetofthingsagenda.techtarget.com/definition/Internet-of-Things-IoT;. (Accessed 18 September 2021).

[10] S. Sharma, X. Wang, Toward massive machine type communications in ultra-dense cellular IoT networks: current issues and machine learning-assisted solutions, IEEE Commun. Surv. Tutorials 22 (1) (2020) 426–471.

[11] B. Bhushan, G. Sahoo, Requirements, protocols, and security challenges in wireless sensor networks: an industrial perspective, in: Handbook of Computer Networks and Cyber Security, 2020, pp. 683–713, https://doi.org/10.1007/978-3-030-22277-2_27.

[12] N. Sharma, I. Kaushik, B. Bhushan, S. Gautam, Applicability of WSN and biometric models in the field of healthcare, in: Deep Learning Strategies for Security Enhancement in Wireless Sensor Networks, 2020, pp. 304–329, https://doi.org/10.4018/978-1-7998-5068-7.

[13] Ondo State Nigerian official Gazete: Administration of Criminal Justice, Law 2015.

[14] Federal Republic of Nigeria (FGN), Administration of Justice 2015, 2015.

[15] J. Mouna, B.A.R. Latifa, Towards new quantitative cybersecurity risk analysis models for information systems: a cloud computing case study, in: B.G. Brij, M.P. Gregorio, P.A. Dharma, G. Deepak (Eds.), Handbook of Computer Networks and Cyber Security: Principles and Paradigms, Springer Nature Switzerland, 2020, ISBN: 978-3-030-22277-2, https://doi.org/10.1007/978-3-030-22277-2.

[16] M. Olusola, O. Samson, A. Semiu, A. Yinka, Cyber crimes and cyber Laws in Nigeria, Int. J. Eng. Sci. 2 (4) (2013) 19–25.

[17] Federal Republic of Nigeria (FGN), Criminal code Act (CAP 77). Laws of the federation, 1990, 1990.

[18] J. Han, M. Kamber, Data Mining: Concepts and Techniques, second ed., Morgan Kaufmann, USA, 2006.

Chapter 7

IoT in modern healthcare systems focused on neuroscience disorders and mental health

S. Varsha[a], K. Adalarasu[a], M. Jagannath[b], and T. Arunkumar[c]

[a]*Department of Electronics and Instrumentation Engineering, School of Electrical and Electronics Engineering, SASTRA Deemed to be University, Thanjavur, Tamil Nadu, India,* [b]*School of Electronics Engineering, Vellore Institute of Technology (VIT), Chennai, Tamil Nadu, India,* [c]*School of Computer Science & Engineering, Vellore Institute of Technology (VIT), Vellore, Tamil Nadu, India*

1. Introduction

The Internet of Things (IoT) connects multiple devices and these devices communicate via networks, mostly based on cloud-based platforms. Its applications have a wide range covering almost every industry in the world, such as the retail, manufacturing, transportation and logistics, grid energy systems, and healthcare fields. Recent automation like the smart home concept is also based on this. Many national governments around the world are investing in this field of research to design and implement smart city concepts using IoT. This technique has its own limitations, including data security, energy consumption, etc., which are also being rectified by advanced technologies such as powerful algorithms, as described in recent studies, and by using fog computing [1–3]. Healthcare is an important sector that focuses on the maintenance and improvement of one's health by providing proper guidance such as diagnosis, treatment, cure, and prevention. It also includes work done in contributing primary, secondary, and tertiary care. Healthcare services include health policies that support patients financially, the healthcare system, the healthcare industry, healthcare research, healthcare information technology, and administration and regulation.

Applying IoT in healthcare [4] helps in remote patient monitoring and provides medical officers and families authorized access to their records, which helps in consultation, treatment, and alerts in case of emergencies. This applies

Blockchain Technology Solutions for the Security of IoT-Based Healthcare Systems.
https://doi.org/10.1016/B978-0-323-99199-5.00006-9
133

to both physical and mental health monitoring. In this chapter, we discuss the application of IoT in the neuroscience field, especially in neurological disorders like Alzheimer's and Parkinson's diseases, and mental health [5]. Most of the reviewed articles have used IoT technology for monitoring and assisting people, optimization of the classification model to achieve a higher prediction rate of the desired output, and also to improve the performance of cloud computing [6,7]. Fig. 1 shows a modern IoT-enabled healthcare system, which includes patients with wearable or handheld devices, IoT cloud networks, and healthcare service providers.

The IoT links a massive number of devices and services to the Internet for a variety of uses. The Internet protocol (IP) is commonly used to link IoT devices to the Internet. Message queue telemetry transport (MQTT), constrained application protocol (CoAP), and advanced message queuing protocol (AMQP) are three commonly used and important IoT protocols. The MQTT protocol is appropriate for small devices that demand economical bandwidth and battery utilization, such as automotive sensors, smoke alarms, smartwatches, and text-based messaging apps, and is generally utilized for restricted networks that enable connections to remote locations. The Internet Engineering Task Force (IETF) created the CoAP as an application-layer protocol for resource-constrained devices. CoAP is a lightweight machine-to-machine (LWM2M) communication protocol that can be implemented using the user datagram protocol (UDP). AMQP is a lightweight application layer protocol that has been designed for increased security and dependability, as well as ease of provisioning and interoperability. Different messaging protocols may be chosen depending on the messaging requirements of IoT use cases.

This chapter interprets the research challenges in IoT-based mental health diagnosis studies that have been presented in the literature and discusses the

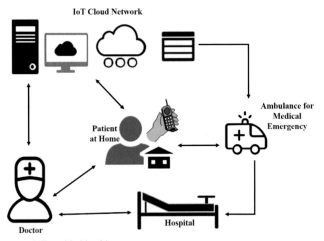

FIG. 1 Modern IoT-enabled healthcare system.

advancements that are likely to be necessary for the future, as well as the research possibilities that are likely to become exciting as more studies yield more detailed results and key areas for improvement. The chapter includes recent studies and research works carried out during the years 2018–21 in the field of IoT and healthcare. Papers with keywords such as IoT, along with at least one of the following, such as, neuroscience, EEG, mental health, Alzheimer's and Parkinson's are taken for the review. Among them, review papers, case studies, and studies related to specific populations have been excluded. Significant contributions of this chapter include:

- The main concentration of this chapter is around IoT applications in neurological disorders like Alzheimer's and Parkinson's and mental health.
- This work also discusses biosignal collection, processing, and storage.
- This chapter gives an overall idea about the current concerns and challenges in the field of biosignal processing, Alzheimer's, Parkinson's, and mental health, and discusses the future scope for work that can be carried out in these fields.

The chapter is divided into four sections. Section 1 gives a general discussion on the IoT field, the healthcare industry, and IoT applications in healthcare. Section 2 explains the recent methodologies of IoT in human healthcare, which includes IoT in the neurophysiological signal collection, assisting and monitoring people with neurological disorders (Parkinson's and Alzheimer's), and IoT in monitoring mental health. Section 3 describes the review summary and discussion. Section 4 concludes the chapter.

2. IoT applications in human healthcare

IoT applications can be used in the healthcare sectors [4] for maintaining the patient's health record, known as the Electronic Health Record (EHR), where the data can be made available for authorized users like healthcare centers, professionals, and nurse practitioners for sensing with the help of wearable sensors [8,9] and collecting real-time data such as user input, or any biopotential signals like neurological-related signals [5]. By analyzing the signal in the cloud to detect any abnormality in patients and assist them in emergency situations, for maintaining the drug records and eliminating any fraud records, telemedicine is enabled, where diagnosis, treatment, and even rehabilitation can be done remotely and for clinical research. The ever-increasing advances in medical data transmission have ushered in a new era of development for networks based on the Internet of Healthcare Things (IoHT). People enrolled in IoHT can get a full range of medical services through a variety of healthcare providers [10]. This chapter explains modern IoT research work and solutions in the neuroscience field, especially for some neurological disorders like Alzheimer's and Parkinson's, and mental health monitoring systems.

2.1 Neurophysiological signals

Wai et al. [11] described an IoT-enabled multimodal headwear system called iMESH, which was designed to collect a subject's physical and physiological data through electroencephalogram (EEG), inertial motion unit (IMU), and photoplethysmography (PPG) sensors installed in wearable headwear. A driver fatigue assessment application was also developed to test the feasibility of the module. The EEG sensor for iMESH was designed by testing various types of materials used for the electrodes and design of the hardware. The iMESH hardware consists of submodules such as an instrumentational amplifier (for the acquisition of EEG unipolar brain waves), analog to digital converter (ADC), transimpedance amplifier, light-emitting diode, photodetectors, 3-axis accelerometer and a 3-axis gyroscope, microcontroller unit, and Bluetooth low energy (BLE) wireless module. The iMESH software consists of headwear (for collecting, processing, and wireless transfer), gateway (for interfacing a PC or a mobile phone with headwear), and a cloud-based platform.

A multichannel wearable brain-sensing system obtains physiological signals, like ECG, EMG, and EEG, for 18 h [12]. This is performed by using a Raspberry Pi 2 (RPI 2) board powered by a power bank, which makes it a convenient portable system. The biosignals undergo analog to digital conversion via low noise ADC for biopotential measurements using an ADS1299 chip, which is communicated through a Texas Instruments ADS1299EG-FE daughter card. SPI protocol is used for interfacing the RPI 2 and ADS1299. The RPI 2 communicates with the MongoDB cloud server through Wi-Fi or Ethernet for data transfer for processing, analyzing, and computing in real time and the feedback mechanism is provided to send back the information from the server end to the device. The live stream of signals extracted from MongoDB are displayed in real time by the web-based application created by them.

In a cloud-based IoT architecture, the brain-inspired trust management model (TMM) is employed for secure multichannel and multilayer brain data transfer, i.e., end to end communication (E2E) [13]. The adaptive neuro-fuzzy inference system (ANFIS) is used in this study to ensure data reliability. This model calculates node behavioral trust and data trust, as well as detecting a node's trustworthiness and identifying malicious nodes. The model is made up of three primary parts: the IoT end collects data from various devices and sends it to the IoT gateway. The IoT end defines the access and network, as well as data analysis, storage, and user interface-visibility and access to processed data based on rights and privileges granted. Each node's trust value is changed in four steps. The nodes collaborate via "trust compositions," which are then broadcast to the IoT. Trust metrics of each node are collected by static weighted sum, neuro-fuzzy approach, and Bayesian inference, which is known as "trust aggregation," and ultimately, trust value is updated for each node, known as trust updation. The trust level in E2E is calculated based on relationships such as node profile information—guaranteed authentication, node behavioral trust—ANFIS, and data trust—weighted sum approach. Relative frequency of interaction (RFI), intimacy, and honesty are all factors that go into determining behavioral trust. The variance between immediate data and historical data of a node is calculated to determine data trust through direct and indirect contact among nodes. The following performance indicators are used to assess data trust: packet forwarding ratio (PFR), network throughput (NetT), average energy consumption ratio (AECR), and F-measure.

Sowmiya and Padmini [14] implemented an IoT-based system where a person is monitored through his/her EEG signal, and their death notified to concerned people without any delay. It has four modules: *Virtual brain module* consists of an EEG headset to sense active functioning of the brain, AVR microcontroller to process the data and fast sign handling, Universal Asynchronous Receiver Transmitter (UART) for communication with IoT, IoT modem, Transformer and Thin Film Transmitter (TFT) Display, *Privacy information module* is used to store person's information under authentication. *Access privilege module* allows information to convey to related people and *Remainder module* gives notification on feeding privacy data. Once no brain activity is detected, all the information will be sent to the concerned people via their mail ID or phone number through the registered mail ID or phone number.

2.2 IoT applications in neurological disorders

2.2.1 Alzheimer's

Alzheimer's disease (AD) is one type of dementia where people experience memory loss and deterioration of their cognitive abilities interfering with their daily activities [15,16]. Generally, this condition arises with aging, where the majority of people suffering the condition are of the age of 65 and older. If the patient is below 65 years old, then it is considered younger-onset. They can be in the early, middle, or late stages of the disease. The reason for the origin of this disease remains unclear but it is said to prevent certain brain cells from coordinating efficiently due to abnormal buildup of proteins in and around the brain cells. It may cause memory lapses, ranging from forgetting small things at the early stages, to losing the ability to respond to the environment, which produces difficulty in communicating with people as the patient loses the memory of their acquaintances. Consequently, it is important to provide intensive care to Alzheimer's patients where caregivers shouldn't allow them to fall "under the radar." This becomes difficult for the caregiver, and produces feelings of stress over time. With the new advances in IoT technologies, it is possible to monitor Alzheimer's patients, to allow patients with not-so-serious symptoms to move around individually, and even to assist them at times when they are lost.

Adardour et al. [17] designed and implemented an IoT prototype system for locating AD people with a GPS module attached to a dorsal belt. The tracking system has NodeMCU ESP8266 and a GPS receiver where the device captures the current coordinates of the position of AD patients and sends them to the server to a mobile application. The data transaction is through Wi-Fi communication protocol. They use an API for IoT called ThingSpeak, an open-source application as a web application where its users may build sensor data logging apps, location tracking apps, and a social network for linked gadgets that includes status updates. As for mobile applications, the Blynk platform is used to control Raspberry Pi and Arduino boards. The location of the patient becomes unclear when they move from inside to outside environments, and so an itinerary trace algorithm is used, where the location is decided based on their frequent visits. The problem arises when the location of the patient is equidistant from two or more structures. To resolve this issue, a predictive mathematical model of the Kalman filter is applied. In this way, the AD patient can be followed via any smart device, both iOS and Android, by knowing their speed, direction, and exact location when connected to the Internet. Future works can include more sensors to monitor patients' health conditions like heart rate, SpO2, etc.

Oskouei et al. [18] proposed a model that helps to provide treatment based on the patient's behavior and movement at their home during the COVID-19 period. Their activities are monitored based on the output of multiple sensors that are positioned in the patient's house, and smartwatches. The sensors used are smart stickers on patients' clothes, smart cameras, and smartphone apps. The smartwatch monitors the blood pressure level, diabetes level, and temperature of the patient. These sensors or devices use different communication protocols like message queue telemetry transport (MQTT), hypertext transfer protocol (HTTP), and WebSocket, which are used here for secure data transfer from the devices. The NodeJS tool is used in developing the communication methods between the IoT devices. Based on the threshold assigned for each parameter, alert signals are sent to the persons whose contact information is associated with the patient's identification number and name. The patient's privacy and detection of fake devices are taken care of by the method they developed for the WebSocket connection as well as for MQTT protocol with devices where a database has been created to collect data and storage of required information. This provides information about patients to the relevant administration. An algorithm has been developed over HTTP-supported devices and smartphone applications that assists AD patients in transportation and medicine delivery, which is done through the application. Their secure backend admin panel traces the doctor's location, patient history, and ambulances. The data is secured during transit and rest by their proposed algorithm for the purpose of security and privacy of information. Altogether, a method has been developed for live tracking of AD patients, also providing transportation and medical facilities with patients' emergency alarms and conditions, such as blood pressure, heartbeat, and sugar level, with a 95% accuracy rate.

IoT-based assistance for AD patients based on deep learning has been developed [3]. It consists of three phases: recurrent neural network (RNN)

Alzheimer's detection using sensor data, abnormal behavioral tracking done by convolutional neural network (CNN) for emotion analysis and time stamp window for natural language processing, and IoT-based assistance for AD patients. The RNN algorithm is trained to produce results where predictions are made based on input at each time step and data from prior time steps. Its current state is calculated (Eqs. 1 and 2) from a set of current input and the previous state.

$$a_k = f(a_{k-1}, x_k) \tag{1}$$

where a_k represents current state, a_{k-1} is previous state, and x_k is input state.

After applying the activation function (e.g., $\tan h$):

$$a_k = \tan h(w_a a_{k-1} + w_k x_k) \tag{2}$$

where w_a is weight at recurrent neuron and w_x represents weight at input neuron.

For the next time-step input, the current state becomes the previous state. One can go as many time steps as necessary according to the problem and join the information from all the previous states. On the completion of all the time steps, the final current state is used for the calculation of the output (Eq. 3):

$$y_k = w_y a_k \tag{3}$$

where y_k represents output and w_y is weight at output layer.

The error is generated from the comparison of output with the target value. The error is then back-propagated to the network to update the weights and hence the network (RNN) is trained. The CNN's working algorithm is as follows: Pixels from the image are fed to the convolutional layer that performs the convolution operation (Eq. 4) done by various filters to form a convolved feature map, followed by applying the convolved feature map to a ReLU (rectified linear unit) function to generate a rectified feature map. For locating the features, the image is processed with multiple convolutions and ReLU layers. The rectified feature map is fed to the pooling layer, which downsamples by reducing the dimension of the feature map to generate a pooled feature map. Identification of specific parts of the image is achieved through different pooling layers with several filters. Flattening of the pooled feature map is done to convert the 2-dimensional map to a single linear vector and is fed to a fully connected layer to get the final output:

$$S(i,j) = (I * K)(i,j) = \sum_m \sum_n I(m,n) K(i-m, j-n) \tag{4}$$

where S represents feature map, I is input, and K is kernel.

The architecture is comprised of IoT supported by machine learning, which has a user layer that consists of humans in an installed sensors environment, fog layer, which is a computational layer that performs data processing and analytics on data provided by the sensor layer, core network layer, where the entire transmission of data happens, and finally, a cloud layer to store the forwarded data for future use. When the fog layer lacks resources for computation, it can be passed to the cloud layer, which compliments the constraints in the resource region. To improve energy efficiency, they employ a trigger-based activation where the slave sensors are activated by the message queue telemetry transport (MQTT).

Roopaei et al. [16] developed a model to assist the early-stage AD patient to recognize and identify people who come in contact with them. This is done by taking the picture of the person and extracting the name and relationship from the matched face, which is displayed on the patient's glasses. The author used a deep learning model to recognize a set of facial images from the patient's circle and help them to re-identify on the next encounter. The system is made up of three parts: a facial perception model for recognizing people and extracting facial features, a personalized patient micro database for recording the ground truth of facial features related to people around the patient, and a matching metric to compare the distinct facial feature vectors extracted from a real-time captured image with the existing features as ground truth. A matching measure is used to compare the unique facial feature vectors generated from an image taken in real time to the existing features saved as ground truth for every specific person in the patient's circle of relevance. The facial perception model (FPM) is a deep ConvNet that recognizes five facial landmarks: two eye centers, a nose tip, and two mouth corners. Patients or family members could use an app or website created specifically for the platform to upload facial images. To avoid fraudulent behaviors, it is also necessary to create a policy and constraints for persons who have access to the platform for posting facial images.

It is possible to monitor AD patients using an Apple smartwatch and iOS application, which should be downloaded on a caregiver's phone interfaced to the AD patient's smartwatch to get and store their related data, like heart rate and location [19]. This enables the caregivers to track the patients when they go out by themselves. As an additional feature, it has a reminder to schedule tasks like medication and medical appointments. This also provides the caregiver's information related to Alzheimer's disease. The architecture has three main parts: a model where data and documents collected are stored, a view that is front-end monitored by the user, and a controller which handles the interaction between user end inputs and the view and model. This iCare system was tested for its real-time usability by 36 users and all users felt the application to be user-friendly and most people don't use other mobile applications for Alzheimer's caregiving.

2.2.2 Parkinson's

Parkinson's disease is caused due to dead nerve cells in certain parts of the brain reducing dopamine production, which regulates the movement of the body and this damage progresses over many years. There are five stages:

- Stage 1. The mildest form of PD where tremors and difficulty in movement can be seen.
- Stage 2. Moderate, with noticeable symptoms like trembling, tremor, stiffness, and occurrence of facial expression changes.

- Stage 3. Middle stage, which shows symptoms of Stage 2 along with loss of balance and reduced reflexes.
- Stage 4. The patient requires assistance for walking.
- Stage 5. The most advanced stage, where the patient must always depend on others for regular tasks like standing.

Research has been made to predict PD as early as possible by making a hybrid model for improving optimization monitoring and assisting the patients.

A hybrid algorithm has been developed to optimize the ANFIS model for the early prediction of Parkinson's disease from the voice data of the patients [2]. The IoT structure consists of an IoT layer for data collection from the sensors, and a fog layer that overcomes the basic barrier faced in past IoT systems by data processing on the network edge and getting immediate feedback from the local community—this layer stores data when cloud link is absent, provides the status of patients with its local model on Internet disturbance, has an expert system for real-time query and alerts in emergency conditions, and is also responsible for data preprocessing that depends on the collected data's nature and the analysis process—and finally, a cloud layer for storage and management. In preprocessing, data normalization and feature selection are important as they have to provide high-quality data for feeding the prediction model. The correlation feature selection (CFS) is used for picking the optimal feature for predicting Parkinson's disease.

A model was developed to reduce the delay in the prediction of Parkinson's disease by using data collected from deep brain stimulation (DBS), a wearable IoT-based mental health sensor, and processing it through a heuristic tubu-optimized sequence modular neural network (HTSMNN) to detect the changes in brain functionality [6]. The traditional system for automatic brain disease diagnosis doesn't process continuously and in real time and also has lower accuracy. This proposed model enhances the performance of Parkinson's prediction. The wearable DBS has electrodes on both sides of the head, which enter the brain through small holes in the skull. These electrodes, on the other side, are connected via a wire to a pulse simulator placed on the chest. The electrical pulses are sent by the simulator according to the patient's symptoms, nerve details, and other details. The heart data is used for sequence analysis, which reduces misclassification and complexity and increases prediction accuracy. The data obtained undergoes data cleaning, feature extraction, and classification. In feature extraction, a total of 19 features are extracted to be fed to HTSMNN for prediction. HTSMNN produces effective results based on the inputs. The network analyzes the input and divides it into subtasks, which are processed by HTSMNN to get the outputs.

A hybrid classifier model was used to improve the accuracy of the fog computing-based prediction of Parkinson's disease [1]. The architecture consists of smart devices, a fog layer, and a cloud layer. Via a smartphone with a web application, the sensor captures the voice signal and the 3D accelerometer senses the gait symptoms from the patient, which are transmitted over Wi-Fi, Bluetooth, or ZigBee to the fog layer. In addition, the universal scale for Parkinson's disease, which is analyzed from the motor performance of patients, called the Unified Parkinson's Disease Rating Scale (UPDRS) score, is assessed from the simple actions that categorize the level or stage of PD into mild (0–20), moderate (21–35), and severe (36–56). The fog layer does some data preprocessing on voice samples, like data aggregation, filtering, compression, and analysis. It also reduces latency, bandwidth, dimensionality, and transmission delay by data reduction. The cloud layer stores data for remote access from anywhere. Cloud databases are divided into shareable, for general information that isn't personal, and nonshareable sections, like users' data, their health condition, and treatment history; the only people who have access to the data are professionals or clinicians for treatment purposes, and patients or family members to check patient reports and provide feedback on therapy.

Pathak et al. [20] propose a health care system for PD patients using efficient and compressive IoT. The components include an EEG sensor to get brain signals, Arduino to process the data, Bluetooth for wireless connectivity between sensor and computation system, and a cloud server for connection with online data during either physical absence or presence. ThingSpeak application, a free IoT cloud tool, is used. The data is collected from the EEG sensor by the processor and this is sent to the cloud server based on conditions defined. If the data is to be sent, compressive sensing is used to compress and encrypt the data. This is decompressed and decrypted in the cloud server where data is analyzed and a decision is taken. The proposed model is simulated using MATLAB and the reconstruction on the cloud side is tested using the same and different CS matrix, which showed that only the same CS matrix can reconstruct the correct signal.

2.3   IoT and mental health

The vital importance of taking care of a person's mental health is equivalent to that of their physical health. During this pandemic era, people often get stressed [21] about staying indoors most of the time where the chance of their mental health getting affected is maximum and unavoidable. In addition, education has come to be based on online systems, where students of all age categories are forced to sit in front of the system for hours for their classes. Many of these classes have become unproductive due to the environment of the student or student's distraction and lack of interest during online classes. It is also essential to monitor people with a mental disorder, as there is an increased risk of them attempting suicide, losing their awareness in public places, or getting lost while trying to go out on their own. Fig. 2 depicts the modalities associated with IoT and mental health.

An IoT (LoRa)-based system has been designed that can track and monitor a patient with a mental disorder [22]. LoRa stands for long range radio operating

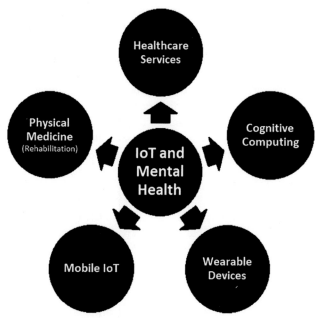

FIG. 2   Modalities associated with IoT and mental health.

at ISM frequency bands of 433, 868, and 915 MHz, and supports IoT networks. It has technical advantages such as the ability to serve as the network platform in a long-distance communications environment and long-term battery life. The LoRa end device is attached to the patient and serves as a tracking device. This comprises the Dragino LoRa Shield Wireless, which provides data transmission using a LoRa radio frequency, GPS sensor for location tracking, and Wi-Fi module for connectivity with local/cloud server assembled in an Arduino. The module can be worn on the upper arm without impeding the patient's daily activities. On the side of hospitals and public spaces, there are LoRa gateways with a star topology that spans a large area and are linked to local or cloud servers by Wi-Fi or cellular modules. The medical officer has a mobile application where the live data of the patient is transmitted along with their location to monitor and keep track of their location. This means that when notification is sent that the patient is outside the treatment area, they can be brought back to a safer place as the next step. To access the patient's medical information, the caregiver or the psychiatrist has to enter their username and password for security and privacy reasons. In the app, an emergency button is provided to inform related people about the patient's location when the place is considered as high risk or when the chance of the patient running away from the hospital is high, and a psychiatrist button to update the current state of the patient's condition.

It is known that music can alter the state of subjects' brains to improve mental health by integrating music with the help of IoT with neural feedback [23].

The existing music applications can induce a meditative state in the user's brain, but because the music is prerecorded, they don't take into account the user's current mental state when playing music. This study introduces neural feedback to overcome this issue. The feedback is taken from the EEG headband and transferred to a mobile application through an Internet connection. The application plays music and records the EEG pattern, processes and analyses the data in the cloud server, and decides the state of the brain. The app tunes the music in such a way that the brain signals are dominated by delta waves, which indicates the deep relaxation state of the brain. By doing this continuously, mental health is improved, and the brain and body become energized due to deep relaxation without any side effects.

Sundaravadivel et al. [24] developed a suicidal ideation detection system (M-SID), an edge-intelligent IoT-based platform for early detection of suicidal ideation, and implemented suicidal ideation elicitation learning approaches. The authors developed a wearable M-SID in real time, which collects the data from different sensors such as accelerometer, pulse oximeter, temperature, and humidity sensor, and then analyzes the pattern of suicidal ideation. Suicidal ideation can be detected using activity and heart rate data, as previously stated. The user input value is also obtained to monitor the state of the patient. The user input values protocol is as follows: Recording a simple questionnaire to assess the distress and anxiety levels of the user before using the M-SID wearable. Before employing the M-SID wearable, a preliminary assessment of the user's suicide vulnerability and frequency of suicidal ideation is taken. The user is instructed to press the input buttons whenever they are distressed at any time of day, and informed about rewards such as "brownie points" that will be given to the user every time a pattern of a healthy active lifestyle is detected, such as exercising regularly or providing reliable user inputs on distress and craving. This is correlated with sensor data and the vulnerability coefficient is calculated with which the current state of the patient is labeled as a critical event.

An embedded smart IoT-based system for emotion analysis was developed [25]. A wearable body area sensor (BAS) with a multisensory embedded cyber-human system (CHS) was designed and implemented for the prediction of emotion. The sensors used are pulse sensor to collect heart rate, temperature sensor, and galvanic skin response sensor, which is based on the perspiration produced by the person wearing it, as a person perspires when they are stressed or angry. The GSR sensors are placed on the middle fingers, whereas the module is designed as a wristband. The system alerts if it detects any emergency issue faced by the user through Bluetooth communication. For the states of happy, stressed, depressed, and calm, experiments were conducted under different test scenarios. As future work, it is planned to test the system on people with mental problems and also measure different physiological parameters in real time, which amounts to a smart home monitoring wireless system.

Using an IoT framework with high-performance long short term memory (LSTM)-based emotion recognition from multimodal physiological signals through wireless communication [26], a system was developed to monitor health and support distance learning for students during the Covid-19 pandemic. The parameters from the sensor are respiration, located high on the torso above the chest, galvanic skin response of the nondominant hand's index finger, ECG, EMG (two on the face and one on the neck), skin temperature, and blood volume pressure of the nondominant hand's middle finger. The experiment was conducted for 30 participants where 8 videos were shown based on 4 types of emotions to be classified under the respective label—relaxing, boring, amusing, and scary. LSTM is a deep neural network that memorizes long-term dependencies of time-series data. The IoT framework proposed enables low latency and reliable communication. Two MAC protocols, reliability-enabled MAC and time-sensitive MAC, are compared with the traditional low latency deterministic network (LLDN), which schedules communication of sensor data periodically and has shared slots to improve reliability through retransmission of failed slots but has a delay in its transmission. To achieve both retransmissions of failed slots and reduction of delay, a MAC protocol was designed.

3. Results and discussion

The iMESH module was evaluated with driver fatigue assessment application, which is complex, since fatigue assessment involves various intrinsic and extrinsic facts in both technical and usability aspects [11]. Their future work involves evaluation in real-world scenarios and reducing fatigue by providing some countermeasures. In Ref. [12], the total operation of the proposed multichannel, multisignal, wearable brain and physiological sensing system takes about 18 h on a fully charged 10,000 mAh battery and 12 h of continuous streaming. In future work, emotions and stress levels will be measured using physiological signals. Two cases were tested based on the classification labels or linguistic terms: Case 1—very low, low, medium, high, and very high; and Case 2—low, medium, and high. The TMM showed higher accuracy (0.967 in Case 1 and 0.957 in Case 2) and F-measure (0.97 in Case 1 and 0.96 in Case 2) values in comparison with FIS (accuracy: 0.89 and F-measure: 0.90) in Ref. [13].

In streaming physiological signals like EEG, ECG, EMG, etc., the challenges commonly faced are applying the module in real time, reducing the power consumption, data reliability, and latency. Future works are based on real-time implementation using IoT-based storage systems for data storage and usability.

The results of the experiments in tracking the position of the Alzheimer's patients from an outdoor to an indoor environment conducted in Ref. [17] showed the estimated error lowered after the use of Kalman filter; that is, the estimated results were closer to the Kalman filter estimator. The results of the proposed model demonstrate that RNN is more accurate than other models in the second prediction of abnormal behavior using video and audio from patients. For the video feed, the MMI, FER, and SEFW datasets were used to compare the performance of the proposed deep CNN network with that of SVM. CNN outperformed

SVM in all three datasets. For the audio feed, Naive Bayes and decision trees were evaluated, and Naive Bayes performed better. Accuracy, precision, recall, true-positive rate, false-positive rate, F-score, and correctly classified cases are among the characteristics assessed in Ref. [16]. FPM's recognition accuracy for people's faces in Ref. [16] is around 90.68%, with more or less precision adjustable by changing the size of the DeepFace layer. In Ref. [19], around 91% of users are satisfied with the location monitoring feature, and 97% believe it helps with the caregiving process. In the same app, 80% thought the heart rate monitoring feature was amazing, 16% thought it was decent, and only 2% thought it was okay, while the design received more than 94% approval.

For the adaptive neural-network-based fuzzy inference system (ANFIS) model optimization purpose, particle swarm optimization, along with gray wolf optimization is realized in Ref. [2]. Results are evaluated from evaluation metrics like mean square error, accuracy, standard deviation, and root mean square error. The proposed model outperformed other optimization models in all three parameters for all five datasets. This was tested and compared with the results of other literature proposed model outperforms other studies and produces high accuracy. In the future, the proposed model will be extended to a broader variety of datasets for different fog learning machine learning techniques. In Ref. [6], the efficiency of the HSTMNN for analyzing the data collected through DBS is evaluated using mean absolute error, mean square error, precision, recall, and accuracy. The parameters are compared with other classifiers such as particle swarm optimized neural network, particle swarm optimized radial basis neural networks, Genetic algorithm-based extreme machine learning network, and tubu-optimized deep neural network, and HSTMNN achieves the lowest error rate, highest accuracy, and minimum time complexity among others. A Parkinson's disease dataset was acquired from UCI Machine Learning Repository and tested through various classifiers such as naive Bayes, J48, support vector machine, random tree, K-nearest neighbor with CBR, and their FKNN-CBR algorithm for performance comparison [3]. These are evaluated using sensitivity, specificity, and accuracy, and the proposed FKNN-CBR produced higher accuracy and sensitivity with lower specificity than other classifiers. The health care system is simulated using MATLAB and the reconstruction on the cloud side is tested using the same and different CS matrix, which showed that only the same CS matrix can reconstruct the correct signal. In addition, the network lifetime of the proposed algorithm showed way better performance when compared with ECEG and RSA-1024 algorithms, which use the behavior of public algorithms, increasing the complexity and computation.

The research studies based on Parkinson's are mostly based on the optimization of the prediction model for higher performance. The models proposed are hybrids of two or more algorithms for better prediction of early-stage Parkinson's. The battery capacity in standby mode for the LoRa model to monitor and track patients with mental illnesses is 7777.78 h (about 324 days). The battery capacity for LoRa in transmit mode is 482.76 h (about 20 days). Future

FIG. 3   Proposed block diagram for diagnosing the neurological disorder.

work is expected to build this system as a real-time working module. The M-SID sends the sensor data to be reviewed by healthcare professionals periodically to detect the suicidal ideation pattern and performs decision making at the edge level. With the use of data obtained from FDA-authorized medical-grade wearables, the proposed design's accuracy and overall system efficiency are validated. The results in distinguishing between different emotional states showed higher accuracy. It is found that the GSR value increased with stable heart rate in a calm state, as the GSR wasn't smooth as in a calm state even though the heart rate was almost stable for a stressed state [25]. There were fluctuations in heart rate during the sad state but the GSR seemed to be the same as the stressed state. In the happy state, the heart rate fluctuates more with irregular spikes in the GSR curve. The technique could also be useful for detecting behaviors in people with various disabilities. As future work, this is planned to be tested on people with mental problems and also to measure different physiological parameters in real time, which amounts to a smart home monitoring wireless system.

The R-MAC algorithm used in LSTM for emotion recognition in Ref. [26] showed that the results are very positive in failure rate evaluation. To obtain high dependability and low latency, data precision is sacrificed, which is acceptable in the provided scenario but can cause problems in other applications. The final result from the model is sent to the educational institution and healthcare infrastructure to achieve effective online or distance learning along with optimal mental health maintenance. Fig. 3 shows the proposed block diagram for diagnosing the neurological disorder.

To maintain or monitor the mental health of a person, emotion recognition-based models are implemented, which involve various sensors, especially GSR, whose data are shown reliable for emotion identification. Reporting patients' mental state or assisting them with music to relax them, and tracking patients with mental disorders is also essential as it is unpredictable what happens to them when they are alone, which might become dangerous, so continuous monitoring is required, which drains energy resources. Reliable energy sources or alternating continuous monitoring with other alternatives should be implemented [23].

4.   Conclusion

In this chapter, we have seen various recent technologies and researches to apply the IoT concept effectively in neuroscience. In the future, many works with more powerful and economical systems, such as IoT along with AI, are will be developed to improve optimization and accuracy and these types of works are expected to be implemented in real life and help people in improving their conditions in order to better lead a normal healthy life.

References

[1] M. Devarajan, L. Ravi, Intelligent cyber-physical system for an efficient detection of Parkinson disease using fog computing, Multimed. Tools Appl. 78 (23) (2019) 32695–32719.

[2] I.M. El-Hasnony, S.I. Barakat, R.R. Mostafa, Optimized ANFIS model using hybrid metaheuristic algorithms for Parkinson's disease prediction in IoT environment, IEEE Access 8 (2020) 119252–119270.

[3] S. Sharma, R.K. Dudeja, G.S. Aujla, R.S. Bali, N. Kumar, DeTrAs: deep learning-based healthcare framework for IoT-based assistance of Alzheimer patients, Neural Comput. & Applic. (2020) 1–3.

[4] G. Aceto, V. Persico, A. Pescapé, Industry 4.0 and health: internet of things, big data, and cloud computing for healthcare 4.0, J. Ind. Inf. Integr. 18 (2020) 100129.

[5] M. Chmielewski, S. Sławińska, F. Głowacki, P. Witowski, Biomedical sensors and IoT platform utilisation for neurological applications and health event recognitions, Procedia Manuf. 44 (2020) 528–535.

[6] A.A. AlZubi, A. Alarifi, M. Al-Maitah, Deep brain simulation wearable IoT sensor device based Parkinson brain disorder detection using heuristic tubu optimized sequence modular neural network, Measurement 161 (2020) 107887.

[7] A. Goyal, S. Kaushik, R. Khan, IoT based cloud network for smart health care using optimization algorithm, Inform. Med. Unlocked 27 (2021) 100792.

[8] F. Ali, S. El-Sappagh, S.R. Islam, A. Ali, M. Attique, M. Imran, K.S. Kwak, An intelligent healthcare monitoring framework using wearable sensors and social networking data, Futur. Gener. Comput. Syst. 114 (2021) 23–43.

[9] H. Fouad, A.S. Hassanein, A.M. Soliman, H. Al-Feel, Analyzing patient health information based on IoT sensor with AI for improving patient assistance in the future direction, Measurement 159 (2020) 107757.

[10] S.S. Rani, J.A. Alzubi, S.K. Lakshmanaprabu, D. Gupta, R. Manikandan, Optimal users based secure data transmission on the internet of healthcare things (IoHT) with lightweight block ciphers, Multimed. Tools Appl. 79 (47) (2020) 35405–35424.

[11] A.A. Wai, H. Dajiang, N.S. Huat, IoT-enabled multimodal sensing headwear system, in: 2018 IEEE 4th World Forum on Internet of Things (WF-IoT), IEEE, 2018 Feb 5, pp. 286–290.

[12] P.K. Yong, E.T. Ho, Streaming brain and physiological signal acquisition system for IoT neuroscience application, in: 2016 IEEE EMBS Conference on Biomedical Engineering and Sciences (IECBES), IEEE, 2016 Dec 4, pp. 752–757.

[13] M. Mahmud, M.S. Kaiser, M.M. Rahman, M.A. Rahman, A. Shabut, S. Al-Mamun, A. Hussain, A brain-inspired trust management model to assure security in a cloud based IoT framework for neuroscience applications, Cogn. Comput. 10 (5) (2018) 864–873.

[14] R. Sowmiya, V. Padmini, A virtual cloud based brain connectivity analysis using Iot (internet of things), J. Phys. Conf. Ser. 1717 (1) (2021) 012032. IOP Publishing.

[15] S.D. Machado, J.E. Tavares, M.G. Martins, J.L. Barbosa, G.V. González, V.R. Leithardt, Ambient intelligence based on IoT for assisting people with Alzheimer's disease through context histories, Electronics 10 (11) (2021) 1260.

[16] M. Roopaei, P. Rad, J.J. Prevost, A wearable IoT with complex artificial perception embedding for Alzheimer patients, in: 2018 World Automation Congress (WAC), IEEE, 2018 Jun 3, pp. 1–6.

[17] H.E. Adardour, M. Hadjila, S.M. Irid, T. Baouch, S.E. Belkhiter, Outdoor Alzheimer's patients tracking using an IoT system and a Kalman filter estimator, Wirel. Pers. Commun. 116 (1) (2021) 249–265.

[18] R.J. Oskouei, Z. MousaviLou, Z. Bakhtiari, K.B. Jalbani, IoT-based healthcare support system for Alzheimer's patients, Wirel. Commun. Mob. Comput. 2020 (2020).

[19] S.S. Aljehani, R.A. Alhazmi, S.S. Aloufi, B.D. Aljehani, R. Abdulrahman, iCare: applying IoT technology for monitoring Alzheimer's patients, in: 2018 1st International Conference on Computer Applications & Information Security (ICCAIS), IEEE, 2018 Apr 4, pp. 1–6.

[20] V. Pathak, K. Singh, A. Aziz, A. Dhoot, Efficient and compressive IoT based health care system for Parkinson's disease patient, Procedia Comput. Sci. 167 (2020) 1046–1055.

[21] A. Kumar, K. Sharma, A. Sharma, Hierarchical deep neural network for mental stress state detection using IoT based biomarkers, Pattern Recogn. Lett. 145 (2021) 81–87.

[22] N. Hayati, M. Suryanegara, The IoT LoRa system design for tracking and monitoring patient with mental disorder, in: 2017 IEEE International Conference on Communication, Networks and Satellite (Comnetsat), IEEE, 2017 Oct 5, pp. 135–139.

[23] B.M. Krishna, V.C. Jhansi, P.S. Shama, A.B. Leelambika, C. Prakash, B.V. Manikanta, Novel solution to improve mental health by integrating music and IoT with neural feedback, J. Comput. Inf. Syst. 15 (3) (2019) 234–239.

[24] P. Sundaravadivel, P. Salvatore, P. Indic, M-SID: an IoT-based edge-intelligent framework for suicidal ideation detection, in: 2020 IEEE 6th World Forum on Internet of Things (WF-IoT), IEEE, 2020 Jun 2, pp. 1–6.

[25] A.J. Majumder, T.M. Mcwhorter, Y. Ni, H. Nie, J. Iarve, D.R. Ucci, sEmoD: a personalized emotion detection using a smart holistic embedded IoT system, in: 2019 IEEE 43rd Annual Computer Software and Applications Conference (COMPSAC), vol. 1, IEEE, 2019 Jul 15, pp. 850–859.

[26] M. Awais, M. Raza, N. Singh, K. Bashir, U. Manzoor, S. ul Islam, J.J. Rodrigues, LSTM based emotion detection using physiological signals: IoT framework for healthcare and distance learning in COVID-19, IEEE Internet Things J. 8 (23) (2020) 16863–16871.

Chapter 8

Blockchain implementation for IoT devices: Blockchain of Things

Marko Šarac[a], Nikola Pavlović[a], Saša Adamović[a], Muzafer Saračević[b], and Dalibor Radovanović[a]

[a]*Faculty of Informatics and Computing, Singidunum University, Belgrade, Serbia,* [b]*Department of Computer Science, University of Novi Pazar, Novi Pazar, Serbia*

1. Introduction

Even though the Internet of Things (IoT) is widely implemented today and capable of solving a wide range of problems, and although it is not a new technology anymore, security challenges still exist. Most Internet of Things implementations are done by end-users in small office home office (SOHO) computer networks. These implementations often lack the necessary user knowledge for proper network implementation of IoT devices. The concerns are related to security and privacy.

The basis of the IoT consists of various wireless networking technologies such as Wi-Fi, Zigbee, Z-Wave, Bluetooth, etc. Zigbee is wireless technology that was developed as an open global standard. The standard should respond to uniform requirements in terms of low power consumption of wireless devices and low cost. Zigbee technology is defined on standard IEEE 802.15.4 of personal computer networks PAN (personal area network), which uses the unlicensed frequency bands in Europe 868 MHz, worldwide 2.4 GHz, and in the United States 900 MHz. It is used in cases where a high bit rate of data transfer is not necessary. Zigbee cannot be used to transmit time-sensitive signals, video, or audio. The advantage of the protocol from this group is reflected in the low power consumption, which ensures a long battery life of the IoT device. Zigbee devices can communicate in different network topologies. The physical (PHY) layer and media access control (MAC) layers of the data link layer are defined by the IEEE 802.15.4 standard, while the Zigbee alliance defines multiple protocol layers.

Blockchain Technology Solutions for the Security of IoT-Based Healthcare Systems.
https://doi.org/10.1016/B978-0-323-99199-5.00007-0
151

Z-Wave is a wireless communication standard that is predominantly used in IoT devices and home automation systems. This technology is used in home electronic devices such as alarms, air conditioners, thermostats, as well as in audio and video equipment for electronic surveillance, etc. Within the Z-Wave MESH-based network topology, each device in the network can send and receive control commands as well as data. Devices based on this technology do not use the same frequency bands as other IoT devices, which typically operate at 2.4 GHz. The band used by Z-Wave technology in the United States is 908.42 MHz and in Europe is 868 MHz. There are two types of Bluetooth technology: BR/EDR (basic rate/enhanced data rate, covered by the IEEE 802.15.1 standard) and BLE (Bluetooth low energy), designed for IoT applications.

The research for the associated work is described in the following. Other researchers have discovered the most prevalent security issues in IoT hubs, as well as the most popular attacks and strategies used against IoT devices. Following the development of the proposed method, we conduct a real-world experiment to see if our work gives greater security. The assessment concludes with a summary of what has been accomplished and recommendations for further work.

The paper is organized into six sections. New blockchain technology layer implementation is provided in the second section. In the third section, we describe the state of art, while in the fourth section, we present our proposed solution. In the fifth section, we note challenges for the proposed solution. Concluding remarks and future works are given in the last section.

2. New blockchain technology layer implementation

Design methods, a lack of standards, and policies are all security issues. Privacy concerns are most visible in data collecting and use and bad privacy implementation within designs. Many Internet of Things device manufactures are collecting user activity under the agreement to improve service. Some of the manufacturers even specify which data they are collecting. This is, however, a big privacy concern due to the user's inability to opt-out of this process. Other IoT devices come with insufficient information on maintainability and upgradeability, which means there is a high probability that it could have a 0-day vulnerability to attack and there will be no way to resolve it.

Fig. 1 presents the implementation of a new blockchain technology layer on the transport and session layer compared to an OSI reference model. The idea is to use blockchain technology to achieve higher security of IoT devices with blockchain implementation on the transport and session layer.

It is worth mentioning that most manufacturers will focus on the development and production of new models and devices, and the support and upgrades for old models will be limited. This also raises the question that, even if a vulnerability is to be discovered, will the manufacturer in any way be obliged to solve the issue and offer the solution for older models.

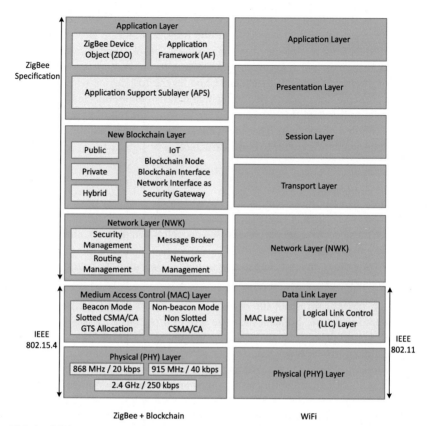

FIG. 1   OSI layer model representation of new blockchain technology layer implementation.

Blockchain of Things could be a solution for some security aspects, at least from the perspective of unsecured network communication between IoT devices. The use of blockchain technology eliminates the need for servers, which are at the heart of IoT infrastructure. One way to resolve privacy and security challenges is the synthesis of blockchain technology with the Internet of Things. This means that IoT data flows through blockchain nodes and each transaction has appropriate authentication. Traditional IoT data is usually sent in plaintext format or with a very weak protection algorithm. The core of blockchain technology is blocks that are generated by participants' transactions, and each block's transaction details are validated if they are preserved correctly. This ensures that tampering of the data is not allowed inside the block. Due to data flow inside IoT architecture, blockchain is a great solution. Blockchain, by its nature, will force IoT devices to maintain the flow of information while it will also increases security and privacy by gradually verifying for each transaction and network request.

It is usual behavior for IoT devices to have constant network communication. The quantity of data is small, but the transmission rate is constant. The standard data flow for IoT devices is as follows Sensors send data using local network resources and Internet communication to the central server [1]. The central server works with big data and provides the IoT device with a specific set of commands on what to do, and which data is being collected. If we add blockchain to this data flow, the central server would be removed and replaced with distributed blockchain. The following are among the possibilities of using blockchain technology with IoT infrastructure:

- Elimination of single control authority.
- Built-in trust between IoT devices.
- History of activities taken by IoT devices in the past.
- Each device's info is treated with confidentiality.
- Since these devices are part of a closed decentralized network, their reliability is enhanced.
- Allowing other, much stronger, cryptography algorithms to be implemented in this network.

However, blockchain is not the perfect solution that would fix all of the IoT architecture problems. Some of the more serious problems are a lack of storage, scalability, and processing speed within IoT devices. Limitation of storage is directly linked to how blockchain works: it requires a single database with a list of all sequential transactions. Adding more IoT devices to one decentralized network will create a scalability issue, which means that more storage is directly linked to having more IoT devices. Processing time is linked to allowing other much stronger cryptography algorithms to protect data. More devices mean more actions and more data processing, which will essentially end up with higher hardware IoT devices specifications.

In 2016, the Mirai botnet took over 8.4 million IoT devices. The attack was conducted by using unsecured implementations of IoT devices, targeting an opened Telnet port with a default password. DDoS (distributed denial of service) assaults were carried out using affected IoT devices that became botnet armies. Even now, some measures are taken to discover harmful malware on devices. The issue here is that there is no documented history of device activity, making it much more difficult to locate rogue devices in a network.

Silex/Brickerbot was first reported in 2017, but then it was rediscovered in 2019. This malware looks for public Internet connectivity and attempts to locate IoT devices there. If the IoT unit is discoverable, it tries to access it using the most common weak login combinations. If malware obtains the right to use the device, it removes all networks, storage data, and firewall rules from the smart device, rendering it useless unless someone logs on to it and restores factory defaults. Some scenarios where device firmware was corrupted were also recorded, and the only solution was firmware reinstall; tasks often too difficult for most end users. The malware's sole aim is to destroy the gadget and render it useless.

In 2019, multiple hacking of Amazon Ring home-security cameras were reported. Ring provides home security using smart cameras that are commonly used as doorbells or as room/baby monitors within people's homes. Hackers could turn on and off cameras and use built-in microphones to communicate with residents. Hackers used exploited devices to encourage destructive behavior in children and to ask for a ransom to leave them alone. The Ring cameras attracted customers who wanted to talk to their children at home. However, the devices, which should be used as security devices, become a source of privacy invasions. Ring, which is owned by Amazon, is accused of having inadequate security procedures, according to a class action complaint that merges many claims filed in recent years. Amazon blamed a third-party site for a security flaw and for releasing the usernames and passwords that were being used for Amazon Ring devices, and encouraged Ring users to use multilevel authentication. When the same username and password are used across numerous services, malicious actors can obtain access to a large number of services/devices.

Another noticeable incident of hacking happened in the spring of 2019. Amazon Echo and Google Home were the gadgets used in this scenario. The microphone of the Google Home or Amazon Echo would transform the laser's light into an electrical signal by directing a high-powered laser at it and adjusting the intensity of the laser, exactly as it would with sound. Hackers could use this gadget to unlock garage doors, make online transactions, and run any program they wanted. As a way to protect these devices, some of the manufacturers design their devices to respond only to the voice of the authenticated user or to use two-factor authentication when executing secure commands like opening/closing garage, making a purchase, or setting up security or alarm systems.

Some smart devices can only be used by the authenticated user, and only the voice of the authenticated user can execute commands. A surfing attack allows attackers to send ultrasonic commands to a smart device. Since the voice of the authenticated user is just a soundwave on a specific frequency, the attacker could record the voice and reproduce it to exploit the device. A remote laptop can use a text-to-speech module to send ultrasonic attacks via Bluetooth or Wi-Fi.

All these records are kept using blockchain, making it much easier to check for abuse, alteration, or deletion of the gathered data by an unauthorized individual. Public blockchains are made to be fully decentralized. No individual or entity cannot control which transactions are recorded or not. This blockchain type is open and anyone can join it. Private blockchain is also known as permission blockchain. This type of blockchain is most widely used by businesses. The reason for this is the ease of sharing the data but still making it private. These chains are centralized by their nature, since one entity allows others to join or leave the network. Consortium blockchains are controlled by the group, unlike private ones. This approach has all the same benefits as private. Therefore, some consider it a subcategory of private blockchains.

The dispersed architecture of the Internet of Things is a considerable problem. Each IoT device is a single node that can be exploited and used to get at more devices in the network to launch, for example, a denial of service (DoS) attack. Another security concern is its centralized configuration. IoT devices in their current state most likely are communicating with cloud service providers. The cloud service provider, if hacked, becomes the central point of failure of the entire system.

Important preconditions for blockchains are:

- It has a distributed database system with rules that allow data to flow across entries.
- It is trustless, since the participants don't know each other and don't have digital signatures, yet they may still communicate data without knowing who they are.
- It is permissionless, as nobody in the network can decide who will operate on it, there are no permissions or controllers.
- It is censorship-resistant, as a transaction once sent from one node to another cannot be censored or stopped.

There is one special case of blockchain where permission is required, but this means that only selected nodes can validate the transactions.

The four ideas that underpin blockchain technology are as follows:

- All users communicate with the network using a private/public key in a peer-to-peer network. The public key is used as a network address, while the private key is used to sign transactions.
- An open and distributed ledger, which is a database of all transactions, is available to everyone.
- Syncing ledger copies across all participants is possible using ledger copies synchronization.
- Because the chain must be legitimate and organized, mining is a method of preventing nodes from being added to it.

Fig. 2 displays the content of one blockchain block. Each block contains two elements, header, and block content. The timestamp, prior block's hash value, and current block's hash value are all included in the headers. The use of hash values in links avoids replay attacks. Each transaction's inputs and outputs are contained in the block content.

In the case of a public blockchain, the only method to tamper with it is to obtain control of 51% of the network's processing power. In the case of private blockchain, there is no way to tamper with the network, since all transactions are controlled by one person or entity.

3. State of art

Kumar and Mallick [2] looked at the problems that existing IoT infrastructure faces. The authors of the study discussed confidentiality and safety issues. They identified the most pressing concerns with the present organization and offered

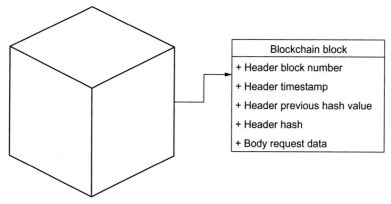

Blockchain block
+ Header block number
+ Header timestamp
+ Header previous hash value
+ Header hash
+ Body request data

FIG. 2   Blockchain block data.

a comprehensive list of them. In addition to providing an overview, the authors explain why the blockchain concept is important for the IoT. Agriculture, business, distribution, energy, cuisine, economics, health care, transportation and logistics, and smart cities are some of the areas where blockchain and IoT may be combined and bring significant advantages. The authors also listed several advantages, including the integrity of data, being temper proof, the removal of a single management agency, robustness, and the ability to store data from previous transactions in smart devices.

Miraz [3] provided an overview of blockchain and the fundamentals of how it works, as well as IoT fundamentals. After providing fundamentals of IoT and blockchain, the author proposed a merging of these two technologies and presented the benefits of the merge: improved security, immutability of the data, verifiability, and access to smart contracts [4] from the blockchain; whereas the benefit IoT provides to blockchain is by actively participating in the consensus process. The authors indicated forecasts that IoT devices will become widespread technology in the next 5 to 10 years, and therefore, justified by its widespread adoption in multifaceted applications and the security concerns raised thus far, the authors also concluded that both of these technologies are distributed, autonomous, and mostly decentralized systems with inherent potential for complementing one another.

Hassija et al. [5] offered a summary of historical changes of IoT infrastructure, from cloud-based to present IoT infrastructure with many servers with a single point of failure and future blockchain-based infrastructure. In the survey, the authors presented security threats at different layers of the network. Some types of attacks are discussed and solutions provided for them on different network layers. The survey the authors provided is expected to serve as a resource for future research and resolve the challenges with security and privacy that exist in the current IoT infrastructure.

Atlam et al. [6] addressed the issues with the client/server model that is using the current IoT infrastructure. Out of many issues that exist, the most important ones are scalability and security. In this paper, the authors provided an overview of using blockchain in conjunction with IoT. The merging of these two leading tools would bring many benefits and challenges that should be addressed. The challenges that are faced with merging are scalability, legal compliance, processing power and time, and storage.

Khanji et al. [7] offered a summary of Zigbee attacks, divided into attacks on the transport layer, network layer, MAC layer and physical layer. They defined and classified the types of attacks on Zigbee as sink attacks, source attacks, neighbor attacks, member attacks, and energy depletion attacks (ghost attacks). Zigbee is sensitive to many network attacks due to its ease of construction, small memory size, low processing speed, and low processing power. For this reason, it is very important to evaluate threats and attacks on Zigbee.

Pavlovic et al. [8] addressed the issue of centralized IoT infrastructure and the security of IoT devices. The paper concluded that IoT devices offer solutions for many modern and real-life problems, but have very low and limited processing power and that they support only very weak or absolute encryption algorithms. The paper proposed the introduction of a security gateway as a solution for more efficient encryption algorithms but failed to solve the issue of centralized infrastructure.

4. Proposed solution

Using blockchain technology in the current IoT infrastructure provides a network with the possibility to add or remove any device to the network and enforce custom access control policies. In the proposed solution we are using a private blockchain. The reason for this is to move control of the network to a single point of security, so that if some of the IoT devices get compromised it would cause no harm to the network. Another important fact is that to get access to a private blockchain network, a device would need an invitation. All the devices in this network would be hidden from the public network and for someone or something to access the smart device it would need to send a request to the control point of the blockchain network.

For one IoT device to work without any problems and get data from cloud services it would need to do the following actions. For IoT devices to send requests to the cloud service and get data, first it would need to send requests to blockchain interfaces that authenticate, record, and enforce access policies. A request to the blockchain interface is one blockchain transaction. The transaction is successful if it is done from devices that are approved in a private network and if it provides the proper hash and data that is needed to validate a transaction in the blockchain. Once the transaction is successful the blockchain interface will send a request—that is a copy of the blockchain body data—to the cloud service. The cloud service would respond to the blockchain interface with a command. The blockchain interface parses the request from the cloud service and creates a new transaction to the IoT device that requested the data from the cloud. Each transaction includes the following in its request body:

- Current block number.
- Previous block hash.
- Timestamp of the creation.
- Request body.

The mentioned request body always has a request for action if the request is leaving the local network and needs access to the cloud service or a response from the cloud service to perform a specific set of actions.

All requests within the private network are transactions, and they cannot be faked or altered. Each transaction is recorded in a database called the distributed ledger, which may be accessed using the blockchain port. A blockchain port may be installed on a Raspberry Pi, with the distributed ledger stored on the computer, a local web server, or even in the case of smart households, no local machine at all. The RSA [9] algorithm may be used to request a distant database that has been encoded with a powerful encoding technique.

We have tested different approaches when integrating the IoT with blockchain technologies. To make sure all data shared by the blockchain nodes is secure, we have used a private blockchain approach in the protocol.

To make sure the proposed solution will work, we have created a demo [10] version of it and tested it on a simple humidity and air temperature sensor and cloud service that provided actions depending on values sent by sensors. The code for the demo should be built in a programming language that can operate on a wide range of devices. Node.js is used in our solution. Most devices are well-supported by Node.js. The container technique is well supported by several Node.js process managers, such as PM2. This implies that our demo would be in a container, making it difficult for an attacker to connect to it. Cluster mode is also supported by PM2. Networked Node.js applications (http(s)/tcp/udp server) may be scaled over all CPUs available in cluster mode. Depending on the number of core CPUs, this dramatically improves server performance. Each process is started in a separate cluster. If an attacker attempts to exploit any process on our server, the cluster will terminate the process after a set length of time to ensure that the server functions properly.

The data provided by sensors is sent to the blockchain interface, which creates a new transaction, checks the validity of the block, and writes to a distributed ledger. The data is then sent to the cloud, and the blockchain interface receives the cloud's answer. The interface creates new transactions for response and provides smart devices with commands.

With this approach, we have created a private blockchain network with a single point where data from the cloud is received, validated, and properly parsed then sent via blockchain transactions to smart devices. The following can be added to this proposed solution to make it even better:

- Filtering allows cloud services to connect to the blockchain network by authorizing access to specific IP addresses or ranges of IP addresses.
- Combining an extra degree of security by including a port that encrypts and decrypts data exiting the blockchain network.
- Combining a technique of storing cloud replies with a method of preventing queries from leaving the blockchain network. If the same request is sent to the cloud, we may use a distributed ledger to transmit previous cloud replies to the smart device.

The following attacks can be prevented using our proposed solution:

- With man-in-the-middle, attackers will be unable to sniff data straight from our smart devices. They will only be able to obtain data from our router to the Internet. There will be very little likelihood of exploitation if the data is adequately secured.
- Connecting directly to a smart device and performing any exploitation of it. All connections from the remote to the smart device are sent to the demo, which verifies that the requests are coming from trusted sources.
- Devices in a local area network that do not have authentication will gain a new layer of protection based on demo authentication. Authentication and permission on the demo would be required to obtain access to any smart device.

In future work, we will integrate all previously mentioned features and provide solutions that can be easily set up in any IoT network.

5. Challenges

Because it is built on a centralized approach with a central authority, the security of present IoT designs is a big concern, as it is subject to a single point of failure. Zigbee network uses two modes of communication, beacon and nonbeacon mode. Beacon mode is used by the battery-operated coordinator to save energy. The device waits for beacons that the coordinator periodically sends and requests messages sent to him/her. If the message transmission is complete, the coordinator sets the schedule for the next beacon for that device. After learning about the next schedule, the device can fall asleep. On the other hand, the nonbeacon mode is used by the mains-powered coordinator. All devices on a network know the schedule to communicate with each other and must wake up in the allotted time so as not to miss a beacon. Therefore, a fairly precise time cycle needs to be applied to the devices. It means that there will be an increase in energy consumption. Nonbeacon communication is suitable for applications such as smoke detectors and burglar alarms where the devices sleep almost all the time. There is a type of attack on energy consumption called a ghost attack, where the attacker sends fake messages to lure the node to consume energy due to redundancy security-related responses. This will shorten the lifespan of the node and make it possible for an attacker to launch several attacks, as is the case with DoS attacks. In this scenario, if the node stop is caused by this attack, the whole network will go down. In addition, this kind of implementation is vulnerable to a man-in-the-middle attack scenario.

In the case of public blockchain infrastructure, single points of failure are eliminated, and decision-making is moved to a shared network of devices, or to a single entity in the case of private blockchain infrastructure. This implementation enhances the security of IoT devices on the transport layer, which is extremely vulnerable with IoT devices [11].

When developing the architecture for IoT to operate with blockchain technology, there are four key problems to consider:

- The major issue when working with a high number of devices in a single network is scalability. The pace of network transaction processing slows when additional devices are added. Furthermore, more hardware resources are utilized such as CPU time and memory allocation [12].
- The anonymity of transaction history in a shared ledger for a network of IoT devices is challenging to establish on public blockchains.
- Interfering with the accurate measurement of the conditions that must be satisfied to complete a transaction might jeopardize the dependability of IoT sensors.
- To provide a safe environment for data flow and transactions, measures to protect the integrity of IoT devices so that they cannot be tampered with by external interventions are required.

We propose an approach with the following advantages:

- The system can be isolated and free to add any device to the network while still enforcing access control policies.
- In case of failure of some device, the entire network will still be visible and operating properly.
- There would not be any single point of failure, since there would not be any central authority.
- The approach has no issue with scalability, which means any device can be added or removed from the network without causing any issues.
- The system hides all IoT devices behind blockchain.

It is unavoidable that the usage of existing technology will alter as a result of the merger of blockchain and IoT technologies—it is not easy to get them all together. To maintain consensus, blockchain uses two main consensus mechanisms: proof-of-work and proof-of-stake. Proof-of-work is the first compromise algorithm and up to this day the most used one. This algorithm prevents double spend. Double spend is when the same data is used twice or in the case of cryptocurrency the same funds are spent twice. In proof-of-work, the miners solve cryptographically hard puzzles by using their computational resources. In proof-of-stake, instead of miners, there are validators. The validators confirm the blocks and add them to the chain.

Since proof-of-work consumes too much power, it is not a good combination with IoT. A good combination, in this case, is proof-of-stake.

In this chapter, each node (IoT device) has access to the distributed ledger—a digital ledger that can be shared but can't be tampered with. A distributed ledger is a database of all transactions that are time-stamped and chronologically documented, it is append-only, and existing blocks cannot be updated or removed. The benefits of this strategy include the elimination of a single point of failure. Even if one node in the network goes down or is hacked, the IoT network will continue to function normally. Furthermore, each device will not be able to communicate directly with the cloud infrastructure. The communication will have to go through the proposed secure interface.

Since IoT devices cannot do blockchain validation due to limited processing and memory resources, as well as receiving and sending requests, we propose a hub architecture in which the devices would communicate with the hub regarding blockchain validation. All IoT devices will have access to the IoT hub. Each request from the IoT device (or sensor) will be directed to the hub [13]. In cases where IoT devices are connected to LAN and try to send requests to cloud services, this request will be forwarded to the hub first. This can be done with firewall rules that can be updated on the home router.

Each request made to the IoT hub is treated as a transaction. It must have sender, receiver, and additional data (which is a response from a cloud computer). As previously explained, each transaction is validated, which prevents any kind of data tampering by third parties. With blockchain implementation in IoT, adding any additional device is quite flexible and requires no additional work on the protocol. The device requests will go through the hub and will get responses from the hub (forwarded from the cloud server).

In our previous research, we proposed an approach to adding a simple interface as security gateway architecture for IoT devices. We may further strengthen the security of the whole IoT infrastructure by applying the approach presented in this previous research, since blockchain and IoT implementation is adaptable. Since the blockchain body has additional data that we are passing from the cloud, we can add a simple interface that will encrypt/decrypt this data and prevent attackers from recording remote requests. The interface would work between blockchain and the cloud. A simple interface as a security gateway can provide an additional layer of security that can perform cryptographic operations, which means that it can perform AES, DES [14] or Triple DES, RSA, or any other strong cryptographic algorithm. However, to use this layer of security, IoT device manufacturers have to follow up on their security standards and add support for strong cryptographic algorithms. Papers [15–18] present a specific blockchain implementation for IoT devices, with an emphasis on data privacy and trustworthy blockchain gateways.

The single threaded nature of Node.js is a disadvantage. This is due to concerns with interoperability across platforms and integrations. It must run under a process manager such as PM2 to be multithreaded. The approach necessitates the use of a distributed ledger. This means that if something goes wrong with the distributed ledger, the solution will be rendered useless. Memory databases can be used to solve this problem. When the proposed solution expects a response from a remote service but does not receive one, the server operation is halted. The current method uses timeouts to wait for remote services to react; if they do not respond within that timeframe, the process is terminated, and no data is delivered back to the smart device. The most significant barrier is that much of the code running on smart devices is not open source, making it impossible to obtain data from a smart device, parse it, and send it encrypted to a remote service without first contacting the manufacturer. Some manufacturers, on the other hand, supply developers with documentation and a dashboard where data may be altered, improved, and sent to a remote service in various formats.

With the merging of blockchain, IoT, and a simple interface as security gateway we achieved the following:

- Any remote request, from the moment the request leaves LAN and goes to the Internet, it is encrypted. The security gateway will encrypt data in any cryptographic algorithm (which is supported by the cloud).
- Response from the cloud will be encrypted by the same algorithm that is used when sending the request.
- When a remote request is received by the router, it will be forwarded using firewall rules to the IoT hub.
- The IoT hub will decrypt the request and proceed to blockchain implementation.
- Once the request is decrypted, the blockchain has the following parameters (receiver—to whom the request is sent, sender—from whom the request is sent, additional data (in the body)—command or any info from cloud).

Once The request is decrypted, blockchain has the following:

- Blockchain implementation will validate the request and create a new block.
- The newly created block will be appended to a distributed ledger.

Fig. 3 depicts the recommended proposal's format. Every Internet of Things device is connected to the blockchain network, and each web request is a transaction. As formerly stated, the protection port sits between the blockchain port and the router, monitoring all Internet requests.

As previously mentioned this method also provides a decentralized model of connecting IoT devices. This model of connection also provides more security, since eliminating or compromising one of the devices will not affect infrastructure as a whole.

IoT Device   Blockchain node   Blockchain interface   Network interface   Router   Cloud service
                                                         as security gateway

FIG. 3 Network infrastructure of the proposed solution.

6. Conclusions

With the provided approach, we were able to secure LAN and WAN demands. Not only did we increase protection, but we also obtained a catalog (distributed ledger) that included a list of all demands. So, if an incident occurs, we may investigate it in the catalog and add an extra layer of security to the presented design, as well as patch infrastructure flaws. We will continue our study by describing the types of attacks that may be made against present IoT infrastructure, as well as how effective our suggested solution is against them.

This method would vastly increase smart device security. Smart gadgets are now vulnerable to a variety of assaults, and most of them have lax or nonexistent security standards. The approach we propose improves the security of smart devices by restricting it from making direct requests to the Internet. All requests are authenticated by the blockchain interface and approved if they are correct. Another layer of security from the Internet is added by implementing a simple interface as a security gateway. This interface protects the devices from third parties that are not allowed by network rules to access local networks.

Our approach has no issue with scalability, any device can be added or removed from the network and the network will still enforce control policies. The IoT devices in the network are hidden. If some of the devices fail to work properly, the distributed ledger will save its request/response block and with additional logic, we can force it to execute it later if needed.

Smart homes, healthcare, private businesses, etc., are all industries where our proposed solution could be used. The flexibility of the solution provides a high level of security to all the devices in the environment, where private data of the residents, in the case of smart home, or highly valuable data of the private businesses or data on patients needs to be hidden and only saved on the local hard drive. Another layer of security provided by a simple interface as a network gateway could be used in this case as encryption logic to protect the data in the blockchain body when saving it in storage.

References

[1] A. Panarello, N. Tapas, G. Merlino, F. Longo, A. Puliafito, Blockchain and IoT integration: a systematic survey, Sensors 18 (2018), 2575.

[2] N. Kumar, P. Mallick, Blockchain technology for security issues and challenges in IoT, Procedia Comput. Sci. 132 (2018) 1815–1823.

[3] M. Miraz, Blockchain of Things (Bcot): The Fusion of Blockchain and Iot Technologies, 2020, Available from: https://arxiv.org/pdf/1910.06898. (Accessed 1 November 2020).

[4] M. Andersen, J. Kolb, K. Chen, G. Fierro, D. Culler, R. Popa, WAVE: A Decentralized Authorization System for Iot Via Blockchain Smart Contracts, 2017, Available from: https://www2. eecs.berkeley.edu/Pubs/TechRpts/2017/EECS-2017-234.pdf. (Accessed 4 November 2020).

[5] V. Hassija, V. Chamola, V. Saxena, D. Jain, P. Goyal, B. Sikdar, A Survey on Iot Security: Application Areas, Security Threats, and Solution Architectures, 2020, Available from: https://www.ece.nus.edu.sg/stfpage/bsikdar/papers/access_19.pdf. (Accessed 4 November 2020).

[6] H.F. Atlam, A. Alenezi, M.O. Alassafi, G. Wills, Blockchain with internet of things: benefits, challenges, and future directions, Int. J. Intell. Syst. Appl. 10 (2018) 40–48.

[7] S. Khanji, F. Iqbal, P. Hung, ZigBee security vulnerabilities: exploration and evaluating, in: Proceedings of the 10th International Conference on Information and Communication Systems 2019, Jordan, 2019, https://doi.org/10.1109/IACS.2019.8809115.

[8] N. Pavlović, M. Šarac, S. Adamović, et al., An approach to adding simple interface as security gateway architecture for IoT device, Multimed. Tools Appl. (2021), https://doi.org/10.1007/s11042-021-11389-8.

[9] X. Zhou, X. Tang, Research and implementation of RSA algorithm for encryption and decryption, in: Proceedings of 2011 6th International Forum on Strategic Technology, Harbin, Heilongjiang, 2011, 2011, pp. 1118–1121, https://doi.org/10.1109/IFOST.2011.6021216.

[10] M. Andriansyah, M. Subali, I. Purwanto, S.A. Irianto, R.A. Pramono, E-KTP as the basis of home security system using Arduino UNO, in: 2017 4th International Conference on Computer Applications and Information Processing Technology (CAIPT), Kuta Bali, 2017, pp. 1–5.

[11] I. Makhdoom, M. Abolhasan, W. Ni, Blockchain for IoT: the challenges and a way forward, in: Proceedings of the 15th International Joint Conference on e-Business and Telecommunications – SECRYPT, 428–439, 2018, Porto, Portugal, 2018, pp. 594–605, https://doi.org/10.5220/0006905605940605.

[12] A. Dwivedi, G. Srivastava, S. Dhar, R. Singh, A decentralized privacy-preserving healthcare blockchain for IoT, Sensors 19 (2) (2019) 326.

[13] N. Tariq, M. Asim, F. Al-Obeidat, M. Farooqi, T. Baker, M. Hammoudeh, I. Ghafir, The security of big data in fog-enabled IoT applications including blockchain: a survey, Sensors 19 (2019) 1788, https://doi.org/10.3390/s19081788.

[14] B. Bhat, A.W. Ali, A. Gupta, DES and AES performance evaluation, in: International Conference on Computing, Communication & Automation, Noida, 2015, pp. 887–890, https://doi.org/10.1109/CCAA.2015.7148500.

[15] Y. Zhao, et al., Privacy-preserving blockchain-based federated learning for IoT devices, IEEE Internet Things J. 8 (3) (2021) 1817–1829, https://doi.org/10.1109/JIOT.2020.3017377.

[16] M. Debe, K. Salah, R. Jayaraman, I. Yaqoob, J. Arshad, Trustworthy blockchain gateways for resource-constrained clients and IoT devices, IEEE Access 9 (2021) 132875–132887, https://doi.org/10.1109/ACCESS.2021.3115150.

[17] F. Loukil, C. Ghedira-Guegan, K. Boukadi, A. Benharkat, E. Benkhelifa, Data privacy based on IoT device behavior control using blockchain, ACM Trans. Internet Technol. 21 (1) (2021), 23, https://doi.org/10.1145/3434776.

[18] C.-L. Chen, Z.-Y. Lim, H.-C. Liao, Blockchain-based community safety security system with IoT secure devices, Sustainability 13 (24) (2021) 13994, https://doi.org/10.3390/su132413994.

Chapter 9

Emergence of blockchain technology in the healthcare and insurance industries

Nick Rahimi and Sai Sri Vineeth Gudapati

University of Southern Mississippi, Hattiesburg, MS, United States

1. Introduction

At the turn of the 21st century, the healthcare industry came under immense pressure to provide high-quality services while managing costs. But thanks to the rise of new technologies, the industry has been innovating and developing toward the accomplishment of these goals [1]. For instance, the concept of smart healthcare is currently providing great progress in transforming the healthcare sector [2,3]. Smart healthcare is a concept that combines technologies such as electronic medical records, cloud computing, and electronic health archives using technologies such as exchange technologies, the internet of things, and data transmission to build optimal management of health services. Potential benefits of this system have become attractive to the research community, plus the case for its benefits was made evident during the recent Covid-19 epidemic, in which remote patient monitoring and other healthcare services became increasingly useful as a means of containing the situation [4]. A similar case of technological deployment has marked the 21st century for developments in the insurance industry.

Unfortunately, as these technological developments mature, so do the research and operational challenges. For example, both the healthcare and insurance industries' technological systems employ a centralized server model; a model that exposes the industries to security and privacy limitations attributed to a centralized server system, particularly those dealing with performance failures such as performance bottleneck and a single point of failure [5,6]. Furthermore, for the case of the healthcare industry, systems such as electronic health records (EHRs) are becoming commonplace, users of which may unknowingly, or in other cases covertly, expose patients' data to insecure agents while conducting their normal activities [7]. On the other hand, among the greatest

Blockchain Technology Solutions for the Security of IoT-Based Healthcare Systems.
https://doi.org/10.1016/B978-0-323-99199-5.00013-6
167

challenges facing the insurance industry amidst the 21st century's radical technological transformations are fraud and big data management [8]. These examples represent areas of serious concerns that challenge the technological development of the two industries. Nevertheless, in what could be argued is the greatest solution from the fourth industrial revolution, blockchain technology possesses characteristics that are responsive to the weak points of the above-discussed traditional technologies. Precisely, blockchain's characteristics, such as decentralization, auditability, being tamper proof, and anonymity imply an adequate capacity for emerging challenges in the healthcare and insurance industries such as privacy maintenance, data security, and establishment of multiparty data alliance chains comprising related enterprises, government agencies, and individual customers [9]. Aside from creating a link between blockchain and the above-stated healthcare and insurance technological challenges, this study conducts a literature review and analysis to determine the feasibility of blockchain technology in the two industries.

This chapter is organized as follows. In Section 2, we summarize the background work, and the current state of healthcare and insurance technological systems. Section 3 presents a brief review of blockchain technology. Section 4 discusses opportunities and needs for blockchain technology in the healthcare and insurance industries. In Section 5, we investigate the feasibility of implementing blockchain in applications in the healthcare and insurance industries. Section 6 introduces several real-world cases of blockchain-based applications in the abovementioned industries. Finally, in Section 7, we offer the chapter's conclusion.

2. A background review

Both the healthcare and insurance industries acknowledge the importance of interaction among various stakeholders in delivering quality services. For instance, taking the example of a healthcare insurance organization, a healthy interaction among the insurers, healthcare providers, individual patients, and government regulatory agencies must precede any chances of quality service [10]. On the other hand, an apt interaction between patients and healthcare practitioners, healthcare institutions, and healthcare devices generates a platform upon which to provide effective devices and quality healthcare services. Considering the significance that a healthy interaction holds in both cases, nothing is as important as information management in these industries. This explains why the industries are making the most out of technological developments to generate technological systems mainly equipped for the information management task [11].

Shi et al. [12] cite the electronic health record (EHR) as the perfect example of these systems for the case of the healthcare industry. According to the researchers, EHR describes a collection of patients' electronic health information reserved in terms of electronic medical records (EMRs) or personal health records (PHRs). EMRs serve in the capacity of data source for EHR generated throughout the entire interaction between a patient and a healthcare practitioner, detailing a patient's medical history, while PHRs serve as data source for patients' personal healthcare information such as that generated from wearable devices. Conversely, an insurance firm in a field such as that of medical insurance must operate a technological system on which insurers, healthcare institutions, insurance providers, and related government agencies submit and access information [13]. These systems are beneficial in that they support the availability of large volumes of data, which, upon effective analysis, underlie appropriate medical decisions and correct responses to insurance claims. Furthermore, the significance of data available on these systems could be extended to other functions such as machine learning, for example, to support medical research efforts as disease forecasting in the case of the healthcare industry.

From a theoretical point of view, the above-discussed systems must support the availability, confidentiality, and integrity of stored data. From the context of the research community, the implementation of healthcare and insurance technological systems must support the cause that data be shared securely among only authorized users and that the systems significantly reduce chances of data replication and the risk of lost records. However, whether at rest or in transit, the challenge of securing data in these systems is exponentially growing thanks to the increasing connectivity of the systems. For example, the current state of technological growth implies that devices as simple as mobile devices can sync with electronic medical systems, serving as potential attack vectors that could easily be targeted [14]. Similar cases of fraud and data management challenges are cited in the insurance sector owing to technological development [15,16]. These similarities in data security problems from both ends suggest serious concerns with the current state of healthcare and insurance systems.

2.1 The current state of healthcare and insurance technological systems

Currently, a centralized architecture underpins both the conventional healthcare and insurance electronic information systems [17]. This form of architecture implies that a central institution is assigned the responsibility of coordinating, managing, and controlling the entire network. Two of the most immediate challenges to availability, integrity, and security of information held in these systems are performance bottleneck and single-point attacks or failures, whereby an attack of failure at any point of management or access renders the entire information vulnerable to malicious agents.

Meanwhile, data sharing is increasingly growing into one of the most crucial functions of not just the above two sectors, but almost every single economic sector within human society. American society can only secure quality service delivery by leveraging interconnectivity among various economic entities.

Other than the case of security challenges accompanying centralized systems of networks, the architecture sees to it that information is fragmented across a multitude of organizations—another challenge making it difficult to overcome the problem of information silos. For example, the problem of information fragmentations has been blamed for a number of healthcare challenges such as incomplete patient information at the point of care and the incapacity to track patients in real time, two problems that undermine any promise of success in coordinated care. One particular study on this issue was a survey study by the American hospital association, whose findings suggested that only 18% of healthcare providers are able to often formulate their care delivery using patient information generated from outside sources [9]. However, up to 36% of healthcare providers have problems accessing, or rarely or never use, patient information from outside sources.

While assessing insurance organizations, Malhotra et al. (2016) claim that one reason as to why insurance transactions today may take up to weeks to locate and process is that the sector faces a multitude of challenges with the manner of acquiring, sharing, processing, and securing information. In one of the consumer surveys conducted in 2007, the study findings suggested that the provider directory—one of the health insurers' most used website functions—comprises mostly out-of-date or incorrectly filled information. In another related study in 2014, California-based regulators reported that about 18.2% in one of the healthcare plans and 12.5% in another plan had wrong addresses on their websites [6]. Other forms of inaccuracies include hospital affiliations and phone numbers. Considering that the system is centralized, any one of these inaccuracies signifies a significant problem in service delivery.

Fraud is another challenge strongly affecting insurance service delivery. It has been estimated that fraud costs the insurance industry about $80 billion each year [18]. There is a wide range of potential for fraud in the insurance industry, beginning with the application process; for example, when applicants withhold important information such as a history of cardiovascular conditions. In other cases, people are prone to life-changing predicaments, changes such as going through a divorce, the outcome of which renders an ex-wife or an ex-husband who previously was covered on behalf of a partner's coverage ineligible. If the individual responsible for the coverage fails to report such changes, an insurance provider stands to suffer fraud challenges. However, the most common forms of fraud in the insurance industry are committed via acts such as submission of claims for services not rendered or up-scaling the services to earn higher payments [6]. Whether in the healthcare or the insurance industry, these many challenges signify conventional technological systems' incapacity to serve the industries' current needs. On the contrary, blockchain technology, which is built on a peer-to-peer (P2P) decentralized network [19,20], has features of auditability, tamper proofing, and anonymity that make it a perfect fit for the current challenges in healthcare and insurance industries.

3. The concept of blockchain technology

Blockchain technology is a concept that came to light in the event of the successful development of the cryptocurrency bitcoin by Nakamoto [21]. The technology describes a distributed form of ledger on which authorized multiple parties can transparently and securely access and add information. Precisely, a blockchain defines a chronological sequence of blocks comprising a record of complete and valid transactions. Each of these blocks is linked to the previous block by a reference, usually referred to as a hash value, which together form a chain. The first block is referred to as the genesis block, while that preceding a given block is referred to as a parent block [21]. Considering it in terms of a ledger, a blockchain's distribution allows identical copies of a given chain to be kept on multiple computers owned by various entities. It is because of this structure that data can be exchanged, stored, and verified across the entire system via fixed structures that own the name blocks. In other words, blockchain technology supports secure and trustworthy transactions on an untrusted network without the need for a centralized third party.

As illustrated in Fig. 1, each block within a blockchain is made up of a block header and block body. The block header comprises the block version, the previous block hash, the timestamp, the nonce, the body root hash, and the target hash. The block version represents the validation rules applicable on the block, the timestamp, the time at which the block was created, and the previous block hash, the hash value for the preceding block [19]. At the other end, the nonce defines the random field that a miner must adjust to in the hash calculation

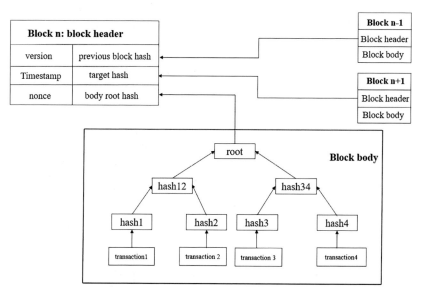

FIG. 1 Block structure.

aimed at solving the proof of work (PoW) puzzle while the target it has is the hash value target threshold that dictates the new valid block. Conversely, the block body defines the blockchain structure that represents all validated transactions within a given period of time. The Merkle tree is the exact name given to the body storing valid transactions. The tree consists of leaf nodes that mark every given transaction and nonleaf nodes representing the hash value of two combined child nodes [19]. Ultimately, this Merkle tree structure is the function that allows for verification of the existence and integrity of a transaction.

One blockchain feature, particularly important for fields such as financial, healthcare, and government services, is the smart contract. The feature defines a self-executing program necessary for the execution of predefined terms automatically and within a secure environment. Precisely, as a result of the function, every time an event meeting predefined parameters occurs on the blockchain, the next step is automatically triggered. For instance, in the case of the healthcare industry, the smart contract function would perfectly serve in the role of linking a healthcare provider to a patient's insurance provider [12].

For example, when the smart contract is applied in the EHR system, the moment a patient visits a physician and the activity is confirmed to the blockchain via the new data entered on the chain, the smart contract function authorizes automatic payment from the insurance provider. In one of the outcomes that would be considered an important advantage of this feature, smart contract shortcuts the need for traditional intermediaries, including broker relationships and banks [18,22]. Ultimately, blockchain technology's advantages cut across diverse needs ranging from security to efficiency.

4. Opportunities for blockchain technology in the healthcare and insurance industries

A multitude of the above-discussed challenges in the healthcare and insurance industries serve as great opportunities for blockchain technology, owing to its superior qualities. One of the technology's most critical qualities that would be strongly considered to serve the present-day challenges in the two industries is decentralization. The American healthcare and insurance sectors are two of the best examples of industries that work best in effective interaction with other sectors, including the interaction between the two themselves. As suggested earlier, one of the largest negative effects of the centralized case of technological systems is the creation of information silos, an outcome that significantly hampers two industries or related organizations from accessing information from external source points [18,23]. Blockchain's capacity to establish trust between different entities gives it an opportunity to solve this interoperability problem better than any of the currently existing technologies.

The second quality that earns blockchain technology an opportunity to serve the healthcare and insurance sectors better than the current technologies is security. As of now, concerns over privacy and security serve as the greatest obstacles against the current technological systems. Even when not worrying about violation of regulations such as the Health Insurance Portability and Accountability Act, security provision still represents one of the measures by which healthcare organizations could protect their customers [24]. Blockchain technology provides a more secure environment in which to fulfill the goals of privacy and security. There are multiple mechanisms in blockchain technology with which to regulate privacy and security concerns. For example, a decentralized technological system means that attacks such as a single-point attack do not necessarily endanger all the information in the entire system. Every participant in the system has equal privileges, and so long as he or she can navigate security terms such as proof of work, proof of stake, or practical byzantine fault tolerance, there are higher chances that he or she could pursue alterations that would identify the exact point of attack or protect his/her own resources from attacks [24,25]. Furthermore, blockchain's auditability quality makes it easy in general to trace the source point of every single operation, even if not made by an individual participant, considering that every historical transaction is recorded in the blockchain.

Most importantly, blockchain technology comprises the digital signature function that effectively serves as its own source of natural security. As illustrated in Fig. 2, blockchain employs the asymmetric cryptography mechanism to send and verify each of the transactions involved in the system [26]. For example, prior to sending any form of a transaction into a blockchain-supported network, one must first sign the transaction using the sender's private key. Once in the system, the sent transaction is broadcasted to the neighboring nodes via the P2P network. At this moment, the senders' public key is employed as the verification and authentication tool for the received transaction based on the predefined block validation rules. If confirmed as valid, the transaction is

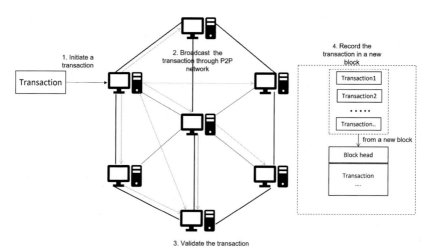

FIG. 2   Blockchain transaction workflow structure.

passed on to other nodes until all the nodes receive and verify it. Otherwise, the transaction is discarded in the process. All these mechanisms adequately serve to prove the practicality of blockchain technology in both the healthcare and insurance industries.

5. Feasibility of blockchain's application in the healthcare and insurance industries

While the above discussion ascertains the advantages of blockchain technology in the healthcare and insurance industries, there are serious concerns over the practicality of the technology within the current economic context. For instance, who would incur the investment costs given that the subject industries are under pressure to reduce their operational costs. Other challenges highlighted in the research community include the lack of standards, blockchain's capacity for data scalability, and whether the technology would require further security measures to tackle constantly emerging threats [27,28]. In response to these challenges, various researchers such as Eklund et al. (2019) have been proposing countermeasures such as reliance on the cloud and storing only pointers to data on the blockchain to confront the issue of scalability and pursuing comprehensive policy reforms to address the needs of this technology [28].

Nevertheless, in order to develop a strong theoretical foundation that would support blockchain adoption, this study conducted a critical literature review and analysis on some of the recent research studies to test for the technology's practicality. The analysis was based on three research questions:

- What are the cases of blockchain application in healthcare and insurance?
- What blockchain-based applications in healthcare and insurance have been developed?
- How to address challenges in blockchain application in healthcare and insurance?

With these questions, the categorization phase selected investigations belonging to only three categories: those addressing blockchain applications in healthcare, those addressing cases of blockchain-based developments in healthcare, and those addressing response measures against blockchain-based applications in healthcare.

The most immediate outcome of the above analysis was an indication that more of the research studies emphasize the advantages of blockchain technology in EMR than any other healthcare issue. As shown in Fig. 3, almost half of the recent research papers on blockchain-based healthcare emphasize blockchain application in electronic medical records systems. Nonetheless, there is also notable emphasis in areas such as healthcare insurance, biomedical research, and supply chain.

Subsequently, there is agreement in most of the research studies on several countermeasures to confront blockchain barriers. One such agreement is the

Percentage Distribution of Blockchain Application in Healthcare

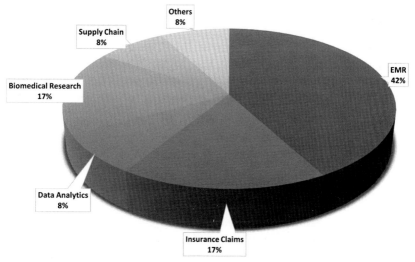

FIG. 3   Percentage distribution of blockchain in healthcare systems.

reliance on cloud computing handling data scalability, which is currently viewed as a serious challenge considering the amount of data employed in healthcare [12,29]. Conversely, another measure uniformly emphasized in strengthening privacy and security measures is the employment of private blockchain networks such as the IBM Blockchain Hyperledger Fabric deployed on Bluemix [28].

Similarly, the provision of adequate policy addressing the technology counts as a key measure in supporting the adoption of the technology. Two already working blockchain-based developments that researchers feel should serve as perfect examples are the Guardtime and MedRec projects [30,31]. Guardtime is a blockchain-based platform that is successfully serving more than 1 million patients in Estonia, while MedRec is an MIT Media Lab and Beth Israel Deaconess Medical Center project successfully demonstrating blockchain's capacity in patient data sharing. On the grounds of all these arguments, it is evident that blockchain stands a greater chance of succeeding in both the healthcare and insurance industries.

6.   Blockchain companies in healthcare

Confidentiality, integrity, control, and availability are the promises of blockchain systems, and these are the factors that healthcare and insurance industries are seeking to provide more than ever. Below is a list of several frontier businesses that are actively bringing blockchain technology to the healthcare and insurance sectors.

6.1 Change healthcare

Change Healthcare is based in Tennessee, United States. They provide several software services for the health sector. They built a blockchain based on Hyperledger Fabric for running the claim process, which is an open-source protocol developed by Linux. They use proof-of-concept as their consensus mechanism. With help of blockchain, they are processing around 50 million transactions per day. For better scalability, Change Healthcare is now moving to an AWS-managed service called AWS Blockchain which supports Hyperledger Fabric [32].

6.2 Chronicled

Chronicled was established in the year 2017 and is based in San Francisco. They developed Mediledger in collaboration with the life science industry. Chronicled is providing solutions for drug and device supply chain and product manufacturers with the help of blockchain. It works on permissioned-based blockchain [33]. Mediledger has implemented all requirements and regulations introduced by the FDA [34].

6.3 Lumedic

This Seattle-based company provides a blockchain-based platform for revenue cycle management. Lumedic was acquired by Providence St. Joseph Health in 2019. Prior authorization request is needed for approval of a claim for patients' treatment. Here they are improving the prior authorization process by establishing a trusted environment where healthcare providers and insurers can safely, securely, and quickly exchange sensitive patient data so treatment can be processed. With the help of this prior authorization process, manual involvements are reduced, and approvals are becoming easier. These changes help reduce the time period for patients to receive the care they need. The application is also offering digital wallets on patients' mobile devices and letting them control their healthcare information and whom it should be shared with. By using blockchain they are reducing delays in delivering care, making test results accessible more quickly, removing ambiguity from medical bills, and in addition, streamlining insurance billing and payments [35,36].

6.4 HSBlox

This Atlanta-based company was founded in 2017. They are focused on value-based and population health, patient permissioned data, analytics, and chain of custody/supply chain. HSBlox launched a digital sampler manager solution using distributed ledger technology (DLT) in January 2019. The sampler manager is used in clinical trials where multiple biological samples are collected at various clinical sites, and it always keeps track of all the information about the samples. By using distributed ledger and the use of smart contracts to automate tracking and a permissioned blockchain mechanism, only the trial sponsors, clinical sites, labs, clinical research organizations, auditors, shippers, local third-party labs, and patients can access their data [37].

6.5   BurstIQ

Based in Denver, Colorado, BurstIQ provides services using an application platform that can handle data from electronic health records (EHR), personal health records (PHR), and smart devices (IoT data). The patient data is shared across physicians, researchers, and developers. Depending upon data from the BurstIQ application, a doctor can provide adequate and timely care for their patients. Using the BurstIQ application, patients can directly sell their data for further investigations. In other words, researchers can use the data for new medical breakthroughs and the developers can build smarter and custom-designed, personalized products [38].

6.6   Modum

This Switzerland-based company was founded in 2016. Modum came into the picture by developing a technology to keep track of medicines that are affected by environmental conditions during transport. This company introduced an innovative idea of using smart devices that were placed into packages and monitor the temperatures of the package until its delivery or sale. The sensor sends the data, and the data gets stored into a distributed ledger by using smart contracts.

Modum introduced a system called tokens where the data in blockchain can be verified by validators. The validator gets their share upon verifying their transactions in the distributed ledger system [39].

6.7   DHL and Accenture

These companies combined to develop an application for supply chains in the pharmaceutical sector where it is necessary to check the authenticity of the drugs produced. By use of blockchain, it is possible to keep track of the drugs or medicines by pharmaceutical serialization (assigning a unique ID) and keeping track of transportation from the plant to the hospitals or the delivery locations, which will eliminate the flow of fake medicines that are entering into the market [40,41].

6.8 Spiritus

Spiritus is interested in the medical device management chain. By utilizing blockchain they can carefully trace medical equipment and its repair process records. With the assistance of distributed ledger, a platform is supplied to the parties involved in the repair and servicing of the medical equipment. This helps them in checking who has made repairs to the device, whether servicing is done by an experienced professional, and whether he/she has the proper training to perform the service. Clearly, this improves the medical device manufacturing companies' ability to track whether the right spares are being used in the process. Spiritus is based in Edinburgh, United Kingdom [42].

6.9 Guardtime

This Estonian company produces blockchain Health API, patient engagement for clinical trials and follow up, efficient supply chain management, value-based contracting, regulatory compliance of health data processing, and other services [43].

6.10 Medibloc

Medibloc is developing multiple blockchain-based health information platforms. They developed a technology called Panacea, which confidentially stores all a patient's related data and tasks. Panacea is a health information protocol that is integrated into a public blockchain and with independent P2P network [44]. The core function of Panacea is to prove the integrity and ownership of the data through hash value. Medibloc introduced cryptocurrency and a token that is called MED coin [45]. It utilizes proof of stake consensus mechanism in which validators are decided by the votes of network participants. MED coins are used as an incentive. Each user receives incentives after the successful creation of a block [46].

6.11 Patientory

This mobile-based application is designed for maintaining population health management. Patientory uses three-tier smart contract architecture. Only a subset of features of a smart contract are implemented in Ethereum blockchain. It meets HIPAA compliance, and it is based in Atlanta, GA [47,48].

6.12 Medable

Medable, based in California, is a blockchain-based platform that helps in exchanging information between patients, medical researchers, and biopharmaceutical companies. Its blockchain network is called insight. Individual participants are given the power to consent and be rewarded for sharing requested research data and/or consideration of a related clinical trial utilizing self-sovereign digital participant IDs. All of this information is accessible through their smartphone app. This data can be utilized to derive useful insights [49–54].

7. Conclusion

Ultimately, while conventional technological systems in the healthcare and insurance industries might be effective in support of quality and cost reduction, the current case of privacy and security concerns rise above their capacity. On the contrary, blockchain technology demonstrates sufficient technological maturity to confront privacy and security challenges. As a decentralized technological system, blockchain technology boasts of qualities such as auditability, accountability, being tamper proof, and anonymity, all of which are necessary for critical functions, including privacy maintenance, security management, and support for effective alliances between the healthcare industry and other economic sectors. Furthermore, with feasibility support from a multitude of research articles and already functioning blockchain-based projects, the future of the healthcare and insurance industries will arguably be more productive with the adoption of blockchain technology.

References

[1] HealthTech, What Happens to Stolen Healthcare Data? 2019, (Online). Available from: https://healthtechmagazine.net/article/2019/10/what-happens-stolen-healthcare-data-perfcon. (Accessed 20 August 2021).

[2] S.B. Baker, W. Xiang, I. Atkinson, Internet of things for smart healthcare: technologies, challenges, and opportunities, IEEE Access 5 (2017) 26521–26544.

[3] J. Qiu, X. Liang, S. Shetty, D. Bowden, Towards secure and smart healthcare in smart cities using blockchain, in: 2018 IEEE International Smart Cities Conference (ISC2), IEEE, 2018, September, pp. 1–4.

[4] D. Ford, J.B. Harvey, J. McElligott, K. King, K.N. Simpson, S. Valenta, L.A. Lenert, Leveraging health system telehealth and informatics infrastructure to create a continuum of services for COVID-19 screening, testing, and treatment, J. Am. Med. Inform. Assoc. 27 (12) (2020) 1871–1877.

[5] N. Rahimi, Security consideration in peer-to-peer networks with a case study application, Int. J. Netw. Secur. Appl. 12 (2) (2020).

[6] N. Rahimi, B. Gupta, S. Rahimi, Secured data lookup in LDE based low diameter structured P2P network, in: Proceedings of CATA, 2018.

[7] S. Ajami, T. Bagheri-Tadi, Barriers for adopting electronic health records (EHRs) by physicians, Acta Inform. Med. 21 (2) (2013) 129.

[8] S. Ajami, R. Arab-Chadegani, Barriers to implement electronic health records (EHRs), Mater. Sociomed. 25 (3) (2013) 213.

[9] N. Rahimi, I. Roy, B. Gupta, P. Bhandari, N.C. Debnath, Blockchain technology and its emerging applications, in: Blockchain Technology for Data Privacy Management, CRC Press, 2021, pp. 133–157.

[10] C.H. Lien, J.J. Wu, Y.H. Chen, C.J. Wang, Trust transfer and the effect of service quality on trust in the healthcare industry, Manag. Serv. Qual. 24 (2014) 399–416.

[11] C. Doukas, T. Pliakas, I. Maglogiannis, Mobile healthcare information management utilizing cloud computing and android OS, in: 2010 Annual International Conference of the IEEE Engineering in Medicine and Biology, IEEE, 2010, August, pp. 1037–1040.

[12] S. Shi, D. He, L. Li, N. Kumar, M.K. Khan, K.K.R. Choo, Applications of blockchain in ensuring the security and privacy of electronic health record systems: a survey, Comput. Secur. 97 (2020), 101966.

[13] L. Morris, Combating fraud in health care: an essential component of any cost containment strategy, Health Aff. 28 (5) (2009) 1351–1356.

[14] C.L. Chen, Y.Y. Deng, W.J. Tsaur, C.T. Li, C.C. Lee, C.M. Wu, A traceable online insurance claims system based on blockchain and smart contract technology, Sustainability 13 (16) (2021) 9386.

[15] H. Wang, Y. Song, Secure cloud-based EHR system using attribute-based cryptosystem and blockchain, J. Med. Syst. 42 (8) (2018) 1–9.

[16] X. Zheng, R.R. Mukkamala, R. Vatrapu, J. Ordieres-Mere, Blockchain-based personal health data sharing system using cloud storage, in: 2018 IEEE 20th International Conference on e-Health Networking, Applications and Services (Healthcom), IEEE, 2018, September, pp. 1–6.

[17] C. Thota, R. Sundarasekar, G. Manogaran, R. Varatharajan, M.K. Priyan, Centralized fog computing security platform for IoT and cloud in healthcare system, in: Fog computing: Breakthroughs in research and practice, IGI Global, 2018, pp. 365–378.

[18] R. Malhotra, C. Mcdaniel, F. Quarre, A. Israel, M. Filipova, L. Lauterbach, B. Naaz, Blockchain in Insurance: Turning a Buzzword into a Breakthrough for Health and Life Insurers, Deloitte Center for Financial Services, 2016, pp. 1–28.

[19] Y. Sun, R. Zhang, X. Wang, K. Gao, L. Liu, A decentralized attribute-based signature for healthcare blockchain, in: 2018 27th International Conference on Computer Communications and Networks (ICCCN), 2018, pp. 1–9.

[20] N. Rahimi, K. Sinha, B. Gupta, S. Rahimi, N.C. Debnath, LDEPTH: a low diameter hierarchical p2p network architecture, in: 2016 IEEE 14th International Conference on Industrial Informatics (INDIN), IEEE, 2016, July, pp. 832–837. S. Rahimi, A Novel Linear Diophantine Equation-Baesd Low Diameter Structured Peer-to-Peer Network, Southern Illinois University, Carbondale, USA, 2017.

[21] S. Nakamoto, Bitcoin: A Peer-to-Peer Electronic Cash System, Bitcoin Organization, 2008, pp. 1–11. https://www.google.com/url?q=https://www.ussc.gov/sites/default/files/pdf/training/annual-national-training seminar/2018/Emerging_Tech_Bitcoin_Crypto.pdf&sa=U&ved=2ahUKEwiWrKiwt_7yAhVJfMAKHfDpD2sQFnoECAgQAg&usg=AOvVaw2hAoRZZy9ucqoefRjBkws8.

[22] M. Raikwar, S. Mazumdar, S. Ruj, S.S. Gupta, A. Chattopadhyay, K.Y. Lam, in: A Blockchain Framework for Insurance Processes, 2018 9th IFIP International Conference on New Technologies, Mobility and Security (NTMS), IEEE, 2018, February, pp. 1–4.

[23] T. McGhin, K.K.R. Choo, C.Z. Liu, D. He, Blockchain in healthcare applications: research challenges and opportunities, J. Netw. Comput. Appl. 135 (2019) 62–75.

[24] L. Bell, W.J. Buchanan, J. Cameron, O. Lo, Applications of blockchain within healthcare, Blockchain Healthc. Today 1 (2018), https://doi.org/10.30953/bhty.v1.8.

[25] N. Rahimi, B. Gupta, Security issues, vulnerabilities, and defense mechanisms in wireless sensor networks: state of the art and recommendation, in: Integration of WSNs into Internet of Things, CRC Press, 2021, pp. 1–15.

[26] N. Rahimi, J.J. Reed, B. Gupta, On the significance of cryptography as a service, J. Inf. Secur. 9 (4) (2018) 242–256.

[27] E. Gökalp, M.O. Gökalp, S. Çoban, P.E. Eren, Analysing opportunities and challenges of integrated blockchain technologies in healthcare, in: Eurosymposium on Systems Analysis and Design, Springer, Cham, 2018, September, pp. 174–183.

[28] J.M. Eklund, C.C. Agbo, Q.H. Mahmoud, Blockchain technology in healthcare: a systematic review, Healthcare 7 (56) (2019) 1–30, https://doi.org/10.3390/healthcare7020056.

[29] D.C. Nguyen, P.N. Pathirana, M. Ding, A. Seneviratne, Blockchain for secure ehrs sharing of mobile cloud-based e-health systems, IEEE Access 7 (2019) 66792–66806.

[30] M. Mettler, Blockchain technology in healthcare: the revolution starts here, in: 2016 IEEE 18th International Conference on e-health Networking, Applications and Services (Healthcom), IEEE, 2016, September, pp. 1–3.

[31] A. Ekblaw, A. Azaria, J.D. Halamka, A. Lippman, A case study for blockchain in healthcare: "MedRec" prototype for electronic health records and medical research data, in: Proceedings of IEEE Open & Big Data Conference, vol. 13, 2016, August, p. 13.

[32] Change Healthcare, 2021. (Online). Available from: https://www.changehealthcare.com/. (Accessed 18 September 2021).

[33] Chronicled Healthcare, 2021. (Online). Available from: https://www.chronicled.com/. (Accessed 18 September 2021).

[34] S. De Angelis, L. Aniello, R. Baldoni, F. Lombardi, A. Margheri, V. Sassone, PBFT Vs Proof-of-Authority: Applying the CAP Theorem to Permissioned Blockchain, 2018.

[35] Lumedic-a Targia Company, 2021. (Online). Available from: https://www.lumedic.io/about. (Accessed 18 September 2021).

[36] Can Blockchain Heal What Ails Healthcare? Lumedic Launches New Quest for Digital Identity Standards, 2021. (Online). Available from: https://www.geekwire.com/2020/can-blockchain-heal-ails-healthcare-lumedic-launches-new-quest-digital-identity-standards/. (Accessed 18 September 2021).

[37] HSBlox, 2021. (Online). Available from: https://hsblox.com/. (Accessed 25 September 2021).

[38] BurstIQ, 2021. (Online). Available from: https://www.burstiq.com/. (Accessed 25 September 2021).

[39] M.L. Gagnon, R. Labonté, Understanding how and why health is integrated into foreign policy-a case study of health is global, a UK government strategy 2008–2013, Glob. Health 9 (1) (2013) 1–19.

[40] DHL and Accenture Unlock the Power of Blockchain in Logistics, 2018. (Online). Available from: https://newsroom.accenture.com/news/dhl-and-accenture-unlock-the-power-of-blockchain-in-logistics.htm/. (Accessed 25 September 2021).

[41] DHL and Accenture Working on Blockchain-Based Pharma Supply Chain Project, 2020. (Online). Available from: https://supplychaindigital.com/technology-4/dhl-and-accenture-working-blockchain-based-pharma-supply-chain-project. (Accessed 25 September 2021).

[42] Medical Device Servicing – A Shared "Middle Ground", 2019. (Online). Available from: https://www.spirituspartners.com/blog-stories/2018/6/11/stuck-in-the-middle-with-you. (Accessed 25 September 2021).

[43] Solving Real Healthcare Challenges with Blockchain, 2020. (Online). Available from: https://guardtime.com/health/#. (Accessed 25 September 2021).

[44] K. Maddali, S. Kaluvakuri, N. Rahimi, B. Gupta, N. Debnath, On designing secured communication protocols along with anonymity for CRT based structured P2P network architecture, in: EPiC Series in Computing, 75, 2021, pp. 59–68.

[45] J.Y. Kim, A comparative study of block chain: bitcoin Namecoin·MediBloc, J. Sci. Technol. Stud. 18 (3) (2018) 217–255.

[46] Medibloc, (Online). Available from: https://medibloc.co.kr/en/. (Accessed 20 September 2021).

[47] C. McFarlane, M. Beer, J. Brown, N. Prendergast, Patientory: A Healthcare Peer-to-Peer EMR Storage Network v1, Entrust Inc., Addison, TX, USA, 2017.

[48] N. Rahimi, J. Nolen, B. Gupta, Android security and its rooting—a possible improvement of its security architecture, J. Inf. Secur. 10 (2) (2019) 91–102.

[49] Medable, 2021. (Online). Available from: https://www.medable.com/. (Accessed 25 September 2021).

[50] Medable, 2021. (Online). Available from: https://www.globenewswire.com/en/news-release/2018/03/13/1421347/0/en/Medable-Inc-Introduces-Blockchain-for-Healthcare.html. (Accessed 25 September 2021).

[51] B. Bhushan, P. Sinha, K.M. Sagayam, J. Andrew, Untangling blockchain technology: a survey on state of the art, security threats, privacy services, applications and future research directions, Comput. Electr. Eng. 90 (2021), 106897.

[52] B. Bhushan, C. Sahoo, P. Sinha, A. Khamparia, Unification of blockchain and internet of things (BIoT): requirements, working model, challenges and future directions, Wirel. Netw 27 (1) (2021) 55–90.

[53] B. Bhushan, A. Khamparia, K.M. Sagayam, S.K. Sharma, M.A. Ahad, N.C. Debnath, Blockchain for smart cities: a review of architectures, integration trends and future research directions, Sustain. Cities Soc. 61 (2020), 102360.

[54] V. Gatteschi, F. Lamberti, C. Demartini, C. Pranteda, V. Santamaría, Blockchain and smart contracts for insurance: is the technology mature enough? Future Internet 10 (2) (2018) 20.

Chapter 10

The use of blockchain technology in IoT-based healthcare: A concise guide

Deepak Sharma[a] and Sudhir Kumar Sharma[b]

[a]*Department of Information and Technology, Institute of Innovation Technology & Management, Guru Gobind Singh Indraprastha University, Delhi, India,* [b]*Department of Information and Technology, Institute of Information Technology & Management, Guru Gobind Singh Indraprastha University, Delhi, India*

1. Introduction

Blockchain technology has permeated every element of digitalization, and its use has accelerated in recent years. The rise of cryptocurrencies for the startup of financial assets by using blockchain technology is popular. The market for blockchain technology was predicted to expand through 2021 [1]. There are presently around 1500 cryptocurrencies [2], all of which were developed within a few years after Bitcoin's launch [3]. Bitcoin was the first digital currency [4]. Miners, who get coins for their computational labor in verifying and storing transactions (payments) on the Bitcoin blockchain, are essential to the Bitcoin network [5]. Network has further information about Bitcoin for the interested reader [6]. Blockchain technology is used in a variety of ways, including cryptocurrencies [7]. There are three main elements to distinguish in a cryptocurrency: the blockchain, the protocol, and the currency. These elements help to create a currency system in which a coin can leverage the blockchain of another coin, such as Bitcoin or Ethereum [8]. The blockchain serves as a distributed ledger, storing all completed coin transactions in the cryptocurrency realm. A blockchain grows sequentially over time with the addition of new blocks.

Most well-known cryptocurrency blockchains are open to the public, and online tools like blockchain.com allow anyone to inquire about the Bitcoin blockchain's transactions. Blockchain eliminates the requirement for a (trusted) third party to facilitate transactions between entities. It is based on validators (typically miners) that operate as third parties and decentralize transaction

Blockchain Technology Solutions for the Security of IoT-Based Healthcare Systems.
https://doi.org/10.1016/B978-0-323-99199-5.00015-X

validation. To accomplish the task for decentralized trade through distributed consensus, the capacity of numerous people working together [9]. Thus, this problem is time consuming in the cryptocurrency world. Several surveys on the use of blockchain in various sectors have already been published [10,11]. An overview of blockchain technology offered by Zheng et al. [12] gave the architecture and several processes for execution. In addition, prominent authors like Karafiloski and Mishev [13] and Ahram et al. [14] have given overviews of blockchain technology, focusing on its use in big data and applications. Systematic reviews of blockchain application domains and associated research subjects have been published by Conoscenti et al. [15–17] and Yli-Huumo et al. [4]. A few publications [4,16–25] discuss blockchain technology in healthcare, but none of them have taken a systematic approach to reviewing the topic.

1.1 Motivation

Unlike the other studies, this one provides a thorough assessment and analysis of current blockchain research in the healthcare field. The study's objective is to show how blockchain can be utilized in the healthcare sector, its challenges, and the future directions of blockchain research. This systematic review includes analysis that offers a unique solution, algorithm, technique, approach, or architecture for the issue of healthcare. Review articles, presentations on potential blockchain uses and applications, and other nonrelevant publications are not included.

The rest of this chapter is laid out as follows. The background information on blockchain technology, its ideas, and the necessity for blockchain in healthcare are presented in Section 2. Section 3 discusses the study's research objectives, including databases, study selection, and literature quality evaluation. The data analysis is presented in Section 4, which includes research methods with the experimental setup, analysis of the obtained data and its characteristics, and the findings of the literature quality evaluation. Section 5 contains implications and discussion of the results and responses to the research questions. Fig. 1 shows year-wise publications on blockchain technology in the IoT healthcare sector.

2. Background

To assist the reader in comprehending the rest of this chapter, we will go through the basics of blockchain technology in this part. A blockchain is a distributed ledger that allows a network of peers to share data [4,12]. It was released in tandem with Bitcoin and solved a long-standing issue known as the double-spend problem. The blockchain technique is accomplished in Bitcoin by most of the so-called mining nodes reaching a consensus and adding

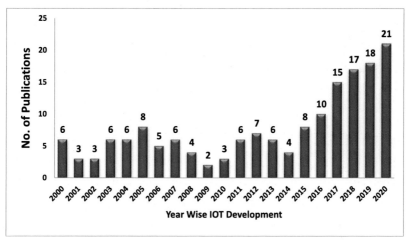

FIG. 1   Year-wise publications on blockchain technology in the IoT healthcare sector.

legitimate transactions to the blockchain. The initial use of blockchain technology was in cryptocurrencies. However, it is not necessary to use blockchain in order to establish a cryptocurrency [26].

A blockchain is a collection of time-stamped blocks linked together by cryptographic hashes. These blocks are securely and irreversibly sealed [26,27]. The chain is continually expanding, with new blocks being added to the end, each of which contains a reference (i.e., a hash value) to the preceding block's content [28]. The shareholders, also known as blockchain nodes, are connected in a peer-to-peer (P2P) network. Each node in the network has two keys [29,30]: a public key for encrypting messages transmitted to it and a private key for decrypting communications and allowing a node to read them.

The communications encrypted with the associated public key can only be decrypted with the appropriate private key. Asymmetric cryptography is the term for this idea. Further information can be obtained in Ref. [31], as a full explanation is beyond the scope of this article. The hash, which is created via a cryptographic one-way hash function, links all the blocks in the blockchain. It also assures the block's anonymity, immutability, and compactness [32]. Before being broadcast to the network for subsequent confirmation, each transaction carried out by a node is signed. A private key to digitally sign marketing allows for transaction authenticity and integrity. One reason for this is the fact that only a single user with a specific private key may sign the transaction, and the second is related to the fact that a data transmission mistake renders decryption impossible, e.g., verifying a digital signature. When the network uses particular consensus techniques, such as proof-of-work or proof-of-stake, specialized nodes, known as miners, arrange and bundle transactions distributed in the network and recognized as legitimate by the network into time-stamped

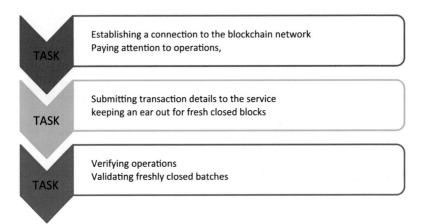

FIG. 2 Essential tasks involved in the blockchain technique for IoT.

blocks. The consensus process determines how the miners are picked and what data is included in the league (a more detailed definition of a consensus protocol is given later). The blocks are then broadcast to the network, where validation nodes verify that the received block contains valid transactions and refers to the previous block in the chain using the matching hash.

We introduced to network nodes and their functions through technology. Because the blockchain network is a peer-to-peer network, a node may be considered a peer after it connects and communicates with other nodes in the web; therefore, the proper term is peer node. For the sake of clarity, we'll refer to it as a "node" from now on. In layman's terms, a full node is any machine that hosts the primary blockchain host states and runs a complete copy of the whole blockchain ledger [33].

A customer that wishes to engage with the blockchain uses a node to connect to the network [34]. The previously mentioned miners are a subset of nodes, since all miners must also operate a fully functional node. As a result, while every miner is also a node, this is not the case for every node. This scenario is well-known due to the employment of the concrete evidence consensus method in a particular public blockchain type. Proof-of-stake [16], for example, is a sort of blockchain network that does not require extraction since it uses other decentralized consensus types. Fig. 2 summarizes essential tasks involved in the blockchain technique for IoT.

3. Objectives of the study

Wearables and other IoT-enabled home monitoring devices can help physicians keep a better eye on their patients' health. They can monitor if the patients are adhering to their treatment plans and if they require emergency medical care. Healthcare practitioners can be more watchful and proactive in their contact with patients thanks to the internet of things. IoT device data can help physicians choose the best treatment technique for their patients and get the desired results.

Apart from monitoring patients' health, hospitals may benefit from IoT devices in various ways. Medical equipment such as wheelchairs, defibrillators, nebulizers, oxygen pumps, and other monitoring equipment can be tracked in real-time using IoT devices with sensors. Medical personnel deployment at various places may also be examined in real-time. Infectious diseases are a big problem among hospital patients. IoT-enabled hygiene monitoring devices aid in the prevention of infection in patients. Asset management, such as pharmaceutical inventory control, and environmental monitoring, such as checking refrigerator temperature, can also be aided by IoT devices. With IoT-connected innovative technologies, insurance companies have several options they can use with data collected by health monitoring devices for assessment and claims processing. They will easily detect fraud claims and discover underwriting prospects using this information. In the underwriting, pricing, claims management, and risk assessment procedures, IoT devices provide transparency between insurers and consumers. Customers will have appropriate insight into the underlying logic behind every decision taken and process outcomes resulting from the internet of things information decisions in all operating processes.

3.1 Primary benefits of IoT in healthcare

The following are some of the primary benefits of IoT in healthcare:

(a) Cost Savings: IoT allows for real-time patient monitoring, reducing the number of needless doctors' appointments, hospitalizations, and readmissions.
(b) Improved Treatment: IoT allows doctors to make evidence-based, well-informed judgments while also providing complete openness.
(c) More Rapid Diagnosis: Using continuous patient monitoring and real-time data, illnesses can be diagnosed at an early stage, even before symptoms appear.
(d) Providing Proactive Medical Care: Continuous health monitoring allows for proactive medical treatment.

4. Research methodology and experimental setup

The public permissionless (commonly referred to simply as public) blockchain contains data all of which is available and transparent to the whole public. However, a few sections of the blockchain might be encrypted to protect the anonymity of participants [12]. In a public permissionless blockchain, anybody may join and function as a primary node or a miner without authorization (node). For example, in bitcoin networks, these forms of blockchains are generally provided with an economic incentive. Bitcoin, Ethereum, and Litecoin are examples of such blockchains [3,8,35]. For instance, only specified nodes can join a local Ethereum blockchain and, as a result, it's a network that's both decentralized and centralized [12]. Private blockchains are cryptocurrency networks that restrict nodes to perform transactions, executing intelligent contracts or mining. A single organization, a responsible third party, is in charge of them. It is only used for personal purposes. Only private blockchain platforms are supported by blockchain technologies like Hyperledger Fabric [36] and Ripple [37].

It's worth noting that categories like these are still up for dispute, and other meanings can be found in the literature. Healthcare is one of the industries where blockchain is thought to have a lot of promise [38]. The emphasis should be on managing data to change healthcare, integrating fragmented systems and improving EHR accuracy. Access control, data sharing, and the management of an audit trail of medical activities can all be supported by blockchain technology. It can also be used to allow drug prescription, medications and logistics, pregnancy and any risk. Provider credentials, medical billing, contracts, medical record interchange, clinical studies, and pro-government medicine are areas where blockchain technology might help.

Medical services are evolving to allow for a more patient-centered approach. Because it would allow people to have authority over their medical information, blockchain-based healthcare solutions might improve the security and dependability of patient data. These systems may also aid in the consolidation of patient data, allowing for the sharing of medical information between different healthcare facilities. Blockchain technology is very resistant to assaults and failures, and it offers a variety of access control options. As a result, blockchain is an excellent foundation for healthcare data.

In June 2018, a search of online digital libraries was done. The search query was purposefully broad in order to evaluate as many outputs as possible relating to the research study issues given in this systematic literature. Fig. 3 summarizes an approach for doing searches and selecting articles.

4.1 Selection of research

Over 610 publications were acquired from existing online collections to begin the screening process. The papers were either included or excluded from the comprehensive study based on the established criteria. There were four stages to the selection process:

- Phase 1: The findings were filtered based on the criteria for inclusion and exclusion. We looked at research from the year 2000 to the year 2020. The year 2000 was chosen as the start of the range since Bitcoin was introduced in that year, and it was the first publicized implementation of

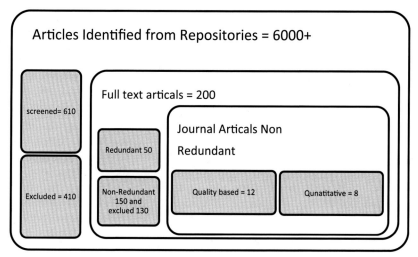

FIG. 3 Approach for doing searches and selecting articles.

blockchain technology. As a result, there was no cryptocurrency research before the year 2000.

- Phase 2: Using simply the title and abstract, we evaluated and chose the results based on their relevance to the study questions.
- Phase 3: Redundant papers were deleted from nine distinct databases. Some publications were detected, with few remaining after the duplicates were removed.
- Phase 4: A thorough reading was used to examine the remaining data in further detail. The article under consideration needed to be directly relevant to the study's subjects. The remaining results must use blockchain technology to make a unique and meaningful contribution to healthcare. Many findings were discarded since the offered concept was broad, and no more information was provided on its design or execution. Some results were also eliminated.

In total, 20 (quality based (12)+quantitative (8)) papers were included in the literature review.

The identification procedure was rigorous to guarantee that only relevant studies of high quality were examined. The Critical appraisal skills Systematic Study Process [39], which covers the appraisal of study in literature reviews, was used to regulate acquiring, selecting, and assessing data for this review.

We got data from those 20 papers after gathering the necessary publications. We started with the basics: title with id, author(s), type of publication (e.g., symposium proceedings, journal article, etc.), release year, and the number of citations (based on Google Scholar Citations [40]). After gathering essential facts, we concentrated on the two key sectors of interest in this paper: healthcare and blockchain. A representation or analysis of engineering (i.e., a system or design), algorithms or procedure, a key agreement, or a metric is a conventional offering.

We were also curious about what function or industry a blockchain in healthcare was being used in. Because blockchain technology may be used for various applications, we've made it possible to pick more than one. We discovered that blockchains are commonly utilized in the following areas: sharing of data, controlling access, health-related information audit trail management, supply chain, and others.

Keeping records is discussed in a lot of books. Health records are used by the majority, whereas medical records and personal health records are proposed or discussed by the minority. In this study, we apply these concepts to the realm of medical records. We also looked at whether the articles presented a current solution or proposed an idea with real-world application potential, including a possible set of evidence of concept implementation. The next step was to extract information regarding blockchain aspects from the evaluated articles. We identified a blockchain platform, a consensus method, and a blockchain type based on the contents of the articles. Lastly, we looked to see if any offered solutions using smart contracts. "Not defined" was assigned to any information not found in the publications. Only seven books have received a lot of attention (e.g., more than 11 citations per publication). Between 2014 and 2020, these articles were presented at conferences and published in journals. The bulk of publications were published during the preceding 2 years, which explains the low number of citations (after 2016 and 2020). There wasn't enough time to collect sources because they are new, but we may expect such articles to receive more in the future. All zero-citation articles were published in 2019 and 2020, whereas all multiple-citation papers were published in 2018. Conference proceedings make up 14 papers, journal papers make up 11 papers, patents make up five papers, and gray literature make up six papers. The bulk of the articles published in 2017 were in peer-reviewed conference proceedings. This paradigm altered in 2018 when most publications were published in peer-reviewed journals. Fig. 4 also demonstrates that the overall volume of research in 2015 was lower than the previous year.

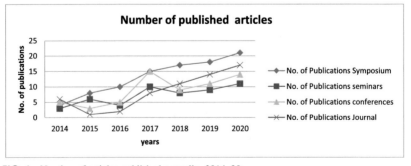

FIG. 4   Number of articles published annually, 2014–20.

The statistics for 2018 are within the first part of the year, and the review of publications papers has already nearly equaled, and much exceeded that of 2017. This demonstrates that blockchain research in healthcare is important and in the process of expanding.

We noticed that most articles do not give a workable solution after gathering data on the execution of the concepts mentioned in publications, although this tendency has begun to reverse, as shown in Figs. 4 and 5. There have been articles that offer a functioning solution since 2018, although there were none in the previous years. Since we conducted our search in 2019, there will likely be additional publications with the strategies above in 2019 and beyond.

Due to inadequate data, we intended to find technical information on cryptocurrency from the selected articles. In most cases, the blockchain components are loosely defined or not specified. Most reports are highly theoretical and do not include a prototype or a real-life application, which explains the lack of specifics. Nonetheless, we collected information on blockchain systems and consensus techniques when feasible. We also attempted to determine the sorts of blockchains utilized and whether or not the usage of a smart contract was suggested.

Not all blockchain systems enable intelligent contracts; for example, the Platform does, while Bitcoin does not. The dataset shows that the most widely utilized platforms are Bitcoin and the private blockchain Fabric, with proof-of-work being the most prevalent consensus mechanism specified in the papers. None of the documents employed a public blockchain-based forum, opting for the public to make these changes (coalition) or for a private blockchain instead. Almost half of the papers examined suggested using smart contracts to solve their problems.

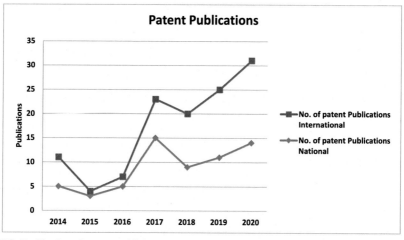

FIG. 5 Number of patents published annually, 2014–20.

The essential component of our comprehensive study was the examiners' score to determine the quality of the examined articles and the relevance of cryptocurrency usage, i.e., how bitcoin usage is presented in the study. Fig. 4 shows the average overall score for each publishing type by year and a trendline that shows the average overall score for all articles published in that year. In 2014 and 2015, fewer categories of writings with a relatively high score were published. Periodicals were published in 2014, yet the overall quality of the publications was slightly lower than for the year before. The quality of the most recent nine papers released in 2018 had improved.

Fig. 5 shows the score for each patent. A more in-depth analysis, as well as total scores, is offered below.

Compared to conference and gray literature publications, the data demonstrate that patents and journal papers are of better quality. It should be emphasized, however, that the variances are not significant. It is also worth noting that, according to Fig. 4, the overall quality of conference papers is somewhat declining, but the actual quality of scientific journals is slightly improving each year.

5. Results and discussion

This section contains a description of the data gathered from the reviewed articles. Research questions were proposed, and they are covered below.

RQ1: How well-established is blockchain in healthcare, and how has it evolved?

This systematic review looked for papers on blockchain technology in healthcare published between 2000 and 2020. All the documents that were found to be acceptable for analysis were all published after 2015, showing that the technology is relatively new and is just now making its way into the healthcare profession. We found 20 articles throughout the assessment process, but only seven of them showed a fully constructed and deployed solution, as shown in Fig. 3. Most publications include ideas that could be adopted but have rarely been so.

The established solutions were released in 2018 and 2019, indicating that blockchain in healthcare is becoming more popular. Another sign of blockchain's application in healthcare throughout time is represented in Fig. 2, which shows that more articles on the issue have been produced each year. We undertook this search in 2019, and the only first half of 2019 is included. During this time, nine articles on health applications were released. In 2017, there were just two patents published, but in 2016, there were three or more. The majority of publications (11+) were released in 2019.

RQ2: What are the latest blockchain research trends in healthcare?

The topics covered in the assessed papers reflect current research trends in healthcare. As shown in Figs. 3 to 5, the results show that the majority of the periodicals employ blockchain techniques of data sharing, health records, and access control. Furthermore, blockchain is seldom utilized in logistics, audit trail governance, or other scenarios such as medicine prescription administration and auditing. We may claim that cryptocurrency, as a decentralized technology, is therefore appropriately utilized in the examined literature in the field of healthcare decision models [35]. According to the International Joint Committee of the Radiological, Operational Responsibilities, and Medical IT Industry [38], there are still numerous applications for artificial intelligence in healthcare, such as medical billing and generally pro medications.

RQ3: What are the components of blockchain technology that are employed in medical publications?

We looked at the aspects of blockchain that were utilized or suggested in the articles and analyzed the contributions. The majority of the papers included a structural design, such as a framework, architecture, or model, for application in healthcare and using blockchain technology.

A novel algorithm or technique was offered in far fewer papers. A novel consensus technique and a metric for measuring healthcare distributed apps were also described in one report [8]. We discovered that writers are very few when looking for particular blockchain aspects, either utilized or recommended, in the research. This might be because the study we found is very theoretical, or it could be because these elements can be changed to better fit needs, and the writers did not want to prescribe a standard answer. According to the sources that identified the blockchain parts, the most popular blockchain platforms are Bitcoin and Ultra Fabric.

A private or a coalition (open make these changes) blockchain was utilized in the nine articles that defined the blockchain type. This is expected in healthcare, since having control, access, and publishing to the blockchain is desired, while writing is undesirable. Healthcare is an industry in which transaction speed is critical, yet real proof of work is a very slow popular algorithm.

The actual proof of work is also seldom employed in consortium or private chains where the participants are well-known (in this example, physicians, people, health insurers, and so on), and trust is more easily established. Cooperative or proprietary chains are often more centralized than open networks, where somebody can be a node and real proof of work is the primary consensus mechanism. Finally, the real explanation of the work method is a highly computational one. It would be unfeasible for hospitals to build big computer centers only to mine transaction information. We were astonished to see the actual proof of work utilized so frequently for all of these reasons. The reason was they work around all of the stated solid proof of work restrictions; we anticipated techniques like confirmation or factual evidence to be far more popular. We believe real evidence of work was viral in the investigation because, as we saw in the preceding part, health applications are still in their early stages. The program's innovators sought existing approaches for inspiration. Cryptocurrencies, which use actual proof of work, are the most well-known and well-publicized public blockchain.

In addition, 13 articles stated (clearly) that smart contracts will be used in their proposal. It is surprising to see that less than half of the recommendations didn't include an intelligent contract aspect. They also provide blockchain applications in healthcare as a new functionality and possibilities, such as limiting access and automating specific operations. In conclusion, the scope of blockchain elements employed in the research is vast, as one may assume. Researchers create networks with various participant constraints to provide the network with greater control and access and record production. Bitcoin and the private blockchain Circuit, both of which feature intelligent contracts, are the most regularly utilized platforms in the selected publications. Smart contracts provide a lot of capability to a network, but they don't appear to be used as frequently as one might expect.

The essential premise of logistic regression is that the linear model has well-fit data if the discrepancies among observable and projected values are modest. The goodness-of-fit is a mathematical model that may explain and account for the disparity between observed and expected data. To put it another way, goodness-of-fit is a statistical hypothesis test that determines how well sample data fits a normality test from a population. When it comes to regression analysis, one common misperception is that a low R-squared number is necessarily a bad thing. This is not the case. Some large datasets or topics of research, for example, have an intrinsically higher proportion of variability.

As a result of Fig. 6, we believe that expanding the usage of intelligent contracts and introducing less limiting consensus protocols should be the key focus of future research and improved inclusion of distributed ledger technology in healthcare.

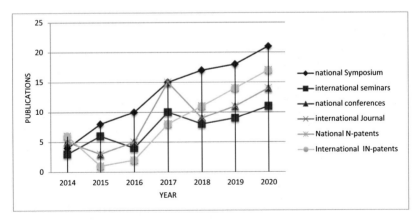

FIG. 6 Number of publications annually, 2014–20.

6.   Conclusions and future work

The existing blockchain-correlated features in healthcare were studied in this chapter. Due to the obviously sensitive nature of the data being processed and handled, blockchain technology has significant potential for usage in healthcare. The study's goal was to determine the present state of blockchain research and its use in the healthcare industry. We developed study questions and used a predetermined technique to restrict the evaluated literature down to 20 papers to accomplish this goal. These were then dissected further. For documents between 2000 and 2020, we examined seven relevant internet resources.

Two reviewers looked through the 20 papers for the in-depth examination. We gathered data in response to our study questions and evaluated the articles using predetermined criteria.

According to our data, public blockchain research and its use in healthcare are on the rise. Blockchain studies in healthcare show that it is usually utilized for information sharing, patient records, and password protection; whereas, it is seldom employed for other situations like logistics or medicine prescribing management. As a result, much of blockchain's potential remains untapped. The majority of research in healthcare uses blockchain technology to propose a new framework, design, or paradigm. Furthermore, technical data regarding the blockchain features employed are frequently omitted, such as the blockchain, consensus method, blockchain type, or usage of payment systems.

As shown in Figs. 3 to 5, the results show that the majority of the periodicals employ blockchain techniques of data sharing, health records, and access control. Furthermore, blockchain is seldom used in logistics, audit trail governance, or other scenarios such as medicine prescription administration and auditing. We may claim that cryptocurrency, as a decentralized technology, is therefore appropriately utilized in the examined literature in the field of healthcare decision models [35]. According to the International Joint Committee of the Radiological, Operational Responsibilities, and Medical IT Industry [38], there are still numerous applications for AI in healthcare, such as medical billing and generally pro medications.

Figs. 3 and 4 show importance of analysis which gave everything being equal to factors. The most evident distinction between values is that adjusted R-squared considers and tests several independent factors against the stock index, whereas R-squared doesn't seem to. As a result, many investors prefer to utilize modified values since they can be more accurate. Additionally, investors may learn more about a stock's impact by using the modified R-squared model to assess numerous independent factors. R-squared, on the other hand, has several drawbacks. The fact that R-squared cannot be utilized to determine whether or not the coefficient estimations are correct is one of the most critical limitations of using this model.

As the capacity of modern computing devices increases and their cost decreases, intelligent systems, and hence soft computing approaches, are becoming increasingly significant. Intelligent systems must use complicated algorithms to make complex judgments and pick the optimal conclusion from various options. This necessitates high processing power and huge storage space, both of which have lately become affordable to so many research institutes, universities, and technical institutions. The importance of adopting soft computing approaches and constructing intelligent systems has never been more significant due to the power and awareness of the internet of things (IoT) concept.

A study of state-of-the-art blockchain research in healthcare is undertaken in this comprehensive study. The results are analyzed with a quantitative overview, an evaluation of the acquired data and its attributes, and literary quality assessment results. Finally, there is a discussion of the analysis and findings. According to the findings, blockchain technology research in healthcare is increasing, and is mainly utilized for data exchange, health record management, and other applications.

Blockchain networks, in particular, might be more widely employed since they allow for the automation of activities on a blockchain platform. Most studies could additionally give a working prototype or at the very least outline the implementation specifics of their suggestions. Further study is needed, since blockchains are relatively new technology in healthcare, and new ways to use them are continuously being discovered and investigated. To summarize, blockchain should be employed in instances where it is both reasonable and necessary.

References

[1] M. Engelhardt, Hitching healthcare to the chain: an introduction to blockchain technology in the healthcare sector, Technol. Innov. Manag. Rev. 7 (2017) 22–34.

[2] B. Bhushan, C. Sahoo, P. Sinha, A. Khamparia, Unification of blockchain and internet of things (BIoT): requirements, working model, challenges and future directions, Wirel. Netw. 27 (1) (2021) 55–90.

[3] B. Bhushan, A. Khamparia, K.M. Sagayam, S.K. Sharma, M.A. Ahad, N.C. Debnath, Blockchain for smart cities: a review of architectures, integration trends and future research directions, Sustain. Cities Soc. 61 (2020) 102360.

[4] J. Yli-Huumo, D. Ko, S. Choi, S. Park, K. Smolander, Where is current research on blockchain technology?—a systematic review, PLoS One 11 (2016) e0163477.

[5] G. Isaac, Museums and the revitalization of endangered languages and knowledge, in: Indigenous Languages and the Promise of Archives, 2021, p. 429.

[6] H. Jo, H. Park, H. Shefrin, Bitcoin and sentiment, J. Futures Mark. 40 (12) (2020) 1861–1879.

[7] M. Mettler, Blockchain technology in healthcare: the revolution starts here, in: Proceedings of the 2016 IEEE 18th International Conference on e-Health Networking, Applications and Services (Healthcom), Munich, Germany, 14–17 September, 2016, pp. 1–3.

[8] P. Zhang, D.C. Schmidt, J. White, G. Lenz, Blockchain technology use cases in healthcare, in: Advances in Computers, Elsevier, Amsterdam, The Netherlands, 2018.

[9] K. Christidis, M. Devetsikiotis, Blockchains and smart contracts for the internet of things, IEEE Access 4 (2016) 2292–2303.

[10] S. Singh, N. Singh, Blockchain: future of financial and cyber security, in: Proceedings of the 2016 2nd International Conference on Contemporary Computing and Informatics (IC3I), Noida, India, 14–17 December, 2016, pp. 463–467.

[11] S. Nakamoto, Bitcoin: A Peer-to-Peer Electronic Cash System, Portal Unicamp, Campinas, Brazil, 2008.

[12] Z. Zheng, S. Xie, H. Dai, X. Chen, H. Wang, An overview of blockchain technology: architecture, consensus, and future trends, in: Proceedings of the 2017 IEEE International Congress on Big Data (BigData Congress), Boston, MA, USA, 11–14 December, 2017, pp. 557–564.

[13] E. Karafiloski, A. Mishev, Blockchain solutions for big data challenges: a literature review, in: Proceedings of the IEEE EUROCON 2017—17th International Conference on Smart Technologies, Ohrid, Macedonia, 6–8 July, 2017, pp. 763–768.

[14] T. Ahram, A. Sargolzaei, S. Sargolzaei, J. Daniels, B. Amaba, Blockchain technology innovations, in: Proceedings of the 2017 IEEE Technology Engineering Management Conference (TEMSCON), Santa Clara, CA, USA, 8 June, 2017, pp. 137–141.

[15] M. Conoscenti, A. Vetro, J.C.D. Martin, Blockchain for the internet of things: a systematic literature review, in: Proceedings of the 2016 IEEE/ACS 13th International Conference of Computer Systems and Applications (AICCSA), Agadir, Morocco, 29 November–2 December, 2016, pp. 1–6.

[16] B. Holmes, Blockchain Technology Battles Counterfeiting, 2015, (Cited 30 January 2017). Available from: http://bravenewcoin.com/news/blockchain-technology-battles-counterfeiting/.

[17] I. Allison, Chronicled Launches Blockchain-Registered Supply Chain and Pharmaceutical Packaging, 2016, (Internet). (Cited 30 January 2017). Available from: http://www.ibtimes.co.uk/chronicled-launches-blockchain-registeredsupply-chain-pharmaceutical-packaging-1592220.

[18] M. del Castillo, Hyperledger Project Explores Fighting Counterfeit Drugs with Blockchain, 2016, (Internet). (Cited 30 January 2017). Available from: http://www.coindesk.com/hyperledger-counterfeit-drugs-blockchain/.

[19] IEEE Launches World's First Virtual Blockchain Workshop Dedicated to Advancing Health-Tech for Humanity, 2016. (Cited 30 January 2017). Available from: http://standards.ieee.org/news/2016/virtual_blockchain.html.

[20] Blockchain for Pharma, 2017. (Internet). (Cited 30 January 2017). Available from: http://beyondstandards.ieee.org/tag/blockchain-for-pharma/.

[21] The BlockRx Project, 2016. (Cited 30 January 2017.) Available from: http://www.blockrx.com/.

[22] N. Zadbuke, S. Shahi, B. Gulecha, A. Padalkar, M. Thube, Recent trends and future of pharmaceutical packaging technology, J. Pharm. Bioallied Sci. 5 (2) (2013) 98–110.

[23] M. Jamrógiewicz, Application of the near-infrared spectroscopy in pharmaceutical technology, J. Pharm. Biomed. Anal. 66 (2012) 1–10.

[24] M.J. Culzoni, P. Dwivedi, M.D. Green, P.N. Newton, F.M. Fernández, Ambient mass spectrometry technologies for the detection of falsified drugs, Med. Chem. Commun. 5 (1) (2014) 9–19.

[25] S.N. Pal, S. Olsson, E.G. Brown, The monitoring medicines project is multinational pharmacovigilance and public health project, Drug Saf. 38 (4) (2015) 319–328.

[26] N. Richards, I. Hudson, UK medicines regulation: responding to current challenges, Br. J. Clin. Pharmacol. 82 (6) (2016) 1471–1476.

[27] N.F. Fayzrakhmanov, Fighting trafficking of falsified and substandard medicinal products in Russia, Int. J. Risk Saf. Med. 27 (Suppl. 1) (2015) S37–S40.

[28] R.N. Das, F.D. Egitto, H. Lin, Anti-counterfeit, miniaturized, and advanced electronic substrates for medical device applications, in: 2013 IEEE 63rd Electronic Components and Technology Conference, IEEE, 2013, pp. 523–528.

[29] WHO, Safety and Security on the Internet: Challenges and Advances in the Member States, WHO, 2011. (Internet). (Cited 5 March 2013). Available from: http://www.who.int/goe/publications/goe_security_web.pdf.

[30] A. Fittler, G. Bősze, L. Botz, Evaluating aspects of online medication safety in long-term follow-up of 136 internet pharmacies: illegal rogue online pharmacies flourish and are long-lived, J. Med. Internet Res. 15 (9) (2013) e199.

[31] R. Fadlallah, F. El-Jardali, F. Annan, H. Azzam, E.A. Akl, Strategies and systems-level interventions to combat or prevent drug counterfeiting: a systematic review of evidence beyond effectiveness, Pharm. Med. 30 (5) (2016) 263–276.

[32] A.S. Kesselheim, J. Avorn, A. Sarpatwari, The high cost of prescription drugs in the United States: origins and prospects for reform, JAMA 316 (8) (2016) 858–871.

[33] G. Orizio, S. Rubinelli, P.J. Schulz, S. Domenighini, M. Bressanelli, L. Caimi, et al., "Save 30% if you buy today." Online pharmacies and the enhancement of peripheral thinking in consumers, Pharmacoepidemiol. Drug Saf. 19 (9) (2010) 970–976.

[34] B. Naughton, L. Roberts, S. Dopson, S. Chapman, D. Brindley, Effectiveness of medicines authentication technology to detect counterfeit, recalled and expired medicines: a two-stage quantitative secondary care study, BMJ Open 6 (12) (2016) e013837.

[35] L. Li, Technology designed to combat fakes in the global supply chain, Bus. Horiz. 56 (2) (2013) 167–177. PWC, Digitization in Pharma: Gaining an Edge in Operations, 2016, (Cited 30 January 2017). Available from: http://www.strategyand.pwc.com/reports/digitization-in-pharma.

[36] Press Release: ITU Releases 2016 ICT Figures, International Telecommunication Union, 2016. (Cited 30 January 2017). Available from: http://www.itu.int/en/mediacentre/pages/2016-PR30.aspx.

[37] H. Isaiah, Information and Communication Technology in Combating Counterfeit Drugs, 2012. S. ur Rehman, R. Ur Rasool, M.S. Ayub, S. Ullah, A. Kamal, Q.M. Rajpoot, et al., Reliable identification of counterfeit medicine using camera-equipped mobile phones, in: IEEE, 2011, pp. 273–279.

[38] B.A. Liang, T. Mackey, Searching for safety: addressing search engine, website, and provider accountability for illicit online drug sales, Am. J. Law Med. 35 (1) (2009) 125–184.

[39] B.A. Liang, T. Mackey, Direct-to-consumer advertising with interactive internet media: global regulation and public health issues, JAMA 305 (8) (2011) 824–825.

[40] A.H. Masoumi, M. Yu, A. Nagurney, A supply chain generalized network oligopoly model for pharmaceuticals under brand differentiation and perishability, Transport. Res. E-Log. 48 (4) (2012) 762–780.

Chapter 11

Applications of blockchain technology for improving security in the internet of things (IoT)

Qasem Abu Al-Haija[a], Mohammad Alnabhan[a], Eyad Saleh[a], and Mohammad Al-Omari[b]

[a]Department of Computer Science/Cybersecurity, King Hussein School of Computing Sciences, Princess Sumaya University for Technology (PSUT), Amman, Jordan, [b]Department of Business Information Technology, King Talal School of Business Technology, Princess Sumaya University for Technology (PSUT), Amman, Jordan

Abbreviations

ACE	authentication and authorization for constrained environments
BC-IoT	blockchain and IoT
BCT	blockchain technology
BTC	bitcoin
CC	certificateless cryptography
CHs	cluster heads
CPU	central processing unit
DNS	domain name system
DTLS	datagram transport layer security
DTM	distributed throughput management
IoT	internet of things
MAC	media access control
MLP	multilayer perceptron
OBM	overlay block manager
ODT	optimizable decision trees
OSCAR	object security architecture for the internet of things
PoS	proof of stake
PoW	proof of work

Blockchain Technology Solutions for the Security of IoT-Based Healthcare Systems.
https://doi.org/10.1016/B978-0-323-99199-5.00003-3

SHA-256   secure hash algorithm 256-bit
SSL   secure sockets layer
SSN   shallow neural network

1. Introduction and preliminaries

A blockchain is a public, decentralized, and distributed database of records (i.e., blocks) connected through a network. It acts as a ledger where observers can verify digital events (e.g., transactions) taking place at any time in the past or present without a trusted third-party authority [1,2]. Moreover, it offers a secure and democratic consentaneous way of growing the database over time while keeping the data immutable and irrefutable [3].

1.1 Background

The anatomy of a blockchain consists of nodes that represent computer participants over a network, as shown in Fig. 1. Each node has a full copy of the ledger (i.e., blocks). A block consists of multiple transactions (i.e., data) [4]. A transaction is recorded in the ledger when initiated by one of the nodes by creating a block with a hash using an algorithm (e.g., SHA 256), and broadcasting it to all the nodes [5,6]. Receiving nodes need to verify the sent block and, once accepted, add it to the chain of blocks [7]. The blocks are linked together chronologically and cannot be modified after they are recorded without writing the entire ledger history again [8]. Nodes use a defined algorithm to reach a consensus on what ledger version is true and accurate [9].

The history of blockchain technology goes back to 1982, where it all started with a dissertation written by David Chaum titled "Computer Systems Established, Maintained, and Trusted by Mutually Suspicious Groups." Additional effort was made in 1991–92 by Stuart Haber, W. Scott Stornetta, and Dave Bayer to increase the security and efficiency of a chain of blocks [5]. The first noteworthy blockchain design was conceived in 2008 by the brilliant yet unknown Satoshi Nakamoto [2]. Satoshi enhanced the blockchain design by

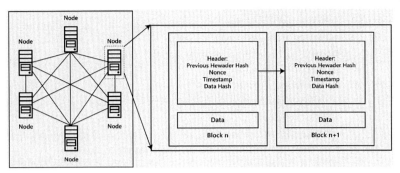

FIG. 1   The anatomy of a blockchain.

implementing a hashcash-like method of blocks' timestamps to eliminate the trusted party signer requirement. This method requires a participant to spend some CPU time to show that it has done work to be considered legitimate, this concept is referred to as proof of work, and represents the consensus component in a Blockchain structure [2,6].

Months after Satoshi's design, an implementation using blockchain technology was born: Bitcoin. According to Satoshi, Bitcoin was a peer-to-peer electronic cash system that would eliminate the need for a trusted intermediary such as a bank [2]. He claimed that trust could be established by cryptographic signatures and challenging mathematical puzzles to be solved by nodes (i.e., proof of work) to prove commitment to the network and legitimacy. However, the validity and security of the system depend on maintaining a majority of "honest" nodes; the reason being that in case of the existence of attacker blocks or different arrival times (i.e., race conditions), the nodes adjust and recover by looking for the longest chain from the majority of nodes, maintaining the accuracy of the block records. In Satoshi's implementation, some of the participant nodes are called miners; these nodes validate any new block that needs to be added to the ledger. The miners race to validate these blocks due to the incentive they earn once a validated block done by them is accepted and added to the blockchain [10].

The workflow of a bitcoin transaction occurs as follows. The sender (i.e., owner) of the Bitcoin sends the transaction to all nodes in the network. Nodes create a block and put the transaction in it, and then they compete in solving the mathematical puzzle, and once a node finds the solution, it broadcasts the block with the answer to all other nodes [11]. Nodes will accept the block only if the solution is correct and all transactions in the block are valid (i.e., the sender has sufficient funds) and have not been spent before. Accepting a block means recording it and linking it with the previous block. This becomes the new ledger until proven otherwise [12].

The popularity of blockchain technology is increasing fast. It has gained such great attention and traction in the past decade that some tech enthusiasts describe it as the greatest invention since the rise of the internet [12]. Blockchain is a technology that is not limited to cryptocurrency; it has uses in many systems that require security, immutability, cost reduction, and speed [13]. For example, blockchain technology can be used in elections so that everyone is guaranteed to have cast their vote securely. It starts by giving every registered voter a digital token or identity, voters can cast their votes online, and the blockchain will have a verifiable record of them taking action at a specific time and location [14]. It becomes nearly impossible to tamper with the votes. As a result, this will reduce fraud, cost, and time spent, and could increase voter turnout.

Furthermore, blockchain technology can be utilized with a smart contract, which is a piece of software that can be programmed to execute contract terms contingent on predefined conditions automatically [15]. The contract could be a financial contract, such as stock options, or non-financial such as marriage certificates [16]. The utilities of intelligent contracts are endless, and this area will become very prosperous shortly, especially with the Ethereum smart contract platform, where people can execute any intelligent contract on the Ethereum network [15].

1.2 Motivation

New talks and discussions have been rising about moving the domain name system (DNS) service to blockchain. Other voices raise the point about secure sockets layer (SSL) certificates and certificate authorities and the need to be on the blockchain for validity, visibility, and consensus. Even legal enthusiasts contend that notarizing legal documents should be done through blockchains to preserve anonymity and privacy. It is pretty clear where the train is heading. Blockchain technology is forming the future, and the more widely it is adopted, the more attention and enhancements need to be applied to the technology because it will be a target for bad actors [17].

Blockchain technology is indeed secure as it uses digital cryptography for verification and consensus to battle fraud and false transactions [18]. The fact that the transaction data is immutable and irrefutable, and the nature of it is decentralized, which means that every node is autonomous and can hold the entire actual ledger, makes it truly powerful and not easy to hack or break. On the other hand, blockchain technology does have some weaknesses in specific scenarios. For example, an assumption is made that at least 51% of the nodes have to be honest to maintain integrity [19]. If this is not the case, the validity of the system breaks down. Another issue is the potential use of weak cryptographic encryption that could jeopardize the system, especially in the era of quantum computing [18].

1.3 Major contributions

The main contributions of this chapter can be summarized as follows:

- We provide a systematic review of blockchain technology characterizing the principles of blockchain technology along with its secure transactions.
- We provide analytical summarization for the most recent trends in blockchain security, characterizing the three major blockchain security applications including cryptocurrency, the internet of things (IoT), and healthcare.
- We provide a thorough analysis of the security of blockchain technology including blockchain authentication and trust management, blockchain attacks and vulnerability vectors, several security algorithms, protocols of blockchain (such as consensus theorem, hashing, smart contrast, proof of work, and proof of stake), the security services of blockchains and the cybersecurity triad, and the potential security applications of blockchains.

- We provide a comprehensive assessment of using blockchain technology to improve IoT security by evaluating the security of IoT, blockchain competence for improved IoT security, and blockchain integration into the IoT

1.4 Chapter organization

In addition to the aforementioned discussion about the principles and fundamentals of blockchain technology along with its secure transactions, the motivation of this chapter, and the summary of the major contributions of this chapter; the remaining parts of this chapter are organized as follows. Section 2 provides the most recent trends and active blockchain security applications, structured into three major subsections including cryptocurrency, the internet of things, and healthcare. Section 3 presents the security of blockchain technology by investigating the robustness of authentication via blockchain technology in which the nodes are devoid of any arbitrator or third-party and the communications can be certified by the nodes themselves; a discussion of blockchains and its main attack and vulnerability vectors (such as ransomware attacks, DDoS attacks, 51% attacks, endpoint vulnerabilities, insider attacks, smart contracts vulnerabilities, and publicity vulnerabilities); discussion of blockchains and the cybersecurity triad; and discussion of potential security applications. Section 4 provides comprehensive detail about the blockchain technology for improved IoT security including a security evaluation of IoT, blockchain competence for improved IoT security, and blockchain integration into the IoT. Finally, Section 5 concludes the chapter.

2. Current trends in blockchain security

Blockchain is widely used to achieve security in several domains, such as cryptocurrency [20,21], healthcare [22–24], and the internet of things [25,26]. We discuss below some of the approaches in those domains.

2.1 Cryptocurrency

Al-Haija et al. [20] propose a classification model for early detection of ransomware payments for heterogeneous bitcoin networks. Basically, two supervised machine learning algorithms were utilized to recognize data patterns and hence construct the classification model, namely optimizable decision trees (ODT) and shallow neural network (SSN). SSN is a feedforward multilayer perceptron (MLP) neural network that is widely used in pattern recognition and classification tasks in different artificial intelligence and machine learning applications. Moreover, ODT is widely used in classification tasks due to its high accuracy. Therefore, SSN is used at the detection stage to flag whether the ransomware exists or not. After which, both ODT and SSN are used to classify ransomware attacks into three families: (1) ransomware—Montreal family, (2) ransomware—Padua family, and (3) ransomware—Princeton family.

2.2 Internet of things

Several approaches have been proposed by researchers to increase security in the IoT domain by using blockchain. For instance, ELIB—efficient lightweight integrated blockchain—represents a security model for IoT that is applied to a smart home environment [25]. The model is basically built on the concept of replacing the resource-intensive proof of work (PoW) and proof of stake (PoS) mechanisms that are mainly used by cryptocurrencies with a consensus-period approach that restricts the number of new blocks added via the cluster heads (CHs). The consensus technique has two main goals. First, to restrict the number of newly created blocks by an arbitrarily selected block generator; and second, to increase the arbitrary nature of block creation by forcing every overlay block manager (OBM) to wait for an arbitrary time window before creating the new block. To avoid the restriction of the throughput caused by the traditional consensus algorithms, ELIB introduces distributed throughput management (DTM) as a replacement of the throughput technique that is used in a typical blockchain (BC) setup. The main goal of DTM is to be able to handle better throughput while verifying that α stays in a particular range (α min, α max). Finally, ELIB utilizes certificateless cryptography (CC) as ID-based cryptography to effectively authenticate the IoT devices.

Alternatively, IoT Chain [26] proposes a scheme for secure and authorized access to IoT resources that combines object security architecture (OSCAR) for the internet of things [27] and authentication and authorization for constrained environments (ACE) [28]. The basic idea is to make the authorization phase of ACE more flexible and reliable by replacing the authorization server with an authorization blockchain. To have a successful attack on the consensus protocol of the blockchain, the attacker needs to control at least 51% of the blockchain before gaining access to tokens. The main improvement of IoT Chain over ACE is that in IoT Chain the access tokens of the clients are generated based on the access rights described by the resource owner that are stored in smart contracts; whereas, in ACE, the tokens are transmitted to the client.

Furthermore, IoT Chain uses OSCAR [27] to generate personal keys that are transmitted to resource servers over a datagram transport layer security (DTLS) channel in order to use them to encrypt and protect the resources. It is worth mentioning that different resources might be encrypted using different keys even if the keys are generated on the same resource server, mainly to enforce access control and privileges. When a client requests access to a certain resource, it sends a request to join the key distribution group associated with the desired resource; afterwards, the key server checks the contract on the blockchain to verify if the client is authorized or not.

2.3 Healthcare

Recently, blockchain has received wide attention regarding being used in securing several healthcare applications, such as public healthcare management, drug prevention, and clinical trials [24,28–35]. Researchers think that blockchain can help in bridging the gap between privacy and the accessibility of electronic healthcare records [31]. We discuss below some of the proposals in that direction.

The Ancile project has introduced a privacy-preserving framework that sends the actual query in a private transaction over HTTPS while creating and storing the hash of the data reference. Similarly, JP Morgan's Quorum [36] follows a similar approach but lacks some elements such as the proxy re-encryption that Ancile uses to streamline the secure transfer of EHRs. Another advantage of proxy re-encryption is that it allows Ancile to store small, encrypted records as well as keys directly on the blockchain, which makes it easier to transfer medical records.

One design aspect of Ancile is that data ownership is the right of the patient. Therefore, the system does not include any form of mining incentive. Finally, smart contacts are used to manage the access control of the different parties on the blockchain, namely the patients, providers, and third parties.

Esposito et al. proposed that when a new treatment or medical data for a patient comes in, a new block will be created and distributed to all peers in the network [24]. After majority approval of the new block, it will be inserted into the chain. If the approval is not achieved, a fork is created, and the block is considered an orphan and not added to the main chain. Tampering with the data is easily detected because you can't tamper with the data in one block without affecting the subsequent blocks. They also proposed that the medical data has to be obfuscated or encrypted before placing it into the block.

3. Security of blockchain technology

Blockchain technology is a global predominant cybernetic digital database that stores time-stamped bunches of data in unchallengeable virtual blocks that are sequentially interconnected. Blockchain utilizes peer-to-peer (P2P) network nodes devoid of any arbitrator or third party where the communications can be certified by the nodes themselves. Indeed, the main reason that blockchains are an attractive solution for numerous industrial applications such as supply chain, healthcare, financial services, and government entities, is that blockchain is new and different from the traditional distributed ledger technology (DLT). DLT can be employed in commercial applications to enhance the security and efficiency of data sharing and transactions processing between several entities. Whereas, the genius of blockchain relies on its capability to authenticate communications among the different communication parties and then accumulate

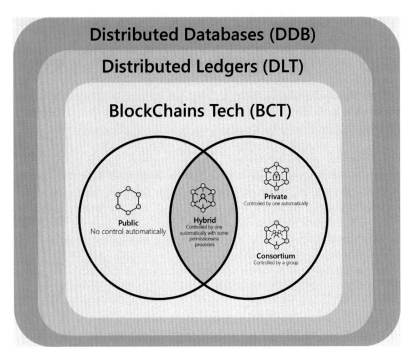

FIG. 2 Blockchain's relationship with databases.

the communication records perpetually on a decentralized network; such a dedicated process makes it tremendously hard to forge any of the blockchain ledger records. Fig. 2 illustrates the architecture for blockchain's relationship with distributed databases in the e-security world (a clear distinction between blockchain and DLT). Furthermore, blockchains are distinctive from other DLTs because of their structures, arrangements, requirements, realistic implementation, the utilization of tokens, and the use of multiple approaches to realize consensuses such as proof of stake (PoS) and proof of work (PoW).

3.1 Blockchains and ransomware attacks

Even though blockchain technology has demonstrated extraordinary proficiency in securing diverse industrial applications (financial systems are a great example), their transactions are susceptible to several kinds of ransomware attack. Ransomware is a malware-type cyberattack that can block the user from accessing their own data/records/screens. The basic idea of blockchain ransomware is to access the user data and encrypt them; subsequently, the data became unreadable to the user, and then the user will not be able to decrypt his/her data, and therefore, the user is requested to pay a ransom [33]. Ransomware is a comparatively innovative cyberattack launched originally against the

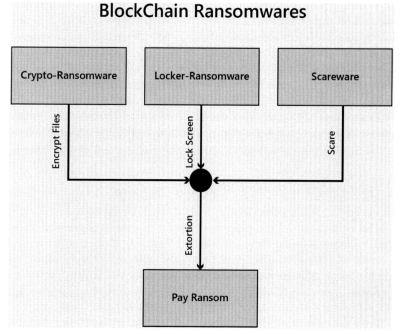

FIG. 3 Main ransomware types against blockchain.

cryptocurrency data of Bitcoin consumers [37]. Principally, according to the functionality of the attack, ransomware cyberattacks can be categorized into three families, as denoted in Fig. 3.

The three types of ransomware attacks can be defined as follows:

- Crypto-ransomware: This attack employs cryptographic techniques while accessing the private data/files for the authorized users. In other words, once the attacker has reached the user (victim) data, he/she encrypts the private data/files and then demands that the victim (who needs to get back the data) pay a ransom. Such attacks are classified as extremely intimidating ransomware attacks, and consequently, they have to be discovered and treated early [37].
- Locker-ransomware: This attack employs locking/bot techniques while accessing the private data/screens for the authorized users. In other words, once the attacker has reached the user (victim) screens, he/she will have control over the user's screen and then demands that the victim (who needs to get back the screen) pay a ransom [37].
- Scareware: This attack employs scaring techniques that influence the victims to download/buy harmful or inadequate programs such as fake antivirus. Usually, the attacker uses pop-up ads and social engineering attacks to scare the users to take advantage of their fear and asks for a ransom to be paid [38].

While encipherment/decipherment techniques are principal and commonly implemented in blockchains, networks, and information security systems to provide data confidentiality and privacy, such approaches can be used to prevent ransomware attacks targeting user's data/files/screens [39]. Indeed, it has been declared that over 500 types of ransomware attack can be launched against blockchain data; and thus, solutions are required to address the detection and classification problem for the different ransomware families [40]. For that reason, recently, researchers have devoted plenty of effort to developing identification and classification systems to detect, mitigate, and prevent such dangerous cyberattacks using machine and deep learning techniques [20,41–45].

3.2 Blockchains and DDoS attacks

Distributed denial of service (DDoS) attack is a malicious endeavor to interrupt the usual data stream of the target host (server, organization, service, or network) by overwhelming the victim with a flood of malignant traffic. Like any traditional network, blockchains are vulnerable to such cyberattacks and are not impenetrable to this hail of communication traffic and transactions. DDoS attacks severely affect blockchains as they can slow down the processing of blockchain transactions even if they don't surpass the total transactions of which the network is capable, or they can ruin the access if they surpassed the transactions total. Fig. 4 demonstrates how a DDoS attack is launched against a blockchain-enabled cloud.

3.3 Blockchains and endpoint vulnerabilities

In modern networks, endpoints are remote computers for personnel or clients, and represent barrier blocks that are dynamically processed. Due to the general orientation of cybersecurity inclinations such as zero-trust pushing the focus inward, governments and corporations should continuously contemplate susceptibilities and weaknesses of the endpoint devices. To this, blockchains are no exception, as they also have endpoint devices. In blockchain networks, all

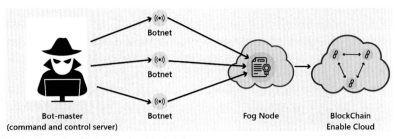

FIG. 4 Example of DDoS against blockchain.

nodes ate endpoint devices, by definition, and thus they are susceptible to false transactions/communications to the chain by attackers. Blockchains are usually composed of a sufficient number of nodes in which compromising a single or more node (a portion of nodes in the blockchain network) will not influence the reliability of the other blocks in the chain. The severity of endpoint attacks depends on the nature of nodes employed in the design of the blockchain network:

- For a blockchain network with homogenous nodes, a deficiency of a single system/node is a deficiency in systems/nodes.
- For a blockchain network with heterogeneous nodes, the node heterogeneity offers more alternatives for discovering weaknesses/susceptibilities.

3.4   Blockchains and insider threats

Insider threats are security risks that arise from the persons with legal access to the institution's data and resources. Insider threats have always been one of the most critical challenges to cybersecurity. Security analysis and planning phases must consider prevention and detection techniques to countermeasures insiders' attacks. This will reduce impact level of these attacks on institutions. According to the most recent security studies by Cybersecurity Insiders [46], it has been reported that 99% of organizations believe they are susceptible to insider threats. In blockchain, new sorts of insider threats originate from the users (miners) who update the chain by adding new blocks to the chain. The key facilitating risks are the large number of actors with extreme access rights (37%), a growing amount of devices with privileges to key resources (36%), and the accumulative complication of information technology (35%). Although blockchain uses proof-of-work (PoW) techniques to stimulate blockchain nodes to maintain data integrity to safeguard the accuracy of blockchain communications and transactions, blockchain is still vulnerable to a well-known attack, known as a 51% attack [47]. A 51% attack is a blockchain attack caused by a cluster of actors (miners) who have compromised the majority of the nodes in the chain network (more than 50%) so that they can disrupt the registering of new blocks in the chain. The process of a 51% attack is demonstrated in Fig. 5.

3.5   Blockchains and publicity vulnerabilities

Blockchains are distinctively connected through a public decentralized topology span across an external network of nodes. Such a structure will keep the blocks of the chain publicly visible, while the used data employed to process their transactions are not public. However, in many cases, the users of a blockchain network fulfill their transactions using a web explorer or browser, which

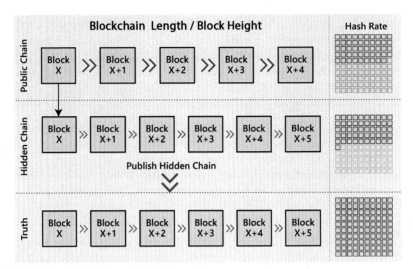

FIG. 5 How 51% attacks on blockchain work.

might unintentionally make their private information vulnerable to hijacking, tampering, or keylogging [48]. Fig. 6 summarizes public blockchain vulnerabilities [49].

3.6 Blockchains and smart contracts vulnerabilities

A smart contract is a digital scheme accomplishing a dual arrangement among communication entities. The main idea of smart contracts in blockchains is shown in Fig. 7. Similar to real-life contracts, smart contracts are delineated by the regulating code describing the regulations on what means both actors should perform by to accomplish the arrangement of the contract (for example the task compensation once the job is done). However, smart contracts can become serious vulnerabilities with widespread consequences in blockchains due to the absence of a central authority to resolve faults when errors appear in smart contract codes such as Botract breaches [48].

3.7 Blockchains and the cybersecurity triad

Like an ant communication network, a security system should highlight and enforce the cybersecurity triad, which is composed of the three main pillars/services that each network is guaranteed to offer, namely confidentiality, integrity, and availability (also known as the CIA triangle). However, for a blockchain security system, since blockchain is a decentralized communication network system, blockchain provides the user/data integrity services using a distributed validation paradigm whereas the availability service is provided by openly (in public) exhibiting the communications and transactions for the blocks in the

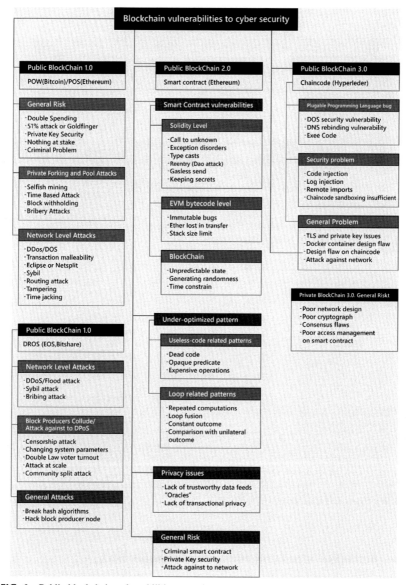

FIG. 6   Public blockchain vulnerabilities.

chain. Blockchain confidentiality is not considered to be a concern, since blockchain is not designed to sustain a data confidentiality service; on the contrary, blockchain data retained by an organization is only that information that is meant to be made public. The correlation of the cybersecurity triad and blockchains is illustrated in Fig. 8.

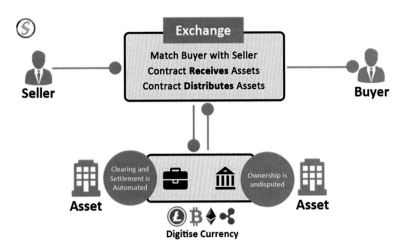

FIG. 7 Smart contracts in blockchains.

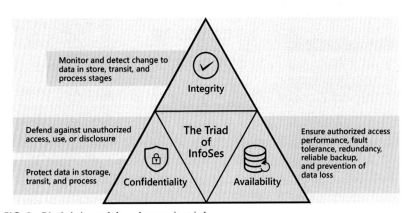

FIG. 8 Blockchains and the cybersecurity triad.

3.8 Blockchains and potential security applications

Blockchain is an emerging technology that can integrate several technologies including advanced cryptography, digital signature and machine leaning, thus it can be utilized to design typical secure applications and protocol. Furthermore, blockchain can be used to address message privacy concerns through developing uniform application programming interfaces (APIs) that facilitate mutual messaging abilities. To sum up, several examples of prospective security applications of blockchain are summarized in Fig. 9.

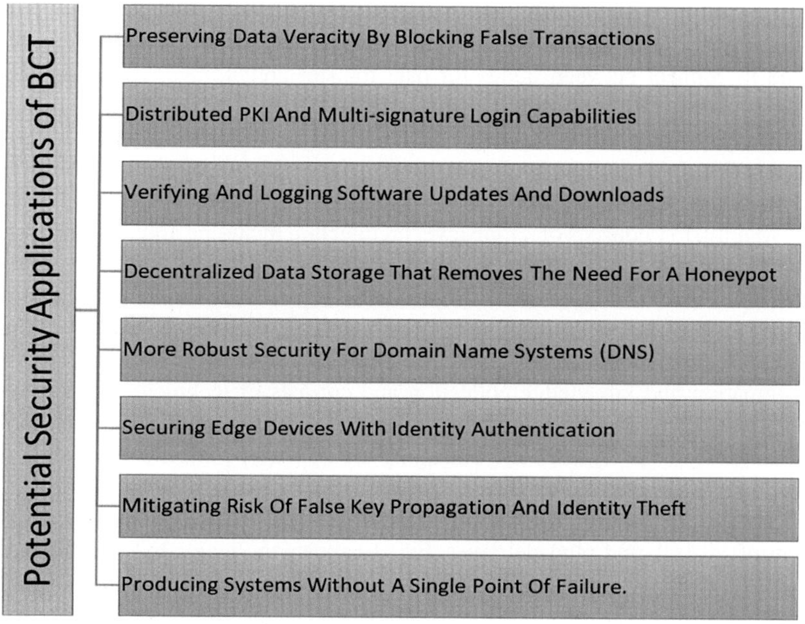

FIG. 9   Potential security applications of blockchain technology (BCT).

4.   Blockchain technology for improved IoT security

The internet of things (IoT) is an emerging technology that has contributed greatly to developing mainstream industries. IoT is utilized in several intelligent application areas, including smart homes, smart cities, smart transportation, smart grids, smart logistics, and smart healthcare systems. The key challenges of IoT deployment are security, privacy, and scalability [50]. IoT integration with blockchain technology represents a revolutionary solution to address these challenges. Blockchain implements complete decentralization, strong public-key cryptography, and strong cryptographic hash. These features provide high scalability and strong tamper-resistance, and offer a distributed and immutable storage of records for all stakeholders [50,51].

4.1   Security evaluation of IoT

IoT is responsible for connecting a vast range of physical objects to the internet using various implementations. This continuously leads to new privacy and security concerns due to several reasons; areas of concern include the architecture of IoT, internet environment, information flows, validity and authenticity of connected nodes, capability limitations of nodes, and different security appliances being implemented [50].

The IoT network is implemented either as a client/server or centralized communication model, in which a single gateway—most likely a cloud server—is used to connect between nodes for data transfer and storage. However, this model implies a set of security and performance limitations especially with an increased number of IoT devices and transaction volume. The IoT communication model is divided into several layers. Several works have described IoT communication models [51,52].

Mainly, IoT consists of a four-layer architecture including application layer, support layer, communication layer, and perception layer. The application layer is responsible for the implementation and utilization of IoT networks. The support layer provides computing and storage services and facilities the rest of the layers. The perception layer connects directly to the physical environment for information and knowledge collection and consists of technical components such as sensors and actuators. The communication layer is responsible for connecting various IoT nodes and managing the transfer of information between different OSI (open systems interconnection) sublayers. This layer includes six sublayers, namely, application, session, transport, network, media access control (MAC), and physical layer. Fig. 10 shows the major IoT architecture layers [52,53].

Concerning security, the IoT application layer is sensitive to various attacks, allowing the whole network to be compromised; this includes code injection, sniffing attack, cross-site scripting, and phishing [53]. The network layer is concerned with transmitted and received data integrity and authenticity. Hence, this layer is vulnerable to packet sniffing, masquerading, man-in-the-middle, and denial of service attacks. The perception layer is in contact with the physical environment and is vulnerable to device replacement and/or the addition of new nodes by attackers, which could provide illegitimate access to IoT resources. The unsecure perception layer can facilitate a set of attacks such as timing attacks, node capturing, eavesdropping, reply attacks, and node capturing [53,54].

Nodes connected in an IoT can have different hardware capabilities and specifications (i.e., computation, power, memory storage). This leads to limited

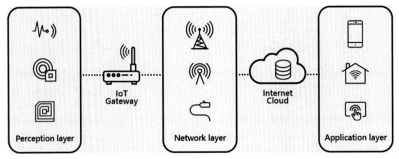

FIG. 10 IoT architecture layers.

interoperability in terms of security implementations and implies a customized security service considering the capacity constraints of these nodes. In addition, the capability and performance limitations of IoT nodes result in high reliance on the cloud as a centralized server for data storage and processing. This increases the vulnerability level and attack surface of IoT architecture and prevents strong security policies being implemented due to resources constraints [54,55].

IoT presents a network with a lot of open-ended links with no measures for data integrity and high levels of threat in resource access and user authentication. Furthermore, IoT centralized-cloud architecture is highly vulnerable to single point of failure (SPOF) and limited scalability especially with an increased number of connected devices [55]. These vulnerabilities make IoT unreliable for secure transactions. Hence, a countermeasure is required to meet the security challenges of IoT and ensure the integrity and confidentiality of transactions and immutability and transparency of records. This can be achieved by utilizing the competencies of blockchain technology [56]. Blockchain decentralized architecture supports IoT scalability, advanced cryptography is used for data confidentiality and privacy, and authentication and integrity modules are implemented for nodes' accountability and data integrity. Blockchain provides a distributed validation for each transaction to detect any malicious act. Nodes are validated before joining the network and utilizing available resources.

4.2 Blockchain competence for improved IoT security

Blockchain can act as an efficient solution to the previously mentioned IoT vulnerabilities. The following features make blockchain a perfect match for developing IoT security: decentralization, secure data and reliable transactions, and nodes authentication and user authorization.

4.2.1 Decentralization

Distribution of data storage and processing among various nodes effectively eliminates the need for a trusted third party and removes the probability of a single point of failure. Hence, it is very resistant to technological failure and provides optimized resource allocation and utilization. BC architecture employs a peer-to-peer communication model and requires all participants' agreement on data transactions through the network. This validates IoT data and transactions, as well as supporting immutability against various forms of malicious activities [57].

4.2.2 Secure data and reliable transactions

In blockchain, transactions between network participants are secured and validated by encryption and chaining with previous records among approval of all participating nodes. This is conducted by utilizing public key infrastructure to securely generate and distribute keys among network participants. Strong hash functions are used for linking transactions through immutable hash chains and providing improved traceability [58]. Access to previous data transactions supports the authenticity of current resources and allows the monitoring of transactions across the network for preserved integrity. This offers greater transparency and immutability of records since transaction histories are time-stamped, linked, and available to all nodes. In addition, blockchain employs the use of consensus to ensure the overall verification of any transaction and provides equal opportunity to all participants to verify and track transactions. BC supports smart contracts, which provide a set of predefined, controlled, and automatically executed controls and services. This includes providing authorization and control of data to network participants. Hence, using blockchain will prevent malicious access to IoT resources and will guarantee high data accuracy, robustness, and transparency [59].

4.2.3 Nodes authentication and user authorization

Before gaining access to the network, Blockchain authenticates both sender and receiver. Means of users' authentication in BC include the use of public-key cryptography and a strong access policy [60,61]. Using blockchain, every node will have a unique ID and a special wallet, which is used for nodes registration and authorization. In addition, smart contracts used in BC will manage access to resources. This protects resources from unauthorized access and eliminates malicious access activities such as packet sniffing, session hijacking, and man-in-the-middle attacks.

4.3 Blockchain integration into IoT

The secure, reliable, distributed, and autonomous features of blockchain technology make it a major advance in the IoT's overall security, scalability, and efficiency. Fig. 11 describes a framework for the integration of Blockchain technology within the IoT architecture [62,63]. The integrated BC-IoT architecture is divided into three major components:

- The IoT environment includes IoT nodes and different smart implementations of wireless technologies.
- The blockchain network is the backbone system for ensuring security and scalability for the IoT environment; blockchain miners are responsible for securing and verifying transactions, and smart contracts are used to automate the execution of predefined rules and consensus between all network participants.
- The cloud environment provides scalable access for the computing resources that are required for supporting the implementation of the overall service.

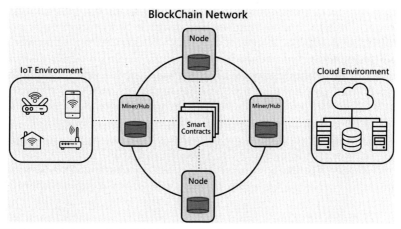

FIG. 11   Blockchain and IoT (BC-IoT) integration framework.

The integration of blockchain in the IoT framework leads to the following advantages:

- Blockchain is used to create a mesh network for secure and reliable connections between IoT devices. This avoids the threats of device spoofing and impersonation.
- Blockchain provides active solutions to preserve data logs and traceability of transactions. It ensures data control is distributed among all participating IoT nodes. This provides data integrity, which is a major demand for IoT applications.
- Blockchain operates communication and transactions between multiple distributed nodes; this provides high computing capability and reliability. This distributed nature makes IoT more reliable and assists in resolving the single point of failure problem. The decentralized structure of Blockchain also offers essential characteristics such as integrity, authentication, privacy, and fraud protection.
- Blockchain provides a solid access and identification policy for participating nodes. This maintains the accountability and validity of IoT nodes. In addition, smart contracts support IoT in setting up effective and automotive resource-consuming procedures that will assist in resolving the high computational demands of IoT.

5.   Conclusions and remarks

Blockchain technology was first proposed in 2008 by Satoshi Nakamoto as a public and distributed ledger that is replicated among several nodes in a peer-to-peer (P2P) network. The blockchain contains a list of immutable and verified records called "blocks." Each block contains a previous hash to link the previous block because the nature of blockchain is linked to the backlist; in addition, it contains a nonce, transaction root, and network timestamp to indicate the time that a block is added to the chain. The characteristics of the blockchain are immutability and anonymity. Blockchain security provides solutions in many fields such as cryptocurrency, healthcare, and IoT technology. In this chapter, we have studied the decentralized blockchain technology along with its different features correlating the blockchain system with a range of security applications and the most recent trends of blockchain security. Furthermore, several possible security contraventions and susceptibilities of blockchain technology have been investigated and reported. Moreover, an inclusive inspection and evaluation for the e-security services and blockchain technology for improved IoT security applications and services was carried out. In conclusion, blockchain technology can be used to provide a distributed database that relies on a P2P network and provides the highest level of trust, availability, and reliability without needing a trusted third party.

References

[1] C.S. Wright, Bitcoin: a peer-to-peer electronic cash system, SSRN Electron. J. (2019), https://doi.org/10.2139/ssrn.3440802.

[2] S. Nakamoto, Bitcoin: A Peer-to-Peer Electronic Cash System, 2008. www.bitcoin.org. (Accessed 22 October 2021).

[3] M. Mettler, Blockchain Technology in Healthcare: The Revolution Starts Here, November 2016, https://doi.org/10.1109/HEALTHCOM.2016.7749510.

[4] T. Ahram, A. Sargolzaei, S. Sargolzaei, J. Daniels, B. Amaba, Blockchain technology innovations, in: 2017 IEEE Technology and Engineering Management Society Conference, TEMSCON 2017, July, 2017, pp. 137–141, https://doi.org/10.1109/TEMSCON.2017.7998367.

[5] D. Drescher, Blockchain Basics: A Non-Technical Introduction in 25 Steps, first ed., Apress, 2017.

[6] Z. Zheng, S. Xie, H. Dai, X. Chen, H. Wang, An overview of blockchain technology: architecture, consensus, and future trends, in: Proceedings—2017 IEEE 6th International Congress on Big Data, BigData Congress 2017, September, 2017, pp. 557–564, https://doi.org/10.1109/BIGDATACONGRESS.2017.85.

[7] J. Yang, H. Shen, Blockchain consensus algorithm design based on a consistent hash algorithm, in: Proceedings—2019 20th International Conference on Parallel and Distributed Computing, Applications and Technologies, PDCAT 2019, December, 2019, pp. 461–466, https://doi.org/10.1109/PDCAT46702.2019.00090.

[8] D. Yaga, P. Mell, N. Roby, K. Scarfone, Blockchain Technology Overview, 2018, https://doi.org/10.6028/NIST.IR.8202.

[9] M. Crosby, Nachiappan, P. Pattanayak, S. Verma, V. Kalyanaraman, Blockchain Technology: Beyond Bitcoin—Applied Innovation Institute, 2016. https://www.appliedinnovationinstitute.org/blockchain-technology-beyond-bitcoin/. (Accessed 22 October 2021).

[10] A. Kaci, A. Rachedi, Toward a machine learning and software defined network approach to manage miners' reputation in blockchain, J. Netw. Syst. Manag. 28 (3) (2020) 478–501, https://doi.org/10.1007/S10922-020-09532-1.

[11] M.J.W. Rennock, A. Cohn, J.R. Butcher, Blockchain Technology and Regulatory Investigations, 2018. https://www.steptoe.com/images/content/1/7/v3/171269/LIT-FebMar18-Feature-Blockchain.pdf. (Accessed 22 October 2021).

[12] D. Efanov, P. Roschin, The all-pervasiveness of the blockchain technology, Procedia Comput. Sci. 123 (2018) 116–121, https://doi.org/10.1016/J.PROCS.2018.01.019.

[13] S.S. Panda, B.K. Mohanta, U. Satapathy, D. Jena, D. Gountia, T.K. Patra, Study of blockchain-based decentralized consensus algorithms, in: IEEE Reg. 10 Annu. Int. Conf. Proceedings/TENCON, vol. 2019-October, 2019, pp. 908–913, https://doi.org/10.1109/TENCON.2019.8929439.

[14] U. Jafar, M.J.A. Aziz, Z. Shukur, Blockchain for electronic voting system—review and open research challenges, Sensors 21 (17) (2021), https://doi.org/10.3390/S21175874.

[15] S.N. Khan, F. Loukil, C. Ghedira-Guegan, E. Benkhelifa, A. Bani-Hani, Blockchain smart contracts: applications, challenges, and future trends, Peer-to-Peer Netw. Appl. 14 (5) (2021) 2901–2925, https://doi.org/10.1007/S12083-021-01127-0.

[16] A. Singh, R.M. Parizi, Q. Zhang, K.K.R. Choo, A. Dehghantanha, Blockchain smart contracts formalization: approaches and challenges to address vulnerabilities, Comput. Secur. 88 (2020) 101654, https://doi.org/10.1016/J.COSE.2019.101654.

[17] B.K. Mohanta, D. Jena, S.S. Panda, S. Sobhanayak, Blockchain technology: a survey on applications and security privacy challenges, Internet Things 8 (December) (2019) 100107, https://doi.org/10.1016/J.IOT.2019.100107.

[18] B. Bhushan, P. Sinha, K.M. Sagayam, J.A. Onesimu, Untangling blockchain technology: a survey on state of the art, security threats, privacy services, applications and future research directions, Comput. Electr. Eng. 90 (March) (2021), https://doi.org/10.1016/J.COMPELECENG.2020.106897.

[19] R. Zhang, R. Xue, L. Liu, Security and privacy on blockchain, ACM Comput. Surv. 52 (3) (2019), https://doi.org/10.1145/3316481.

[20] Q.A. Al-Haija, A.A. Alsulami, High performance classification model to identify ransomware payments for heterogeneous bitcoin networks, Electronics 10 (17) (2021) 2113.

[21] A.A. Monrat, O. Schelén, K. Andersson, A survey of blockchain from the perspectives of applications, challenges, and opportunities, IEEE Access 7 (2019) 117134–117151.

[22] S. Shi, D. He, L. Li, N. Kumar, M.K. Khan, K.K.R. Choo, Applications of blockchain in ensuring the security and privacy of electronic health record systems: a survey, Comput. Secur. (2020) 101966.

[23] F.A. Khan, M. Asif, A. Ahmad, M. Alharbi, H. Aljuaid, Blockchain technology, improvement suggestions, security challenges on smart grid and its application in healthcare for sustainable development, Sustain. Cities Soc. 55 (2020) 102018.

[24] C. Esposito, A. De Santis, G. Tortora, H. Chang, K.K.R. Choo, Blockchain: a panacea for healthcare cloud-based data security and privacy? IEEE Cloud Comput. 5 (1) (2018) 31–37.

[25] S.N. Mohanty, K.C. Ramya, S.S. Rani, D. Gupta, K. Shankar, S.K. Lakshmanaprabu, A. Khanna, An efficient lightweight integrated blockchain (ELIB) model for IoT security and privacy, Futur. Gener. Comput. Syst. 102 (2020) 1027–1037.

[26] O. Alphand, et al., IoTChain: a blockchain security architecture for the Internet of Things, in: 2018 IEEE wireless communications and networking conference (WCNC), IEEE, 2018, April, pp. 1–6.

[27] M. Vučinić, B. Tourancheau, F. Rousseau, A. Duda, L. Damon, R. Guizzetti, OSCAR: object security architecture for the Internet of Things, Ad Hoc Netw. 32 (2015) 3–16.

[28] L. Seitz, G. Selander, E. Wahlstroem, S. Erdtman, H. Tschofenig, Authentication and authorization for constrained environments (ace). Internet Engineering Task Force, Internet-Draft draft-ietf-aceoauth-authz-07, 2017.

[29] T. McGhin, K.R. Choo, C.Z. Liu, D. He, Blockchain in healthcare applications: research challenges and opportunities, J. Netw. Comput. Appl. 135 (2019) 62–75.

[30] K. Peterson, R. Deeduvanu, P. Kanjamala, K. Boles, A Blockchain-based approach to health information exchange networks, in: Proc. NIST Workshop Blockchain Healthcare, vol. 1, 2016, pp. 1–10.

[31] G.G. Dagher, J. Mohler, M. Milojkovic, P.B. Marella, Ancile: privacy-preserving framework for access control and interoperability of electronic health records using Blockchain technology, Sustain. Cities Soc. 39 (2018) 283–297.

[32] A.F. Hussein, N. ArunKumar, G.R. Gonzalez, E. Abdulhay, J.M.R. Tavares, V.H.C. de Albuquerque, A medical records managing and securing Blockchain based system supported by a genetic algorithm and discrete wavelet transform, Cogn. Syst. Res. 52 (2018) 1–11.

[33] H. Kaur, M.A. Alam, R. Jameel, A.K. Mourya, V. Chang, A proposed solution and future direction for blockchain-based heterogeneous medicare data in cloud environment, J. Med. Syst. 42 (8) (2018) 1–11.

[34] W. Liu, S.S. Zhu, T. Mundie, U. Krieger, Advanced block-chain architecture for e-health systems, in: 2017 IEEE 19th International Conference on e-Health Networking, Applications and Services (Healthcom), IEEE, 2017, October, pp. 1–6.

[35] V. Patel, A framework for secure and decentralized sharing of medical imaging data via blockchain consensus, Health Inform. J. 25 (4) (2019) 1398–1411.

[36] Quorum Whitepaper. https://github.com/jpmorganchase/quorum-docs/blob/master/Quorum%20Whitepaper%20v0.1.pdf.

[37] S. Mohurle, M. Patil, A brief study of Wannacry Threat: Ransomware Attack 2017, Int. J. Adv. Res. Comput. Sci. 8 (5) (2017) 1938–1940.

[38] S.H. Kok, A. Abdullah, N. Jhanjhi, M. Supramaniam, Prevention of crypto-ransomware using a pre-encryption detection algorithm, Computers 8 (4) (2019) 2–15.

[39] M. Paquet-Clouston, B. Haslhofer, B. Dupont, Ransomware payments in the Bitcoin ecosystem, J. Cybersecur. (2019) 1–11.

[40] M. Warkentina, C. Orgeronb, Using the security triad to assess Blockchain technology in public sector applications, Int. J. Inf. Manag. 52 (2020) 1–8.

[41] A. Al Badawi, Q.A. Al-Haija, Detection of anti-money laundry in bitcoin transactions, in: Accepted, 4th Smart Cities Symposium (SCS), IET, IEEE, 2021.

[42] A. Yazdinejad, H. HaddadPajouh, A. Dehghantanha, R.M. Parizi, G. Srivastava, M.-Y. Chen, Cryptocurrency malware hunting: a deep recurrent neural network approach, Appl. Soft Comput. J. 96 (2020) 106630.

[43] O.M.K. Alhawi, J. Baldwin, A. Dehghantanha, Leveraging machine learning techniques for windows ransomware network traffic detection, Cyber Threat. Intell. Adv. Inf. Secur. 70 (2018) 93–106.

[44] K. Kolesnikova, O. Mezentseva, T. Mukatayev, Analysis of bitcoin transactions to detect illegal transactions using convolutional neural networks, in: Proceedings of the 2021 IEEE International Conference on Smart Information Systems and Technologies (SIST), Nur-Sultan, Kazakhstan, 28–30 April, 2021, pp. 1–6.

[45] C. Lee, S. Maharjan, K. Ko, J. Woo, J.W.K. Hong, Machine learning based bitcoin address classification, in: Z. Zheng, H.N. Dai, X. Fu, B. Chen (Eds.), Blockchain and Trustworthy Systems. BlockSys 2020. Communications in Computer and Information Science, vol. 1267, Springer, Singapore, 2020.

[46] J. Umawing, Report: organizations remain vulnerable to increasing insider threats, in: Cybersecurity Insiders Reports, 2019.

[47] C. Ye, G. Li, H. Cai, G. Yonggen, A. Fukuda, Analysis of security in Blockchain: case study in 51%-attack detecting, in: 2018 5th International Conference on Dependable Systems and Their Applications (DSA), IEEE, 2018, pp. 15–24.

[48] N.A.I. Malaika, A. Majid, O. Al Ibrahim, Botract: Abusing Smart Contracts and Blockchains for Botnet Command and Control, 2017-11-15 [2019-04-02] https://sector.ca/sessions/botract-abusing-smart-contracts-and-blockchain-for-botnet-command-and-control.

[49] H. Hasanova, U. Baek, M. Shin, K. Cho, M.-S. Kim, A survey on Blockchain cybersecurity vulnerabilities and possible countermeasures, Int. J. Netw. Manag. 29 (2019) e2060, https://doi.org/10.1002/nem.2060.

[50] L.S. Burks, A.E. Cox, K. Lakkaraju, M.J. Boyd, E. Chan, Bitcoin Address Classification (No. SAND2017-8407C), Sandia National Lab.(SNL-NM), Albuquerque, NM, USA, 2017.

[51] A. Srivastava, S. Gupta, M. Quamara, P. Chaudhary, V. Aski, Future IoT-enabled threats and vulnerabilities: state of the art, challenges and future prospects, Int. J. Commun. Syst. 33 (8) (2020) 384–391.

[52] Q. Abu Al-Haija, S. Zein-Sabatto, "An efficient deep-learning-based detection and classification system for cyber-attacks in IoT communication networks" Electronics, MDPI 9 (12) (2020) 2152, https://doi.org/10.3390/electronics9122152.

[53] K. Santosh, K. Sanjeev, Communication models in Internet of Things: a survey, Int. J. Sci. Technol. Eng. 3 (11) (2017) 87–91.

[54] H.-N. Dai, Z. Zheng, Y. Zhang, Blockchain for Internet of Things: a survey, IEEE Internet Things J. 6 (5) (2019) 1–19.

[55] M.A. Uddin, A. Stranieri, I. Gondal, V. Balasubramanian, A survey on the adoption of blockchain in IoT: challenges and solutions, Blockchain Res. Appl. 2 (2021) 1–49.

[56] M. Picone, S. Cirani, L. Veltri, Blockchain security and privacy for the internet of things, Sensors 21 (3) (2021) 1–4.

[57] Z. Zheng, S. Xie, H. Dai, X. Chen, H. Wang, An overview of Blockchain technology: architecture, consensus, and future trends, in: 6th IEEE International Congress on Big Data, 2017, pp. 557–564.

[58] K. Abbas, L.A. Tawalbeh, A. Rafiq, A. Muthanna, I. Elgendy, A. Abd El-Latif, Convergence of blockchain and IoT for secure transportation systems in smart cities, Secur. Commun. Netw. 2021 (2021). Article ID 5597679.

[59] Y. Zhong, M. Zhou, J. Li, J. Chen, Y. Liu, Y. Zhao, M. Hu, Distributed blockchain-based authentication and authorization protocol for smart grid, Wirel Commun. Mob. Comput. vol. 2021 (2021). 15 p., Article ID 5560621.

[60] J.G. Song, E.S. Kang, H.W. Shin, J.W. Jang, A smart contract-based P2P energy trading system with dynamic pricing on ethereum blockchain, Sensors 21 (6) (2021) 1985.

[61] M. Yavari, M. Safkhani, S. Kumari, S. Kumar, C. Ming, An improved blockchain-based authentication protocol for IoT network management, Secur. Commun. Netw. 2020 (2020). Article ID 8836214, 16 p.

[62] R. Garg, P. Gupta, A. Kaur Secure, IoT via blockchain, IOP Conf. Ser.: Mater. Sci. Eng. 1022 (2021).

[63] N. Iqbal, Imran, A. Shabir, A. Rashid, K. Do-Hyeun, A scheduling mechanism based on optimization using IoT-tasks orchestration for efficient patient health monitoring, Sensors 21 (16) (2021).

Chapter 12

Blockchain for medical insurance: Synthesizing current knowledge and problematizing it for future research avenues

A.K.M. Bahalul Haque[a] and Bharat Bhushan[b]
[a]*Software Engineering, LUT University, Lappeenranta, Finland,* [b]*School of Engineering and Technology (SET), Sharda University, Greater Noida, Uttar Pradesh, India*

1. Introduction

Healthcare has been one of the basic human needs since the dawn of civilization [1]. The civic societies of this world cannot potentially survive without adequate healthcare facilities for their people. State-of-the-art healthcare is required nowadays to improve the living standard of modern urbanized environments. A smart healthcare system is connected to an IoT and a cloud-based system [2], and decentralization, digitization, affordability, and availability are the buzzwords of such a system. In and of itself, the traditional healthcare system is a vast network of people, procedures, and technology. Cash flow, regulations, infrastructure, employees, and medical records are just a few components. Competent healthcare makes all systems and procedures more convenient for all parties involved. Insurance facilities are among the most critical facilities to ensure patients' health security and maintain standard health services [3,4]. Medical insurance helps a governing body to maintain healthcare facilities for both emergency and general conditions [5,6].

Blockchain is a distributed ledger technology (DLT) that creates an immutable, decentralized, cryptographically secured, and shared database [7,8]. It is a technique that achieves a significant advance in trustworthy computation by decentralizing most interactions. This implies that blockchain empowers

Blockchain Technology Solutions for the Security of IoT-Based Healthcare Systems.
https://doi.org/10.1016/B978-0-323-99199-5.00002-1

people to connect and conduct business as individuals without the need to contract with a third party, which make it more protected from criminal cyberattacks [9,10]. Blockchain technology is the foundation of Bitcoin and is known as a cybersecurity technique containing algorithms, economic models, mathematics, cryptography techniques, etc. After the invention of Bitcoin and the operating platform blockchain in 2009, the developers made the whole network and its code open source. Since then, it has facilitated people contributing to blockchain network development [11]. Since the inception of Bitcoin, the network has changed constantly. Since Bitcoin is based on a public network, anyone could participate in it, and the network became vast quickly. Later, other blockchain networks like Ethereum came into existence, which has contributed to the proliferation of blockchain applications across various domains. The blockchain application now exists in almost every domain, including finance, automobile, healthcare, data storage, internet of things (IoT), and other domains. In the case of financial organizations, blockchain technology allows transactions without the help of any kind of intermediary or bank [12,13]. Since it removes the intermediary, the technology can be used as an enabler for trust, transparency, accountability, and visibility in other financial application sectors [14,15].

Blockchain has become a widely used assistive technology that enables various healthcare features, including insurance. Blockchain as an enabling technology for medical insurance has been discussed in other literature. Therefore, it is crucial to discuss the recent advancements and limitations of blockchain technology in medical insurance claims. This chapter aims to provide a state-of-the-art comprehensive review of blockchain as an enabler for medical insurance claims based on recent pieces of literature. Blockchain fundamentals will be discussed initially to give the readers a sound understanding. In addition, blockchain in smart healthcare is discussed briefly to outline the other sectors of healthcare that use blockchain technology. To facilitate the review, articles that have been published in peer-reviewed conferences and journals with significant novelty and empirical research have been used. The comprehensive summary regarding blockchain for medical insurance claims also provides guidelines for future research. Another crucial novelty of this chapter that has not been used other in blockchain-based medical insurance reviews is the problematization approach [16]. Using this approach, we have summarized the literature, research gaps, and possible future research avenues.

The contributions of this chapter include:

1. A comprehensive outline of the attributes, architecture, and working principles of blockchain.

2. A detailed description of various types of blockchain and their characteristics.
3. A comprehensive outline of the use of blockchain in various sectors of smart healthcare.
4. Recent studies are synthesized to represent the current knowledge of blockchain in smart healthcare.
5. Current knowledge is problematized to investigate the research gaps from existing literature synthesis.
6. Future research avenues are presented based on the critical analysis of existing research gaps.

The rest of the chapter is structured and organized as follows: Section 2 contains the background of blockchain, which covers characteristics, block structure, and blockchain classification; Section 3 outlines a brief description of blockchain use in smart healthcare; Section 4 briefly discusses the synthesis of current literature, research gaps, and future research avenues; and Section 5 concludes the chapter.

2. Blockchain fundamentals

The primary goal of blockchain technology is to have no intermediary. Several techniques follow from this. All committed transactions are stored in a list of blocks in chronological order called a public ledger. Distributed database or public ledger is one of the critical features or techniques of the blockchain principle [17]. A public ledger exists across a decentralized network of computers, forming a peer-to-peer network with no solitary entity to control the network. As part of the network, every device is deemed to have an identical copy of the ledger. The ledger is immediately copied when the machine is turned on. Blockchain uses both public and private key concepts for encrypting the data. As a result, there is no requirement for a mediator. As a result, blockchain significantly decreases the cost of transactions, shortens transaction times, and increases operational productivity.

2.1 Characteristics of blockchain

In order to produce a proper review of blockchain, first, we need to understand the characteristics of blockchain. Blockchain is not only for cryptocurrency but also for those industries that demand resource management and transaction handling. Security, privacy, immutability, decentralization, and sustainability are the core characteristics of blockchain. These features facilitate the development of secure and trustworthy applications for consumer and business use [18]. These characteristics are as follows.

2.1.1 Decentralization

In a centralized transaction system, a specific group or organization is responsible for storing data, recording data, and updating data. Central trusted agencies validate these transactions [19]. However, in a decentralized system, there is no central authority. Every node connected implements a peer-to-peer network. Due to decentralization, every layer of intermediaries has been eliminated. Hence, blockchain reduces the development cost, operation cost, and server cost.

2.1.2 Immutability

Blockchain technology has a ledger that is open to all. All the transaction data are stored in the ledger in each node. So, it is not possible to trace or change the data [20]. When information is stored in the ledger, it is impossible to alter it. No one can modify or delete the ledger data due to the massive range of participants. This characteristic is highly beneficial for auditing data and for financial transactions. Nevertheless, in a private blockchain, there are only a few users, so sometimes, it could be altered. It is important to remember that at least 50% of nodes must be controlled to tamper with the data.

2.1.3 Persistency

The theory of persistency is that other nodes verify every block. If any nodes contain invalid transactions, other features of blockchain will discover this immediately and resolve the transaction quickly. Every block contains transaction data. Once a transaction's data is written into the ledger, no one can modify or tamper with the data. However, some dishonest miners perform invalid or fake transactions to break the blockchain chain. To combat this specific problem, consensus algorithms work to track the transaction. After tracking the transaction, they audit the whole block and notify the other blocks about the current block. The consensus algorithm also eliminates fake transactions.

2.1.4 Anonymity

Blockchain never reveals the real identity of the user, and successful transactions can be accomplished with the blockchain address only. Sometimes, users create more than one Bitcoin address to hide their real identity. Name, phone number, residential address, and passport ID are not required in blockchain technology to complete a transaction [21]. The anonymous transaction is vital to building sustainable privacy. It also increases the trust issue among the nodes [22]. Every anonymous transaction has two sets: sender and recipient set.

2.1.5 Auditability

The advantages of audibility include traceability and transparency of the network data. Blockchain retains the complete information of any transactions, like timestamp, validation, and other attributes. Users can trace previous records by accessing any node.

2.1.6 Transparency

After completing a transaction, people can see their record and store it for further verification. A public ledger makes the records visible to the users [23]. Blockchain networks self-audit their ecosystem every 10 min. It is important to reunite the transactions in the network. All the united data of transactions are stored in a block. As a result, no one can make a fake transaction or enact any kind of corruption. The openness of public ledger increases transparency and also improves the trust issue.

2.1.7 Distributed ledger

The main goal of blockchain technology is to end the use of centralized systems. As we all know, decentralized systems reduce the development cost and increase the transaction speed. Therefore, the public ledger is one of the core principles of blockchain technology. All the connected nodes in a network can access the public ledger. They only can check or verify the transactions. Users cannot remove or modify any transactions from the ledger once a transaction is submitted.

A synchronized distributed ledger is too responsive for any kind of tampering or unauthenticated activity. If any users want to place a new block in the network, other blocks would have to verify the transaction according to the distributed ledger. Then the user can participate easily. Every user gets the same kind of privileges from the ledger.

2.1.8 Autonomy

The main idea of autonomy is to build trust from a single centralized authority to the whole system. However, in a decentralized system, there is no central authority to audit the transactions. All nodes connected with the distributed network can transfer and update information securely without any interference.

2.2 The block structure

A block structure has two parts, block body and header. The block's body generally contains information regarding the transaction counter and the transaction itself. The header contains information regarding the data stored in the blockchain and information required for block validation. The size of the block body is not fixed and contains data or verified transactions. The size of the block header is 80 bytes. The starting block of a chain in a blockchain network is called the genesis block. The core part of a block is structured as a Merkle tree [24].

2.2.1 Hash function

A hash function is a code generator that gives a unique value within a fixed length [25]. This unique output value depends on the input value. It works like a fingerprint for digital data or documents. If the input value is modified or changed, the hash value will also be different. A single dot, letter, or space is enough to change the whole hash value. Blockchain generally uses the SHA-256 algorithm. SHA means "secure hash algorithm." It takes 256 bits in memory. Hash is a hexadecimal number consisting of 64 characters. Each character holds 4 bits of memory [26].

Every block has its hash value, but this is only helpful for the next block. The current block uses the previous block's hash to connect, and this is how it maintains the chain. The previous block is considered as the current block's parent block. The first block of the blockchain system has no parent block and is named the genesis block. A hash function is executed after the transactions in the block execute.

2.2.2 Timestamp

Timestamping is a function that is used to track the creation time of a block securely, because it is essential in storing the data to record when a block was created and entered into the blockchain network. The timestamp shows the current time as seconds in universal time since 01 January 1970 in the following format: 1970-01-01T00:00 UTC. Timestamp also maintains a record of when any block data have been modified. It creates a particular date and time so that this is easier to track and verify [27].

2.2.3 Merkle tree root hash

Merkle tree is the central part of any block. In a Merkle tree, every node is labeled with a block as a leaf. Merkle tree increases the efficiency to store the large data structures securely within a specific time. This method considers all the hash values of all the transactions in the block. Every transaction is connected with a Merkle tree. This Merkle tree has a function named hash process, which generates a different Merkle root for processing transactions. The block header consists of the generated Merkle root.

2.2.4   Nonce

A nonce (number once) value is a 4-byte value first initialized with 0. With the calculation of hash value, the nonce changes. Every node of the network must calculate a hash value, which the miners frequently change to get unique hash values. The block header contains the nonce. If a nonce is changed, the hash will change entirely following the avalanche effect. Nonce guessed by the miner must be lower than the randomly fixed nonce to be validated. This calculation operates by the proof of work (PoW) method. If any node reaches the target value, the block is broadcast with other nodes. All the nodes then verify the newly broadcast node and mutually confirm the correctness of the hash value. The nonce can be a number up to four billion [28].

2.3   Blockchain classification

According to the data access mechanisms, blockchain can be classified into three classes: public, private, and consortium [27,28].

2.3.1   Public blockchains

A public blockchain is structured based on the decentralized concept of blockchain. This is a type of blockchain where anyone can join the network without permission. It enables everyone to access the transparent transaction history and join the process of attaining consensus [29]. The participants can make their identities anonymous. The transaction follows the peer-to-peer method for creating a block, which ensures a decentralized environment. Before a transaction is written to the system, it must be associated with the blockchain. All the participants of the network can control the operations in the system. Every user can access the transaction information and formulates the mining process. Public blockchains are very effective against attacks and node failures for the consensus mechanism they follow. Mostly, proof of work (PoW) or proof of stake (PoS) are utilized to help public blockchains overcome issues like Sybil attacks, which involve mining by unknown participants, or the freedom of every node to create a block [30]. Public blockchains are highly secure, but slow and inefficient, with increasing electric power needs as more nodes are added to the system. The most valuable parts of public blockchains are the user's anonymity and a distributed ledger. They are is inefficient in cost and speed compared to private blockchains but faster and less expensive than the systems used before blockchain. Systems like Bitcoin, Ethereum, and Litecoin follow the method of public blockchains.

2.3.2   Private blockchains

Private blockchains allow a single entity or organization to control the system by setting some definite rules for the network. It is similar to a centralized system in giving access permission by some specific nodes but also increases the privacy with strict management. Some individuals or a dedicated team control the mining process following a deterministic distributed consensus— practical byzantine fault tolerance (PBFT) [30,31]. This algorithm not only restricts the access of unknown or new users, but also ensures transparency. The main shortcoming of private blockchains is that they do not entirely uphold the decentralized characteristics of public blockchain. On the other hand, private blockchains are faster and more efficient than public blockchains for establishing the consensus by the trusted entity. This benefit encourages government-based or private companies or organizations to partake in this privately-run version of blockchain, which is more efficient, secure, and faster than any other blockchain technology.

2.3.3 Consortium blockchains

Consortium blockchains are the union of a public and private blockchain that is partly decentralized. There are some controlling nodes to verify and validate transactions or blocks. The miner blocks are valid only when approved and signed by these controlling nodes. The data or transaction details can be open source, like public blockchains, but the nodes can verify and validate transactions instead of a specific individual or a single company. Consortium blockchain has a problem of immutability and irreversibility, and its nodes have a higher chance of being malicious [32]. However, it provides a great advantage to organizations that involve partners.

3. Blockchain for smart healthcare

Health is one of the fundamental rights of every citizen. In a smart city, the healthcare system has to be modernized and secured. Smart healthcare includes smart hospitals, smart ambulances, efficient data management among the patients, doctors, and pharmacies, a smart diagnostic system, and a smart administration that includes doctors, nurses, orderlies, and all the components of a hospital. It is essential to share the data on the health condition of a patient to enable the doctors to make fast decisions [33]. Blockchain ensures this sharing procedure in an efficient and immutable manner. A major task in healthcare systems is to manage patient information, digital health records, and treatment data. A health bank method is proposed that can provide immutable, decentralized, and distributed ledger properties to the system [34]; this is referred to as a user-oriented healthcare management system. There is also a method named "decentralized application" (DApp) that can ensure transparent, secure, and anonymous transactions [35]. Healthcare data gateway (HDG) is a system architecture that helps patients manage and control their data [36]. The structure has three layers: data storage layer, data management layer, and data usage layer. Patients are connected with HDG architecture. They can store data in the blockchain cloud and pass it to a physician, researcher, or a particular center in the data usage layer. It forbids the access of patients' data without consent, ensuring security and immutability. There is also a system named body sensor network (BSN) that collects physiological signals from a patient's body [37]. This signal is automatically stored in a blockchain network where doctors can respond in real-time.

The data stored in the system must also be shared efficiently and securely in order for a proper healthcare service to be provided. This data can be highly sensitive for patients, due to which, the patient must have complete control and protection from unauthorized access. To maintain electronic medical records (EMRs) a management system named MedRec is proposed [38]. It uses a smart contract to transmit the data. Researchers and medical stakeholders are encouraged to participate in the process of mining. There is also a system called MedShare for auditing, controlling access to the cloud, and data provenance [39]. It also uses smart contracts to perform actions on medical data and prevent malicious access activity. We can see that blockchain has a great deal of potential in managing big medical data. The most fantastic benefit of applying blockchain is that patients can control their data and also use it from anywhere at any time.

4. Synthesis of literature and problematization for the future research agenda

This section synthesizes the current knowledge of blockchain-based insurance claim systems to problematize it for future research directions. The current knowledge outlines the following benefits of using blockchain technology:

- Substantial performance benefits, operational efficiencies, clarity, speedier payments, and fraud prevention will be enabled by blockchain technology, which enables the legitimate exchange of data across various parties in what seems like a responsible and identifiable way. Additionally, blockchains can enable new insurance practices to develop quality, value, and marketplaces.[a]
- Insurers compete in a hypercompetitive climate where both retail and corporate clients want great value and an exceptional service offered. The financial sector has achieved positive business transformation thanks to blockchain technology.
- Insurance may be done using smart contracts and autonomous apps, bringing further automation and tamperproof audit trails. Furthermore, the cheap

---

a. https://consensys.net/blockchain-use-cases/finance/insurance/.

cost of smart contracts and business records enables certain items to be somewhat more accessible in the developing world's constrained markets.

- Eventually, the nascent blockchain sector will purchase insurance of its own. Cyber insurance can serve as a starting point for covering additional costs, financial drawbacks, liabilities, and other issues. Manufacturers may collaborate with technology businesses to analyze vulnerability and guide loss control and mitigation methodologies.

- The conveyance of any area of virtual proof for insurance purposes, such as using electronic health data, is one possible application of distributed ledger technology. When it becomes simpler to include electronic information for insuring, we should expect improvements in other areas like product and brand innovation to follow. The interplay between IoT and AI in insurance procedures will become more automated in the coming years, resulting in a radically altered landscape for the sector. Nonetheless, since these are still emerging technologies, sufficient reasonable care must be performed before insurers can effectively utilize them.

The problematizing approach uses the existing knowledge to identify possible limitations or research gaps [16]. The synthesis has shown that blockchain-based systems for medical insurance have not flourished to date. Although researchers are trying to design and develop blockchain-based systems for medical insurance, it is implausible to some extent due to scalability issue, transaction speed issue in blockchain etc. To the best of our knowledge, no comprehensive guidelines or frameworks have been developed to date. Blockchain is a new kid on the block that has its doubters among researchers. In addition, technological shock also exists as an obstacle to the implementation of such ecosystems.

Furthermore, blockchain systems are not known for privacy regulations compliance, such as GDPR compliance, which has also created some issues for European companies [40,41]. Therefore, although blockchain has some remarkable features of tamperproof nature, immutability, transparency, trustworthiness, and inherent cryptographic nature, blockchain has not yet been successful in the insurance claim domain. Despite the drawbacks, blockchain is seen as a suitable storage provider for insurance data so that no one can tamper with it and the data is secure. Data stored in the blockchain can be insurance transaction data or patient data. However, if patient data and medical history are stored in the blockchain, they cannot be deleted or altered; therefore, if someone wants to change data, it is almost impossible to do that [42]. Moreover, it might require the creation of new blocks, which is also a waste of resources since blockchain is already known for its high processing power consumption and energy consumption. Hence, the research questions mentioned in Table 1 can be applied to the problem.

TABLE 1 Research gaps and future research agenda.

References	Current knowledge	Research gaps	Future research avenues
Zhou et al. [43]	Blockchain-based medical insurance framework based on Ethereum blockchain	The users don't have the scope to delete the data if needed or if the information needs to be updated	RQ1. What techniques can be applied to design an editable (modifying the customer data if needed) blockchain-based insurance framework?
	Insurance storage platform	Any information update needs a new block creation, which is resource-exhausting and time-consuming	RQ2. What security measures can be developed for physical blockchain nodes?
	Tamper-resistant and trustworthy insurance storage platform for patients and hospitals	The data privacy issue is not considered in this work	RQ3. How to train insurance fraud detection against various real-life use cases?
	Requires less memory processing power	Although it is a blockchain-based system, still, user-level security measures should be considered from each node perspective	RQ4. How to design a secure and privacy-preserving blockchain-based medical insurance management system?
Zhang et al. [44]	Uses artificial intelligence and analysis of two real datasets to identify medical insurance frauds	The framework is not tested against versatile use cases	RQ5. How to address the privacy issues of the medical insurance data?
	Proposes a framework to prevent insurance fraud that is based on a consortium blockchain	No physical level of security is mentioned at any point. Although blockchain is immutable, there should be mention of access control mechanisms for the users	RQ6. How to design a GDPR-compliant blockchain-based medical insurance management system?
	The framework facilitates medical data to be tamperproof and immutable		RQ7. What type of blockchain is suitable for the medical insurance framework and why is it suitable?
Thomas et al. [45]	Outlines the medical insurance storage system	Did not discuss any solid, comprehensive framework for medical insurance that considers infrastructural security issues	RQ8. How to manage the access and control the data flow of blockchain-based healthcare insurance management systems?
	Uses blockchain as tamperproof storage of medical data	Did not contribute toward the privacy issues of the healthcare data	

Continued

TABLE 1 Research gaps and future research agenda—cont'd

References	Current knowledge	Research gaps	Future research avenues
Chang et al. [46]	Contributes toward outlining the usage of blockchain for medical insurance storage and credit investigation systems	Limits the contribution of a comprehensive framework that addresses the discussed implications	**RQ9.** How to effectively design a smart contract to send requests, and accept or reject insurance claims in the healthcare domain?
		The study did not consider the security and privacy issues of the system	**RQ10.** How to conduct a proper requirements analysis among different stakeholders to identify the items to be addressed?
		Healthcare data being sensitive data, separate security measures should be taken to tackle these issues	**RQ11.** Is blockchain-based insurance suitable for compliance with privacy regulations?
Mohan and Praveen [47]	Contributes toward a privacy-preserving medical insurance framework	The study did not consider any privacy regulations, for example, GDPR, HL7, etc., for designing the system	**RQ12.** How to design a scalable blockchain-based insurance framework?
	Used blockchain as tamperproof storage of medical insurance information		
Liu et al. [48]	Cloud-based healthcare insurance management system that is based on blockchain technology	The study does not discuss any potential real-life security and privacy issues and measures (GDPR) required for the blockchain	
	The framework contributed toward preventing the fraud of the medical insurance ecosystem	A comprehensive framework with the minimum viable product is not present in this study	
Saeedi et al. [49]	Contributes to proposing a blockchain-based framework for the healthcare insurance scheme	Lacks discussion of a privacy-preserving system	
		Did not consider the addition or deletion of patient data from the system	
	Discussed the business value of the proposed scheme and the design requirements	Did not discuss in depth which blockchain platform should be used and why that is the suitable platform	

Reference	Contributions	Limitations
Ismail and Zeadally [50]	Contributed to designing a fraud-detection framework for healthcare insurance	Lacks discussion of the technical requirements of such a system Analysis of the design with an actual use case implementation is not present The type of blockchain used in this system is not specified
Alhasan et al. [51]	Contributes to the prevention of illicit insurance Designed and developed a blockchain-based insurance framework to prevent insurance fraud Creates a trustworthy system for insurance management	A comprehensive framework does not include the data flow among different entities starting from the patient, hospitals, and companies A smart contract algorithm is not present that can effectively tell the reader about the access control of the system The proposed framework uses a consensus algorithm that also lacks proper performance evaluation by other researchers
Goyal et al. [52]	Proposes a framework that utilizes machine learning and blockchain Blockchain will be used to store insurance transactions, claims, and histories Immutable record for insurance history	Lacks discussion of a privacy-preserving system Did not discuss in depth which blockchain platform should be used and why that is the suitable platform
Thenmozhi et al. [53]	Designs a blockchain-based system to facilitate the insurance companies to claim insurance Utilizes smart contract to manage insurance claim/rejection requests from different stakeholders	A smart contract algorithm is not present that can effectively tell the reader about the access control of the system Did not consider the addition or deletion of patient data from the system Did not discuss in depth which blockchain platform should be used and why that is the suitable platform

Continued

TABLE 1 Research gaps and future research agenda—cont'd

References	Current knowledge	Research gaps	Future research avenues
Kumar and Kumar [54]	Proposes a privacy-preserving and transparent model for medical insurance claims	Verification of following different privacy and data privacy guidelines especially GDPR is not present	
		The proposed model does not comprehensively discuss anything	
		The requirement analysis phase is missing	
Purswani [55]	Proposed medical insurance framework for parametric insurance data	The framework is not tested against versatile use cases	
	Conceptualized blockchain and smart contract as an enabling technology to promote immutability and trustworthy insurance claims	No physical level of security is mentioned at any point. Although blockchain is immutable, there should be mention of access control mechanisms for the users	
		Did not discuss any solid, comprehensive framework for medical insurance that considers infrastructural security issues	
		A smart contract algorithm is not present that can effectively tell the reader about the access control of the system	

5. Conclusion

There are low-performance issues and procedural complicacy in existing health insurance procedures, which must be addressed. Currently, patients who wish to file insurance claims must first visit the hospital to obtain a treatment report and voucher. They then have to submit the necessary paperwork to the insurer and, in order to be compensated, the firm must first conduct clearance with the person's hospital. Blockchain, on the other hand, has the potential to alleviate the current predicament. This technology can revolutionize the whole insurance file and claim process with better efficiency and less complexity. However, based on the comprehensive discussion outlined in this chapter, it is observed that there are no industry or academic standards to date to design a blockchain-based medical insurance ecosystem. The benefits of using blockchain in insurance systems are many, although a holistic system requires a proper understanding of the underlying technology and design requirements. Research gaps and future research directions summarized in this chapter can work toward solving these problems.

References

[1] A.B. Haque, B. Bhushan, G. Dhiman, Conceptualizing smart city applications: requirements, architecture, security issues, and emerging trends, Expert. Syst. 39 (2022) e12753.

[2] S. Goyal, N. Sharma, B. Bhushan, A. Shankar, M. Sagayam, Iot enabled technology in secured healthcare: applications, challenges and future directions, in: Cognitive Internet of Medical Things for Smart Healthcare, Springer, Cham, 2021, pp. 25–48.

[3] W. Zhao, X. Luo, T. Qiu, Smart healthcare, Appl. Sci. 7 (11) (2017) 1176.

[4] S. Tian, W. Yang, J.M. Le Grange, P. Wang, W. Huang, Z. Ye, Smart healthcare: making medical care more intelligent, Glob. Health J. 3 (3) (2019) 62–65.

[5] D.H. Mills, Medical insurance feasibility study: a technical summary, West. J. Med. 128 (4) (1978) 360.

[6] S.W. Zhao, X.Y. Zhang, W. Dai, Y.X. Ding, J.Y. Chen, P.Q. Fang, Effect of the catastrophic medical insurance on household catastrophic health expenditure: evidence from China, Gac. Sanit. 34 (2021) 370–376.

[7] S. Nakamoto, Bitcoin: a peer-to-peer electronic cash system, Decentralized Bus. Rev. (2008) 21260.

[8] S. Saxena, B. Bhushan, M.A. Ahad, Blockchain based solutions to secure Iot: background, integration trends and a way forward, J. Netw. Comput. Appl. 181 (2021) 103050, https://doi.org/10.1016/j.jnca.2021.103050.

[9] A.K.M. Haque, M. Rahman, Blockchain technology: methodology, application and security issues, Int. J. Comput. Sci. Netw. Secur. 20 (2) (2020) 21–30.

[10] B. Bhushan, P. Sinha, K.M. Sagayam, J. Andrew, Untangling blockchain technology: a survey on state of the art, security threats, privacy services, applications and future research directions, Comput. Electr. Eng. 90 (2021) 106897, https://doi.org/10.1016/j.compeleceng.2020.106897.

[11] A.P. Joshi, M. Han, Y. Wang, A survey on security and privacy issues of blockchain technology, Math. Found. Comput. 1 (2) (2018), https://doi.org/10.3934/mfc.2018007.

[12] A.B. Haque, B. Bhushan, Blockchain in a nutshell: state-of-the-art applications and future research directions, in: Blockchain and AI Technology in the Industrial Internet of Things, IGI Global, 2021, pp. 124–143.

[13] B. Bhushan, N. Sharma, Transaction privacy preservations for blockchain technology, in: Advances in Intelligent Systems and Computing International Conference on Innovative Computing and Communications, 2020, pp. 377–393, https://doi.org/10.1007/978-981-15-5148-2_34.

[14] P. Zhang, Z. Liu, S. Han, L. He, H.S. Müller, T. Zhao, Y. Wang, Visualization of rapid penetration of water into cracked cement mortar using neutron radiography, Mater. Lett. 195 (2017) 1–4, https://doi.org/10.1016/j.matlet.2017.02.077.

[15] A.B. Haque, B. Bhushan, Emergence of blockchain technology: a reliable and secure solution for IoT systems, in: Blockchain Technology for Data Privacy Management, CRC Press, 2021, pp. 159–183.

[16] M. Alvesson, J. Sandberg, Generating research questions through problematization, Acad. Manag. Rev. 36 (2) (2011) 247–271.

[17] T.H. Pranto, A.A. Noman, A. Mahmud, A.B. Haque, Blockchain and smart contract for IoT enabled smart agriculture, PeerJ Comput. Sci. 7 (2021) e407.

[18] G. Madaan, B. Bhushan, R. Kumar, Blockchain-based cyberthreat mitigation systems for smart vehicles and industrial automation, in: Studies in Big Data Multimedia Technologies in the Internet of Things Environment, Springer, 2020, pp. 13–32, https://doi.org/10.1007/978-981-15-7965-3_2.

[19] I.-C. Lin, T.-C. Liao, A survey of blockchain security issues and challenges, Int. J. Netw. Secur. 19 (2017) 653–659.

[20] Z. Zheng, S. Xie, H. Dai, X. Chen, H. Wang, Blockchain challenges and opportunities: a survey, Int. J. Web Grid Serv. 14 (4) (2018) 352–374.

[21] M. Bani Yassein, F. Shatnawi, S. Rawashdeh, W. Mardin, Blockchain Technology: Characteristics, Security and Privacy; Issues and Solutions, IEEE, 2019.

[22] M. Möser, Anonymity of bitcoin transactions: an analysis of mixing services, in: Proceedings of Münster Bitcoin Conference, Münster, Germany, 2013, pp. 17–18.

[23] P. Rathee, Introduction to blockchain and IoT, advanced applications of blockchain technology, in: Studies in Big Data, vol. 60, 2020, https://doi.org/10.1007/978-981-13-8775-3_1.

[24] G. Cui, K. Shi, Y. Qin, L. Liu, B. Qi, B. Li, Application of block chain in multi-level demand response reliable mechanism, in: Proceedings of the IEEE ICIM'17, Chengdu, China, April, 2017, pp. 337–341.

[25] Y. Yuan, F. Wang, Towards blockchain-based intelligent transportation systems, in: 2016 IEEE 19th International Conference on Intelligent Transportation Systems (ITSC), 2016.

[26] B. Bhushan, C. Sahoo, P. Sinha, A. Khamparia, Unification of blockchain and internet of things (BIoT): requirements, working model, challenges and future directions, Wirel. Netw 27 (1) (2021) 55–90.

[27] B. Bhushan, A. Khamparia, K. Martin Sagayam, S. Kumar Sharma, M. Abdul Ahad, N.C. Debnath, Blockchain for smart cities: a review of architectures, integration trends and future research directions, Sustain. Cities Soc. 2210-6707, 61 (2020) 102360, https://doi.org/10.1016/j.scs.2020.102360.

[28] A. Biswal, B. Bhushan, Blockchain for internet of things: architecture, consensus advancements, challenges and application areas, in: 2019 5th International Conference on Computing, Communication, Control and Automation (ICCUBEA), 2019, https://doi.org/10.1109/iccubea47591.2019.9129181.

[29] A. Manimuthu, V.R. Sreedharan, G. Rejikumar, D. Marwaha, A literature review on bitcoin: transformation of crypto currency into a global phenomenon, IEEE Eng. Manag. Rev. 47 (1) (2019) 28–35, https://doi.org/10.1109/emr.2019.2901431.

[30] J.R. Douceur, The sybil attack, in: Peer-to-Peer Systems Lecture Notes in Computer Science, 2002, pp. 251–260, https://doi.org/10.1007/3-540-45748-8_24.

[31] D. Puthal, N. Malik, S.P. Mohanty, E. Kougianos, G. Das, Everything you wanted to know about the blockchain: Its promise, components, processes, and problems, IEEE Consum. Electron. Mag. 7 (4) (2018) 6–14.

[32] X. Huang, Y. Zhang, D. Li, L. Han, An optimal scheduling algorithm for hybrid EV charging scenario using consortium blockchains, Futur. Gener. Comput. Syst. 91 (2019) 555–562,- https://doi.org/10.1016/j.future.2018.09.046.

[33] T.-T. Kuo, H.-E. Kim, L. Ohno-Machado, Blockchain distributed ledger technologies for biomedical and health care applications, J. Am. Med. Inform. Assoc. 24 (6) (2017) 1211–1220,- https://doi.org/10.1093/jamia/ocx068.

[34] M. Mettler, Blockchain technology in healthcare: the revolution starts here, in: 2016 IEEE 18th International Conference on E-Health Networking, Applications and Services (Healthcom), 2016, https://doi.org/10.1109/healthcom.2016.7749510.

[35] G. Zhang, X. Zhang, M. Bilal, W. Dou, X. Xu, J.J. Rodrigues, Identify fraud of medical insurance based on blockchain and deep learning, Futur. Gener. Comput. Syst. 130 (2021) 140–154.

[36] X. Yue, H. Wang, D. Jin, M. Li, W. Jiang, Healthcare data gateways: found healthcare intelligence on blockchain with novel privacy risk control, J. Med. Syst. 40 (10) (2016) 218.

[37] H. Zhao, Y. Zhang, Y. Peng, R. Xu, Lightweight backup and efficient recovery scheme for health blockchain keys, in: Proc. IEEE ISADS'17, Bangkok, Thailand, March, 2017, pp. 229–234.

[38] A. Azaria, A. Ekblaw, T. Vieira, A. Lippman, MedRec: using blockchain for medical data access and permission management, in: Proc. IEEE OBD'16, Vienna, Austria, August, 2016, pp. 25–30.

[39] Q. Xia, E.B. Sifah, K.O. Asamoah, J. Gao, X. Du, M. Guizani, MeDShare: trust-less medical data sharing among cloud service providers via blockchain, IEEE Access 5 (2017) 14,757–14,767.

[40] A.B. Haque, A.N. Islam, S. Hyrynsalmi, B. Naqvi, K. Smolander, GDPR compliant blockchains—a systematic literature review, IEEE Access 9 (2021) 50593–50606.

[41] G.A. Teixeira, M.M. da Silva, R. Pereira, The critical success factors of GDPR implementation: a systematic literature review, Digit. Policy Regul. Gov. 21 (2019) 402–418.

[42] F. Hofmann, S. Wurster, E. Ron, M. Böhmecke-Schwafert, The immutability concept of blockchains and benefits of early standardization, in: 2017 ITU Kaleidoscope: Challenges for a Data-Driven Society (ITU K), IEEE, 2017, November, pp. 1–8.

[43] L. Zhou, L. Wang, Y. Sun, MIStore: a blockchain-based medical insurance storage system, J. Med. Syst. 42 (8) (2018) 1–17.

[44] W. Zhang, C.P. Wei, Q. Jiang, C.H. Peng, J.L. Zhao, Beyond the block: a novel blockchain-based technical model for long-term care insurance, J. Manag. Inf. Syst. 38 (2) (2021) 374–400.

[45] C. Thomas, V. Bindu, A.A. Aby, U.R. Anjalikrishna, A. Kesari, D. Sabu, Blockchain-based medical insurance storage systems, in: Recent Trends in Blockchain for Information Systems Security and Privacy, CRC Press, 2021, pp. 219–235.

[46] S.E. Chang, Y. Chen, M. Lu, H.L. Luo, Development and evaluation of a smart contract-enabled blockchain system for home care service innovation: mixed methods study, JMIR Med. Inform. 8 (7) (2020), e15472.

[47] T. Mohan, K. Praveen, Fraud detection in medical insurance claim with privacy preserving data publishing in TLS-N using blockchain, in: International Conference on Advances in Computing and Data Sciences, April, Springer, Singapore, 2019, pp. 211–220.

[48] W. Liu, Q. Yu, Z. Li, Z. Li, Y. Su, J. Zhou, A blockchain-based system for anti-fraud of healthcare insurance, in: 2019 IEEE 5th International Conference on Computer and Communications (ICCC), December, IEEE, 2019, pp. 1264–1268.

[49] K. Saeedi, A. Wali, D. Alahmadi, A. Babour, F. AlQahtani, R. AlQahtani, Z. Rabah, Building a blockchain application: a show case for healthcare providers and insurance companies, in: Proceedings of the Future Technologies Conference, October, Springer, Cham, 2019, pp. 785–801.

[50] L. Ismail, S. Zeadally, Healthcare insurance frauds: taxonomy and blockchain-based detection framework (Block-HI), IT Prof. 23 (4) (2021) 36–43.

[51] B. Alhasan, M. Qatawneh, W. Almobaideen, Blockchain technology for preventing counterfeit in health insurance, in: 2021 International Conference on Information Technology (ICIT), July, IEEE, 2021, pp. 935–941.

[52] A. Goyal, A. Elhence, V. Chamola, B. Sikdar, A blockchain and machine learning based framework for efficient health insurance management, in: Proceedings of the 19th ACM Conference on Embedded Networked Sensor Systems, November, ACM, 2021, pp. 511–515.

[53] M. Thenmozhi, R. Dhanalakshmi, S. Geetha, R. Valli, Implementing blockchain technologies for health insurance claim processing in hospitals, Mater. Today Proc. (2021).

[54] S. Kumar, A. Kumar, Addressing transparency vis-a-vis privacy in portability of health insurance through blockchain, in: Innovations in Information and Communication Technologies (IICT-2020), Springer, Cham, 2021, pp. 407–411.

[55] P. Purswani, Blockchain-based parametric health insurance, in: 2021 IEEE Symposium on Industrial Electronics & Applications (ISIEA), July, IEEE, 2021, pp. 1–5.

Chapter 13

Blockchain embedded security and privacy preserving in healthcare systems

Avinash Kumar[a], Bharat Bhushan[a], Sonal Shristi[a], Saptadeepa Kalita[a], Raj Chaganti[b], and Ahmed J. Obaid[c]

[a]*School of Engineering and Technology (SET), Sharda University, Greater Noida, Uttar Pradesh, India,* [b]*Department of Computer Science, University of Texas at San Antonio, San Antonio, TX, United States,* [c]*Kufa University, Faculty of Computer Science and Mathematics, Kufa, Iraq*

1. Introduction

The internet of things (IoT) can be understood as the method or underlying theory that facilitates the interconnection of devices, which basically implies that these devices are interconnected to each other through the internet and are allowed to exchange information [1]. Among the many applications of IoT, medicine is the most common, mainly because of how important improving healthcare quality has become [2,3]. The uneven patient to doctor ratio observed in many countries—a trend that can render patients incapable of acquiring appropriate care from a doctor—provides a plausible explanation behind the efforts that are being made to make the medical field technologized. The deployments of IoT-enabled devices in scenarios such as these would lead to an improvement in the quality of healthcare services, for instance, by remote patient monitoring (RPM) [4]. RPM introduces a way for doctors and other medical practitioners to monitor patients outside the traditional clinical environment, thereby resulting in an increase in the number of patients that can be treated as compared to the number that could be treated in the traditional face-to-face setup. Another benefit of RPM is that it makes getting a clinical checkup a convenient service for the patients, since they can now remain connected with their doctor as and when required. It also decreases, among other things, the cost invested to maintain state-of-the-art antisepticised on-site hospitals and clinics. These are among the many reasons why healthcare providers are looking for

Blockchain Technology Solutions for the Security of IoT-Based Healthcare Systems.
https://doi.org/10.1016/B978-0-323-99199-5.00005-7

241

various means to make RPM devices widely available. In an IoT setup, RPMs can be visualized as a wearable device commissioned with an array of actuators and sensors that allow the device to interact and share information with whomever it may concern [5].

Another requirement that comes up when often sensitive patient data is to be shared, for example, with a network of smart hospitals, is the minimum security constraints that need to be employed. A contemporary example of this is the necessitated data sharing that arises as a result of the affiliation between the health insurance companies and the hospitals in many countries like the United States. Federal laws like the Health Insurance Portability and Accountability Act (HIPAA) require creation of national standards to prevent breach of a patient's confidentiality; and while sharing this information might enhance the treatment options, doing so while abiding by these laws and standards poses another challenge [6]. Moreover, the contemporary data sharing systems use a centralized model that at its foundation works with centralized trust. IoT, however, is intended to address these issues inherent to the traditional systems by migrating to blockchain as a means of sharing of data, the advancements in the hospital technology making the idea fairly reasonable. In smart environments such as smart hospital networks, IoT-based devices can either be fixed to a set location or be mobile. Most health applications suffer from security limitations, mainly due to digitization-induced privacy concerns. Moreover, collecting health data and then dealing with its secure interaction imposes certain constraints [7,8]. Secure communication necessitates the usage of some type of authentication methodology to facilitate the interactions between these IoT-enabled devices.

As evidenced by the interest shown by the research community, blockchain is a fairly viable solution to overcome the issue of secure communication, preventing any breach in patient privacy [9–11]. Dwivedi et al. [12] demonstrated a blockchain for IoT that was capable of protecting privacy and was decentralized. The paper presented a framework that was related to models of embedded blockchain for IoT-based devices. The framework relied on the network's distributed nature. Irving et al. [13] presented timestamped protocols and their possible role in increasing the trustworthiness of medical science, providing a method of using blockchain in a hospital setting to give evidence of endpoints that were defined beforehand. Srivastava et al. [14] demonstrated a medical blockchain that employed directed acyclic graphs [15]. The transactional protocol for RPM specifically made use of a private as well as a public blockchain. The approach was primarily devised to deal with the already known security issues, without making any drastic impact on scalability. Yazdinejad et al. [16] demonstrated a blockchain-based approach to benefit the authentication process in the 5G networks. The approach also utilized software defined networking (SDN). These blockchain-enabled methods removed the requirement of re-authentication every time the calls/devices moved between the cells present in the network [17].

Considering a typical scenario in a hospital where the medical staff interact among themselves with every node being monitored by a nurse station, the authentication in the secure communication mode of new staff present in the network that is not necessarily a part of a division or a region tends to be complex, the reason being that the authentication of members that are new needs the authority managing the authentication process to be decentralized. Many traditional authentication methods tend to be centralized and, generally, need an intervention from a trusted third party. Therefore, in scenarios that require a broad range of settings, there is an urgent need for decentralized approaches that remain scalable as well as flexible, qualities like security, trust, and privacy being necessitated by the nature of the sector. Arising as a result of user mobility (between parts of the same hospital or between different hospitals), re-authentications or frequent authentications have become the norm. This imposed need to identify and authenticate devices and people every so often incurs high costs of computation and introduces latency in the system, which, in a time-sensitive environment such as a hospital, can lead to extremely dangerous consequences. Moreover, these overheads are impractical in the application in question. One should always bear in mind the variable architecture of security systems and the need to authenticate if one is to ensure the robustness of the designed security solution. Yazdinejad et al. [18] proposed an interconnected healthcare system that uses peer-to-peer connections and a shared ledger, and also allows the users to migrate to affiliated hospitals through their distributed identity, eliminating the need for repeated authentication, and thereby significantly reducing the overheads discussed above.

Blockchain in its most simple terms can be described as a chain or sequence of blocks that are capable of holding an all-inclusive list of the history of transactions similar to how a traditional registry would be maintained. The first block present in a blockchain has no parents and is called a genesis block.

A block consists of a block header and a body, with the block header containing the following components: block version (which is indicative of the set of rules for block validation that are to be followed), Merkle tree root hash (which is the hash of all the transactions that are contained in a particular block), timestamp (current time in seconds since 1 January 1970), nBits (which is a valid block hash's target threshold), nonce (a counter of sorts that starts with the value 0 and is incremented for every hash calculated), and parent block hash (a 256 bit hash pointer that points to the current block's parent block). The block body is made up of a counter for transactions and the actual transactions. The maximum number of transactions that can be contained inside a given block depends both on the size of the block and the size of the individual transactions. Blockchain employs an asymmetric cryptographic mechanism to validate and authenticate the transactions [19–21].

This chapter seeks to explain how blockchain, if used efficiently, can prove to be highly beneficial in the field of healthcare. The main contributions made in this chapter include:

- An explanation of the benefits of using blockchain technology to safeguard data.
- A list of all the features of blockchain that could achieve the integrity of data.
- A brief overview of the embedded use of blockchain and IoT to protect the healthcare system.
- Enumeration of all the security challenges that the field of healthcare is susceptible to regarding various forms of cyberattacks.
- A list of the applications of blockchain-powered smart healthcare.

The remainder of this paper is organized as per the following scheme: Section 2 gives a detailed overview of the use of blockchain in healthcare along with its various features; Section 3 discusses all the security challenges that are prominent in the field of healthcare; Section 4 sheds light on the various applications that blockchain-powered smart healthcare has in real life; and Section 5 concludes the chapter by stating the future research directions.

2. Use of blockchain in healthcare

The recent advances in technology have made tremendous changes to human lives. These technologies have affected various sectors in order to make human lives better and more secure. One of the most prominent emerging domains is the integration of technology in healthcare [22]. Smart healthcare is a vital need for the rising global population. The conventional ways to store medical data were paper-based systems that were less efficient, less organized, insecure, easily tampered with, and are now redundant. This has made people move toward e-healthcare systems. The functions of e-healthcare systems are storing medical records in electronic form, managing patients' appointments and billing, keeping records of lab tests, etc. These generate a huge amount of medical data, like medical records, radiographs, ECG data, etc., and require transmission of these data from one device to another [23]. Healthcare data generally stores patients' confidential information, which is prone to privacy breaches. Therefore, the greatest challenge faced by the e-healthcare systems is security of the devices connected via the internet. Applications based on blockchain technology in the domain of medical science offer an incredible contribution for healthcare support. The advantages of implementation of blockchain in healthcare are improvement of security of medical records, user-related experiences, and various other aspects in the medical field [24]. Primarily, there are three applications of blockchain in healthcare, which are resources for fast healthcare interoperability, counterfeit drug prevention and detection, and user-oriented medical research. In the subsections below, a more detailed description of the uses of blockchain in healthcare is given.

2.1   Blockchain features for e-healthcare

Blockchain technology has various features that can be applied to the healthcare domain. These features are integrated into the systems and implemented in healthcare. Some of the features of blockchain features for e-healthcare are discussed in detail below.

2.1.1   Decentralization

This is one of the most vital features of blockchain, which provides the basis for enhancement of security and authentication of the medical data stored in the systems. Decentralized storage helps to store medical data such as documents as well as contracts by distributing the records stored in a single server to multiple servers with the help of blockchain ledger [25]. This technology makes the system secure by storing information in multiple servers instead of one server, which enables the transmission of data through the blockchain network, thus maintaining the authenticity of the transactions [26].

2.1.2   Transparency

Blockchain is very transparent in nature, as the processing of each transaction can be seen in the public domain. To achieve this transparency, a trust-based relationship must exist among the entities present within the system. The data that is stored in the blockchain is distributed among the servers in the network; therefore, the control of the data is also shared, making the system more transparent and secure from intervention by any other party [27]. This feature enables users to see the data available at any time, keeping all the transactions transparent.

2.1.3   Immutability

The database in blockchain is immutable in nature. The data stored in the blockchain ledger cannot undergo any type of modification, regardless of who the user is. In case any error occurs during a transaction, a new transaction is created in order to reverse the error. During that particular period of time, both the original transaction and the new transaction are visible. Then the original transaction is considered as an error and it is also recorded in the blockchain ledger [28].

2.2   IoT (smart healthcare) and blockchain for e-healthcare

The IoT is a collection of various devices that are interconnected and transfer information to each other via the internet. The demand for IoT applications in healthcare systems is rapidly increasing, as patients are becoming more aware of their health and willing to proceed toward some proactive approaches in healthcare [29]. In this kind of personalized healthcare system, the data is generated from sensors and devices that record the various parameters of the body and send it to a doctor for further diagnosis. Some of the popularly used IoT-enabled devices in healthcare are smart watches, fitness wrist bands, programmed microchips placed under the skin, contact lenses, etc. The data generated from these devices are stored in databanks or databases. IoT systems are vulnerable and prone to various attacks. However, the implementation of blockchain for IoT-based healthcare can make the system more secure [30]. Blockchain preserves the security of a medical database by securing the network as well as providing secure communication among the various devices present in the network [31]. Some shortcomings of IoT-based healthcare applications are discussed in detail below.

Presently, the sectors utilizing IoT-based networks depend on the client-server architecture. The devices within the network have the capacity to store a huge amount of data as well as processing it. These devices are always recognized and validated before connecting to the cloud servers [32]. Moreover, it is essential for the devices to be connected via the internet to exchange data to the other devices, regardless of how close they are to each other. However, such models are only viable in small IoT networks. Large IoT networks require stronger communication links, including maintenance of centralized cloud servers and networking devices. For building such large IoT networks the cost is significant. Moreover, centralized cloud servers are not reliable as they may suffer single point failure. The IoT devices must not be vulnerable to attacks and any kind of tampering with data. Some current technologies can provide security to IoT devices, but these techniques are extremely complex as well as not being applicable to IoT devices with less computational power.

The problem stated above of a single point of failure is overcome by blockchain technology. Moreover, by establishing a peer-to-peer network, the installation cost is minimized. The dependence on centralized cloud servers is also decreased as the data storage and computation is distributed among the devices in the network. This paradigm provides the solution to a single point of failure. In order to preserve the privacy of the IoT networks, the blockchain technology uses various cryptographic algorithms. In addition, application of tamper-resistant ledgers can resolve the reliability issue in IoT networks.

3. Security challenges in healthcare

The healthcare industry faces major challenges in managing and recovering the massive amounts of personal health data created in the course of conducting business and providing services. Devices for the purpose of health-monitoring, for example, wearables, generate large amounts of personal health data. The majority of health related data is not available, not standardized throughout systems, and is also challenging to comprehend, manage, and communicate. Data are received from many different places and are maintained in IT systems that are often centralized, making the data difficult to share and manage. Compiling, collecting, obtaining, and sending patient data requires time and resources. Healthcare systems may generate comprehensive views of patients, which increase the quality of care and treatments, improve communication, and improve health outcomes by properly managing and extracting these data. Standardization, unmanageable patient history, and an absence of appropriate and reliable demographic health data are all issues that the healthcare industry is dealing with. Some healthcare institutions keep sensitive health data in a central location, which is vulnerable to ransomware and other intrusions because of its antiquated IT system. The healthcare industry is still in the early phases of establishing equipment, automated systems, and management procedures that can effectively, safely, and systematically combine the various forms of data available to them. Patients' anonymity and the reliability, trustworthiness, and consistency of the system are all issues with current healthcare data systems. Criminals and cyber threat agents are seeking to exploit the flaws that come with these shifts as the healthcare industry continues to provide life-critical services while seeking effective health and patient treatment with emerging innovations. Cyberattacks in the field of healthcare can lead to problems that are much worse than breach of data and loss of financial assets. In the healthcare industry, there are three categories of cyberattack; these are described in Table 1.

4. Application of blockchain-powered smart healthcare

In recent years, the technologies that are integrated with blockchain have received the world's attention. A blockchain is a list of records that are growing continuously and are secured as well as linked with the help of cryptography. A blockchain that can record the negotiation between two different parties in a verified as well as persistent way is regarded as an open and distributed ledger [52]. The technological development of blockchain has enabled programming logic that is customizable, so that it can be stored in a decentralized manner, which has revived the creation of smart contracts. The software programs that consist of complex instructions on blockchain but are self-executing are known as smart contracts. The trusted agreements as well as transactions that are permitted by the smart contracts are carried out between anonymous parties without any need of legal systems, mechanisms of external enforcement, or central authorities [53]. The smart contracts and the blockchain applications cover digital identity certification, asset exchange, distributed file storage, together with IoT, and many more. Blockchain has some common applications in the healthcare sector, which can be divided into three categories [8,54]: user-oriented healthcare research, counterfeit medical drug detection and prevention, and fast healthcare interoperability resources. The healthcare applications based on blockchain in smart healthcare are explained further below.

TABLE 1 Challenges faced in the healthcare industry.

S. no.	Layer	Definition	Type of attack	Definition
1.	Application layer attacks	Application layer attacks consist of distributed denial-of-service (DDoS) attack, SQL injections, HTTP Floods, Slowloris attack, parameter tampering, and cross-site scripting [33]. Attacks target specific issues as well as vulnerabilities, so that the application layers will not be able to transfer the content to its specific user. The most targeted vulnerabilities of the application layer are web servers. As an attempt to prevent these attacks, most organizations and devices use protection techniques such as a web application firewall and security gateways. It also includes attacks like OpenBSD vulnerabilities, Apache attacks, and others.	Session medjack attack	A medjack attack is a cyberattack involving the hijacking of medical devices [34], which makes devices such as X-ray machines and MRI scanners vulnerable to hackers and cybercriminals. These attacks let attackers tamper with the devices and alter their functionality, allowing them to threaten the lives of patients or access information about their medical histories. These types of attacks can be very hard to detect, so to prevent these attacks from happening, deception techniques such as automation of honeypot or honey-grid networks are used, which can entrap or draw the attackers away as they enter into the network
			Amplification	This is a kind of attack in which the attackers multiply its attacking power with the help of the amplification factor. Amplification allows attackers to cause the malfunction of a large amount of resources with relatively small amount of resources, so it is called asymmetric. It consists of attacks such as Smurf attacks, DNS amplification, ICMP amplification, and Fraggle attacks, as well as UDP amplification and more [35]

Persistent XSS attack	In persistent XSS attacks, the websites as well as web applications are injected with malicious codes so that the end user's devices will become corrupted [36]. Some kinds of XSS attacks don't have a specific target. In this type of attack, the attackers simply try to find the vulnerability of the site so that they can take advantage of that vulnerability. But there are some direct ways, such as e-mails. These attacks exploit vulnerabilities in programming domains, such as Flash, ActiveX, and more
Dynamic host configuration protocol (DHCP) starvation	A DHCP starvation attack is a kind of attack that targets DHCP servers with a hostile digital attack [37]. During DHCP attacks, the server drains out the reserve of the IP addresses with the help of the malicious actor and floods it with discovery packets. This attack can lead to a man-in-the-middle (MITM) attack, as the attacker can challenge the user service network, or substitute the DHCP connection
Hypertext transfer protocol (HTTP) get request exhaustion	An HTTP get request attack is a type of DDoS attack which is very common. The setup or the implementation for this attack is very easy. In this attack the attackers will try to reject the services of the authorized user or the organization to exhaust the server by flooding the server with requests. Such attacks can cause the organization or business the loss of millions of dollars because it prevents the server from offering services to the authorized users [38]

Continued

TABLE 1 Challenges faced in the healthcare industry.—cont'd

S. no.	Layer	Definition	Type of attack	Definition
			Medical resource exhaustion	Medical resource exhaustion is a type of DDoS attack the vulnerabilities to which lie within the network layer as well as the transport layer. In this attack, the attackers drain the resources used for computing that are primary or secondary memories and computational power and create a network which is connected to a false IP address. This attack exploits the vulnerability of the protocol [39]
			Malware injection attacks	In malware injection attacks, the attackers create a hostile application or website and then inject it into the service models, such as SaaS, PaaS, and IaaS, individually. Also, the injection being injected in the cloud infrastructure, the attackers can attack with different types of attacks, such as data manipulation and more. There are many kinds of malware injection attacks, such as structured query languages (SQL) injection attack, XSS attack, and more [40]
			SQL injection DB medical information	This is a kind of cyberattack used by hackers or attackers with a small SQL code, so that they can do database manipulation as well as being able to obtain private data. This attack is among the most threatening as well as prevailing attacks because it can use the database of any websites or applications [41]

2.	Network layer attacks	The goal of network layer attacks is to crash computers, programs, and services. In addition to this, they also intend to exhaust the network capacity of devices. Network layer attacks commonly target infrastructure and network equipment.	IPv6 fragment attacks	IP fragmentation is a procedure of communication that involves the breaking down of IP datagrams into small packets and then their transmission is done across a network, after which they are integrated back together to create the initial datagram [42]. IPv6 fragment attacks come under the umbrella of denial of service attacks. In such attacks, the attacker heavily exploits the datagram fragmentation mechanisms and overwhelms the network
			IPSec flood attacks	IPSec flood attacks occur when the upper limit of the defined threshold is reached by the DoS cookie challenge that is configured. Such attacks are known to be extremely dangerous. This is because the attacker's primary intention is to exhaust all of the resources that belong to the targeted system. When an IPSec flood attack is carried out successfully, the system that is affected overwhelms all of its resources and this prevents it from fulfilling requests that are legitimate. This also hampers the IPSec VPN connections. To mitigate such attacks, organizations should ensure that traffic from only trusted sites that are previously known is allowed. This is because IPSec is mostly used to define VPN connections between sites that are already known and organizations can define the IP addresses of these sites beforehand in the list of infrastructure access [43,44]

Continued

TABLE 1 Challenges faced in the healthcare industry.—cont'd

S. no.	Layer	Definition	Type of attack	Definition
			ARP poisoning	ARP poisoning, otherwise referred to as ARP spoofing, is a man-in-the-middle kind of attack [45]. It gives attackers the chance to intercept the communication being carried out between two networking devices. An ARP poisoning involves an attacker who possesses access to the targeted network. The attacker scans this network in order to determine the IP addresses of a minimum of two different network devices. The attacker then proceeds to use spoofing tools to broadcast false ARP responses. Some spoofing tools that are commonly used are Driftnet and ARP spoof. The false broadcasted responses indicate that the attacker's MAC address is the same as the MAC addresses of both the devices' IP addresses. This allows the network devices to unknowingly connect to the machine that belongs to the attacker under false pretenses. This causes the ARP cache entries of both the devices to be updated and the devices can then only communicate with the attacker instead of each other. This allows the attacker to be the middleman and have access to all the communication happening between the two devices. The attacker, once successful in carrying out the process of ARP poisoning, can steal sensitive data, access all the accounts that the user is logged into, and introduce malicious content into the devices [46,47]

3.	Perception layer attacks	The perception layer incorporates a lot of hardware components like actuators and sensors. These attacks involve the physical presence of the attacker in close proximity to the targeted systems in order to carry out the attack to exhaust them.	RFID sniffing	RFID sniffing can also be referred to as a man-in-the-middle attack. Such an attack takes place when a signal is being transmitted. The attacker first tries to listen for any kind of communication between a reader and a tag. Once communication is detected, the attacker then intercepts it and then manipulates or tampers with the data. Next, the attacker takes the original signal and diverts it. After the diversion, incorrect data is sent under the pretext of it being a regular part of the RFID system [48]
			RFID spoofing	After gaining access to the information stored in a user's RFID card and copying it to another blank RFID card, it becomes easy for an attacker to enter into areas or items that are secured and are only intended to be accessed exclusively by the user. To replicate the information present in an RFID card, the attacker needs to be aware of the kind of information present in it. Therefore, these kinds of attacks are mainly prevalent in asset management operations or access management operations [49]
			RFID cloning	RFID cloning is a very common technique used by attackers. It involves cloning a user's RFID card. To clone an RFID card, an attacker does not necessarily need to have access to it physically. The data stored in an RFID card can easily be procured through off-the-shelf components even from a distance. This data can then be rewritten to a new, blank RFID card that is compatible. The components used to devise these

Continued

TABLE 1 Challenges faced in the healthcare industry.—cont'd

S. no.	Layer	Definition	Type of attack	Definition
				cloning devices are acquired mostly from a large-scale RFID reader. Such readers are commonly used in parking garages. This is because the user does not have an option to be in close proximity to the reader in order to scan their card. The attacker can easily bypass these readers and clone the sensitive information [50]
			RFID denial of service	RFID denial of service attacks are mostly physical. They involve carrying out activities like actively jamming systems by employing noise interference, removing RFID tags, blocking radio signals, disabling RFID tags, physically destroying RFID tags, etc. [51]

4.1   User-oriented healthcare research

Researchers in the healthcare and medical fields require datasets that are comprehensive in order to understand the development of the diseases, to design customizable treatment strategies for an individual based on their genetics, external environment, and lifestyle, as well as to accelerate the biomedical assessment of the patients [55]. With the help of blockchain, the development process of the healthcare system is effectively speeding up [56]. Model-chain is a framework that is proposed to improve the robustness as well as the security of a predictive model based on distributed healthcare using private blockchain [57]. The framework of the model-chain is like a blockchain for a peer-to-peer network with the characteristics of machine learning that are incremental in nature. Model-chain was introduced to adapt the technology of the blockchain for preserving the privacy of machine learning. Each contributor to the site can participate in the parameter estimation of the model without any disclosure of the patient's health data [58]. Model-chain can also help to improve interoperability as follows:

- Maintenance of modularity: Model-chain inherits the blockchain architecture by peer-to-peer, so while interoperating with the other site, it allows the remaining site to be modular.
- In aspects of interoperability protecting privacy and security: The design of the Model-chain is a robust, privacy-preserving, as well as secure interoperability platform. Blockchain helps to increase the security during predictive model processing by preserving the privacy of the data through exchanging zero patient's data.

Healthcare predictive models help to improve patient health care [59]. There have been several algorithms proposed to preserve the privacy of an individual's health data, such as conducting predictive models by transferring partially trained machine learning instead of dispersing the individual private health data [60]. To build an Ethereum blockchain, an indicator provider of blockchain, Gems, announced a partnership with Philips, for the application development of a healthcare enterprise [61].

4.2   Counterfeit medical drug detection and prevention

Counterfeit drugs represent a serious threat to human health [62]. The authenticity, interoperability, and data security of blockchain allows the life science and the healthcare industries to record healthcare data that will combat counterfeiting of prescription drugs effectively as well as protecting intellectual property [63]. The MediLedger project works with the contribution of several of the world's prime pharmaceutical manufacturers together with wholesale distributors [64]. It helps to design as well as implement a process to explore the potential of blockchain technology to improve the track and trace capabilities of prescription medicines. Blockchain makes it easy to track medications and trace them when they move from these manufacturers and distributors safely to the patients. Based on blockchain principles, the MediLedger project uses customizable as well as advanced decentralized supply chain management [65]. It has a dynamic system that helps to innovate the track and trace regulations by evolving the solution, along with providing improvements in terms of supply chain operation. The MediLedger project is creating its own blockchain network, which is permissioned by the industry for the pharmaceutical sector and is based on open specifications and standards. Only industry managers and technology providers who work for the industry can operate the set of network nodes. The MediLedger project has a decentralized network, which is possible because it has solved the sensitive data privacy issue.

In the United States, there was a rampant opioid crisis, which was addressed by BlockMedX [66]. It provided services specifically designed for physicians as well as pharmacies, to help to increase accountability along with security in the drug industry.

Counterfeit medicines and drugs are products that are deliberately and falsely produced, and then their identity and origin is faked to make them appear to be genuine products. False or counterfeit medications include medicines that contain an inferior quality, low, incorrect, or no level of active pharmaceutical ingredients (API), or repackaged products that are already expired. Counterfeit medication can be detrimental both for the consumer and for producers of generic products.

4.3 Fast healthcare interoperability resources

Previously, in the healthcare industry, patients did not have the ability to have control over their EHRs and most were completely unaware that their private medical data has tremendous value [67,68]. The users as well as the providers of healthcare systems can manage the medical records along with the data of clinical trials while maintaining regulatory observance with the help of the technology of blockchain. For instance, there is a health records management system, which is decentralized as well as novel, known as MedRec [69]. It provides services because of which the patients can authorize the viewership of their data and can build a record of their health data. It is a system which prioritizes patients by giving them access to view their medical history [70]. There is also another powered blockchain system, known as MedShare, which provides auditing and data provenance, as well as control over the shared healthcare data in cloud storage among researchers in the medical and healthcare fields, healthcare providers, and healthcare entities [3]. It is designed to employ smart contracts along with procedures that authenticate and track the behavior of the data effectively.

5. Conclusion and future research directions

This chapter has summarized all the vital aspects pertaining to preserving privacy and security by embedding blockchain in healthcare by anomaly detection. The paper first thoroughly explained the different uses that blockchain has in the field of healthcare. Along with this, the different features that blockchain provides in the e-healthcare domain were also listed with brief explanations. Furthermore, the chapter delved into how IoT and blockchain paired together can greatly benefit the field of e-healthcare. Their benefits were discussed in detail. The chapter then went on to elucidate the many challenges the field of healthcare faces due to the highly personal data it deals with. The different forms of cyberattacks in the application, network, and perception layers were defined. This chapter provides a solution and platform for each individual attack that has been explained in Section 3 and relates threat and risk mitigation for every attack within the IoT domain of smart healthcare. Finally, the chapter listed the various applications of blockchain-powered smart healthcare, such as counterfeit drug detection and prevention, fast healthcare interoperability resources, and user-oriented healthcare research. In terms of future work, this study can be used as a reference to devise more efficient blockchain-powered systems. Furthermore, this study can be treated as a base to acquire a deeper understanding of such systems. This study aims to make contributions to studies and future research that take place in the field of blockchain-based healthcare and give rise to technological advancements in this field.

References

[1] S. Liu, Y. Liu, X. Liang, N. Wang, Uncertainty observation-based adaptive succinct fuzzy-neuro dynamic surface control for trajectory tracking of fully actuated underwater vehicle system with input saturation, Nonlinear Dyn. 98 (3) (2019) 1683–1699, https://doi.org/10.1007/s11071-019-05279-w.

[2] M. Mettler, Blockchain technology in healthcare: the revolution starts here, in: 2016 IEEE 18th International Conference on e-Health Networking, Applications and Services (Healthcom), 2016, https://doi.org/10.1109/healthcom.2016.7749510.

[3] M. Wang, Y. Guo, C. Zhang, C. Wang, H. Huang, X. Jia, MedShare: a privacy-preserving medical data sharing system by using blockchain, IEEE Trans. Serv. Comput. (2021) 1, https://doi.org/10.1109/tsc.2021.3114719.

[4] C.E. Puig, Remote Monitoring Enhanced Patient and Clinician Confidence in Home Dialysis, 2017, https://doi.org/10.26226/morressier.59a56f96d462b8028d895d3e.

[5] M. Jayson Baucas, P. Spachos, Fog and IOT-based remote patient monitoring architecture using speech recognition, in: 2020 IEEE Symposium on Computers and Communications (ISCC), 2020, https://doi.org/10.1109/iscc50000.2020.9219649.

[6] C. DeLeon, Y.B. Choi, Blockchain and the protection of patient information in line with HIPAA, in: Research Anthology on Blockchain Technology in Business, Healthcare, Education, and Government, 2021, pp. 1373–1379, https://doi.org/10.4018/978-1-7998-5351-0.ch076.

[7] H. Al Rasyid, M. U., Astika Saputra, F., & Kurniawan, A., Surveillance monitoring system based on internet of things, in: 2020 International Electronics Symposium (IES), 2020, https://doi.org/10.1109/ies50839.2020.9231634.

[8] N. Sharma, I. Kaushik, B. Bhushan, S. Gautam, A. Khamparia, Applicability of WSN and Biometric Models in the Field of Healthcare, in: Deep Learning Strategies for Security Enhancement in Wireless Sensor Networks Advances in Information Security, Privacy, and Ethics, 2020, pp. 304–329, https://doi.org/10.4018/978-1-7998-5068-7.ch016.

[9] S. Gupta, S. Sinha, B. Bhushan, Emergence of blockchain technology: fundamentals, working and its various implementations, 2020, SSRN Electron. J. https://doi.org/10.2139/ssrn.3569577.

[10] S. Dash, P.K. Gantayat, R.K. Das, Blockchain technology in healthcare: opportunities and challenges, Intell. Syst. Ref. Libr. (2021) 97–111, https://doi.org/10.1007/978-3-030-69395-4_6.

[11] A. Malik, S. Gautam, S. Abidin, B. Bhushan, Blockchain technology-future of IoT: including structure, limitations and various possible attacks, in: 2019 2nd International Conference on Intelligent Computing, Instrumentation and Control Technologies (ICICICT), 2019, https://doi.org/10.1109/icicict46008.2019.8993144.

[12] A. Dwivedi, G. Srivastava, S. Dhar, R. Singh, A decentralized privacy-preserving healthcare blockchain for IOT, Sensors 19 (2) (2019) 326, https://doi.org/10.3390/s19020326.

[13] G. Irving, J. Holden, How blockchain-timestamped protocols could improve the trustworthiness of medical science, F1000Research 5 (2016) 222, https://doi.org/10.12688/f1000research.8114.2.

[14] G. Srivastava, R.M. Parizi, A. Dehghantanha, K.-K.R. Choo, Data sharing and privacy for patient IOT devices using blockchain, in: Communications in Computer and Information Science, 2019, pp. 334–348, https://doi.org/10.1007/978-981-15-1301-5_27.

[15] Y. Sompolinsky, S. Wyborski, A. Zohar, Phantom Ghostdag, in: Proceedings of the 3rd ACM Conference on Advances in Financial Technologies, 2021, https://doi.org/10.1145/3479722.3480990.

[16] A. Yazdinejad, R.M. Parizi, A. Dehghantanha, K.-K.R. Choo, Blockchain-enabled authentication handover with efficient privacy protection in SDN-based 5G networks, IEEE Trans. Netw. Sci. Eng. 8 (2) (2021) 1120–1132, https://doi.org/10.1109/tnse.2019.2937481.

[17] K. Nabben, Blockchain security as "people security": applying sociotechnical security to Blockchain technology, Front. Comput. Sci. 2 (2021), https://doi.org/10.3389/fcomp.2020.599406.

[18] A. Yazdinejad, G. Srivastava, R.M. Parizi, A. Dehghantanha, K.-K.R. Choo, M. Aledhari, Decentralized authentication of distributed patients in hospital networks using blockchain, IEEE J. Biomed. Health Inform. 24 (8) (2020) 2146–2156, https://doi.org/10.1109/jbhi.2020.2969648.

[19] B. Bhushan, C. Sahoo, P. Sinha, A. Khamparia, Unification of Blockchain and Internet of Things (BIoT): requirements, working model, challenges and future directions, Wirel. Netw (2020), https://doi.org/10.1007/s11276-020-02445-6.

[20] S. Saxena, B. Bhushan, M.A. Ahad, Blockchain based solutions to secure IoT: background, integration trends and a way forward, J. Netw. Comput. Appl. (2021), https://doi.org/10.1016/j.jnca.2021.103050. 103050.

[21] B. Bhushan, P. Sinha, K.M. Sagayam, J. Andrew, Untangling blockchain technology: a survey on state of the art, security threats, privacy services, applications and future research directions, Comput. Electr. Eng. 90 (2021) 106897, https://doi.org/10.1016/j.compeleceng.2020.106897.

[22] S. Khatri, F.A. Alzahrani, M.T.J. Ansari, A. Agrawal, R. Kumar, R.A. Khan, A systematic analysis on blockchain integration with healthcare domain: scope and challenges, IEEE Access 9 (2021) 84666–84687, https://doi.org/10.1109/ACCESS.2021.3087608.

[23] A.A. Mazlan, S. Mohd Daud, S. Mohd Sam, H. Abas, S.Z. Abdul Rasid, M.F. Yusof, Scalability challenges in healthcare blockchain system—a systematic review, IEEE Access 8 (2020) 23663–23673, https://doi.org/10.1109/ACCESS.2020.2969230.

[24] E.M. Abou-Nassar, A.M. Iliyasu, P.M. El-Kafrawy, O.-Y. Song, A.K. Bashir, A.A.A. El-Latif, DITrust chain: towards blockchain-based trust models for sustainable healthcare IoT systems, IEEE Access 8 (2020) 111223–111238, https://doi.org/10.1109/ACCESS.2020.2999468.

[25] P.G. Shynu, V.G. Menon, R.L. Kumar, S. Kadry, Y. Nam, Blockchain-based secure healthcare application for diabetic-cardio disease prediction in fog computing, IEEE Access 9 (2021) 45706–45720, https://doi.org/10.1109/ACCESS.2021.3065440.

[26] A. Aderibole, et al., Blockchain technology for smart grids: decentralized NIST conceptual model, IEEE Access 8 (2020) 43177–43190, https://doi.org/10.1109/ACCESS.2020.2977149.

[27] M. Zarour, et al., Evaluating the impact of blockchain models for secure and trustworthy electronic healthcare records, IEEE Access 8 (2020) 157959–157973, https://doi.org/10.1109/ACCESS.2020.3019829.

[28] D.C. Nguyen, P.N. Pathirana, M. Ding, A. Seneviratne, BEdgeHealth: a decentralized architecture for edge-based IoMT networks using blockchain, IEEE Internet Things J. 8 (14) (2021) 11743–11757, https://doi.org/10.1109/JIOT.2021.3058953.

[29] A.P. Singh, et al., A novel patient-centric architectural framework for blockchain-enabled healthcare applications, IEEE Trans. Industr. Inform. 17 (8) (2021) 5779–5789, https://doi.org/10.1109/TII.2020.3037889.

[30] S. Goyal, N. Sharma, B. Bhushan, A. Shankar, M. Sagayam, IoT enabled technology in secured healthcare: applications, challenges and future directions, in: Cognitive Internet of Medical Things for Smart Healthcare, 2020, pp. 25–48, https://doi.org/10.1007/978-3-030-55833-8_2.

[31] R. Sethi, B. Bhushan, N. Sharma, R. Kumar, I. Kaushik, Applicability of industrial IoT in diversified sectors: evolution, applications and challenges, in: Studies in Big Data Multimedia Technologies in the Internet of Things Environment, 2020, pp. 45–67, https://doi.org/10.1007/978-981-15-7965-3_4.

[32] J. Sun, H. Xiong, X. Liu, Y. Zhang, X. Nie, R.H. Deng, Lightweight and privacy-aware fine-grained access control for IoT-oriented smart health, IEEE Internet Things J. 7 (7) (2020) 6566–6575, https://doi.org/10.1109/JIOT.2020.2974257.

[33] K. Salunke, U. Ragavendran, Shielding Techniques for Application Layer DDoS Attack in Wireless Networks: A Methodological Review, 2021, https://doi.org/10.21203/rs.3.rs-240485/v1.

[34] S. Khazaei, J. Kolahi, Journal hijacking: a new challenge for medical scientific community, Dent. Hypotheses 6 (1) (2015) 3, https://doi.org/10.4103/2155-8213.150858.

[35] D.R. Thomas, R. Clayton, A.R. Beresford, 1000 days of UDP amplification DDoS attacks, in: 2017 APWG Symposium on Electronic Crime Research (ECrime), 2017, https://doi.org/10.1109/ecrime.2017.7945057.

[36] B.B. Gupta, P. Chaudhary, Fundamentals of cross-site scripting (XSS) attack, in: Cross-Site Scripting Attacks, 2020, pp. 53–74, https://doi.org/10.1201/9780429351327-3.

[37] N. Hubballi, N. Tripathi, A closer look into DHCP starvation attack in wireless networks, Comput. Secur. 65 (2017) 387–404, https://doi.org/10.1016/j.cose.2016.10.002.

[38] T.R. Sree, S.M. Bhanu, HADM: detection of HTTP get flooding attacks by using analytical hierarchical process and Dempster-Shafer theory with MapReduce, Secur. Commun. Netw. 9 (17) (2016) 4341–4357, https://doi.org/10.1002/sec.1611.

[39] M. Aridoss, Defensive mechanism against ddos attack to preserve resource availability for IOT applications, in: Securing the Internet of Things, 2020, pp. 1429–1442, https://doi.org/10.4018/978-1-5225-9866-4.ch065.

[40] P. Tripathi, R. Thingla, Cross site scripting (XSS) and SQL-injection attack detection in web application, SSRN Electron. J. (2019), https://doi.org/10.2139/ssrn.3356292.

[41] S. Gupta, About SQL injection attack, in: SQL Injection Attacks, 2020, https://doi.org/10.1007/978-1-4842-6505-5_1.

[42] D. Forte, Fragmentation attacks: protection tools and techniques, Netw. Secur. 2001 (12) (2001) 12–13, https://doi.org/10.1016/s1353-4858(01)01219-3.

[43] IPSec architecture., A Technical Guide to IPSec Virtual Private Networks, 2000, https://doi.org/10.1201/9780203997499.ch7.

[44] A.S. Dhaliwal, Detection and Mitigation of SYN and HTTP Flood DDoS Attacks in Software Defined Networks, 2021, https://doi.org/10.32920/ryerson.14647329.

[45] W. Enck, ARP spoofing, in: Encyclopedia of Cryptography and Security, 2011, pp. 48–49, https://doi.org/10.1007/978-1-4419-5906-5_100.

[46] M. Data, The defense against ARP spoofing attack using semi-static ARP cache table, in: 2018 International Conference on Sustainable Information Engineering and Technology (SIET), 2018, https://doi.org/10.1109/siet.2018.8693155.

[47] R.K. Kanna, R. K., Sunkari, V., & Chander, P., DOS and ARP spoofing attacks analysis through agent software, Indian J. Appl. Res. 3 (5) (2011) 253–255, https://doi.org/10.15373/2249555x/may2013/77.

[48] Classification of RFID Attacks, Proceedings of the 2nd International Workshop on RFID Technology—Concepts, Applications, Challenges, 2008, https://doi.org/10.5220/0001738800730086.

[49] B.-Z. Jing, P.P. Chan, W.W. Ng, D.S. Yeung, Anti-spoofing system for RFID access control combining with face recognition, in: 2010 International Conference on Machine Learning and Cybernetics, 2010, https://doi.org/10.1109/icmlc.2010.5580562.

[50] J. Abawajy, Enhancing RFID tag resistance against cloning attack, in: 2009 Third International Conference on Network and System Security, 2009, https://doi.org/10.1109/nss.2009.101.

[51] Y. Fu, C. Zhang, J. Wang, A research on denial of service attack in passive RFID system, in: 2010 International Conference on Anti-Counterfeiting, Security and Identification, 2010, https://doi.org/10.1109/icasid.2010.5551848.

[52] N. Singh, M. Vardhan, Distributed Ledger technology based property transaction system with support for IOT devices, in: Research Anthology on Blockchain Technology in Business, Healthcare, Education, and Government, 2021, pp. 299–319, https://doi.org/10.4018/978-1-7998-5351-0.ch018.

[53] M. Sokolov, Smart legal contract as a future of contracts enforcement, SSRN Electron. J. (2018), https://doi.org/10.2139/ssrn.3208292.

[54] A. Biswal, B. Bhushan, Blockchain for internet of things: architecture, consensus advancements, challenges and application areas, in: 2019 5th International Conference on Computing, Communication, Control and Automation (ICCUBEA), 2019, https://doi.org/10.1109/iccubea47591.2019.9129181.

[55] P. Mehta, Framework of Indian healthcare system and its challenges, in: Healthcare Community Synergism Between Patients, Practitioners, and Researchers, 2017, pp. 247–271, https://doi.org/10.4018/978-1-5225-0640-9.ch011.

[56] M.S. Gross, R.C. Miller, Ethical implementation of the Learning Healthcare System with Blockchain technology, Blockchain in Healthcare Today 2 (2019), https://doi.org/10.30953/bhty.v2.113.

[57] M. Kiruthika, V. Gupta, T. Poongodi, B. Balamurugan, Architectural framework of 5G-based smart healthcare system using Blockchain technology, in: Blockchain for 5G Healthcare Applications: Security and Privacy Solutions, 2021, pp. 197–225, https://doi.org/10.1049/pbhe035e_ch8.

[58] T. Fukuhara, Y. Hori, Parameter estimation without confidence intervals? Epidemiol. Health 38 (2016), https://doi.org/10.4178/epih.e2016036r.

[59] L. Dormer, How can real-world evidence be used in practice to demonstrate drug value and improve patient care? J. Comp. Eff. Res. 6 (3) (2017) 183–184, https://doi.org/10.2217/cer-2017-0016.

[60] D. Liu, K. Fox, G. Weber, T. Miller, Confederated Learning in Healthcare: Training Machine Learning Models Using Disconnected Data Separated by Individual, Data Type and Identity for Large-Scale Health System Intelligence (Preprint), 2020, https://doi.org/10.2196/preprints.24951.

[61] S. Palladino, Blockchains, in: Ethereum for Web Developers, 2019, pp. 1–16, https://doi.org/10.1007/978-1-4842-5278-9_1.

[62] A. Behura, A. Behura, H. Das, Counterfeit product detection analysis and prevention as well as prepackage coverage assessment using machine learning, in: Advances in Intelligent Systems and Computing, 2020, pp. 483–496, https://doi.org/10.1007/978-981-15-2414-1_49.

[63] R. Yousuf, D. Ashraf Khan, Z. Jeelani, Security and privacy concerns for blockchain while handling healthcare data, in: Blockchain for Healthcare Systems, 2021, pp. 177–192, https://doi.org/10.1201/9781003141471-12.

[64] R. Ishii, Manufacturers' and distributors' capabilities influencing Dual Channel Choice, Mark. Intell. Plan. 39 (1) (2020) 151–166, https://doi.org/10.1108/mip-06-2019-0336.

[65] N. Kshetri, Blockchain in supply chain management, in: Blockchain and Supply Chain Management, 2021, pp. 1–37, https://doi.org/10.1016/b978-0-323-89934-5.00009-x.

[66] V.A. Canady, Depression care addressed as way to deal with opioid crisis, Ment. Heal. Wkly. 28 (22) (2018) 4–5, https://doi.org/10.1002/mhw.31471.

[67] T. Ziminski, S. Demurjian, T. Agresta, Extending the fast healthcare interoperability resources (FHIR) with Meta Resources, in: Proceedings of the 16th International Conference on Software Technologies, 2021, https://doi.org/10.5220/0010546500002992.

[68] S.S. Bhuyan, S. Bailey-DeLeeuw, D.K. Wyant, C.F. Chang, Too much or too little? How much control should patients have over EHR data? J. Med. Syst. 40 (7) (2016), https://doi.org/10.1007/s10916-016-0533-2.

[69] J. Nichols, Becoming reconciled to MedRec, Caring for the Ages 18 (4) (2017) 4–5, https://doi.org/10.1016/j.carage.2017.03.006.

[70] I. Taskent, Evaluation of the patient's data forms which arrives at Emergency Medical Services by ambulance, J. Surg. Curr. Trend. Innov. 4 (1) (2020) 1–13, https://doi.org/10.24966/scti-7284/100025.

Chapter 14

Blockchain-based decentralized management of IoT devices for preserving data integrity

Avinash Kumar[a], Bharat Bhushan[a], Sonal Shristi[a], Raj Chaganti[b], and Ben Othman Soufiene[c]

[a]*School of Engineering and Technology (SET), Sharda University, Greater Noida, Uttar Pradesh, India,* [b]*Department of Computer Science, University of Texas at San Antonio, San Antonio, TX, United States,* [c]*PRINCE Laboratory Research, ISITcom, Hammam Sousse, University of Sousse, Sousse, Tunisia*

1. Introduction

Blockchain can be defined as a way of securing data in a distributed manner such that it is immutable, auditable, and resistant to faults. Blockchain technology was introduced in the year 2009 and has gained popularity due to its capacity to eliminate the need for a third party to make transactions between multiple devices [1–3]. It removes the need for centralization to validate the transactions; instead, validation is performed by a network of peers [4,5]. However, it also comes with some disadvantages, such as high cost, as blockchain that needs to be maintained on a very large scale is costly. Additionally, it requires high computational power and storage capacity [5].

Nowadays, smart devices and other electronic devices are being designed in such a way that they carry storage and computational capabilities on board [6]. This is a direct result of the lowering of the cost of manufacturing in terms of electronic devices, and is also due to the widespread prevalence of the internet. A traditional smart device is a combination of actuators and sensors and is designed as a single unit, keeping in mind particular tasks that it needs to perform. Smart appliances and sensor nodes typically do not have very high computational power [7,8]. This makes them incapable of locally executing tasks that require intensive use of the CPU. This challenge is overcome by outsourcing the computational tasks to another central device that possesses high computational power, like a cloud-based server [9,10]. The system encountering network latency is the weakness of this technique [11]. This challenge is

Blockchain Technology Solutions for the Security of IoT-Based Healthcare Systems.
https://doi.org/10.1016/B978-0-323-99199-5.00009-4

overcome by employing an edge device that acts as an intermediary between the cloud and the end smart device. The edge device processes tasks locally, since it is local to the smart devices, and the remaining tasks are outsourced to the cloud [12,13]. This model incorporating edge computing along with the cloud is extremely helpful [14].

Pairing blockchain with internet of things (IoT)-based devices can help to solve many challenges and each of those technologies also helps in compensating for the demerits of the other [15]. For instance, blockchains are extremely expensive due to their requirement of high computational power and consumption of memory. IoT systems, on the other hand, are designed to be quite low in terms of cost [16]. One of the main reasons blockchain is so popular is the use of a ledger to ensure the security of data. Instead of using a centralized system, blockchain technology focuses on decentralization, which overcomes the challenge of single point of failure [17]. Each node that is involved in the process possesses a replica of the blockchain ledger. Tampering and making modifications to the ledger is a very tough task if there isn't a proper consensus of a fairly large number of involved individuals [18]. Incorporating blockchain technology in an IoT-based system is a very effective way to decentralize the way in which numerous devices are managed. Furthermore, the immutable nature of blockchain facilitates the tracking and auditing of sources of data and transactions [19,20].

This chapter seeks to give a detailed analysis of the approaches that are used in the decentralization of IoT devices as well as the role of blockchain. The major contributions in the paper can be summarized as follows:

- This chapter analyses and discusses the background of blockchain, which is crucial for IoT-based systems.
- This chapter elaborates the essential features of blockchain that enhances the security of IoT-based systems.
- This chapter describes the need for and benefits of using the decentralized features of blockchain in IoT.
- This chapter discusses the applications of blockchain in real-life scenarios.

The remainder of this chapter is organized as per the following scheme: Section 2 provides a detailed analysis of the background of blockchain and its role in the IoT; Section 3 addresses the decentralized use of blockchain along with trusted execution environment and distributed management in networks in the IoT; Section 4 describes the applications of blockchain in the IoT decentralized concept; an lastly, Section 5 concludes the paper and suggests future research directions.

2. Background of blockchain and its role in the IoT

Blockchain has now become one of the essential technologies to detect anomalies in any system where transaction or confidential communication is needed. The following subsection provides a deep analysis of the technology of blockchain.

2.1 Background of blockchain

A blockchain can be referred to as a list of records that are also given the term blocks [21]. These blocks keep growing continuously and are linked to each other with the help of cryptography [22]. Every single block constitutes a cryptographic hash that belongs to the preceding block [23]. Essentially, blockchain can be seen as a simple yet efficient method of sending information from point A to point B in a way that is safe and completely automated. The first party involved in a transaction starts the process by making a block. That block, after verification through a huge number of computers that are present in the net in a distributed manner, is integrated into a chain that is also stored in the net. This results in the creation of a new and distinct record, which also has a very distinct history as compared to other records. A ledger, by definition, is a book that keeps and maintains records of all the kinds of transactions an organization makes. The blockchain is essentially the public ledger that contains information about all the transactions that will be made and transactions that have already been executed. Such a ledger of transactions is known as blockchain because it is a chain made of blocks.

This chain of blocks grows continuously and constantly because new blocks are added to the chain by the miners involved whenever a new transaction is made. The addition of blocks is always done in a chronological and linear manner. The mining of blockchain is a process that includes adding the transactions of records to the private/public ledger belonging to the blockchain. A miner that belongs to a blockchain network is essentially a node. This means that it is a part of the network that can validate the transactions of records after a kind of consensus is offered. When a miner or a group of multiple miners collectively try to take control of over 50% of a given network's computational power, hash rate, and mining power, it is referred to as an attack made on a blockchain [24]. If someone takes over the control of such a large part of the mining power, it gives them the power to block any new transactions from being executed and confirmed.

Another term that is very important in terms of blockchain technology is smart contract [25]. A smart contract is a term that is used to refer to a program created to fulfill the purpose of following a particular set of computer protocols in order to carry out digital verification, digital facilitation, and to enforce the execution and negotiation of a given contract. A smart contract usually eliminates the need for any third parties and can allow transactions as long as they are credible, trackable, and irreversible. A smart detractor is a unique concept in the context of programming. The purpose of a smart detractor is to discover contracts that might be suspicious in nature and stop them from being able to be executed.

2.2 Features of blockchain

Blockchain has multiple features; these are transparency, decentralization, and immutability:

- When the transaction and holding of every public address can be viewed openly it is known as transparency.
- Decentralization refers to the technology where all assets such as documents, contracts, etc., can be accessed via the internet [26].
- The owner of the assets has all the control over the account and the right to transfer the assets present. The data, once added to the ledger, is no longer available for changes, regardless of the role of the user. This is known as immutability. If, by chance, there is an error, then it can only be fixed through the creation of new transactions to fix the error. In such a case, both, the erroneous transaction and the transaction made to reverse the error are displayed. So there is no way to completely remove the transaction that contains the error from the ledger.

2.3 Working principles of blockchain

There are five steps involved in the working of blockchain. Step 1 involves the making of a request by any individual to make a transaction. Step 2 involves the request being sent to the nodes that are the members. These nodes, which are collectively known as a network of nodes, make use of algorithms that verify and approve the transaction. Step 3 involves the completion of the transaction after it is approved by the network of nodes. Step 4 involves the addition of a distinct new block to the blockchain network after the transaction is completely executed. Finally, Step 5 involves the addition of the verified transaction to the other transactions that are already present and this makes up a distinct new data block. In order to perform the addition of information to the blockchain, it is imperative that the individual first provides their unique key and public address to log in. The unique key is a private key that helps in signing the transaction. This kind of information is extremely secure. This is because it is replicated multiple times, which makes it necessary to gain control over at least 51% of the available nodes for a hacker to make any changes.

2.4 Types of blockchain

Currently, there are four different kinds of blockchain networks that are widely used, which are consortium, private, public, and hybrid. A consortium blockchain is a semidecentralized blockchain. This means that various organizations have the right to collectively make decisions that facilitate the process of giving users the provision of blockchain services [27]. This permission-based approach is used to put restrictions on who has rights over the infrastructure of blockchain and to what extent. A private blockchain is heavily permission-based. This means that an individual can only access it if an invitation is given by the administrator of the blockchain network [28]. So, there is a heavy restriction on the rights of the validator and the role of participation. Private blockchain infrastructure is usually employed by applications and organizations where there is a need for the keeping of records and management of sensitive data. A public blockchain is not at all permission-based, which means that it has no restrictions applied to it. Any individual present on the internet is allowed to connect to such a network and can also send transactions. Additionally, the individual can also play the role of key validator [29]. Public blockchains are heavily dependent on mechanisms that are economic and based on incentives to secure the system by making use of consensus algorithms that come under a special type. Finally, hybrid blockchain is a combination of the facilities of both private and public blockchain. It is implemented when private as well as public access to data needs to be incorporated. This combination is done in a seamless manner. A user in the hybrid blockchain is offered free or permission-based access depending on what the application requires [30].

2.5 Blockchain and IoT in smart healthcare

Devices with internet connectivity and electronic devices embedded into them are capable of interacting and communicating with other devices present all over the internet. They can also be controlled and monitored without the operator being in close proximity, i.e., remotely. IoT networks have a set of strict requirements and the use of blockchain facilitates avoiding malicious attacks on stored data and keeping the network secure as well as allowing the devices present all over the network to communicate with each other in a very secure manner. However, there are some disadvantages associated with IoT-based systems. For instance, many IoT networks that are used nowadays use the server-client model as their basis. In a server-client model, all the devices present are thoroughly authenticated, identified, and connected through cloud servers. This needs a very large amount of storage capability and processing power. Additionally, any interactions that take place among these devices must pass through the internet regardless of the fact that the devices are already close to each other. A model like this, although viable for IoT networks that are small, is not scalable. Moreover, there is a high cost involved in the creation of such a large number of communication links, networking all the necessary equipment, and maintaining centralized clouds. Since the architecture is heavily dependent on cloud servers, it also becomes vulnerable to problems like a failure at a single point.

Furthermore, devices based on IoT have to be safe from tampering with both the data and the physical hardware. There are many methods that deal with these issues and help in making IoT-based devices more secure but they can sometimes be too complex and not suitable for devices that have low computational power and certain resource constraints. The use of blockchain is very efficient in overcoming these challenges. This is because using blockchain ensures that a peer-to-peer network is established. This lowers the installation and maintenance cost of data centers, equipment used for networking, and centralized clouds, it does so by distributing the storage and computational requirements across all the devices present in the network. This solves the problem of a single point of failure. The privacy of IoT networks is protected using cryptographic algorithms in blockchain. The problem of reliability in IoT networks is solved by making use of blockchain, which is extremely resistant to tampering.

3. Decentralized use of blockchain

Decentralization of management of assets using blockchain technology is extremely helpful as it helps to maintain the transparency, integrity, and security of data. In a decentralized system, the rights to access data are given through smart contracts, and the blockchain stores all the audit trail of data access. The following subsections describe in detail the strategies and techniques that are used to achieve decentralization.

3.1 Managing using trusted environment

The data belonging to users is shared with many third parties every day. This is not always done in a transparent manner. The reason behind this is the authority centralization in how the data generated by IoT devices are managed. The technology of blockchain is becoming more and more popular all across the world and is being employed so that the management of the various assets is done in a decentralized manner. One example of this is Bitcoin. Using a decentralized system for the management of data through IoT-based devices that enforce permission to access data by making use of smart contracts and all of the information regarding access of data being stored in the blockchain is very beneficial. Using applications based on smart contracts, a set of rules can be enforced by various parties to oversee all interactions. These rules can function independently and this eliminates the need for a system that is centralized. This can be done through multiple frameworks. For instance, a framework can use blockchain and store the hash of the available data in it. The raw data is then stored in a storage platform that is highly secure. This is done by making use of a trusted execution environment (TEE), which ensures that the data is secure and the privacy of sensitive data stays intact. The data is protected from being accessed by parties that are not authorized and who could use the data for malicious purposes.

Intel SGX is considered to be an integral part of TEE. SGX provides the protection of the user's data on a hardware level. It does so by employing the isolation of processes through the execution of necessary programs in enclaves that are highly secure. The memory pages that belong to the enclave are protected by the hardware of the CPU. Enclaves can essentially be defined as secure containers that are protected from hypervisor processes, operating systems, and other processes [31,32]. There have been some substantial developments in the area of embedded hardware technology that have proved to be very beneficial to support TEE, for example, ARM Trust Zone, TPM, AMD SVM [33,34]. These have aided service providers in ensuring the integrity and confidentiality of computations and data by employing the protection of data and code within a region of computation that is secure.

Intel SGX is a very popular and reliable architecture in computing. It has been employed in the processors of Intel Skylake [35]. By offering a newly created set of instructions, extending the X64 and X86 architectures, the applications at the user level have been made capable of providing integrity and confidentiality of data by eliminating the trust of the operating system that is in use. With this given set of instructions, the developers of the application can quite easily devise containers that are isolated and secure, known as enclaves, and protect the security-sensitive computations. The content of the memory of an enclave is specifically stored in the enclave page cache (EPC). The EPC is a region of memory that is protected by the hardware. Employing the use of a memory encryption engine (MEE) makes it easier to encrypt all the EPC pages and the hardware restricts any kind of access to them [36]. This is how TEE paired with SGX protects computations and data that are sensitive in nature from the risk of attacks that can come from applications that have high privileges, for example, system management mode, hypervisors, and the operating system.

3.2   Distributed management in a network in the IoT

One of the most prevalent challenges faced in the implementation of blockchain is consuming resources for IoT devices in order to execute protocols based on mining and consensus [37]. Employing edge computing in order to support blockchain integration into IoT networks is extremely helpful [38]. Such a system comprises a huge number of IoT devices and fog nodes (FNs), which have capabilities such as edge computing [39]. It also comprises a primary fog node (PFN), which has a large amount of storage capability [40,41]. FNs come with the ability of edge computing which helps them to connect wirelessly to IoT devices [42]. In addition to this, FNs are free to leave and join networks according to suitability [43]. This means that FN deployment does not encounter frequent and continuous updates [44].

IoT devices that employ the use of blockchain release the tasks related to mining to PFNs, initially. They are responsible for procuring tasks from IoT devices and then incorporating them into blocks using an algorithm known as the proof of word (PoW) algorithm. This block, which is newly generated, is sent to the remaining FNs to attain a consensus. Management of resources and scheduling the different FNs is a disadvantage when it comes to executing blockchain on an IoT network that is enabled based on fog. Auction theory and game theory are some of the techniques that have been used to overcome this issue. The problem that arises due to this is that, in approaches like game theory, it is imperative to be aware of the actions carried out by the other players involved. This is not the most practical when implemented in a blockchain system. In auction theory, the maximization of the utility of the platform is done by eliciting the true cost of a miner [45]. Nowadays, matching theory has become extremely popular given its capability to achieve stability in a market that is two-sided by eliminating the requirement of a centralized controller.

4. Application of blockchain in the IoT decentralized concept

As blockchain is gaining more and more popularity, organizations are migrating to it and implementing it in many domains. For example, waste management in smart cities, pollution level monitoring, and vehicle life cycle tracking. These applications and the inner workings of the implementations are discussed in detail in the following subsections.

4.1 Smart waste management using blockchain technology

Cities all across the globe have been generating huge amounts of waste at an alarming rate. This is affecting the environment and the health of living organisms negatively. According to one estimate, each year billions of tons of waste is generated in the world. This number will only increase as the years pass by. One human is estimated to generate an amount of waste that ranges from 0.11 to 4.54 kg every day [46]. Approximately 33% of the solid waste that is generated in most cities is not being managed in a way that is safe for the environment and has no harmful effects [47]. This management of waste in an improper manner poses a risk of contamination to oceans. It also poses a threat to the health of animals and contributes to the spreading of dangerous diseases. Furthermore, the primary source of food for stray animals is the food that is disposed by humans, mostly in plastic bags.

For waste management to be done in a proper manner, combined effort and coordination between all the stakeholders is required. This involves collectors, waste generators, waste treatment facilities, and shippers. Many systems that exist for this purpose lack this coordination, due to which the task becomes quite challenging as the data related to the waste generated is not shared among all the stakeholders that are involved in the process efficiently [48]. There usually exists a discrepancy between them due to the shortage of means to share the data adequately [49,50]. The use of blockchain technology has proved to be extremely beneficial in overcoming this challenge. It offers a unified and highly integrated platform that all the stakeholders involved in city's waste management can use collectively in order to share the data in a transparent, secure, verifiable, and effective manner [51–53].

Blockchain technology is based on a structure that is decentralized in its design. This makes it robust, extremely tolerant of faults that might occur, and overall, a reliable technology. Most existing cities have to encounter quite a long list of challenges such as polluted air and the deteriorating nature of management of water resources. In addition to these, there are also challenges like sustainable creation of energy and management of waste in an eco-friendly manner. A city is termed as a smart city when the quality of life of citizens residing in the city is quite good, the environment is protected, the local economy increases substantially, and there is a very low rate of traffic congestion due to making use of reliable and efficient information communication technologies (ICT) [54,55]. If employed in a sustainable and effective manner, waste management policies greatly facilitate in improvement of the quality of water and air considerably. Additionally, they contribute to the reduction of carbon emissions, which leads to a cleaner environment. A considerable number of systems that are in place for waste management are based on IoT and make use of centralized cloud-based resources to process data that is related to waste. These systems use IoT-based nodes that monitor, sense, and transmit the type and amount of waste present in bins and the levels of humidity and temperature, and then calculate the route data and time of arrival of the trucks that carry the waste, so that the data can be processed by the cloud servers and decisions can be made accordingly [56]. For example, it is useful to predict the amount of waste that can be carried by smart bins and if there are any vehicles that are available near them [57].

However, this centralized design to store and process data can lead to discrepancies among the stakeholders, which can further lead to poor coordination opportunities among them. Additionally, when data is stored in a system that is centralized it becomes prone to threats like unauthorized modifications, deletion by third parties with malicious intent, and fraud. The reliability of the data pertaining to the management of waste heavily impacts the decisions that are made by the stakeholders. This means that if the data is hampered in any way, it results in the planning of resources by concerned authorities for the management of waste generated in smart cities being poor and ineffective. Furthermore, this centralized design and the lack of coordination reduces the productivity and performance of the processes carried out for the management of waste.

Employing the technology of blockchain for the task of waste management positively impacts the process of decision-making. It also leads to an improvement in cost efficiency and productivity and ensures that the regulations put in place for the processing of waste are being abided by. Blockchain relies on a peer-to-peer (P2P) architectural design to store and process data [58]. It is extremely reliable, transparent, and secure, making it a very trusted technology [59]. A smart contract is a term that is used to represent programs that are stored on the blockchain along with the terms of the agreement among everyone that is a participant in the processes employed for waste management. When a criterion that is determined beforehand in the contract is met, certain trigger events are automatically executed. The stakeholders also benefit as it helps them to perform operations related to business in a much cheaper, more secure, and faster fashion as compared to conventional systems that are rendered ineffective unless certain intermediaries are employed to perform the business-related operations.

According to the lifetime and the characteristics associated with smart contracts, they can be further classified into many kinds such as active, self-destructed, dormant, and prolific. For instance, a smart contract for waste management that is active entails registering the organizations that participate in it and issuing them certificates as a reward for management of identity. In blockchain technology, the waste management data that is stored is done in an immutable and encrypted manner. Additionally, the data along with the transactions are stored in chronological order so that a record of waste provenance can be provided when needed [60,61]. Data pertaining to waste provenance helps to verify that the waste items that are gathered, managed, and processed abide by the rules that are defined for the handling of waste. In addition to this, it also facilitates the identification of recyclers and generators of waste, all while maintaining the privacy of data. The records stored on the blockchain are highly trustworthy, immutable, secure, and transparent. The concerned authorities can access them to gain knowledge on the city that generates the highest amount of waste for the waste treatment facility. In addition to this, the information on ownership of waste generated and information on provenance can assist governments in recognizing and issuing rewards to responsible citizens who direct their waste properly; whereas, the identification of waste handlers who do not comply with the laws defined for the shipment and treatment of waste is done via the audibility feature using blockchain data [62]. Blockchain ensures the protection of privacy through the maintenance of citizens' anonymous identities. These anonymous identities cannot be traced back to the users' real identities.

Nowadays, most of the implementation of smart contracts for automation of services in smart cities focuses on smart healthcare, smart grids, smart homes, supply chain management, agriculture, and smart transportation [63–65]. Systems based on blockchain that are devised for the effective management of waste primarily concentrate on agricultural, electronic, domestic, and medical waste generated by smart cities. There have been many projects done for the purpose of waste management that have employed numerous kinds of services that are related to shipment monitoring and assets tracking, tokens transferring, auditability of waste handler's actions, and waste sorting, along with waste management [66–68]. A lot of systems use Hyperledger Fabric and Ethereum platforms in order to distribute penalties and rewards among the participants. This helps in ensuring that they abide by the laws pertaining to waste management [69–71]. There are many more uses for blockchain technology in the management of waste in smart cities, which also come with a set of social and technical challenges, making them a very popular topic among researchers.

4.2   Decentralized pollution-monitoring systems based on distributed ledger technology

The demand for reliable data on pollution has increased due to the regulations regarding environmental protection becoming stricter. This has helped researchers, planners, and policymakers greatly, as they can use this data to make well-informed decisions on how to manage and improve the environment [72,73]. For effective collection and storage of pollution data and to perform a detailed analysis on the atmospheric conditions it is important to have reliable pollution monitoring systems (PMSs) [74,75]. Nowadays, public environment agencies and various other local authorities have been given the task of operating PMSs and performing the provision to provide clean air. This includes monitoring the pollution level of the air and devising strategies accordingly to help mitigate air pollution [76]. However, the centralization of tasks like maintenance and operation of PMSs in local authorities leads to an absence of transparency in the storage, processing, and collecting of sensor data. For example, the data is lacking in terms of nonrepudiation, integrity, and authenticity [77]. The verification of pollution analysis can prove to be quite a challenging task for external parties due to the fact that there are only a few analysts who perform tasks like data calibration, cleaning, sensor data interpretation, and applied analytical methods [78,79]. This, in turn, can lead to an erroneous assessment of the pollution level in the environment. This can affect the regulations created for pollution control and ultimately impact the health of living organisms.

To mediate this problem, allowing third parties to verify and crosscheck the pollution data and to promote enhanced decision-making in terms of improving air quality can be extremely helpful [80]. This increases the transparency in the storage, collection, and analysis of data pertaining to pollution levels. Local authorities mainly make use of stationary PMSs and mostly look into what the long-term causes will be on a macro scale and in urban areas. The high cost and huge size of stationary PMS only allows a few people to partake in the process of data collection and only a small number of people have access to the data that is stored [80]. In approximation, a stationary PMS costs 30,000 USD annually for maintenance and 200,000 USD initially for installation [81]. Furthermore, PMSs can be detrimental to the procurement of pollution data in a fine-grained and flexible manner [82]. To achieve monitoring of air pollution that is finer-grained, even more detailed data is required. This data should contain parameters like the temporal and spatial variability of the pollutants present in the air, for example, particulate matter.

Technological improvements in the field of portable sensor nodes have allowed for the sensing of pollution in a very efficient manner. This is mostly due to their cost being low and their power supply being battery based, unlike stationary PMS. Integrating portable sensor nodes allows stationary PMSs to make measurements more flexibly. They are also capable of attaining an increased spatiotemporal resolution as a result of them containing large numbers of sensor nodes [83,84]. Even though it has an obvious advantage in terms of monitoring pollution levels, portable sensor nodes-integrated PMS still comes with a set of disadvantages. Some cons are that they have a limited supply of energy due to being battery dependent and they also possess low computational resources [85]. These disadvantages make the creation of portable sensor nodes-integrated PMS quite challenging. Therefore, a better method of pollution monitoring, including portable sensor nodes, is needed to perform an apt analysis on how to devise PMSs that are transparent, viable, and show resistance to fraudulent advances.

Distributed ledger technology (DLT) is another advancement that is known to mediate several challenges that are encountered when PMSs are operated, for instance, data not being authentic or being vulnerable to unwanted modifications [86]. DLT ensures that the database that is being operated is transparent and cannot be tampered with. It has an infrastructure that is highly available and is capable of tolerating faults. It contains a large number of computing and storage devices that can replicate data [87]. Evidently, applications based on DLT can provide efficient identity management to devices and organizations and access management to available data, and storage of data can be done effectively without any interruptions [88–91]. However, DLT also has its fair share of disadvantages. These can include poor scalability, low performance when compared with traditional distributed and central databases, and high consumption of resources like storage as they require extremely large storage space as a result of ledger replications [92]. Extensive consumption of resources is one of the most important challenges faced when designing PMSs that use low-energy and portable sensor nodes. There is still a lot of research that needs to be done in the field of DLT in terms of PMSs using low-energy and portable sensor nodes. Hence, there is not a lot of information available to prove how effective DLT can be when associated with PMS using low-energy and portable sensor nodes and what should be the acceptable solution to the tradeoff between consumption of resources and flexibility.

4.3 Blockchain-based framework for vehicle life cycle tracking

Blockchain is being widely accepted due to the many advantages it offers. Many countries have switched to blockchain to carry out their business-related activities [93]. One example of this is the maintenance and management of the usage and history details of vehicles. This has become a primary concern of many people and organizations all across the globe. Vehicle tracking systems are very important. Developed countries have devised systems exclusively for the purpose of online verification that contain records of millions of driving licenses and those of vehicles, and these records are regularly updated [94–96]. Tracking the life cycle of a vehicle entails interconnecting transportation departments, vehicle manufacturers, vehicle inspection organizations, insurance companies, and agencies whose purpose is to analyze the number of accidents the vehicle has been through. There is one such framework that is very beneficial for this purpose. The framework focuses on tracking the complete life cycle of a vehicle over a blockchain that helps individuals and organizations by providing information regarding vehicles. The customization of the blockchain involved facilitates the inspection's control of usage and renting. The model for usage control is paired with IoT devices so as to monitor the vehicles continuously and revoke access remotely if required [97,98].

The development process of this framework involved consulting numerous implementations of monitoring of life cycle of vehicles that employed the application of blockchain technology all across the globe. It was found that the use of a centralized system for the management of violations had many downsides to it. Some downsides of a centralized system are failure at a single point and how it takes away from the involvement of stakeholders. Stakeholders, for the most part, are interested in being a part of the centralized system in order to offer helpful services to the owners of the vehicles and, due to the closed nature of centralized system, this is not an option for them. This is where blockchain-based systems for tracking the life cycle of vehicles have an advantage over centralized systems. Characteristics such as transparency, decentralization, inherent security, and verification of the transactions made by eliminating the need for a third party are just some of the merits of blockchain-based systems. Blockchain ensures data integrity, data transparency, and distributed trust. Utilizing the pros of blockchain technology for the maintenance of the integrity of the details of vehicles and using an infrastructure that is not prone to threats is highly beneficial for the process of making transactions as well. These transactions include transferring used vehicles, placing orders to purchase new vehicles, estimation of prices of vehicles that are used, insurance, renting, management of violation and accident, and inspection of vehicles as long as they are usable and are not scraped. Table 1 contains some of the most notable implementations in the field of blockchain.

5. Conclusion and future research directions

This chapter has summarized all the important topics associated with blockchain and its role in the decentralized management of IoT devices so far. First, it discussed the background of blockchain and its role in IoT. These were briefly explained along with some important terms associated with blockchain technology. In addition, the features of blockchain, its working principles, and types of blockchain were also discussed. A detailed description of decentralized use of blockchain was given along with an explanation of managing using a trusted execution environment and distributed management in a network in IoT. Their motives, usage, and limitations were discussed as well. After that, light was shed on the topic of the applications of blockchain in the IoT decentralized concept. Some of the applications that were mentioned were blockchain for waste

TABLE 1 Summary of various blockchain-based implementations.

Application	References	Year	Contribution
IoT for solid waste management	Shyam et al. [99]	2017	Manage waste collection dynamically
	Chen et al. [100]	2018	Waste container management
	Gayathri et al. [101]	2021	Management of food waste
	Kumar et al. [102]	2017	GPRS-based garbage clearance
	Al-Masri et al. [103]	2018	Serverless IoT architecture for waste management
	Pranathy et al. [104]	2021	Capacitated vehicle routing in smart dustbins
Cloud-based waste management system	Aazam et al. [105]	2016	Sensor-based waste bins
	Catarinucci et al. [106]	2019	Ultralow-power RFID-based waste management
	Baras et al. [107]	2020	Recycling bin for house waste classification
	Das et al. [108]	2020	Inventorization of e-waste for sustainability
	Rashmi et al. [109]	2019	Sensor-based garbage data collection and processing via AWS kinesis
Blockchain-based waste management system	Ahmad et al. [69]	2021	Integration of Ethereum blockchain with storage system files for effective waste management
	Mondal et al. [110]	2022	Plastic waste management and tracking
	Schmelz et al. [66]	2019	Transborder waste management and tracking
	Dua et al. [111]	2020	Smart waste management for 5G smart communities
	Damadi et al. [112]	2021	Promotes cooperation between companies involved in the process of the waste management chain
	Farizi et al. [113]	2021	Electronic waste management using Hyperledger Fabric

TABLE 1 Summary of various blockchain-based implementations—cont'd

Application	References	Year	Contribution
Blockchain-based smart healthcare	Nguyen et al. [114]	2021	Architecture for data sharing and offloading
	Asad et al. [115]	2020	Proof of authority technology for secure sharing of sensitive data
	Vardhini et al. [116]	2021	Smart contract-based framework for electronic medical records
	Gul et al. [117]	2020	Automation of healthcare tasks using machine learning concepts
	Aich et al. [118]	2021	Protecting personal healthcare records via federated learning technologies
	Ismail et al. [119]	2020	Framework for healthcare records management for better diagnosis
Blockchain and IoT for air pollution monitoring	Nizeyimana et al. [120]	2021	Framework to monitor air pollution spikes
	Niya et al. [121]	2018	LoRaWAN and smart contracts-based pollution monitoring system
	Muthukumar et al. [122]	2018	System for pollution monitoring and control
	Xiaojun et al. [123]	2015	Forecasting and monitoring air pollution
	Parmar et al. [124]	2017	Monitoring presence of different gases like CO, CO_2, SO_2, and NO_2
	Sajjan et al. [125]	2021	Air pollution analysis using Raspberry Pi
Blockchain for vehicle life cycle tracking	Syed et al. [126]	2020	Framework for vehicle life tracking using parameters like renting and inspection parameters
	Subramanian et al. [127]	2021	Hybrid blockchain for tracking previously owned vehicles
	Demir et al. [128]	2019	Vehicle insurance management
	Sharma et al. [129]	2019	Framework for vehicular industry in smart cities
	Wang et al. [130]	2019	Vehicle supply chain management using Hyperledger Fabric

management in smart cities, the advantages of a decentralized pollution-monitoring system based on distributed ledger technology, and a blockchain-based framework for vehicle life cycle tracking. In addition to the applications, the details of their inner working were also explained briefly.

As far as future work is concerned, the study performed above can be referred to, to formulate more efficient systems using blockchain. This study can also be extended to gain a deeper understanding of decentralized systems in order to perform more real-life practical implementations. This study has successfully created a basis and the main aim of it is to make noteworthy contributions to future research and studies in the field of decentralized management of IoT devices using blockchain, where smart healthcare is one of the implementations of IoT that deals with more sensitive and more personal data.

References

[1] J.T. George, Introducing blockchain applications, in: Introducing Blockchain Applications, 2022, https://doi.org/10.1007/978-1-4842-7480-4.

[2] J. Golosova, A. Romanovs, The advantages and disadvantages of the blockchain technology, in: 2018 IEEE 6th Workshop on Advances in Information, Electronic and Electrical Engineering (AIEEE), 2018, https://doi.org/10.1109/aieee.2018.8592253.

[3] S. Rouhani, R. Deters, Data trust framework using blockchain technology and adaptive transaction validation, IEEE Access 9 (2021) 90379–90391, https://doi.org/10.1109/access.2021.3091327.

[4] I. Khan, A. Shahaab, A peer-to-peer publication model on Blockchain, Front. Blockchain 4 (2021), https://doi.org/10.3389/fbloc.2021.615726.

[5] A. Zeiselmair, B. Steinkopf, U. Gallersdörfer, A. Bogensperger, F. Matthes, Analysis and application of verifiable computation techniques in blockchain systems for the energy sector, Front. Blockchain 4 (2021), https://doi.org/10.3389/fbloc.2021.725322.

[6] Securing Smart Devices, Security and Auditing of Smart Devices, 2016, pp. 111–116, https://doi.org/10.1201/9781315369372-14.

[7] L. Binternagel, C4.2—energy efficient sensor nodes, in: Proceedings SENSOR 2009, vol. II, 2009, https://doi.org/10.5162/sensor09/v2/c4.2.

[8] S. Harte, Fault tolerance in sensor networks using self-diagnosing sensor nodes, in: IEE Seminar on Intelligent Building Environments, 2005, https://doi.org/10.1049/ic:20050211.

[9] B. Sawiris, S. El-Gaber, M. Abdel-Fattah, Centralization of big data using distributed computing approach in IOT, Int. J. Intell. Eng. Syst. 14 (4) (2021) 393–409, https://doi.org/10.22266/ijies2021.0831.35.

[10] S.K. Singh, Cloud computing: comparative study own server vs cloud server, in: Recent Advances in Mathematics, Statistics and Computer Science, 2016, https://doi.org/10.1142/9789814704830_0056.

[11] R. Goonatilake, R.A. Bachnak, Modeling latency in a network distribution, Netw. Commun. Technol. 1 (2) (2012), https://doi.org/10.5539/nct.v1n2p1.

[12] Proceedings 2020 IEEE International Conference on Edge Computing Edge 2020, 2020, https://doi.org/10.1109/edge50951.2020.00001.

[13] Proceedings 2020 IEEE 13th International Conference on Edge Computing, 2020, https://doi.org/10.1109/edge50951.2020.00002.

[14] P. Marcer, X. Masip, E. Marin, A. Jurnet, Scaling edge computing security with Blockchain technologies, in: Blockchain-Enabled Fog and Edge Computing, 2020, pp. 187–215, https://doi.org/10.1201/9781003034087-9.

[15] S. Gupta, S. Sinha, B. Bhushan, Emergence of blockchain technology: fundamentals, working and its various implementations, SSRN Electron. J. (2020), https://doi.org/10.2139/ssrn.3569577.

[16] A. Malik, S. Gautam, S. Abidin, B. Bhushan, Blockchain technology-future of IoT: including structure, limitations and various possible attacks, in: 2019 2nd International Conference on Intelligent Computing, Instrumentation and Control Technologies (ICICICT), 2019, https://doi.org/10.1109/icicict46008.2019.8993144.

[17] Introduction: The Decentralization Formula, in: Blockchain + Antitrust, 2021, pp. viii–xii, https://doi.org/10.4337/9781800885530.00005.

[18] B. Bhushan, C. Sahoo, P. Sinha, A. Khamparia, Unification of blockchain and internet of things (BIoT): requirements, working model, challenges and future directions, Wirel. Netw (2020), https://doi.org/10.1007/s11276-020-02445-6.

[19] S. Saxena, B. Bhushan, M.A. Ahad, Blockchain based solutions to secure IoT: background, integration trends and a way forward, J. Netw. Comput. Appl. (2021), https://doi.org/10.1016/j.jnca.2021.103050. 103050.

[20] B. Bhushan, P. Sinha, K.M. Sagayam, J.A. Onesimu, Untangling blockchain technology: a survey on state of the art, security threats, privacy services, applications and future research directions, Comput. Electr. Eng. 90 (2021) 106897, https://doi.org/10.1016/j.compeleceng.2020.106897.

[21] I. Weber, Introduction and background: blockchain and smart contracts, in: Blockchain and Robotic Process Automation, 2021, pp. 1–11, https://doi.org/10.1007/978-3-030-81409-0_1.

[22] K.S. Mohamed, New trends in cryptography: quantum, blockchain, lightweight, chaotic, and DNA cryptography, in: New Frontiers in Cryptography, 2020, pp. 65–87, https://doi.org/10.1007/978-3-030-58996-7_4.

[23] Basic Concepts of Cryptography, in: Hashing in Computer Science, 2010, pp. 94–115, https://doi.org/10.1002/9780470630617.ch6.

[24] S. Dos Santos, C. Chukwuocha, S. Kamali, R.K. Thulasiram, An efficient miner strategy for selecting cryptocurrency transactions, in: 2019 IEEE International Conference on Blockchain (Blockchain), 2019, https://doi.org/10.1109/blockchain.2019.00024.

[25] R. Sujeetha, C.A. Deiva Preetha, A literature survey on smart contract testing and analysis for smart contract based blockchain application development, in: 2021 2nd International Conference on Smart Electronics and Communication (ICOSEC), 2021, https://doi.org/10.1109/icosec51865.2021.9591750.

[26] Decentralization via Blockchain, Toward 6G, 2020, pp. 147–165, https://doi.org/10.1002/9781119658054.ch6.

[27] Retail Blockchain Consortium, Commercializing Blockchain, 2019, pp. 307–309, https://doi.org/10.1002/9781119578048.app1.

[28] G. Dimitropoulos, Blockchain law: between public and private, transnational and domestic, in: New Directions in European Private Law, 2021, https://doi.org/10.5040/9781509935642.ch-008.

[29] Y. Hermstrüwer, Blockchain and public administration, in: Blockchain and Public Law, 2021, pp. 105–122, https://doi.org/10.4337/9781839100796.00012.

[30] S. Zhu, H. Hu, Y. Li, W. Li, Hybrid blockchain design for privacy preserving crowdsourcing platform, in: 2019 IEEE International Conference on Blockchain (Blockchain), 2019, https://doi.org/10.1109/blockchain.2019.00013.

[31] E. Fernandes, J. Jung, A. Prakash, Security analysis of emerging smart home applications, in: 2016 IEEE Symposium on Security and Privacy (SP), 2016, https://doi.org/10.1109/sp.2016.44.

[32] A.T. Gjerdrum, R. Pettersen, H.D. Johansen, D. Johansen, Performance of trusted computing in cloud infrastructures with Intel SGX, in: Proceedings of the 7th International Conference on Cloud Computing and Services Science, 2017, https://doi.org/10.5220/0006373706960703.

[33] N. Santos, H. Raj, S. Saroiu, A. Wolman, Using arm trustzone to build a trusted language runtime for mobile applications, ACM SIGPLAN Not. 49 (4) (2014) 67–80, https://doi.org/10.1145/2644865.2541949.

[34] L. Van Doorn, Hardware virtualization trends, in: Proceedings of the 2nd International Conference on Virtual Execution Environments—VEE '06, 2006, https://doi.org/10.1145/1134760.1134762.

[35] S. Hammond, C. Vaughan, C. Hughes, Evaluating the Intel Skylake Xeon processor for HPC workloads, in: 2018 International Conference on High Performance Computing & Simulation (HPCS), 2018, https://doi.org/10.1109/hpcs.2018.00064.

[36] Y. Han, J. Kim, A novel covert channel attack using memory encryption engine cache, in: Proceedings of the 56th Annual Design Automation Conference 2019, 2019, https://doi.org/10.1145/3316781.3317750.

[37] R. Sethi, B. Bhushan, N. Sharma, R. Kumar, I. Kaushik, Applicability of industrial IoT in diversified sectors: evolution, applications and challenges, in: Studies in Big Data Multimedia Technologies in the Internet of Things Environment, 2020, pp. 45–67, https://doi.org/10.1007/978-981-15-7965-3_4.

[38] A. Arora, A. Kaur, B. Bhushan, H. Saini, Security concerns and future trends of internet of things, in: 2019 2nd International Conference on Intelligent Computing, Instrumentation and Control Technologies (ICICICT), 2019, https://doi.org/10.1109/icicict46008.2019.8993222.

[39] M. Singh, A. Singh, S. Kim, Blockchain: a game changer for securing IOT data, in: 2018 IEEE 4th World Forum on Internet of Things (WF-IoT), 2018, https://doi.org/10.1109/wf-iot.2018.8355182.

[40] X. Wang, Y. Han, C. Wang, Q. Zhao, X. Chen, M. Chen, In-edge ai: intelligentizing mobile edge computing, caching and communication by federated learning, IEEE Netw. 33 (5) (2019) 156–165, https://doi.org/10.1109/mnet.2019.1800286.

[41] Wireless device-to-device caching networks, in: Wireless Edge Caching, 2020, pp. 37–65, https://doi.org/10.1017/9781108691277.004.

[42] Z. He, Y. Zhang, B. Tak, L. Peng, Green fog planning for optimal internet-of-thing task scheduling, IEEE Access 8 (2020) 1224–1234, https://doi.org/10.1109/access.2019.2961952.

[43] M. Debe, K. Salah, M.H. Rehman, D. Svetinovic, IOT public fog nodes reputation system: a decentralized solution using Ethereum blockchain, IEEE Access 7 (2019) 178082–178093, https://doi.org/10.1109/access.2019.2958355.

[44] F. Guo, F.R. Yu, H. Zhang, H. Ji, M. Liu, V.C. Leung, Adaptive resource allocation in future wireless networks with Blockchain and mobile edge computing, IEEE Trans. Wirel. Commun. 19 (3) (2020) 1689–1703, https://doi.org/10.1109/twc.2019.2956519.

[45] Mechanism design and auction theory in computer networks, in: Auction Theory for Computer Networks, 2020, pp. 52–71, https://doi.org/10.1017/9781108691079.003.

[46] S. Kaza, L. Yao, At a glance: a global picture of solid waste management, in: What a Waste 2.0: A Global Snapshot of Solid Waste Management to 2050, 2018, pp. 17–38, https://doi.org/10.1596/978-1-4648-1329-0_ch2.

[47] P. Bocquier, World urbanization prospects, Demogr. Res. 12 (2005) 197–236, https://doi.org/10.4054/demres.2005.12.9.

[48] Smart waste management using internet-of-things (IOT), Int. J. Innov. Technol. Explor. Eng. 8 (9) (2019) 2518–2522, https://doi.org/10.35940/ijitee.g5334.078919.

[49] D. Misra, G. Das, T. Chakrabortty, D. Das, An IOT-based waste management system monitored by cloud, J. Mater. Cycles Waste Manage. 20 (3) (2018) 1574–1582, https://doi.org/10.1007/s10163-018-0720-y.

[50] B. Bhushan, A. Khamparia, K.M. Sagayam, S.K. Sharma, M.A. Ahad, N.C. Debnath, Blockchain for smart cities: a review of architectures, integration trends and future research directions, Sustain. Cities Soc. 61 (2020) 102360, https://doi.org/10.1016/j.scs.2020.102360.

[51] S. Singh, P.K. Sharma, B. Yoon, M. Shojafar, G.H. Cho, I.-H. Ra, Convergence of blockchain and artificial intelligence in IOT network for the sustainable smart city, Sustain. Cities Soc. 63 (2020) 102364, https://doi.org/10.1016/j.scs.2020.102364.

[52] I.J. Orji, S. Kusi-Sarpong, S. Huang, D. Vazquez-Brust, Evaluating the factors that influence blockchain adoption in the freight logistics industry, Transport Res E-Log 141 (2020) 102025, https://doi.org/10.1016/j.tre.2020.102025.

[53] J. Angelis, E. Ribeiro da Silva, Blockchain adoption: a value driver perspective, Bus. Horiz. 62 (3) (2019) 307–314, https://doi.org/10.1016/j.bushor.2018.12.001.

[54] E. Ismagilova, L. Hughes, Y.K. Dwivedi, K.R. Raman, Smart cities: advances in research—an information systems perspective, Int. J. Inf. Manag. 47 (2019) 88–100, https://doi.org/10.1016/j.ijinfomgt.2019.01.004.

[55] M. Poongodi, M. Hamdi, V. Vijayakumar, B.S. Rawal, M. Maode, An effective electronic waste management solution based on blockchain smart contract in 5G communities, in: 2020 IEEE 3rd 5G World Forum (5GWF), 2020, https://doi.org/10.1109/5gwf49715.2020.9221346.

[56] C. Tao, L. Xiang, Municipal solid waste recycle management information platform based on internet of things technology, in: 2010 International Conference on Multimedia Information Networking and Security, 2010, https://doi.org/10.1109/mines.2010.155.

[57] S. Aleyadeh, A.-E.M. Taha, An IOT-based architecture for waste management, in: 2018 IEEE International Conference on Communications Workshops (ICC Workshops), 2018, https://doi.org/10.1109/iccw.2018.8403750.

[58] Y. He, H. Li, X. Cheng, Y. Liu, C. Yang, L. Sun, A blockchain based truthful incentive mechanism for distributed P2P applications, IEEE Access 6 (2018) 27324–27335, https://doi.org/10.1109/access.2018.2821705.

[59] G.G. Dagher, J. Mohler, M. Milojkovic, P.B. Marella, Ancile: privacy-preserving framework for access control and interoperability of electronic health records using Blockchain technology, Sustain. Cities Soc. 39 (2018) 283–297, https://doi.org/10.1016/j.scs.2018.02.014.

[60] M. Moniruzzaman, S. Khezr, A. Yassine, R. Benlamri, Blockchain for smart homes: review of current trends and research challenges, Comput. Electr. Eng. 83 (2020) 106585, https://doi.org/10.1016/j.compeleceng.2020.106585.

[61] S. Hakak, W.Z. Khan, G.A. Gilkar, M. Imran, N. Guizani, Securing smart cities through Blockchain technology: architecture, requirements, and challenges, IEEE Nctw. 34 (1) (2020) 8–14, https://doi.org/10.1109/mnet.001.1900178.

[62] P. Taylor, K. Steenmans, I. Steenmans, Blockchain technology for sustainable waste management, Front. Polit. Sci. 2 (2020), https://doi.org/10.3389/fpos.2020.590923.

[63] B. Bhushan, Anushka, A. Kumar, L. Katiyar, Security magnification in supply chain management using blockchain technology, in: Blockchain Technologies for Sustainability, 2021, pp. 47–70, https://doi.org/10.1007/978-981-16-6301-7_3.

[64] B. Bhushan, K. Kadam, R. Parashar, S. Kumar, A.K. Thakur, Leveraging blockchain technology in sustainable supply chain management and logistics, in: Blockchain Technologies for Sustainability, 2021, pp. 179–196, https://doi.org/10.1007/978-981-16-6301-7_9.

[65] S. Aggarwal, R. Chaudhary, G.S. Aujla, N. Kumar, K.-K.R. Choo, A.Y. Zomaya, Blockchain for smart communities: applications, challenges and opportunities, J. Netw. Comput. Appl. 144 (2019) 13–48, https://doi.org/10.1016/j.jnca.2019.06.018.

[66] D. Schmelz, K. Pinter, S. Strobl, L. Zhu, P. Niemeier, T. Grechenig, Technical mechanics of a trans-border waste flow tracking solution based on blockchain technology, in: 2019 IEEE 35th International Conference on Data Engineering Workshops (ICDEW), 2019, https://doi.org/10.1109/icdew.2019.00-38.

[67] A.S.L. França, J. Amato Neto, R.F. Gonçalves, C.M.V.B. Almeida, Proposing the use of blockchain to improve the solid waste management in small municipalities, J. Clean. Prod. 244 (2020) 118529, https://doi.org/10.1016/j.jclepro.2019.118529.

[68] D. Zhang, Application of blockchain technology in incentivizing efficient use of rural wastes: a case study on Yitong system, Energy Procedia 158 (2019) 6707–6714, https://doi.org/10.1016/j.egypro.2019.01.018.

[69] R.W. Ahmad, K. Salah, R. Jayaraman, I. Yaqoob, M. Omar, S. Ellahham, Blockchain-Based Forward Supply Chain and Waste Management for COVID-19 Medical Equipment and Supplies, 2021, https://doi.org/10.36227/techrxiv.13553942.v1.

[70] T.K. Dasaklis, F. Casino, C. Patsakis, A traceability and auditing framework for electronic equipment reverse logistics based on blockchain: The case of mobile phones, in: 2020 11th International Conference on Information, Intelligence, Systems and Applications (IISA), 2020, https://doi.org/10.1109/iisa50023.2020.9284394.

[71] O. Akter, Blockchain leveraged incentive providing waste management system, Adv. Intell. Syst. Comput. (2021) 429–437, https://doi.org/10.1007/978-981-15-9927-9_42.

[72] B.R. Gurjar, A. Jain, A. Sharma, A. Agarwal, P. Gupta, A.S. Nagpure, J. Lelieveld, Human health risks in megacities due to air pollution, Atmos. Environ. 44 (36) (2010) 4606–4613, https://doi.org/10.1016/j.atmosenv.2010.08.011.

[73] Z. Idrees, L. Zheng, Low cost air pollution monitoring systems: a review of protocols and enabling technologies, J. Ind. Inf. Integr. 17 (2020) 100123, https://doi.org/10.1016/j.jii.2019.100123.

[74] D. Ghanem, J. Zhang, 'Effortless perfection:' do Chinese cities manipulate air pollution data? J. Environ. Econ. Manag. 68 (2) (2014) 203–225, https://doi.org/10.1016/j.jeem.2014.05.003.

[75] C. Yuyu, J.G. Zhe, K. Naresh, S. Guang, Gaming in air pollution data? Lessons from China, B. E. J. Econ. Anal. Policy 13 (3) (2012) 1–43.

[76] C.I. Beattie, J.W.S. Longhurst, N.K. Woodfield, Air quality management: evolution of policy and practice in the UK as exemplified by the experience of English local government, Atmos. Environ. 35 (8) (2001) 1479–1490, https://doi.org/10.1016/s1352-2310(00)00311-3.

[77] Risk governance through transparency: Information disclosure and the global trade in transgenic crops, in: Transparency in Global Environmental Governance, 2014, https://doi.org/10.7551/mitpress/9857.003.0011.

[78] J. Brainard, Publishers try out alternative pathways to open access, Science 367 (6483) (2020) 1179, https://doi.org/10.1126/science.367.6483.1179.

[79] Web based air pollution monitoring system (air pollution monitoring using smart phone), Int. J. Sci. Res. 5 (3) (2016) 266–269, https://doi.org/10.21275/v5i3.nov161795.

[80] W. Yi, K. Lo, T. Mak, K. Leung, Y. Leung, M. Meng, A survey of wireless sensor network-based air pollution monitoring systems, Sensors 15 (12) (2015) 31392–31427, https://doi.org/10.3390/s151229859.

[81] Y. Zheng, F. Liu, H.-P. Hsieh, U-air, in: Proceedings of the 19th ACM SIGKDD International Conference on Knowledge Discovery and Data Mining, 2013, https://doi.org/10.1145/2487575.2488188.

[82] S. Steinle, S. Reis, C.E. Sabel, Quantifying human exposure to air pollution—moving from static monitoring to spatio-temporally resolved personal exposure assessment, Sci. Total Environ. 443 (2013) 184–193, https://doi.org/10.1016/j.scitotenv.2012.10.098.

[83] A. Mukherjee, S.G. Brown, M.C. McCarthy, N.R. Pavlovic, L.G. Stanton, J.L. Snyder, S. D'Andrea, H.R. Hafner, Measuring spatial and temporal PM2.5 variations in Sacramento, California, communities using a network of low-cost sensors, Sensors 19 (21) (2019) 4701, https://doi.org/10.3390/s19214701.

[84] A. Gałuszka, Z.M. Migaszewski, J. Namieśnik, Moving your laboratories to the field—advantages and limitations of the use of field portable instruments in environmental sample analysis, Environ. Res. 140 (2015) 593–603, https://doi.org/10.1016/j.envres.2015.05.017.

[85] K. Hu, V. Sivaraman, B.G. Luxan, A. Rahman, Design and evaluation of a metropolitan air pollution sensing system, IEEE Sensors J. 16 (5) (2016) 1448–1459, https://doi.org/10.1109/jsen.2015.2499308.

[86] A. Sunyaev, Distributed ledger technology, Internet Comput. (2020) 265–299, https://doi.org/10.1007/978-3-030-34957-8_9.

[87] N. Kannengießer, S. Lins, T. Dehling, A. Sunyaev, Trade-offs between distributed ledger technology characteristics, ACM Comput. Surv. 53 (2) (2021) 1–37, https://doi.org/10.1145/3379463.

[88] R. Cornet, Faculty opinions recommendation of omniphr: a distributed architecture model to integrate personal health records, in: Faculty Opinions—Post-Publication Peer Review of the Biomedical Literature, 2017, https://doi.org/10.3410/f.727656142.793533886.

[89] A.G. Abbasi, Z. Khan, Veidblock, in: Companion Proceedings of the 10th International Conference on Utility and Cloud Computing, 2017, https://doi.org/10.1145/3147234.3148088.

[90] H. Shafagh, L. Burkhalter, A. Hithnawi, S. Duquennoy, Towards blockchain-based auditable storage and sharing of IOT data, in: Proceedings of the 2017 on Cloud Computing Security Workshop, 2017, https://doi.org/10.1145/3140649.3140656.

[91] H.G. Do, W.K. Ng, Blockchain-based system for secure data storage with private keyword search, in: 2017 IEEE World Congress on Services (SERVICES), 2017, https://doi.org/10.1109/services.2017.23.

[92] M. Mostafa, Bitcoin's blockchain peer-to-peer network security attacks and countermeasures, Indian J. Sci. Technol. 13 (07) (2020) 767–786, https://doi.org/10.17485/ijst/2020/v13i07/149691.

[93] A. Alkhodre, T. Ali, S. Jan, Y. Alsaawy, S. Khusro, M. Yasar, A blockchain-based value added tax (VAT) system: Saudi Arabia as a use-case, Int. J. Adv. Comput. Sci. Appl. 10 (5) (2019), https://doi.org/10.14569/ijacsa.2019.0100588.

[94] I. Bauer, L. Zavolokina, F. Leisibach, G. Schwabe, Exploring blockchain value creation: the case of the car ecosystem, in: Proceedings of the Annual Hawaii International Conference on System Sciences, 2019, https://doi.org/10.24251/hicss.2019.822.

[95] K.L. Brousmiche, T. Heno, C. Poulain, A. Dalmieres, E. Ben Hamida, Digitizing, securing and sharing vehicles life-cycle over a consortium blockchain: lessons learned, in: 2018 9th IFIP International Conference on New Technologies, Mobility and Security (NTMS), 2018, https://doi.org/10.1109/ntms.2018.8328733.

[96] P. Fraga-Lamas, T.M. Fernandez-Carames, A review on Blockchain technologies for an advanced and cyber-resilient automotive industry, IEEE Access 7 (2019) 17578–17598, https://doi.org/10.1109/access.2019.2895302.

[97] J. Ali, T. Ali, Y. Alsaawy, A.S. Khalid, S. Musa, Blockchain-based smart-IOT trust zone measurement architecture, in: Proceedings of the International Conference on Omni-Layer Intelligent Systems, 2019, https://doi.org/10.1145/3312614.3312646.

[98] T. Ali, M. Nauman, S. Jan, Trust in IOT: dynamic remote attestation through efficient behavior capture, Clust. Comput. 21 (1) (2017) 409–421, https://doi.org/10.1007/s10586-017-0877-5.

[99] G.K. Shyam, S.S. Manvi, P. Bharti, Smart waste management using internet-of-things (IOT), in: 2017 2nd International Conference on Computing and Communications Technologies (ICCCT), 2017, https://doi.org/10.1109/iccct2.2017.7972276.

[100] W.-E. Chen, Y.-H. Wang, P.-C. Huang, Y.-Y. Huang, M.-Y. Tsai, A smart IOT system for waste management, in: 2018 1st International Cognitive Cities Conference (IC3), 2018, https://doi.org/10.1109/ic3.2018.00-24.

[101] N. Gayathri, A.R. Divagaran, C.D. Akhilesh, V.M. Aswiin, N. Charan, IOT based smart waste management system, in: 2021 7th International Conference on Advanced Computing and Communication Systems (ICACCS), 2021, https://doi.org/10.1109/icaccs51430.2021.9441819.

[102] S.V. Kumar, T.S. Kumaran, A.K. Kumar, M. Mathapati, Smart garbage monitoring and clearance system using internet of things, in: 2017 IEEE International Conference on Smart Technologies and Management for Computing, Communication, Controls, Energy and Materials (ICSTM), 2017, https://doi.org/10.1109/icstm.2017.8089148.

[103] E. Al-Masri, I. Diabate, R. Jain, M.H. Lam, S.R. Nathala, A serverless IOT architecture for smart waste management systems, in: 2018 IEEE International Conference on Industrial Internet (ICII), 2018, https://doi.org/10.1109/icii.2018.00034.

[104] M.S. Pranathy, S. Ranjana, P.S. Reenu Rita, S. Rajalakshmi, S. Angel Deborah, Internet of things enabled smart dustbins using capacitated vehicle routing, in: 2021 5th International Conference on Computer, Communication and Signal Processing (ICCCSP), 2021, https://doi.org/10.1109/icccsp52374.2021.9465346.

[105] M. Aazam, M. St-Hilaire, C.-H. Lung, I. Lambadaris, Cloud-based smart waste management for smart cities, in: 2016 IEEE 21st International Workshop on Computer Aided Modelling and Design of Communication Links and Networks (CAMAD), 2016, https://doi.org/10.1109/camad.2016.7790356.

[106] L. Catarinucci, R. Colella, S.I. Consalvo, L. Patrono, A. Salvatore, I. Sergi, IOT-oriented waste management system based on new RFID-sensing devices and cloud technologies, in: 2019 4th International Conference on Smart and Sustainable Technologies (SpliTech), 2019, https://doi.org/10.23919/splitech.2019.8783097.

[107] N. Baras, D. Ziouzios, M. Dasygenis, C. Tsanaktsidis, A cloud based smart recycling bin for in-house waste classification, in: 2020 International Conference on Electrical, Communication, and Computer Engineering (ICECCE), 2020, https://doi.org/10.1109/icecce49384.2020.9179349.

[108] A. Das, B. Debnath, N. Modak, A. Das, D. De, E-waste inventorisation for sustainable smart cities in India: a cloud-based framework, in: 2020 IEEE International Women in Engineering (WIE) Conference on Electrical and Computer Engineering (WIECON-ECE), 2020, https://doi.org/10.1109/wiecon-ece52138.2020.9397960.

[109] G. Rashmi, M. Ameenulla, S.S. Kumar, Cloud based architecture for solid waste garbage monitoring and processing, in: 2019 4th International Conference on Computational Systems and Information Technology for Sustainable Solution (CSITSS), 2019, https://doi.org/10.1109/csitss47250.2019.9031040.

[110] S. Mondal, S.G. Kulkarni, A blockchain based transparent framework for plastic waste management, in: 2022 14th International Conference on COMmunication Systems & NETworkS (COMSNETS), 2022, https://doi.org/10.1109/comsnets53615.2022.9668574.

[111] A. Dua, A. Dutta, N. Zaman, N. Kumar, Blockchain-based e-waste management in 5G smart communities, in: IEEE INFOCOM 2020—IEEE Conference on Computer

Communications Workshops (INFOCOM WKSHPS), 2020, https://doi.org/10.1109/infocomwkshps50562.2020.9162845.

[112] H. Damadi, M. Namjoo, Smart waste management using blockchain, IT Prof. 23 (4) (2021) 81–87, https://doi.org/10.1109/mitp.2021.3067710.

[113] T.S. Farizi, R.F. Sari, Implementation of blockchain-based electronic waste management system with Hyperledger Fabric, in: 2021 2nd International Conference on ICT for Rural Development (IC-ICTRuDev), 2021, https://doi.org/10.1109/ic-ictrudev50538.2021.9656503.

[114] D.C. Nguyen, P.N. Pathirana, M. Ding, A. Seneviratne, A cooperative architecture of data offloading and sharing for smart healthcare with blockchain, in: 2021 IEEE International Conference on Blockchain and Cryptocurrency (ICBC), 2021, https://doi.org/10.1109/icbc51069.2021.9461063.

[115] N.A. Asad, M.T. Elahi, A.A. Hasan, M.A. Yousuf, Permission-based blockchain with proof of authority for secured healthcare data sharing, in: 2020 2nd International Conference on Advanced Information and Communication Technology (ICAICT), 2020, https://doi.org/10.1109/icaict51780.2020.9333488.

[116] B. Vardhini, S.N. Dass, R. Sahana, R. Chinnaiyan, A blockchain based electronic medical health records framework using smart contracts, in: 2021 International Conference on Computer Communication and Informatics (ICCCI), 2021, https://doi.org/10.1109/iccci50826.2021.9402689.

[117] M.J. Gul, A. Paul, S. Rho, M. Kim, Blockchain based healthcare system with artificial intelligence, in: 2020 International Conference on Computational Science and Computational Intelligence (CSCI), 2020, https://doi.org/10.1109/csci51800.2020.00138.

[118] S. Aich, N.K. Sinai, S. Kumar, M. Ali, Y.R. Choi, M.-I.L. Joo, H.-C. Kim, Protecting personal healthcare record using blockchain & federated learning technologies, in: 2021 23rd International Conference on Advanced Communication Technology (ICACT), 2021, https://doi.org/10.23919/icact51234.2021.9370566.

[119] L. Ismail, H. Materwala, Y. Sharaf, Block HR—a blockchain-based healthcare records management framework: performance evaluation and comparison with client/server architecture, in: 2020 International Symposium on Networks, Computers and Communications (ISNCC), 2020, https://doi.org/10.1109/isncc49221.2020.9297216.

[120] E. Nizeyimana, D. Hanyurwimfura, R. Shibasaki, J. Nsenga, Design of a decentralized and predictive real-time framework for air pollution spikes monitoring, in: 2021 IEEE 6th International Conference on Cloud Computing and Big Data Analytics (ICCCBDA), 2021, https://doi.org/10.1109/icccbda51879.2021.9442611.

[121] S.R. Niya, S.S. Jha, T. Bocek, B. Stiller, Design and implementation of an automated and decentralized pollution monitoring system with blockchains, Smart Contracts, and Lorawan, in: NOMS 2018–2018 IEEE/IFIP Network Operations and Management Symposium, 2018, https://doi.org/10.1109/noms.2018.8406329.

[122] S. Muthukumar, W. Sherine Mary, S. Jayanthi, R. Kiruthiga, M. Mahalakshmi, IOT based air pollution monitoring and control system, in: 2018 International Conference on Inventive Research in Computing Applications (ICIRCA), 2018, https://doi.org/10.1109/icirca.2018.8597240.

[123] C. Xiaojun, L. Xianpeng, X. Peng, IOT-based air pollution monitoring and forecasting system, in: 2015 International Conference on Computer and Computational Sciences (ICCCS), 2015, https://doi.org/10.1109/iccacs.2015.7361361.

[124] G. Parmar, S. Lakhani, M.K. Chattopadhyay, An IOT based low cost air pollution monitoring system, in: 2017 International Conference on Recent Innovations in Signal Processing and Embedded Systems (RISE), 2017, https://doi.org/10.1109/rise.2017.8378212.

[125] V. Sajjan, P. Sharma, Analysis of air pollution by using raspberry pi-IOT, in: 2021 6th International Conference on Inventive Computation Technologies (ICICT), 2021, https://doi.org/10.1109/icict50816.2021.9358535.

[126] T.A. Syed, M.S. Siddique, A. Nadeem, A. Alzahrani, S. Jan, M.A. Khattak, A novel blockchain-based framework for vehicle life cycle tracking: an end-to-end solution, IEEE Access 8 (2020) 111042–111063, https://doi.org/10.1109/access.2020.3002170.

[127] G. Subramanian, A.S. Thampy, Implementation of hybrid blockchain in a pre-owned electric vehicle supply chain, in: IEEE Access, vol. 9, 2021, pp. 82435–82454, https://doi.org/10.1109/ACCESS.2021.3084942.

[128] M. Demir, O. Turetken, A. Ferworn, Blockchain based transparent vehicle insurance management, in: 2019 Sixth International Conference on Software Defined Systems (SDS), 2019, https://doi.org/10.1109/sds.2019.8768669.

[129] P.K. Sharma, N. Kumar, J.H. Park, Blockchain-based distributed framework for automotive industry in a Smart City, IEEE Trans. Ind. Inf. 15 (7) (2019) 4197–4205, https://doi.org/10.1109/tii.2018.2887101.

[130] K. Wang, M. Liu, X. Jiang, C. Yang, H. Zhang, A novel vehicle blockchain model based on hyperledger fabric for vehicle supply chain management, in: Z. Zheng, H.N. Dai, M. Tang, X. Chen (Eds.), Blockchain and Trustworthy Systems. BlockSys 2019. Communications in Computer and Information Science, vol. 1156, Springer, Singapore, 2020, pp. 732–739. https://doi.org/10.1007/978-981-15-2777-7_59.

Index

Note: Page numbers followed by *f* indicate figures and *t* indicate tables.

A

Adaptive neural-network-based fuzzy inference
    system (ANFIS) model, 146
Alzheimer's disease (AD)
    CNN's working algorithm, 139
    GPS module, 137–138
    IoT-based assistance, 138–139
    message queue telemetry transport (MQTT),
        139–140
    sensors, 138
Amazon Ring home-security cameras, 155

B

Biometric authentication systems, 78
Bitcoin blockchain, 183
Blockchain technology
    absolute encryption algorithms, 158
    advantages, 161
    anatomy of, 200, 200*f*
    architecture for IoT, 161
    benefits, 231–232
    bitcoin transaction, 201
    block structure
        hash function, 228
        Merkle tree, 228
        nonce, 229
        timestamping, 228
    challenges, 160–163
    characteristics
        anonymous transaction, 226
        audibility, 227
        autonomy, 227
        decentralized system, 226
        distributed ledger, 227
        immutability, 226
        persistency, 226
        transparency, 227
    classification
        consortium blockchains, 230
        private blockchain, 227
        public blockchain, 229
    client/server model, 158
    cluster mode, 159

concept of, 171–172
consortium blockchains, 155
DDoS, 154
decentralization of management
    managing using trusted environment,
        268–269
    primary fog node (PFN), 269
    proof of word (PoW) algorithm, 269–270
distributed ledger technology (DLT), 274
e-healthcare
    counterfeit drugs, 255–256
    decentralization, 245
    fast healthcare interoperability
        resources, 256
    immutability, 245
    IoT in healthcare systems, 245–246
    remote patient monitoring (RPM),
        241–242
    security challenges, 246–247
    software defined networking (SDN)
        approach, 242
    transparency, 245
    user-oriented healthcare research, 255
financial assets, 183
healthcare and insurance industries
    BurstIQ, 177
    change healthcare, 176
    chronicled, 176
    DHL and Accenture, 177
    electronic health records (EHRs), 167–169
    feasibility, 174–175
    fraud, 170
    HSBlox, 176–177
    insurance organizations, 170
    lumedic, 176
    Medable, 178–179
    Medibloc, 178
    Modum, 177
    opportunities, 172–174
    Patientory, 178
    Spiritus, 178
implementations, 276–277*t*
information communication technologies
    (ICT), 271

Printed in the United States
by Baker & Taylor Publisher Services